BEAUTIFUL
TROUBLE

A TOOLBOX FOR REVOLUTION

BEAUTIFUL TROUBLE

TROUBLE

A TOOLBOX FOR REVOLUTION

ASSEMBLED BY ANDREW BOYD
WITH DAVE OSWALD MITCHELL

O/R

OR Books

New York • London

All essays © 2012 Beautiful Trouble by the various authors
www.beautifultrouble.org

Published by OR Books, New York and London
Visit our website at www.orbooks.com

All rights information: rights@orbooks.com

First printing 2012

Cataloging-in-Publication data is available from the Library of Congress.
A catalog record for this book is available from the British Library.

ISBN 978-1-935928-57-7 paperback
ISBN 978-1-935928-58-4 e-book

Art direction and cover design by Cristian Fleming
Cover illustration by Andy Menconi
Book design by The Public Society
www.thepublicsociety.com

Printed by BookMobile in the United States and CPI in the United Kingdom.
The U.S. printed edition of this book comes on Forest Stewardship Council-
certified, 30% recycled paper. The printer, BookMobile, is 100% wind-powered.

BEAUTIFUL TROUBLE TEAM

Co-editor & wrangler-in-chief / *Andrew Boyd*
Co-editor / *Dave Oswald Mitchell*
Master of logistics / *Zack Malitz*
Photo editor / *Margaret Campbell*
Web maker & project agitator / *Phillip Smith*
Art Director / *Cristian Fleming*
Designer / *Stephanie Lukito*
Consultant-in-chief / *Nadine Bloch*
Wordhorse / *Joshua Kahn Russell*
Fellow traveler / *Maxine Schoefer-Wulf*

PARTICIPATING ORGANIZATIONS

Agit-Pop/The Other 98%, The Yes Men/Yes Lab, CODEPINK, smartMeme,
The Ruckus Society, Beyond the Choir, The Center for Artistic Activism,
Waging Nonviolence, Alliance of Community Trainers and Nonviolence International.

CONTRIBUTORS

Rae Abileah, Ryan Acuff, Celia Alario, Phil Aroneanu, Peter Barnes,
Jesse Barron, Andy Bichlbaum, Nadine Bloch, Kathryn Blume, L.M. Bogad,
Josh Bolotsky, Mike Bonanno, Andrew Boyd, Kevin Buckland,
Margaret Campbell, Doyle Canning, Samantha Corbin, Yutaka Dirks,
Stephen Duncombe, Mark Engler, Simon Enoch, Jodie Evans, John Ewing,
Brian Fairbanks, Bryan Farrell, Janice Fine, Lisa Fithian, Cristian Fleming,
Elisabeth Ginsberg, Stan Goff, Arun Gupta, Silas Harrebye, Judith Helfand,
Daniel Hunter, Sarah Jaffe, John Jordan, Dmytri Kleiner, Sally Kohn,
Steve Lambert, Anna Lee, Stephen Lerner, Zack Malitz, Nancy Mancias,
Duncan Meisel, Matt Meyer, Dave Oswald Mitchell, Tracey Mitchell, George Monbiot,
Brad Newsham, Gaby Pacheco, Mark Read, Patrick Reinsborough, Simon Roel,
Joshua Kahn Russell, Leónidas Martín Saura, Levana Saxon, Maxine Schoefer-Wulf,
Nathan Schneider, Kristen Ess Schurr, John Sellers, Rajni Shah, Brooke Singer,
Matt Skomarovsky, Andrew Slack, Phillip Smith, Jonathan Matthew Smucker,
Starhawk, Eric Stoner, Jeremy Varon, Virginia Vitzthum, Harsha Walia,
Jeffery Webber and the Coalition of Immokalee Workers.

**The role of the artist in the social structure follows
the need of the changing times:**

IN TIME OF SOCIAL STASIS: *to activate*

IN TIME OF GERMINATION: *to invent fertile new forms*

IN TIME OF REVOLUTION: *to extend the possibilities of peace and liberty*

IN TIME OF VIOLENCE: *to make peace*

IN TIME OF DESPAIR: *to give hope*

IN TIME OF SILENCE: *to sing out*

—*Judith Malina, "The Work of
an Anarchist Theater"*

A.B.

To my mentors in the struggle, both far away — George Orwell, Abbie Hoffman, Subcomandante Marcos — and close at hand — Bob Rivera, Dennis Livingston, Janice Fine, Mike Prokosch, Chuck Collins, John Sellers & the RTS/B4B crew.

D.O.M.

For the silent leaders behind every victory "who strain in the mud and the muck to move things forward, who do what has to be done, again and again" (Marge Piercy).

CONTENTS

⊕ PRINCIPLES

 # THEORIES

CASE STUDIES

 **PRACTITIONERS**

INTRODUCTION

By Andrew Boyd & Dave Oswald Mitchell

*"The clowns are organizing. They are organizing. Over
and out."*

*—Overheard on UK police radio during action
by Clandestine Insurgent Rebel Clown Army, July 2004 (see p. 304)*

"Human salvation," Dr. Martin Luther King, Jr. argued,
"lies in the hands of the creatively maladjusted," and
recent historical events are proving him as prescient
as ever. As the recent wave of global revolt has swept
through Iceland, Bahrain, Egypt, Spain, Greece, Chile,
the United States and elsewhere, the tools at activists'
disposal, the terrain of struggle and the victories that
suddenly seem possible are quickly evolving. The realization is rippling through the ranks that, if deployed
thoughtfully, our pranks, stunts, flash mobs and encampments can bring about real shifts in the balance of
power. In short, large numbers of people have seen that
creative action gets the goods — and have begun to act accordingly. Art, it turns out, really does enrich activism,
making it more compelling and sustainable.

This blending of art and politics is nothing new.
Tactical pranks go back at least as far as the Trojan
Horse. Jesus of Nazareth, overturning the tables of the
money changers, mastered the craft of political theater
2,000 years before Greenpeace. Fools, clowns and carnivals have always played a subversive role, while art,
culture and creative protest tactics have for centuries
served as fuel and foundation for successful social movements. It's hard to imagine the labor movements of the
1930s without murals and creative street actions, the
U.S. civil rights movement without song, or the youth

upheavals of the late 1960s without guerrilla theater, Situationist slogans or giant puppets floating above a rally.

Today's culture jammers and political pranksters, however, shaped by the politics and technologies of the new millennium, have taken activist artistry to a whole new level. The current political moment of looming ecological catastrophe, deepening inequality, austerity and unemployment, and growing corporate control of government and media offers no choice but to fight back. At the same time, the explosion of social media and many-to-many communication technologies has put powerful new tools at our disposal. We're building rhizomatic movements marked by creativity, humor, networked intelligence, technological sophistication, a profoundly participatory ethic and the courage to risk it all for a livable future.

This new wave of creative activism first drew mainstream attention in 1999 at the Battle in Seattle, but it didn't start there. In the 1980s and '90s, groups like ACT-UP, Women's Action Coalition and the Lesbian Avengers inspired a new style of high-concept shock politics that both empowered participants and shook up public complacency. In 1994, the Zapatistas, often described as the first post-modern revolutionary movement, awakened the political imaginations of activists around the world, replacing the dry manifesto and the sectarian vanguard with fable, poetry, theater and a democratic movement of movements against global capitalism. The U.S. labor movement, hit hard by globalization, began to seek out new allies, including Earth First!, which was pioneering new technologies of radical direct action in the forests of northern California. The Reclaim the Streets model of militant carnivals radiated out from London, and the "organized coincidences" of Critical Mass bicycle rides provided a working model of celebratory, self-organizing, swarm-like protest. Even the legendary Burning Man festival, while not explicitly political, introduced thousands of artists and activists to the lived experience of participatory culture, radical self-organization and a gift economy. The Burning Man slogans "No spectators!" and "You are the entertainment!" were just as evident on the streets of Seattle as they are in the Nevada desert each summer.

Through the last decade, though we've lost ground on climate, civil liberties, labor rights and so many other fronts, we've also seen an incredible flourishing of creativity and tactical innovation in our movements, both in the streets and online. Whether it was the Yes Men prank-announcing the end of the WTO (and everyone believing it!), or the Billionaires for Bush parading their "Million Billionaire March" past the Republican National Convention, or MoveOn staging a millions-strong virtual march on Washington to protest the Iraq War, our movements were forging new tools and a new sensibility that got us through those dark times. Every year, new terms had to be invented just to track our own evolution: flash mobs, virtual sit-ins, denial-of-service attacks, media pranks, distributed actions, viral campaigns, subvertisements, culture jamming, etc.

As a participant in many of these movements, Andrew Boyd, this project's instigator and co-editor, had been kicking around the idea for *Beautiful Trouble* for almost a decade before he teamed up with web maker Phillip Smith and editor Dave Oswald Mitchell to make it happen. Little did we know what kind of a year 2011 would turn out to be.

By the time our expanding team of collaborators was hammering out our first proof-of-concept modules, Egyptian revolutionaries were phoning in pizza orders to the students and workers occupying the Capitol in Madison, Wisconsin. A few months later, as we were gearing up for our big finishing push, Occupy Wall Street went global. Suddenly, half the people we were trying to wrangle modules out of were working double overtime for the revolution. The excuses for why these writer/activists were missing their deadlines were priceless (and often airtight, since we could simply confirm them by checking the day's news!): *Sorry, I had to shut down Wall Street with a blockade-carnival while distracting the cops with 99,000 donuts.* Or: *I'll get that rewrite to you as soon as me and my 12,000 closest friends finish surrounding the White House to save the climate as we know it.* Or: *Hold on, I have to sneak a virtuoso guitarist into the most heavily guarded spot on earth that day (the APEC summit in Honolulu) to serenade Obama and Chinese President Hu Jintao with a battle cry from the 99%.* Or: *Shit, I know I said I'd write up that guerrilla projection tactic thing you wanted, but I can't because, get this, I'm DOING ONE RIGHT NOW see: CASE: 99% bat signal.* Somehow, though, we managed to keep moving the project forward through the thick of the American Autumn.

· ·

Beautiful Trouble lays out the core tactics, principles and theoretical concepts that drive creative activism, providing analytical tools for changemakers to learn from their own successes and failures. In the modules that follow, we map the DNA of these hybrid art/action methods, tease out the design principles that make them tick and the theoretical concepts that inform them, and then show how all of these work together in a series of instructive case studies.

Creative activism offers no one-size-fits-all solution, and neither do we. *Beautiful Trouble* is less a cookbook than a pattern language,[1] seeking not to dictate strict courses of action but instead offer a matrix of flexible, interlinked tools that practitioners can pick and choose among, applying them in unique ways varying with each situation they may face.

The material is organized into five different categories of content:

Tactics
Specific forms of creative action, such as a flash mob or an occupation.

Principles
Hard-won insights that can guide or inform creative action design.

Theories
Big-picture concepts and ideas that help us understand how the world works and how we might go about changing it.

Case studies
Capsule stories of successful and instructive creative actions, useful for illustrating how *principles, tactics* and *theories* can be successfully applied in practice.

---

[1] The originator of the concept of a pattern language, architect Christopher Alexander, introduces the concept thus: "... the elements of this language are entities called patterns. Each pattern describes a problem which occurs over and over again in our environment, and then describes the core of the solution to that problem, in such a way that you can use this solution a million times over, without ever doing it the same way twice." Alexander first introduced the concept of pattern languages in his 1977 book *A Pattern Language: Towns, Buildings, Construction*, in which he sought to develop "a network of patterns that call upon one another" each providing "a perennial solution to a recurring problem within a building context." Pattern languages have since been developed for other fields as varied as computer science, media and communications, and group process work. Though we do not follow the explicit form of a pattern language here, we were inspired by its modular interlocking format, its organically expandable structure and by the democratic nature of the form, which provides tools for people to adapt to their own unique circumstances.

Practitioners
Brief write-ups of some of the people and groups that inspire us to be better changemakers.

Each of these modules is linked to related modules, creating a nexus of key concepts that could, theoretically, expand endlessly. As the form took hold and the number of participating organizations and contributing writers grew, what began as a how-to book of prankster activism gradually expanded into a Greenpeace-esque direct action manual and from there grew further to address issues of mass organizing and emancipatory pedagogy and practice.

While we've sought to cast as wide a net as possible, drawing in over seventy experienced artist-activists and ten grassroots organizations to distill their wisdom, we are painfully aware of the geographical, thematic and cultural limitations of the collection of modules as it currently stands. We've included in the book blank templates for each content type, and the capacity to submit or suggest modules on the website, in the hopes that readers will be inspired to identify, and fill in, some of these gaps.

We encourage readers to explore our website, *beautifultrouble.org*, which is more than simply an appendage to the book, but in fact stands as perhaps the fullest expression of the project. In an easily navigable form, the website includes all the book's content as well as material that, due to constraints of both space and time, we were unable to include in this print edition. With the participation of readers, the body of patterns that constitute *Beautiful Trouble* could continue to evolve and expand, attracting new contributors and keeping abreast of emerging social movements and their tactical innovations.

Millions around the world have awoken not just to the need to take action to reverse deepening inequality and ecological devastation, but to our own creative power to do so. You have in your hands a distillation of ideas gleaned from those on the front lines of creative activism. But these ideas are nothing until they're acted upon. We look forward to seeing what you do with them.

January 2012

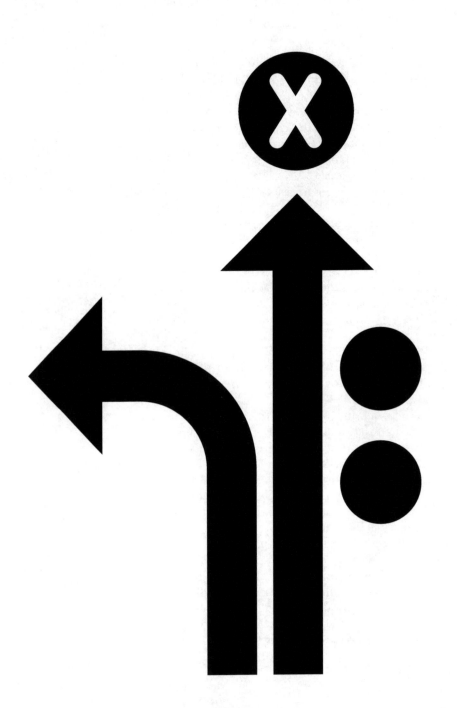

TACTICS

-- -- -- -- -- -- -- -- --

MODES OF ACTION

-- -- -- -- -- -- -- -- --

Specific forms of creative action, such as a flash mob or an occupation.

-- -- -- -- -- -- -- -- --

"Tactics . . . lack a specific location, survive through improvisation, and use the advantages of the weak against the strong."

—Paul Lewis et al.[1]

-- -- -- -- -- -- -- -- --

Every discipline has its forms. Soldiers can choose to lay siege or launch a flanking maneuver. Writers can try their hand at biography or flash fiction. Likewise, creative activists have their own repertoire of forms. Some, like the sit-in and the general strike, are justly famous; others, like flash mobs and culture jamming, have a newfangled pop appeal; yet others — like debt strike, prefigurative intervention, eviction blockade — are mostly unknown but could soon make their appearance on the stage of history. If art truly is a hammer with which to shape the world, it's time to gear up.

[1] Paul Lewis, Marc Tsurumaki, and David J. Lewis, Situation normal– (Princeton Architectural Press, 1999).

TACTIC:
Advanced leafleting

COMMON USES

To get important
information into
the right hands.

PRACTITIONERS

Center for Tactical Magic
Institute for Applied Autonomy
WAG

FURTHER INSIGHT

Institute for Applied Autonomy,
"Little Brother"
http://www.appliedautonomy.com/
lb.html

Center for Tactical Magic,
"The Tactical Ice Cream Unit"
http://trb.la/yOmgjs

CONTRIBUTED BY

Steve Lambert
Andrew Boyd

Leafleting is the bread-and-butter of many campaigns. It's also annoying and ineffective, for the most part. How many times have you taken a leaflet just because you forgot to pull your hand back in time, only to throw it in the next available trash can? Or you're actually interested and stick it in your pocket, but then you never get around to reading it because it's a block of tiny, indecipher-able text? Well, if that's what a committed, world-caring person like you does, just imagine what happens to all the leaflets *you* give out to harried career-jockeys as they rush to or from work.

"If you're doing standard leafleting, you're wasting everybody's time. What you need is advanced leafleting."

In a word, if you're doing standard leafleting, you're wasting everybody's time. What you need is *advanced* leafleting.

In advanced leafleting, we acknowledge that if you're going to hand out leaflets like a robot, you might as well have a robot hand them out. Yes, an actual leafleting robot. In 1998, the Institute for Applied Autonomy built "Little Brother" a small, intentionally cute, 1950s-style metal robot to be a pamphleteer. In their tests, strangers avoided a human pamphleteer, but would go out of their way to take literature from the robot.

Make it fun. Make it unusual. Make it memorable. Don't just hand out leaflets. Climb up on some guy's shoulders and hand out leaflets from there, as one of the authors of this piece did as a student organizer. (He also tried the same tactic hitchhiking, with less stellar results.) The shareholder heading into a meeting is more likely to take, read and remember the custom message inside the fortune cookie you just handed her than a rectangle of paper packed with text.

Using theater and costumes to leaflet can also be effective. In the 1980s, activists opposed to U.S. military intervention in Central America dressed up as waiters and carried maps of Central America on serving trays, with little green plastic toy soldiers glued to the map. They would go up to people in the street and say, "Excuse me, sir, did you order this war?" When the "no" response invariably followed, they would present an itemized bill outlining the costs: "Well, you paid for it!" Even if the person they addressed didn't take the leaflet, they'd get the message.

The point is, leafleting is not a bad tactic. It's still a good way to tell passersby what you're marching for, why you're making so much noise on a street corner or why you're setting police cars on fire. But people are more likely to take your leaflet, read it, and remember what it's all about if you deliver it with flair. Or ice cream.

Related:

TACTICS
Creative petition delivery p. 22
Creative disruption p. 18
Mass street action p. 68
Street theater web
Electoral guerilla theater p. 40
Guerrilla newspaper web

CASE STUDIES
New York Times "Special Edition" web

. . . .

KILL THEM WITH KINDNESS: 'Nuff said. Pissing people off won't do your cause any favors, so don't piss people off. Disarm with charm, and maybe your audience will let their guard down long enough to hear what you have to say.

KEY PRINCIPLE
at work

OTHER PRINCIPLES AT WORK:
Show, don't tell p. 174
Consider your audience p. 118
Balance art and message p. 100
Stay on message p. 178

TACTIC:
Artistic vigil

COMMON USES

To mourn the death of a public hero; to link a natural disaster or public tragedy to a political message; to protest the launch of a war.

PRACTITIONERS

Artists' Network of Refuse & Resist
Women In Black
Mothers of the Plaza de Mayo
Suzanne Lacy
Arlington West
Bread and Puppet Theater
"I Dream Your Dream"

FURTHER INSIGHT

Kelly, Jeff. "The Body Politics of Suzanne Lacy." But Is It Art? Edited by Nina Felshin. Seattle: Bay Press, 1994.

T.V. Reed. The Art of Protest: Culture and Activism from the Civil Rights Movement to the Streets of Seattle. University of MN, 2005.

CONTRIBUTED BY

Andrew Boyd

The word *vigil* comes from the Latin word for wakefulness, and refers to a practice of keeping watch through the night over the dead or dying. Compared to the blustery pronouncements of a rally, a candlelight vigil offers a more soulful and symbolically potent expression of dissent.

Unfortunately, routine and self-righteousness can strip vigils of their power. In the American peace movement of the 1970s, '80s and '90s, the "candlelight vigil" — all too often a handful of dour people silently holding candles — became a standard, and fatally predictable, form of protest.

An *artistic* vigil, on the other hand, brings a more artful touch. This doesn't necessarily mean costumes and face paint and puppets (though it could). It means thoughtful symbolism, the right tone and a distinct look and feel that clearly convey the meaning of the vigil. An artistic vigil often draws upon ritual elements *see PRINCIPLE: Use the power of ritual* to both deepen the experience of participants and demonstrate that experience to observers.

"Our Grief is not a Cry for War" vigils organized by the Artists' Network of Refuse & Resist in New York City in the wake of 9/11. Library of Congress, Prints & Photographs Division, Exit Art's "Reactions" Exhibition Collection [reproduction number, e.g., LC-USZ62-123456]

A good example is the series of "Our Grief Is Not a Cry for War" vigils organized by the Artists' Network of Refuse & Resist in New York City in the wake of 9/11. People were asked to wear a dust mask (common in NYC after 9/11), dress all in black (common in NYC all the time), show up at Times Square at exactly 5 pm, and remain absolutely silent. Each participant held a sign that read "Our Grief Is Not a Cry for War." These vigils were silent and solemn, but there was a precision to the message that gave them a visceral potency in that emotionally raw time, for participants and observers alike.

The most famous vigils of the late twentieth century were probably those organized by the Mothers of the Plaza de Mayo, a group of Argentinian women whose children were disappeared by Argentina's 70s-era military dictatorship. By gathering every Thursday for more than a decade in the plaza in front of the Presidential Palace, they not only kept vigil for their lost loved ones, but also kept pressure on the government to answer for its crimes.

The "artistry" of a vigil can be exceedingly complex, or as simple as a few basic rituals. The simple fact of women wearing black and gathering in silence on Fridays gives shape and presence to the Women in Black worldwide network of vigils. Begun by Israeli women during the First Intifada to protest the occupation of Palestine, it has since expanded across the globe and embraced broader anti-war and pro-justice themes, but nonetheless maintains its distinctive character. At the other end of the spectrum, artist Suzanne Lacy has created complex works of art in which victims of sexual violence stand vigil amidst the art installations that tell their stories.

Related:

TACTICS
Image theater p. 62
Distributed action p. 32
Advanced leafleting p. 8

THEORIES
Action logic p. 208
Ethical spectacle p. 230
Hamoq & hamas p. 236
Narrative power analysis p. 244

USE THE POWER OF RITUAL: Compared to the average political event, a ritual is expected to have a certain gravitas, a higher level of emotional integrity, even a transcendent quality for participants. Like all rituals, a vigil should work at both the personal and political levels. It should offer a sacred experience for participants while effectively reaching out to nonparticipants. The more these two goals align, the more powerful the experience is for the participants and the more powerful the impact on the broader public.

KEY PRINCIPLE
at work

OTHER PRINCIPLES AT WORK:
Know your cultural terrain p. 142
*No one wants to watch a
drum circle* p. 156
Show, don't tell p. 174
*Simple rules can have
grand results* p. 176
Consider your audience p. 176
Balance art and message p. 100

TACTIC:
Banner hang

COMMON USES

To boldly articulate a demand; to rebrand a target; to provide a message frame or larger-than-life caption for an action.

PRACTITIONERS

Ruckus Society
Greenpeace
Rainforest Action Network

FURTHER INSIGHT

The Ruckus Society, "Balloon Banner Manual"
http://ruckus.org/article.php?id=364

Tree Climbing
http://trb.la/xa9dGu

Destructables, "Banner Drops"
http://Destructables.org/node/56

Destructables, "Banner Hoist"
http://Destructables.org/node/57

Steal This Wiki, "Banners"
http://wiki.stealthiswiki.org/wiki/Banners

Freeway Blogger
http://freewayblogger.blogspot.com/

CONTRIBUTED BY

Nadine Bloch

Astoria Bridge Nuclear Free Seas Banner Blockade. Greenpeace climbers hang from the Astoria-Megler Bridge over the Columbia River in Oregon to protest and block the arrival of the nuclear warship USS New Jersey. 1990. Photo by James Perez.

What better way to air the dirty laundry of an irresponsible institution than to hang a giant banner over its front door? A banner drop can also be an effective way to frame or contextualize an upcoming event or protest *see TACTIC: Reframe*. Banner hangs can also function as public service announcements to alert the public of an injustice or a dangerous situation.

Banner hangs can be as low-tech and low-risk as several bedsheets tied to road overpasses decrying the Iraq War, but the ones that really pack a punch involve large pieces of cloth or netting deployed at great heights, often by experienced climbers.

Regardless of the level of risk or complexity, all effective banner hangs start with a clear goal (you *have* a goal, right?!), and fall into two broad categories: *communicative* (concise protest statements), and *concrete* (blockade elements that directly disrupt business as usual) *see PRINCIPLE: Make your actions both concrete and communicative*. In 1991, in a great example of a banner hang with a *concrete goal*, small communities in the Pacific Northwest asked for help to stop nuclear warships from entering Clatsop County, Oregon, a designated nuclear-free zone on the Columbia River. An enormous net banner was deployed from the Astoria Bridge, affixed below the span where it would be difficult to remove, and weighted by the climbers' bodies themselves. The action succeeded in delaying the warships' entrance while educating the area on the issue.

Most banner hangs, however, tend to be *communicative*. Take, for instance, the banner hung from a crane in downtown Seattle in November 1999 *see CASE: Battle in Seattle* just before the opening of the World Trade Organization meeting. The banner messaging was as clear as day: an iconic visual of a street sign with arrows pointing in opposite directions: *democracy* this way, *WTO* that way. This was a classic "framing action." Hung on the eve of a big summit meeting and a huge protest, the banner made it clear what all the fuss to come was really about: a basic struggle of right and wrong; the People vs. WTO.

When there is no crane, bridge or building to hang your banner from, large helium-filled weather balloons have been used to raise everything from CODEPINK's "pink slip for President George Bush" in front of the White House to a banner deployed from a houseboat on the East River in New York with a message for the UN. Smaller balloons have been used to raise banners indoors in the atriums of malls or corporate or government buildings.

POTENTIAL PITFALLS: If the banner hang requires specific climbing skills or tools, *do not* skimp on training, scouting, or the quality of gear. Cutting corners could result in the banner snagging, the team being detained before the banner drops, or someone getting seriously injured or killed. Pay attention to changing weather conditions that could turn a proverbial walk in the park into a life-threatening situation *see PRINCIPLE: Take risks, but take care*. Also, make sure that lighting, lettering, height of building and other factors are taken into account to ensure a readable banner.

. . . .

SAY IT WITH PROPS: If it's worth saying, it's worth saying *loudly*! If it's worth doing, it's worth doing *boldly*! What better way to put your message out there, than to spell it out in twelve-foot-high letters?

Related:

TACTICS
Guerrilla projection p. 52
Giant props web
Media-jacking p. 72
Détournement/Culture
jamming p. 28

THEORIES
Points of intervention p. 250
Ethical spectacle p. 230
Framing web

CASE STUDIES
Battle in Seattle p. 286

KEY PRINCIPLE
at work

OTHER PRINCIPLES AT WORK:
Take risks, but take care p. 182
Reframe p. 168
Everyone has balls/
ovaries of steel p. 136
Do the media's work for them p. 124
Show, don't tell p. 174
Make your actions both concrete
and communicative p. 154

TACTIC: Blockade

PRACTITIONERS

Grassy Narrows First Nation
Penan of Borneo
Civil rights movement
Global justice movement
Greenpeace
Migrant/immigrant rights movement
American Indian Movement
Black Panther Party

FURTHER INSIGHT

The Ruckus Society, "Manuals and Checklists"
http://ruckus.org/section.php?id=82

Praxis Makes Perfect, "Resources for Organizers"
http://trb.la/yTYBj7

The Ruckus Society, A Tiny Blockades Book pamphlet, Oakland California, 2005

Blockades commonly have one of two purposes: first, to stop the bad guys, usually by targeting a *point of decision* (a boardroom), a *point of production* (a bank), or a *point of destruction* (a clearcut) *see THEORY: Points of intervention*; or second, to protect public or common space such as a building occupation or an encampment.

Blockades can consist of *soft blockades* (human barricades, such as forming a line and linking arms) or *hard blockades* (usinggear such as chains, U-locks, lock-boxes, tripods or vehicles. Blockades can involve one person or thousands of people, and can be a stand-alone tactic or an element of a larger tactic like an occupation.

Daguerreotype entitled, "Barricades avant l'attaque, Rue Saint-Maur" ("Barricades Before the Attack, Rue Saint-Maur"). Barricades were a completely new tactic at the time, and spread like wildfire across Europe. This is one of the very first photos ever taken of a street protest. By M. Thibault.

Successful blockades can be primarily *concrete* or *communicative see PRINCIPLE: Make your actions both concrete and communicative*. Either way, all participants should be clear on the goals. For example, if your blockade is symbolic, it does not require a *decision dilemma see: PRINCIPLE: Put your target in a decision dilemma*. If, however, you have an concrete goal, like preventing people from entering a building, you must ensure that your blockade has the capacity to achieve that goal. In other words, make sure you've got all the exits covered.

Whatever the case, it's important to lead with your goals. Don't think in terms of less or more radical; think in terms of what is appropriate to your goals, strategy, tone, message, risk, and level of escalation *see PRINCIPLE: Choose tactics that support your strategy*.

Here are a few tips to keep in mind, adapted from the Ruckus Society's how-to guide, *A Tiny Blockades Book*:

Build a crew. It all begins with a good action team and good nonviolence/direct-action training.

All roles are important. A good support team is essential.

Know your limits. Make a realistic assessment of your capacity and resources.

Scout, scout, scout. Spend a lot of time getting to know your location.

Know your choke points. These are the spots that make you the most secure and pesky blockader. Choose a spot that your target cannot just work, walk, or drive around.

Practice, and prepare contingency plans.

Don't plan for your action; plan through your action. Think of the action as "the middle," and expect a ton of prep work and follow-through — legal, emotional and political.

Have a media strategy. Make sure your message gets out and your action logic is as transparent as possible *see THEORY: Action logic*. Don't let communications be an afterthought.

Eliminate unnecessary risk. Make your action as safe as it can be to achieve your goals *see PRINCIPLE: Take risks, but take care*.

Do not ignore power dynamics within your group or between you and your target. Race, class, gender identity (real or perceived), sexual identity (real

Related:

TACTICS
Direct action p. 32
Banner drop p. 12
Mass street action p. 68
Occupation p. 78

THEORIES
Points of intervention p. 250
Pillars of support p. 248
Action logic p. 208
The commons p. 220
Cycles of social movements web

CASE STUDIES
Battle in Seattle p. 286

or perceived), age, physical ability, appearance, immigration status and nationality all affect your relationship to the action.

Dress for success. Make sure that your appearance helps carry the tone you want to set for your action. Dress comfortably. Ensure that support people bring water, food, and extra layers.

Be creative. Have fun.

POTENTIAL PITFALLS: A complex and confrontational tactic like blockade requires meticulous planning and preparation, and should never be attempted without significant preparation, research and training *see PRINCIPLE: Take risks, but take care.*

. . . .

KEY PRINCIPLE
at work

OTHER PRINCIPLES AT WORK:

Take risks, but take care p. 182
Choose tactics that support your strategy p. 112
Make your actions both concrete and communicative p. 154
Put your target in a decision dilemma p. 166
Escalate strategically p. 134
Maintain nonviolent discipline p. 148
Show, don't tell p. 174
Take leadership from the most impacted p. 180
Anger works best when you have the moral high ground p. 96

PUT YOUR TARGET IN A DECISION DILEMMA: When employing a blockade with a concrete goal, your ability to "hold the space" will depend on your decision dilemma. If you are able to prevent your target from "going out the back door" (metaphorically or literally), you have successfully created a dynamic where you cannot be ignored.

TACTIC: Blockade

Mobilization for Climate Justice activists blockade intersection in San Francisco, 2009. Photo by Rainforest Action Network.

TACTIC:
Creative Disruption

COMMON USES

To expose and disrupt the public relations efforts of the armed and dangerous. Particularly useful at speeches, hearings, meetings, fundraisers and the like.

EPIGRAPH

"Human salvation lies in the hands of the creatively maladjusted."

–Dr. Martin Luther King, Jr.

PRACTITIONERS

CODEPINK Women for Peace
WAG

FURTHER INSIGHT

Thompson, Nato, and Gregory Sholette. The Interventionists: Users' Manual for the Creative Disruption of Everyday Life. North Adams, MA: Massachusetts Institute of Technology and Massachusetts Museum of Contemporary Art, 2004.

Video: "Newt Gingrich Gets Glittered at the Minnesota Family Council" http://www.youtube.com/watch?v=g8OZsJokBBO

Video: "Auctioneer: Stop All the Sales Right Now!" http://www.youtube.com/watch?v=u3X89iViAlw

Video: "Mass Walkout at Wayne State Leaves IDF Spokesman Lecturing to Empty Room" http://trb.la/yWfBd8

CONTRIBUTED BY

Nancy L. Mancias

If a war criminal like Dick Cheney or a corporate criminal like former BP CEO Tony Hayward comes to town, what's the best way to challenge the spin they'll put on their misdeeds? Often, the scale of the misdeeds and the imbalance of power are so great that activists will forgo dialogue and move straight to disruption, attempting to shut down or seriously disrupt the event. Disruption can be an effective tactic, and has been used successfully by small groups of people, often with little advance notice or advance planning.

The problem, of course, is that not only does the target control the mic, the stage, and the venue, but even more importantly, as an invited guest or the official speaker, s/he has the audience's sympathy. A poorly thought-out shout-down or disruption can easily backfire. The target can portray themselves as a victim of anti-free speech harassment, thus gaining public sympathy and a larger platform. The challenge is to disrupt the event without handing your target that opportunity.

> "A well-designed creative disruption should leave your target no good option."

Sometimes an oblique intervention that re-frames the target's remarks or forces a response to your issues without literally preventing anyone from speaking can be more effective than just shouting down someone. When House Speaker Nancy Pelosi held a rare town hall meeting in San Francisco in 2006 during the height of the wars in Iraq and Afghanistan, CODEPINK demonstrators — angry that Pelosi was not pushing for a cut-off in war funding — waited until the Q and A session, then surrounded the stage with their "Stop Funding War" banners and stood there, silently, for the remainder of the meeting.

The creative use of a sign or banner can help you avoid the "it's an attack on free speech" trap. In effect, you're adding an additional "layer" of speech; you're engaging in *more* free speech, not less. Song can can also be used in this way. A 2011 foreclosure auction in Brooklyn, for instance, was movingly disrupted by protesters breaking into song. Song creates sympathy.

A creative disruption needn't be passive. When Newt Gingrich came to the Minnesota Family Council conference for a book signing, a queer activist dutifully waited in line and when it came to his turn, dumped rainbow glitter over Gingrich, shouting, "Feel the rainbow, Newt! Stop the hate, stop anti-gay policies" as he was escorted out of the room. The video documenting the event *see PRINCIPLE: Do the media's work for them* went viral and the disruption gained international press attention, sparking a wave of LGBT activism. The tactic of "glitter-bombing" even made it into an episode of the TV show *Glee*.

Theater is another way to "disrupt without disrupting." When Jeane Kirkpatrick (Reagan's Ambassador to the UN), came to UC Berkeley in the 1980's, activists staged a mock death-squad kidnapping. "Soldiers" (students) in irregular fatigues marched down the main aisle barking orders in Spanish and dragged off a few students kicking and screaming from the audience. Others then scattered leaflets detailing the U.S.'s and Kirkpatrick's support for El Salvador's death-squad government from the balcony onto the stunned audience.

CODEPINK activists re frame a Nancy Pelosi speech at a town hall forum in 2006 with their silent protest – showing how creative disruption can be an effective tactic by putting their target in a lose-lose situation. Chronicle / Michael Macor.

As these examples show, it's critical to tailor your disruption to the specific target and situation. Often, you can be more effective if you step out of the "combative speech box" and consider alternate modalities, like visuals, song, theater, and humor.

Republican Presidential candidate Rick Santorum being glitter-bombed at a Town Hall forum in late 2012 by LGBT rights activists. Not only did the initial hit of glitter creatively disrupt his meet-and-greet, but the continual presence of glitter on his person put him and his homophobic and anti-LGBT sentiments in a decision-dilemma. REUTERS/Sarah Conard

. . . .

KEY PRINCIPLE
at work

OTHER PRINCIPLES AT WORK:

The real action is your target's reaction web
Kill them with kindness p. 140
Show, don't tell p. 174
Reframe p. 168
Think narratively p. 186
Play to the audience that isn't there p. 160
Do the media's work for them p. 124

PUT YOUR TARGET IN A DECISION DILEMMA: Well-designed creative disruption should leave your target no good option. If Nancy Pelosi had acknowledged or engaged with the protesters, she would have only elevated their credibility and drawn further attention to their message. Had security cleared out the silent activists, it would have looked heavy-handed. Had she left the scene, it would have been seen as a capitulation. Her least worst option, and what she chose to do, was continue with the event — whose meaning was then reframed by the silent protest signs around her. A well-designed creative disruption puts you in a win-win — and your target in a lose-lose — situation.

TACTIC: Creative Disruption

THOSE WHO PROFESS TO FAVOR FREEDOM,

AND YET DEPRECATE AGITATION . . .

WANT RAIN WITHOUT THUNDER AND LIGHTNING.

THIS STRUGGLE MAY BE A MORAL ONE;

OR IT MAY BE A PHYSICAL ONE; OR IT MAY BE

H MORAL AND PHYSICAL; BUT IT MUST BE A STRUGGLE.

ER CONCEDES NOTHING WITHOUT A DEMAND. IT NEVER

AND IT NEVER WILL.

—*Frederick Douglass*

TACTIC:
Creative petition delivery

COMMON USES

To translate online outcry into offline action; to make mass public opposition unavoidably visible to a campaign target.

PRACTITIONERS

Avaaz.org
MoveOn.org
Greenpeace

FURTHER INSIGHT

Creative Petition: Bags of Grain to the White House to Prevent War, 1955
http://trb.la/wceMpx

Avaaz, "Highlights"
http://www.avaaz.org/en/highlights.php

CONTRIBUTED BY

Duncan Meisel, with help from Pascal Vollenweider @ Avaaz

Online petitions are an effective way of spreading information, raising an outcry or putting pressure on a target. But online actions alone are easily ignored by targets. To translate virtual signatures into real-world action, a number of netroots organizations have developed the art of creative petition delivery. While publicizing your message and the support it has garnered, creative petition deliveries put public pressure on your target.

It's helpful to find creative ways to physically quantify the number of petition signatures. A number of well-labeled boxes rolled into a target's office is a tried and true approach, but other tactics can be effective as well. For a petition asking the World Health Organization to investigate and regulate factory farms, the international multi-issue campaign organization Avaaz set up 200 cardboard pigs — each representing 1,000 petition signers — in front of the WHO building in Geneva, providing the media with a visual hook on which to peg stories about factory farms and swine flu.

But you don't have to physically occupy the same space as your target. Attracting media attention can be an effective way to reach a target as well. Avaaz sometimes places ads in newspapers that both their target and supporters are likely to read. In one instance, to deliver a petition against nuclear energy to German Chancellor Andrea Merkel, they purchased an ad in *Der Spiegel*, the German paper of record.

Or try a more outlandish media stunt. To deliver a petition against deepwater oil drilling in the Arctic, Greenpeace International sent its executive director to a controversial oil rig in the middle of the ocean, where he trespassed onto the rig to deliver the petition to the ship's captain — at which point he was arrested and held for four days. Between the unusual way it was delivered and the media coverage that resulted, the petition was difficult for the target to ignore.

Sometimes less public tactics can be equally effective: to deliver a petition about cluster bombs to a UN conference debating arms munitions treaties, Avaaz first digitally delivered 600,000 petition signatures to the head of the conference, and then quietly distributed 1,000 fliers to conference attendees, describing the issue and listing the number of people who'd signed the petition. Even the subtle hint of public pressure created a stir in the often obscure world of UN diplomats. The delivery had a big impact on the eventual outcome of the conference, which did not adopt a draft treaty to allow stockpiling of cluster bombs.

Related:

TACTICS

Distributed action p. 36
Artistic vigil p. 10
Advanced leafleting p. 8

THEORIES

Action logic p. 208
Points of intervention p. 250
Ethical spectacle p. 230

38 Degrees members deliver a petition of over 410,000 names to the NHS. Their message: Save Our NHS. Photo by 38 Degrees.

Creative petition deliveries allow organizers to turn online outcry into offline action. By becoming unavoidably visible to a campaign target, creative deliveries make sure the voices of thousands of petition signers are publicly heard.

· ·

MAKE THE INVISIBLE VISIBLE: Creative petition deliveries give an abstract issue a physical and visual presence. Public figures and decision-makers can afford to avoid listening to public outcry as long as it remains distant and exclusively online. By bringing the voices of petition signers to a target (and the media) in a way that makes them impossible to ignore, creative petition deliveries amplify the effectiveness of online organizing efforts.

KEY PRINCIPLE
at work

OTHER PRINCIPLES AT WORK:

Create online-offline synergy web
Show, don't tell p. 174
Bring the issue home p. 106
Consider your audience p. 118
Choose your target wisely 114
Put your target in a decision dilemma p. 166
Play to the audience that isn't there p. 160

TACTIC:
Debt strike

COMMON USES

To fight back against financial exploitation when many people are crushed by debt.

EPIGRAPH

"If you owe the bank $100, that's your problem; if you owe the bank $100 million, that's the bank's problem."

–John Paul Getty

CONTRIBUTED BY

Sarah Jaffe
Matthew Skomarovsky

What does non-cooperation with our own oppression look like? Sometimes it looks like Rosa Parks refusing to sit in the back of the bus, and sometimes it's less visible — for instance, a coordinated refusal to make our monthly debt payments.

With wages in many countries stagnant since the 1970s, people have increasingly turned to debt financing to pay for education, housing and health care. Banks have aggressively pursued and profited from this explosion of debt, fueling economic inequality, inflating a massive credit bubble and trapping millions in a form of indentured servitude.

Most people feel obliged to pay back loans no matter the cost, or fear the lasting consequences of default, but the financial crisis has begun to change that. After watching the government shovel trillions in bailouts and dirt-cheap loans to big banks, growing numbers view our debt burdens as a structural problem and a massive scam rather than a personal failure or a legitimate obligation. But asking politicians and banks for forgiveness is unlikely to get us anywhere, because our payments are their profits. What we need is leverage.

Enter the *debt strike*, an experiment in collective bargaining for debtors. The idea is simple: en masse, we stop paying our bills to the banks until they negotiate. Because they can't operate without these payments — for student loans, mortgages, or consumer credit — they're under severe pressure to negotiate. Such a strike can be connected to demands to reform the financial system, abolish predatory and usurious loan conditions, or provide direct debt forgiveness. Strikers could even pool some or all of the money they're not paying, and put it into a "strike fund" to support the campaign or kick-start alternative community-based credit systems.

Coordination is key. We can't act in isolation, exposing ourselves to retaliation and division. Instead, participants should all sign a pledge — either public or confidential — to stop paying certain bills. When enough people sign up to provide real leverage, strike. In the meantime, organize furiously, publicize a running total, aggregate grievances, collect outrageous debt stories, and watch the financial élite panic.

A debt strike is audacious, simple, and easy to participate in — easier than paying bills, since all you have to do is *not* pay your bills. It takes courage and social support, but provides immediate gratification. Who doesn't despise the monthly ritual of sending away precious cash to line the pockets of dishonest and destructive financial institutions?

Although a massive debt strike has not yet been organized, efforts are underway. People have been mobilizing for years to fight foreclosures and predatory loans. The Occupy Student Debt Campaign aims to gather a million student debt refusal pledges. Another group is building a social pledge system to connect debtors by neighborhood, common lenders and demands. Online social networks, pledge-to-act platforms like ThePoint.com and story aggregators like Tumblr may soon become weapons on the battlefield of debt.

The outrage, organizers, techniques and tools already exist, and the tactic has perhaps never been more justified. The debt strike is out there, waiting to take the world by storm.

FURTHER INSIGHT

Stephen Lerner, "Take the Fight to the Streets," In These Times, April 18, 2011
http://trb.la/wooXp3

Sarah Jaffe, "Debtor's Revolution: Are Debt Strikes Another Possible Tactic in the Fight Against the Big Banks?" AlterNet, November 3, 2011
http://trb.la/wIMxqX

Rortybomb, "Some Quick Thoughts on the Notion of a Debtors' Strike"
http://trb.la/ydZE6e

Occupy Student Debt Campaign
http://www.occupystudent debtcampaign.org/

Debt Strike kick-stopper
http://forum.contactcon.com/discussion/33/kick-stopper#Item_1

Related:

Gan Golan as the Master of Degrees. From the book The Adventures of Unemployed Man by Gan Golan and Erich Origen. Photo by Friedel Fisher.

POTENTIAL PITFALLS: While the initial sign-up is as easy as signing an online petition, unlike a petition, there are potentially serious consequences. Defaulting on a loan impacts your credit rating, which can severely impact your future ability to get a credit card, rent an apartment, buy a car, or even get a job. Thus a successful debt strike will require support networks for strikers, the same way a union has a strike fund to support striking workers.

Achieving the critical mass required for the tactic to be effective may also be a challenge. A debt strike is only effective at large scale.

"A debt strike is easier than paying bills, since all you have to do is not pay your bills."

. . . .

KEY THEORY
at work

OTHER THEORIES AT WORK:
Pillars of support p. 248
Points of intervention p. 250
Capitalism p. 216
The commons p. 220

DEBT REVOLT: Debt is too often treated like a personal failing that shouldn't be discussed in public, rather than a common struggle against systemic exploitation. We also tend to think of debt as a non-negotiable fact rather than a social construct. Once we realize that debts are shared fictions that can be renegotiated or even rejected entirely, we discover we have the power to pull the plug on a system that relies on our separation, shame, and consent. Household debt in the U.S. is around ninety percent of GDP, has grown at nearly twice the rate of real incomes, and as Mike Konczal has noted, impacts the bottom 99% disproportionately. As the slogan for the Occupy Student Debt campaign says: "Can't Pay? Won't Pay? Don't Pay!"

Student protester. Lack of economic opportunity is a threat to students, but what will non-cooperation with their oppression look like, and who will it threaten?

TACTIC:
Détournement/Culture jamming

COMMON USES

Altering the meaning of a target's messaging or brand; packaging critical messages as highly contagious media viruses.

PRACTITIONERS

The Situationist International
Adbusters
Jon Stewart
Stephen Colbert
Center for Tactical Magic
Robbie Conal
Guillermo Gómez-Peña
Gran Fury
Guerrilla Girls
Preemptive Media
Reverend Billy and the
Church of Earthalujah

CONTRIBUTED BY

Zack Malitz

Urban living involves a daily onslaught of advertisements, corporate art, and mass-mediated popular culture *see THEORY: Society of the spectacle.* As oppressive and alienating as this spectacle may be, its very ubiquity offers plentiful oppor-tunities for semiotic jiu-jitsu and creative disruption. Subversive and marginalized ideas can spread contagiously by reappropriating artifacts drawn from popular media and injecting them with radi-cal connotations.

This technique is known as

"Détournement appropriates and alters an existing media artifact, one that the intended audience is already familiar with, in order to give it a new meaning."

détournement. Popularized by Guy Debord and the Situ-ationists, the term is borrowed from French and roughly translates to "overturning" or "derailment." Détourne-ment appropriates and alters an existing media artifact, one that the intended audience is already familiar with, in order to give it a new, subversive meaning.

In many cases, the intent is to criticize the appropri-ated artifact. For instance, the neo-Situationist magazine *Adbusters* has created American flags bearing corporate logos in place of stars. The traditional flag, which is often used to quash dissent by equating America with lib-erty and progress *see THEORY: Floating signifier,* is made to communicate its own critique: corporations, not the people, rule America. Similarly, an *Adbusters* "subvertise-ment" for Camel cigarettes, perfectly rendered in the style and lettering of real Camel advertisements, depicts a bald Joe Chemo in a hospital bed.

Détournement works because humans are creatures of habit who think in images, feel our way through life, and often rely on familiarity and comfort as the final ar-biters of truth *see PRINCIPLE: Think narratively.* Rational arguments and earnest appeals to morality may prove less effective than a carefully planned détournement

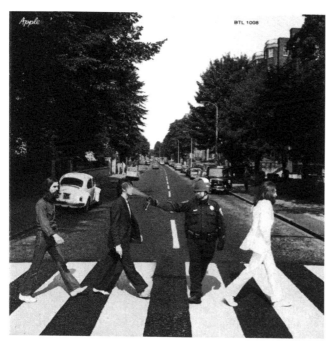

"Pepper spray cop" Lt. Pike strolls through the Beatles' iconic Abbey Road cover, casually pepper spraying Paul McCartney. This doctored image plays on the popularity of the Beatles to emphasize the callous absurdity of Pike's actions.

FURTHER INSIGHT

"A User's Guide to Détournement"
http://trb.la/zvA2dH

"Détournement as
Negation and Prelude"
http://trb.la/zTgoFp

Mark Dery, "Culture Jamming:
Hacking, Slashing, and Sniping
in the Empire of Signs"
http://markdery.com/?page_id=154

Lasn, Kalle. Culture Jam: The
Uncooling of America. New
York: Eagle Brook, 1999.

Heath, Joseph, and Andrew Potter.
The Rebel Sell: Why the
Culture Can't Be Jammed.
New York: Harper, 2005.

Destructables, "The Art and Science
of Billboard Improvement"
http://destructables.org/node/82

Destructables, "Phonebooth
Takeover Tutorial"
http://destructables.org/node/52

Destructables, "Shop-Dropping
Product Lables"
http://trb.la/wLEUjZ

that bypasses the audience's mental filters by mimicking familiar cultural symbols, then disrupting them.

For instance, UC Davis police officer Lt. John Pike began to pop up in some unexpected places after he was captured on film casually pepper spraying students during a peaceful protest. One image depicted Lt. Pike walking through John Trumbull's classic painting *The Declaration of Independence* and pepper spraying America's founding document, while another depicted him in Georges Seurat's *A Sunday Afternoon on the Island of La Grande Jatte*, pepper spraying a woman lounging in the grass. These images, and other détournements of "pepper spray cop," are some of the most visible critiques of police brutality in recent American history.[1]

In addition to its instrumental, critical function, détournement has an important humanistic function.

Related:

TACTICS

Media-jacking p. 72
Identity correction p. 60
Guerrilla projection p. 52
Guerrilla newspaper web

THEORIES

Society of the spectacle p. 266
Ethical spectacle p. 230
Memes p. 242
Alienation effect p. 210
Floating signifier p. 234
Points of intervention p. 250

CASE STUDIES

Billionaires for Bush p. 296
Colbert roasts Bush p. 308
Mining the Museum p. 334
Couple in the Cage p. 312
The Barbie Liberation
Organization p. 282
99% bat signal p. 278

[1] It is worth noting that the "pepper spray cop" meme emerged out of an incident in which the victims of police brutality were mostly white college students. By contrast, the brutal murder of Oscar Grant, a young black man, by BART police officer Johannes Mehserle, which was also filmed, generated nowhere near the same level of outrage. Détournement, as a communicative strategy that closely mimics dominant culture, often replicates—or even relies on—oppressive cultural assumptions and biases.

Détournement can be used to disrupt the flow of the media spectacle and, ultimately, to rob it of its power. Advertisements start to feel less like battering rams of consumerism and more like the raw materials for art and critical reflection. Advertising firms may still generate much of culture's raw content, but through détournement and related culture jamming tactics, we can reclaim a bit of autonomy from the mass-mediated hall of mirrors that we live in, and find artful ways to talk back to the spectacle and use its artifacts to amplify our own voices.

POTENTIAL PITFALLS: Détournement is just a tactic, and like any tactic, it needs to be integrated into a larger strategy to be effective *see PRINCIPLE: Choose tactics that support your strategy.* While détournement can be a highly effective political tool, when divorced from a larger strategy, it can slide into a tool of complacency or complicity *in the guise of resistance.* There's nothing wrong with taking savage pleasure in subverting grossly offensive media images, but take care to avoid using détournement as merely a palliative or a substitute for organizing.

. . . .

KEY PRINCIPLE
at work

OTHER PRINCIPLES AT WORK:
Show, don't tell p. 174
Make the invisible visible p. 152
Reframe p. 168
Brand or be branded p. 104
Balance art and message p. 100
Don't just brainstorm, art-storm! p. 128
Use others' prejudices against them p. 192

KNOW YOUR CULTURAL TERRAIN: As an act of semiotic sabotage, détournement requires the user to have fluency in the signs and symbols of contemporary culture. The better you know a culture, the easier it is to shift, repurpose, or disrupt it. To be successful, the media artifact chosen for détournement must be recognizable to its intended audience. Further, the saboteur must be familiar with the subtleties of the artifact's original meaning in order to effectively create a new, critical meaning.

TACTIC: Détournement/Culture jamming

This altered iconic image undercuts Coca Cola's brand by evoking the company's violent labor-repression strategies.

TACTIC:
Direct Action

COMMON USES

To shut things down; to open things up; to pressure a target; to re-imagine what's possible; to intervene in a system; to empower people; to defend something good; to shine a spotlight on something bad.

EPIGRAPH

"Direct action gets the goods."
—Industrial Workers of the World

PRACTITIONERS

The Ruckus Society
Civil rights movement
Gandhi
Antiwar movement
Quakers
Unions
Jesus of Nazareth
American Indian Movement
Jewish resistance during the Holocaust
The Boston Tea Party (original)
Global justice movement
Anti-nuclear movement
Rastafarianism
GI resistance
Immigrant rights
Earth First
ACT-UP
Mitch Snyder

CONTRIBUTED BY

Joshua Kahn Russell

Direct action is at the heart of all human advancement. Sound like a grandiose claim? It is. But it's also beautifully simple: direct action means that we take collective action to change our circumstances, without handing our power to a middle-person.

We see instances of direct action in indigenous parables and stories, in the Bible, Torah and Koran, in every people's movement and popular revolution in modern history. Direct action is often practiced by people who have few resources, seeking to liberate themselves from an injustice.

Direct action is a physical act that should be designed so that the story tells its self. It seeks to change power dynamics directly, rather than relying on others to make changes for us.

People often conflate direct action with "getting arrested." While sometimes getting arrested can amplify your message, or is strategically necessary to achieve your goal, it isn't the *point* of direct action. (In most liberation struggles throughout history, "getting captured" is actually seen as a *bad* thing!)

Similarly, people often conflate direct action with civil disobedience. Civil disobedience is a specific form of direct action that involves intentionally violating a law because that law is unjust — for instance, refusing to pay taxes that would fund a war, or refusing to comply with anti-immigrant legislation. In these circumstances, breaking the law *is the purpose*. With other kinds of direct action, laws may be broken, but the law being broken isn't the point. For example, we may be guilty of trespassing if we drop a banner from a building, but the violation is incidental: we aren't there to protest trespassing laws.

While associated with confrontation, direct action at its core is about *powe*r. Smart direct action assesses power dynamics and finds a way to shift them.

One way of thinking about power is that there are two kinds: *organized money* and *organized people*. We don't have billions of dollars to buy politicians and governments, but with direct action organized people spend a different currency: we leverage *risk*. We leverage our freedom, our comfort, our privilege or our safety.

As Frederick Douglass said, "power concedes nothing without a demand." Malcolm X elaborated, "Power never takes a step back, except in the face of more power." Rather than deferring to others to make changes for us through votes or lobbying, we seek to change the dynamics of power directly.

"Rather than deferring to others, we seek to change the dynamics of power directly. "

FURTHER INSIGHT

Praxis Makes Perfect - Direct
Action resources
http://trb.la/Awdjso

Gene Sharp's 198 methods
of nonviolent action
http://trb.la/yNUMG2

Video, Book and Interactive Game
on Direct Action: A Force
More Powerful
http://www.aforcemore-
powerful.org/

War Resisters' International
handbook for nonviolent campaigns
http://wri-irg.org/node/3855

Alliance of Community Trainers
http://www.trainersalliance.org/

Ruckus Society
http://www.ruckus.org

RANT Collective
http://www.rantcollective.net

Destructables, "Lockboxes"
http://destructables.org/node/59

Related:

POTENTIAL PITFALLS: Direct action involves significant levels of risk for all involved. It is imperative to be careful, conscious and deliberate about the risks you take. A good action planner distinguishes between the risks she can

Direct action is often practiced by people who have few resources, seeking to liberate themselves from an injustice. Image by Black Mesa Indigenous Support (BMIS) Collective.

(and should) minimize, and the ones she cannot, and will explain to all participants the potential consequences *see PRINCIPLE: Take risks, but take care.*

KEY THEORY
at work

ACTION LOGIC: Because direct action is a physical act, it often speaks louder and deeper than anything you might say or write. Ideally, you should choose your target and design your action so that *the action itself tells the story.*

INSTEAD OF WAGING AN ALL-OUT ASSAULT ON THE CASTLE,

THE PRANKSTER SLIPS THROUGH THE GATES WEARING A FOOL'S OUTFIT...

—*Art Tinnitus*

TACTIC:
Distributed action

COMMON USES

To demonstrate the breadth, diversity and power of a movement; to swarm a large target in diverse locations.

PRACTITIONERS

350.org
Billionaires for Bush
UK Uncut
MoveOn.org

FURTHER INSIGHT

International Solidarity work as Distributed Action for South Africa: http://trb.la/xIwDYd

World AIDS Day Distributed Actions: http://www.worldaidsday.org/

350.org, "International Day of Climate Action" (2009) http://www.350.org/en/october24

Billionaires for Bush, "Do-It-Yourself Manual" (2004) http://trb.la/wEe81W

CONTRIBUTED BY

Phil Aroneanu

October 24, 2009, marked the first 350 International Day of Climate Action, according to CNN "the most widespread day of political action in our planet's history." Pictured here, Poppy and Jarrah hold a 350 kick-board at the Great Barrier Reef. Photo by 350.org.

350 International Day of Climate Action, Cairo. Photo by 350.org.

We use the Internet for news, to be social, and to share information, but it can also be a radical tool for connecting people around the world in service to a common cause. That might mean signing your name to a petition, but it can also involve taking real world action in our own towns and cities. At its best, a distributed action projects the power of the movement and gives activists a sense of being part of a greater whole. This is a particularly useful tactic when a movement is young, dispersed, and minimally networked.

There are a number of ways that distributed action can help propel a campaign forward and bring a critical issue to the fore, but here are a few key elements:

The day of action. A group of people create a call to action, and provide a meme *see THEORY*, message, or framework for others around the world to take similar action at the same time. The fact that the events all happen at the same time projects a sense of power and focuses attention on the issue at hand. Days (or weeks) of action can be highly disciplined and structured, or they can be more like a potluck dinner, where everybody brings the dish s/he feels like cooking up. Organizers might choose to invest time and energy in select "flag-ship" locations to help drive the story and take things to a higher level in a few spots.

The call to action. A call to action should resonate not just with your core supporters and networks, but should tell a story that the general public will understand, and motivate new volunteer leaders to take to the streets. Depending on the situation, a call to action might have an embedded demand of political leaders, or it can simply be an expression of grievances, like the call to #occupywallstreet.

Providing the tools. Hard work, a compelling story, and a healthy dose of inspiration are the most important elements of a successful distributed action. But it can be helpful to provide some extra resources for those activists who have never organized an action before. This can be as simple as posting a web link to a few tips, or as complex as offering in-person trainings and downloadable toolkits with posters, checklists, sample press releases and more. Some kinds of actions, especially those that involve nonviolent direct action, will require more support than others *see PRINCIPLE: Take risks, but take care.*

> "A distributed action projects the power of the movement and gives activists a sense of being part of a greater whole."

POTENTIAL PITFALLS: By its nature a distributed action is risky. Not physically, but politically: You put out a call, and people you've never met respond and roll into action under your banner. Some folks may go way off message or do something foolish that requires you to engage in damage control. This is part of the risk using a tactic with such an open architecture, but should not discourage you from doing it. Most things will probably go swimmingly, but the more you follow the guidelines above — a strong framework, clear call to action, and solid tools to help folks stay on track — the less likely you are to have problems. Many groups also use nonviolence guidelines or a code of conduct that people agree to abide by when signing up online.

KEY PRINCIPLE
at work

OTHER PRINCIPLES AT WORK:

Simple rules can have
grand results p. 176

Make new folks welcome p. 150

Enable, don't command p. 132

Create levels of participation web

Delegate p. 122

Choose tactics that support
your strategy p. 112

Stay on message p. 178

Use the Jedi mind trick p. 194

This ain't the Sistene Chapel p. 188

Do the media's work for them p. 124

Consider your audience p. 118

HOPE IS A MUSCLE: A successful distributed action demands commitment from all involved. It's easy to feel like nobody is listening. Distributed action runs on inspiration, momentum, hope and hard work. If you tell a story that resonates, pour your utmost efforts into empowering others to take action, and keep a positive and fun outlook, you can pull off a great and successful distributed action.

TACTIC: Distributed action

An aerial view of the 344 (just short of 350) people at the Gibsons, B.C, Canada rally. The 350 day of action was the largest distributed action ever recorded. Image by 350.org

TACTIC:
Electoral guerrilla theater

COMMON USES

Running for public office as a creative prank — not to win the election, but to get attention for a radical critique of policy or to sabotage the campaign of a particularly heinous candidate.

PRACTITIONERS

Reverend Billy & the Church of Earthalujah
The Dutch Provos
The Dutch Kabouters
Pauline Pantsdown of Australia
Jello Biafra
Michael Moore ("Ficus 2000")
Joan JettBlakk ("Lick Bush in '92")
Christof Schlingensief (Chance 2000, Germany)

FURTHER INSIGHT

Stephen Colbert Super PAC http://www.colbertsuperpac.com/

World AIDS Day Distributed Actions: http://www.worldaidsday.org/

L. M. Bogad, Electoral Guerrilla Theater: Radical Ridicule and Social Movements (New York: Routledge, 2005)

L. M. Bogad, "Billy Versus Bloomy: Electoral Guerrilla theater In New York City." In ByProduct: On the Excess of Embedded Art Practices, edited by Marisa Jahn (Toronto: YYZ Books, 2010)

CONTRIBUTED BY

L. M. Bogad

A group of eco-anarchist "gnomes" running for city council in Amsterdam; Reverend Billy, an anti-consumerist performance artist, running for mayor of New York City; a drag queen running for the Australian senate as the queer dopplegänger of far-right racist politician Pauline Hanson. These are all examples of electoral guerrilla theater, in which creative activists run for public office to inspire critique of the electoral system or the choices on offer.

The term *electoral guerrilla* yokes two seemingly incompatible approaches. Electoral activists work within the state's most accepted and conventional avenues in an attempt to reform the system peacefully. Guerrillas, in the military sense, exist on the extreme margins of the social system, constantly on the move, launching surprise attacks against the state before disappearing again. This contradiction is what makes electoral guerrilla theater a wild card in the repertoire of resistance, both for the target and the activist. It is an unstable and problematic combination that can take all players involved by surprise.

Winning is rarely the goal. However, by piggybacking on the massive media attention that elections gather, a clever guerrilla campaign can attract much more public attention than might otherwise be possible. Craft a compelling and funny character that fits your critique, say, a pro-corporate pirate who wants to get in on the easy plunder that Wall Street has been enjoying, for example. Craft your persona, and start crashing mainstream political events — or make a scene when you are prevented from crashing. Even better, earn more scandalous attention by crashing your absurdity through the front door of the power structure by getting a slot in an "equal time" debate, or getting on the ballot with your silly character name, or getting interviewed by the straight media in character.

> "The power of the electoral guerrilla is in great part the fact that you are not trying to win state power but to call its core premises into question."

Joan Jett Blakk ran a militant, queer campaign for President in 1992. Photo by Marc Geller.

Related:

TACTICS
Prefigurative intervention p. 82
Media-jacking p. 72
Identity correction p. 60
Détournement/Culture
jamming p. 28
White plan web
Hoax p. 54
Guerrilla theater web
Street theater web

THEORIES
Alienation effect p. 210
Ethical spectacle p. 230
Points of intervention p. 250
Narrative power analysis p. 244
Floating signifier p. 234

CASE STUDIES
The Nihilist Democratic Party p. 342

Couple things to keep in mind:

Do what they do but with a critical difference *see* THEORY: *Alienation effect.* If you're doing this right, by absurdly aping the clichés of the "proper" candidates you can call attention to the fact that they are just as socially-constructed and fake as your pirate/gnome/witch/etc. Cut ribbons. Kiss babies. Bring out the empty symbolism of these rituals, and insert your own radical critique, alternative meanings to them with a few quick jokes.

Combine serious and playful elements in your election platform. You should actually have a serious point you're making, and in the middle of all the absurdity and pranks, while you've got people's attention, make that point. Jello Biafra did a great job illustrating this principle during his run for mayor of San Francisco in 1979. Some of his "if I am elected" platform made folks laugh bitterly; some planks —

★ ★ ★ ★ VOTE ★ ★ ★ ★

REV **BILLY TALEN**
GREEN PARTY Candidate
for **MAYOR** of **NYC**

VOTE
Tuesday
Nov. 3rd

★ ★ ★ ★ ★ ★ ★ ★ ★ ★ ★ ★
Find out more at VoteRevBilly.org

Reverend Billy Talen for Mayor of NYC. Photo: brennan cavanaugh. Graphics by Emily Schuch.

like suggesting that beat cops be elected by the neighborhoods they patrol — made folks think "hmmm...actually that's not a bad idea." Get people's attention with humor and follow up with a few simple, radical, The-World-We-Want-to-See ideas *see TACTIC: Prefigurative intervention*. In this way you're not just talking about what you're against, but what you're for.

When done right, electoral guerrilla theater is *serious play* at its best.

POTENTIAL PITFALLS: If there is a candidate running that you actually do support, take care to craft your campaign in such a way that it amplifies theirs, or at least doesn't interfere with it. Don't let your satire upstage your ally to the point that it detracts from their campaign.

. . . .

MAKE IT FUNNY: Don't forget this is a joke. Elections are a seductive power ritual. If you are doing well as an electoral guerrilla, you'll get a lot of attention due to your clever, critical pranks and incursions into the field of "legitimate" debate. This may lead to you or members of your crew to think, "hey, we might actually win; let's tone this down and get more respectable." The campaign then becomes just like the other boring candidacies, except without the money or insider connections. Yawn. The end. The power of the electoral guerrilla is in great part the fact that you are not trying to win state power but to call its core premises into question.

KEY PRINCIPLE
at work

OTHER PRINCIPLES AT WORK:

Anyone can act p. 98
Use your radical fringe to slide
the Overton window p. 200
Stay on message p. 178
Play to the audience that
isn't there p. 160
Know your cultural terrain p. 142
Reframe p. 168
Do the media's work for them p. 124
Use the law, don't be
afraid of it p. 196
Turn the tables p. 190
Bring the issue home p. 106
Balance art and message p. 100
Put your target in a
decision dilemma p.166

TACTIC:
Eviction blockade

COMMON USES

To organize a strong show of physical resistance to an unjust eviction; to force a moral confrontation with a system that operates amorally.

EPIGRAPH

"Home is where the heart is."
—Proverb

PRACTITIONERS

Take Back the Land (USA)
Landless Workers Movement (MST, Brazil)
Western Cape Anti-Eviction Campaign (South Africa)
Abahlali baseMjondolo (South Africa)
City Life / Vida Urbana (USA)
Occupy Our Homes (USA)

FURTHER INSIGHT

City Life / Vida Urbana, "Resources"
http://clvu.org/resources

Occupy Our Homes, "Resources: How to defending your home"
http://occupyourhomes.org/resources/

Video: "Michael Moore's 'Capitalism, A Love Story': 'You Be Squatters in Your Own Home'"
http://trb.la/zpgVWF

Eviction Stoppers of Spain (article and video)
http://trb.la/zKaVgT

CONTRIBUTED BY

Ryan Acuff

It was a cold March morning in Rochester, NY, when the city marshal approached 9 Ravenwood Avenue in an attempt to carry out what he thought would be a routine eviction. Instead, he was met with eighty people holding signs and banners protesting the foreclosure and imminent displacement of the Lennon-Griffin family, including grandmother Catherine Lennon, her three daughters, and eight small grandchildren. Four people were chained to the stairs of the house. Next to them was a large sign that read, "We shall not be moved." The eviction blockade had been organized by the anti-poverty group Take Back the Land.

The marshal left as quickly as he came, later saying, "this is not what I signed up for." He would not return for weeks.

Eviction blockades are as old as evictions themselves, and like evictions, they tend to surge in numbers in times of economic hardship. In response to the Great Depression in the U.S., for instance, the National Unemployment Council — founded in Chicago in 1930 — formed hundreds of local branches to organize eviction blockades across the country. From January to June 1932, 185,794 families in New York City received eviction notices, and the Unemployment Council helped an estimated 77,000 of those families keep their homes. The eviction blockade can be an extraordinarily effective tactic when it has community support, when it is embedded within a larger movement or campaign, and when it is linked to winnable demands.

In the case of the Lennon-Griffin family, mortgage holder Fannie Mae eventually pushed the City of Rochester to conduct a SWAT-like operation to break the blockade and forcibly remove the family. The eviction created a terrifying spectacle: Special Operations officers stormed the house, crime scene tape was wrapped around the area, traffic enforcement officers blocked access by supporters and media. The police arrested seven people, including an elderly neighbor across the street in her pajamas. Though the eviction went ahead, the family's plight and the actions and goals of the movement were elevated to a new prominence, and more families in the community stepped forward to defend their homes with eviction blockades. The eviction cost the city an estimated $9,000 — one third the value of the original mortgage.

Marshall Cooper, 75, protests the national conference of the American Bankers Association in Copley Square, Boston in October of 2010. Cooper's home in the Dorchester neighborhood of Boston was foreclosed on in early 2010. Photo by Kelly Creedon.

The negative publicity of breaking a community-supported eviction blockade tends to make local governments and banks more reticent to repeat violent evictions in the future. For example, just five weeks after Catherine Lennon was evicted, she publicly moved back into her house without the bank's permission and with zero police interference.[1]

In the wake of a property bubble that saw the banks bailed out while homeowners were left to fend for themselves, the tactic is an increasingly effective one for social movements everywhere. In the summer of 2011 the *Indignados* movement in Spain shifted its actions from public squares to neighborhoods, organizing eviction blockades across the country. Six months later, the Occupy movement followed suit. The organizing potential for such actions is as vast as the injustice it seeks to confront.

* * *

PUT YOUR TARGET IN A DECISION DILEMMA: Effective eviction blockades create a decision dilemma for banks and local governments. If they call off the eviction, the family stays and the movement grows. If they go ahead with the eviction and break the blockade, they dramatically highlight fundamental injustices in the system and raise awareness of the movement.

KEY PRINCIPLE
at work

OTHER PRINCIPLES AT WORK:

[1] As of December 2011, Catherine Lennon and her family were still in their home and it seemed likely the family will find a permanent settlement with Fannie Mae and Bank of America to stay in their home.

TACTIC:
Flash Mob

COMMON USES

To organize a show of dissent on short notice; to quickly replicate a successful tactic in a dispersed yet coordinated way; to create a shared moment of random kindness and senseless beauty.

PRACTITIONERS

Improv Everywhere
Critical Mass
April 6th Movement
Newmindspace
Adbusters
Revolution through the Social Network
Allan Kaprow
UK Uncut

FURTHER INSIGHT

Know Your Meme, "Flash Mob"
http://trb.la/ybFWol

End the Occupation, "B.D.S. Song/ Dance Flash Mob: Step-by-Step How-To Kit"
http://trb.la/zXeGst

Mondoweiss, "Mondo Award Winner, First Runner-Up: Rae Abileah and Colleen Kelly for Flashmob"
http://trb.la/yRnZdb

CONTRIBUTED BY

Dave Oswald Mitchell
Andrew Boyd

Pillow fight on Wall Street, organized by Newmindspace in 2009. The widely circulated invitation read simply: "Bring a pillow to Wall St & Broad St at 3:00pm. Dress in business suits, demand your bailout."

A flash mob is an unrehearsed, spontaneous, contagious, and dispersed mass action. Flash mobs first emerged in 2003 as a form of participatory performance art, with groups of people using email, blogs, text messages, and Twitter to arrange to meet and perform some kind of playful activity in a public location.[1] More rec-ently, activists have begun to harness the political potential of flash mobs for organizing spontaneous mass actions on short notice.

Flash mobs have recently become a powerful tactic for political protest, particularly under repressive conditions. In the midst of a harsh crackdown on protests in Belarus in 2011, for instance, dissidents calling themselves "Revolution through the Social Network" began organizing impromptu demonstrations where protesters would simply gather in public spaces and clap their hands in unison.[2] The result was the bewildering sight of secret police brutally arresting people for the simple act of clapping their hands — a powerful challenge to the legitimacy of an increasingly irrational regime.

The overthrow of President Hosni Mubarak in Egypt also involved flash-mob-like tactics, with organizers calling for protesters to gather initially in alleys and other protected spaces for safety before moving into the streets in larger and larger numbers. Blogger Patrick Meier explains the thinking behind this approach:

> Starting small and away from the main protests is a safe way to pool protesters together. It's also

about creating an iterative approach to a "strength in numbers" dynamic. As more people crowd the smaller streets, this gives a sense of momentum and confidence. Starting in alleyways localizes the initiative. People are likely neighbors and join because they see their friend or sister out in the street.[3]

Another example of effective use of the flash mob tactic is UK Uncut. In October 2010, one week after the British government announced massive cuts to public services, seventy people occupied a Vodaphone store in London to draw attention to the company's record of unpaid taxes. The idea quickly went viral: within three days, over thirty Vodaphone stores had been shut down around the country by flash mobs organizing over Twitter using the hashtag #ukuncut.

The revolutionary potential for dispersed, coordinated action using flash mob tactics has only begun to be realized. As Micah White wrote in Adbusters:

Fun, easy to organize, and resistant to both infiltration and preemption because of their friend-to-friend network topology, flash mobs are positioned to be the next popular tactic with revolutionary potential. . . . With flash mobs, activists have the potential to swarm capitalism globally.[4]

Related:

TACTICS
Creative disruption p. 18
Guerrilla musical web
Invisible theater p. 66
Carnival protest web
Mass street action p. 68
Distributed action p. 26

THEORIES
The social cure p. 264
Movement as network web
The tactics of everyday life p. 268

CASE STUDIES
Orange Alternative web
UK/US Uncut web

. . . .

SIMPLE RULES CAN HAVE GRAND RESULTS: Whether it's a mass pillow fight (bring a pillow, hit anyone else carrying a pillow), or a bank shut-down (get in line, ask the teller for your entire account balance in pennies, and be disarmingly polite), the invitation to participate in a flash mob is easy to share, but when multiplied by tens or hundreds of people, can lead to complex, dispersed and powerfully effective actions.

KEY PRINCIPLE
at work

OTHER PRINCIPLES AT WORK:
No one wants to watch
a drum circle p. 156
Enable, don't command p. 132
If protest is illegal, make
daily life a protest p. 138
Make your actions both concrete
and communicative p. 154

[1] The understanding of "flash mobs" that has filtered into popular culture is generally limited to surprise choreographed dance routines performed in public. But for organizing purposes, those carefully choreographed stunts are better described as "guerrilla" than "flash." see TACTIC: Guerrilla Musicals. The distinct characteristics of a flash mob – an unrehearsed, spontaneous, contagious, and dispersed mass action – has its own unique advantages, and requires a different set of organizing principles than a surprise choreographed dance routine requires.
[2] "Dozens Arrested in Belarus 'Clapping' Protest," Al Jazeera English, July 3, 2011.
[3] "Civil Resistance Tactics Used in Egypt's Revolution," irevolution, Feb. 7, 2011. http://irevolution.net/2011/02/27/tactics-egypt-revolution-jan25.
[4] Micah White, "To the Barricades," Adbusters 94 (March/April 2011).

TACTIC:
Forum theater

COMMON USES

Forum theater is a tool for exploring and rehearsing possible actions that people can take to transform their world. It's often used both in preparation to taking action and in anti-oppression workshops.

PRACTITIONERS

Julian Boal
Brent Blair
Cheryl Harrison
Mark Weinburg
Mark Weinblatt
Rosa Gonzales
Melina Bobadilla
Practicing Freedom

FURTHER INSIGHT

Boal, Augusto. Games for Actors and Non-Actors. London: Routledge, 1992.

Boal, Augusto. Theater of the Oppressed. New York: Theater Communications Group, 1993.

CONTRIBUTED BY

Levana Saxon

Forum theater is one of the more commonly used tools from Theater of the Oppressed. It begins with the crafting and performance of a short play that dramatizes real situations faced by the participants and that ends with the protagonist(s) being oppressed. After the first performance, the play or scene is repeated with one crucial difference: the spectators become "spect-actors" and can at any point yell "freeze" and take the place of an actor to attempt to transform the outcome. Forum theater is an exercise in democracy in which anyone can speak and anyone can act.

"The point is not to show what we think other people should do — it is not theater of advice. The point is to discover what we can do."

One of the first things that spect-actors realize is that, as in life, if they don't intervene, nothing will change. The next thing spect-actors find is that doing "something" is not enough, it must be a *strategic* something. The people acting as oppressors on stage will maintain their oppression until they are authentically stopped — and just like in life, stopping them isn't easy. Forum theater thus becomes a laboratory to experiment with different courses of action.

The protagonists should be characters that all or most of the people in the room can identify with, so that when they intervene, they are rehearsing *their own* action. The point is not to show what we think *other* people should do — it is not theater of advice. The point is to discover what *we* can do.

Forum theater is facilitated by someone called a Joker, who engages the spect-actors both on and off stage in dialogue throughout the process. After an intervention, the Joker may ask, "Did this work?", "Was this realistic?", "Can you do this in real life?"

Forum theater was developed in a context in which it was very clear what the oppression was, who was oppressed and who the oppressors were: its originator, Augusto Boal, was living in exile from the Brazilian military dictatorship, and social movements across the continent were struggling against harsh military

Participants in a Theater of the Oppressed program in Toronto, Canada, run by In Forma Theater. The months-long program addresses life transitions related to family, migration, resettlement and loss. Photo by Adam Perry.

Related:

TACTICS
Image theater p. 62
Invisible theater p. 66
Guerrilla theater web
Street theater web

THEORIES
Theater of the Oppressed p. 272
Pedagogy of the Oppressed p. 246

repression. Since then, the technique has been adapted to countless other contexts around the world, as practitioners seek to grapple with the complicated power relationships of more diverse groups of people. Often interventions will uncover multiple layers of power, dramatizing characters who are simultaneously oppressed and oppressing others.

Forum theater is an effective tool of creative activism, useful for generating interventions, as an intervention itself, and for building common strategic frameworks for movements.

· ·

POTENTIAL PITFALLS: The role of the Joker is a tricky one. It is easy to leave the group with false optimism about what can work, or to run out of time before everyone is satisfied with what has been attempted. The Joker must make many small decisions in every moment, such as whether or not to allow the introduction of additional characters, whether or not to add interventions upon other interventions, how many interventions to allow, when to stop an intervention when it's not going anywhere, and so on.

Another pitfall is to use forum theater to generate solutions *and then fail to act on them*: forum theater "works" to the extent that it prepares participants to intervene critically in their own lives.

PRINCIPLES AT WORK:
Praxis makes perfect p. 162
Anyone can act p. 98
Don't just brainstorm, artstorm! p. 128

TACTIC:
General strike

COMMON USES

To put effective pressure on a corporate or political target by shutting down business as usual; to overcome the challenges of organizing vulnerable workers in isolated sectors.

EPIGRAPH

"Win or lose, mass strikes reveal the truth."

—Jeremy Brecher, Strike!

PRACTITIONERS

Justice for Janitors campaign
Service Employees International Union
Occupy Oakland

FURTHER INSIGHT

The Seattle General Strike of 1919
http://trb.la/wMXduW

Movie : "The Corporation"
http://trb.la/xItXye

Strike! Famous Worker Uprisings (in pictures)
http://trb.la/xmAfET

Jeremy Brecher. Strike! Boston: (South End Press, 1997)

CONTRIBUTED BY

Stephen Lerner

One-day general strikes, like those that took place in the UK and Oakland in November 2011, are primarily symbolic protests, more focused on making a political point than creating real economic pressure. To harness the tactic's true potential, general strikes need to escalate from symbolic one-day protests to ongoing actions that last days and potentially weeks, with a clear goal of inflicting both economic and political damage until the strikers' demands are met.

IWW Sabo Cat tells us to "Strike!" Illustration by Eric Drooker.

Strikes can be a powerful weapon for shifting the balance of power in workplaces and points of production. By withholding their labor and stopping work from continuing, generations of workers over the last 150 years have won better wages, working conditions, and basic bargaining rights.

It is too easy, however, to romanticize the idea of strikes and general strikes. Due to the increasing concentration of transnational corporate power and various laws limiting workers rights, most strikes in the United States are now small and rarely successful rearguard actions to resist wage and benefit cuts. Workers need to creatively reinvent the tactic if strikes are again going to be an effective weapon to win justice. In particular, workers need to recognize, and harness, the power of *general* and cross-industry strikes.

The city-wide general strikes of janitors in Los Angles (2000), Boston (2002) and Houston (2006) are one example of how an industry-wide general strike successfully forced powerful corporations hiding behind cleaning subcontractors to meet the demands of tens of thousands of striking janitors. Undocumented immigrant janitors were able to use sit-ins, street blockades and nonviolent civil disobedience, backed by supporters around the world, to build movements that could win. At various points, striking workers and their supporters effectively shut down business-as-usual in the business districts of the cities. The strikes, pitting poor janitors against rich landlords, won massive public support and saw the workers' demands met.

Key to the success was the fact that striking janitors continued to escalate their tactics. Instead of just engaging in picketing at their work site, each janitor, liberated from work by the strike, became a full-time organizer, campaigning against the corporations and politicians that control and profit from the real estate industry the workers were targeting. In Los Angeles, that meant literally thousands of striker/organizers working full-time, day in and day out, organizing demonstrations that shut down streets and occupied office buildings while mobilizing community and ecumenical support.

The striking janitors learned firsthand that small, isolated strikes are rarely effective, but that going on a city-wide general strike, even in large numbers, doesn't alone lead to victory either. To win, strikers need to have a clear understanding of the target and its vulnerabilities, and develop a plan to exploit those vulnerabilities. No one action or tactic will provide enough pressure. There needs to be constant, creative and courageous escalation.

> *"Instead of just engaging in picketing at their work site, each worker, liberated from work by the strike, became a full-time organizer."*

Related:

TACTICS
Mass street action p. 68
Prefigurative intervention p. 82
Direct action p. 32
Blockade p. 14

THEORIES
Points of intervention p. 250
Cultural hegemony p. 222
The tactics of everyday life p. 268
Narrative power analysis p. 244
Community unionism web

CASE STUDIES
Taco Bell boycott p. 372
Wisconsin Capitol Occupation p. 396
Justice for Janitors (DC) p. 326

. . . .

CHOOSE YOUR TARGET WISELY: Successful workplace actions depend on choosing the right target and determining how best to apply pressure on that target. The most vulnerable target may not always be the most obvious one — the janitors had far more success in targeting the real estate companies in which they worked, rather than the shadowy subcontractors who were their direct employers, and who were far less vulnerable to public pressure and bad press.

KEY PRINCIPLE
at work

OTHER PRINCIPLES AT WORK:
We are all leaders p. 202
Take leadership from the most impacted p. 280
Create levels of participation web
Make cross-class alliances web
Shift the spectrum of allies p. 172
Escalate strategically p. 134

TACTIC: General strike   51

TACTIC:
Guerrilla projection

COMMON USES

To broadcast a message; to frame an action; to rebrand a target; to entertain a crowd.

PRACTITIONERS

Greenpeace
Agit-Pop
Students for a Free Tibet
Glass Bead Collective
Dawn of Man

FURTHER INSIGHT

InterOccupy, "Occupy 'Bat Signal' Source Files": http://interoccupy.org/occupy-bat-signal/

Video: Graffiti Research Lab "All You See Is..." http://trb.la/zpgVWF

Video: "Anti War Guerrilla Projection at Ground Zero 4th Anniversary of Iraq War" http://trb.la/xBZvLs

Video: "Projectionists Light Up New York City Buildings, and Protesters' Spirits, with Occupy-Themed Display." Democracy Now, November 18, 2011. http://trb.la/AcfNAg

Flash: Light (innovative projection art project in New York City) http://www.flashlightnyc.org/

CONTRIBUTED BY

Samantha Corbin
Mark Read

Guerrilla projection, pioneered by artists and advertisers, has been increasingly embraced by activists in recent years as a new medium for delivering messages. The advantages are obvious: with a single high-powered projector, you can turn the side of a building into a huge advertisement for your cause, plastering your message on a spot that would otherwise be out of reach. It's legally kosher, relatively cheap and risk free compared to, say, trespassing onto a building's roof to hang a banner off of it. Most importantly, it's visually powerful: you can literally shine a light on the opposition.

"With a guerrilla projection you can literally shine a light on the opposition, you can enter their space and rebrand it. "

Projections can be low-fi or hi-fi; mobile or stable. Two jerry-riggers can do one out of the back of their car to capture a quick hit-and-run photo op, or a professional VJ can project from a more stable plug-in location to entertain a crowd of thousands *see CASE: 99% bat signal*. They're also a perfect tactic for rebranding your target. Greenpeace projected a huge cartoon "KABLOOM" onto the side of a nuclear reactor to remind people how dangerous nuclear power can be, and a "We have nuclear weapons on board" onto a nuclear equipped air craft carrier that was refusing to acknowledge it. In 1993, the Academy Award-winning documentary, "Deadly Deception," was projected directly onto the San Francisco TV station that was refusing to air it, while hundreds watched, eating popcorn. Under pressure, the station relented and aired the film.

Much of the power of projections is in the medium itself. Unlike hanging a banner, a projection can move and change, and even be interactive. With a medium so versatile, why limit yourself to static slogans? On the eve of the Great American Smokeout in 1994, INFACT hit the Philip Morris building in New York with a running count of the number of children addicted to cigarettes. With simple online tools, your projection can become interactive and crowd-sourced. Supporters on the street — or a continent

Greenpeace Nuclear Free Seas campaign: British aircraft carrier Ark Royal in Hamburg harbor. © Greenpeace / Vennemann, Dieter

away — can text, tweet or email in their own messages to be projected in real time. With a laser pointer, people on the street can write messages to others inside a building, whether they're friends and family in jail or a CEO in his corner office.

Projections help us upend the power dynamic. The buildings of the powerful can feel so big and our voices and protest signs so small. But when a huge "99%" bat signal lights up the night sky, or you see your own handwriting scrawled across a corporate HQ in real time, it begins to level the playing field. Small voices are writ large.

Related:

TACTICS
Human banner p. 56
Banner hang p. 12
Détournement/Culture jamming p. 28
Media-jacking p. 72
Mass street action p. 68

THEORIES
Action logic p. 208
Points of intervention p. 250
Ethical spectacle p. 230

CASE STUDIES
99% bat signal p. 278
Koch guerrilla drive-in web

· ·

POTENTIAL PITFALLS: The technology is very powerful, "spectacular" in nature, and often under the control of one person or a small group who could potentially manipulate a large and impressionable crowd. This power needs to be kept accountable to the broader group, and should be wielded with great care.

BALANCE ART AND MESSAGE: When designing your action, let your imagination range far and wide. Consider, in particular, its site-specific nature, and look for ways the medium itself can highlight your message. Consider all the artful elements at work in the 2008 Free Tibet projection on the Chinese consulate in New York: the persecuted Tibetan activist was at that moment literally in hiding a world away, yet was able to speak directly to — and literally on — a massive institution that was complicit in his repression. His handwriting splaying across the marble facade in real time was at once defiant and intimate. His private act of dissent had become not just public but beautiful.

KEY PRINCIPLE
at work

OTHER PRINCIPLES AT WORK:
Make the invisible visible p. 152
Make your actions both concrete and communicative p. 154
Do the media's work for them p. 124
Know your cultural terrain p. 142
Stay on message p. 178
Show, don't tell p. 174
Consider your audience p. 118
Think narratively p. 186
Reframe p. 168

TACTIC:
Hoax

COMMON USES

To create a momentary illusion that exposes injustice through satirical exaggeration, or that demonstrates how another reality is possible.

EPIGRAPH

"Sometimes it takes a lie to expose the truth."
—Sun Tzu, The Art of War

PRACTITIONERS

Daniel Dafoe
Alan Abel
Joey Skaggs
Abbie Hoffman and The Yippies
The Yes Men
Mark Thomas
Sacha Baron Cohen
Paul Krassner
The Provos

FURTHER INSIGHT

The Yes Lab
http://yeslab.org/

A. Juno & V. Vale. Pranks! San Francisco: RE/Search, 1987.

Mark Dery, "The Merry Pranksters and the Art of the Hoax", New York Times, 1990.
http://trb.la/ynjM4a

Destructables "Make Your Own Newspaper Headlines"
http://trb.la/w6s9P8

CONTRIBUTED BY

Mike Bonanno

On April 15, 2011, when General Electric announced that the company would return its illegitimate (but legal) $3.2 billion tax refund, and also lobby to close the sort of corporate tax loopholes that had allowed them to dodge taxes in the first place, it seemed too good to be true. When was the last time a major American corporation took such a moral leadership role?

Um, never! The announcement was a hoax, created by the tax fairness group U.S. Uncut, with some help from The Yes Lab. On this occasion, the core of the action was a simple press release that masqueraded as a real one from General Electric. An Associated Press writer, as eager as the rest of America to believe that such a thing could be true, picked it up and sent it over the wire. It only took minutes to be debunked, but in the media storm it created (including a temporary $3 billion plunge in GE stock value), U.S. Uncut was able to make their point, at a scale usually only granted to those who can pay for the privilege.

> "With nothing more than a website, a phone line, and some gumption, anyone can be anyone."

Hoaxes are one way for activists to "buy" some airtime that they can't afford. Instead of complaining that the press is set up to give voice to the interests of the powerful *see THEORY: Propaganda model*, the hoax puts that bias to work. By speaking *as* the powerful, and telling a more interesting story than the powerful usually do, one can often commandeer a pretty big soapbox. After the hoax is revealed (usually within minutes or hours) then the activists can explain themselves to the public in their own true voices, with the help of the usually massive numbers of journalists all stirred up by the trick that's just been played on the powerful.

It is generally best to reveal a hoax promptly. The ultimate goal here is more truth for more people. At the Yes Lab, we have an ethos: Never leave a lie on the table. This ethos is the opposite MO of those in power. The grand hoaxes they perpetrate on the people — everything from simple greenwashing campaigns to complex conspiracies

to subvert democracy[1] — are never meant to be debunked. Activists, on the other hand, generally reveal their hoaxes at the earliest opportunity. Speaking of which, the epigraph for this entry is not from Sun Tzu. It's from the DVD box of *The Yes Men Fix the World*.

Liz, Scott and Andy Bichlbaum display the hoax "Iraq War Ends" edition of the New York Times.

POTENTIAL PITFALLS: There is always a certain segment of the population that despises the idea of a lie, regardless of the intent. If you are trying to appeal to this small, sanctimonious, and usually left-wing group, you may want to think twice.

USE THE JEDI MIND TRICK: With nothing more than a website, a phone line, and some gumption, anyone can be anyone. Just use the Force!

Related:

TACTICS

Image theater p. 62
Détournement/Culture jamming p. 28
Infiltration p. 64
Identity correction p. 60
Media-jacking p. 72
Prefigurative intervention p. 82

THEORIES

Ethical spectacle p. 230
The propaganda model p. 256
The tactics of everyday life p. 268
Society of the spectacle p. 266
Floating signifier p. 234
Points of intervention p. 250
Political identity paradox p. 254

CASE STUDIES

Dow Chemical apologizes
for Bhopal p. 318
The Big Donor Show p. 294
The Couple in the Cage p. 312
Bidder 70 p. 290
New York Times "Special
Edition" web
The Yes Men Pose as Exxon web

KEY PRINCIPLE
at work

OTHER PRINCIPLES AT WORK:

The real action is your target's
reaction web
Anyone can act p. 98
Do the media's work for them p. 124
Everyone has balls/
ovaries of steel p. 136
Know your cultural terrain p. 142
Reframe p. 168
Choose you target wisely p. 114
Use the law, don't be
afraid of it p. 196
Think narratively p. 186
Consider your audience p. 118
Seek common ground p. 170
Team up with experts p. 184
Play to the audience that
isn't there p. 160
Make it funny web

[1] In 1991 the PR company Hill and Knowlton created a fake story on behalf of the Kuwaiti government about Iraqi soldiers taking premature babies out of incubators after the invasions of Kuwait. Their story and manufactured "eyewitness accounts" won Bush Sr. the U.S. public support he needed to invade Iraq. That hoax was never meant to be revealed, but thanks to investigative journalists, the truth eventually came out. That's just one example. For more, see gregpalast.com.

TACTIC: Human banner

COMMON USES

To make a single, unified statement with thousands of people.

PRACTITIONERS

Greenpeace
John Quigley
Brad Newsham

FURTHER INSIGHT

Human Banners SF, "Over 1000 Spell Out 'Tax the 1%'" http://www.humanbannersf.com/

Melóncoyote, "Foreign Mining Operations Soundly Rejected" http://trb.la/yZBneq

CBS News, "Anti–Wall Street Protests Coast-to-Coast: Washington, D.C." http://trb.la/xkWLTq

Greenpeace, "Giant Melting da Vinci Artwork Recreated on Arctic Sea Ice" http://trb.la/wKZ7o4

Iowa National Guard, "The Camp Dodge Story" http://trb.la/x2qt51

Spectral Q: Collaborative Art for the Common Good http://spectralq.com/Home.html

CONTRIBUTED BY

Brad Newsham

There's no law saying that the revolution can't be fun — and human banners are excruciatingly fun. No chanting, no harangues; just hundreds of people using their bodies to form enormous words or an image in order to send a message.

I've helped create ten human banners, with crowds ranging from 300 to 1,500. Each event was powerful, cathartic, and the feedback was always something along the lines of: "The most enjoyable, most fun, best demonstration I've ever been to!"

The human banner is a powerful, expressive tactic. It has some of the political virtues of a rally: it turns out numbers that physically demonstrate public support and the movement's ability to mobilize, but it does so with elegance, like a work of art.

"A human banner can be spur of the moment — a milling crowd can be quickly arranged and photographed from a nearby building or lamppost — but conscientious planning can produce staggering works of aerial art."

CODEPINK 2006.

"Tax the 1%" human banner organized by The Other 98%, 2011. (The other 1% remains unaccounted for.)

Related:

TACTICS
Flash mob p. 46
Artistic vigil p. 10
Banner hang p. 12
Art intervention web

THEORIES
Action logic p. 208
Ethical spectacle p. 230
Expressive & instrumental
actions p. 232

It works well for media coverage, too. Journalists need fresh story angles and compelling visuals, and the human banner delivers: it's unusual, remarkable, notable, people-powered, and made up of a thousand individual human interest stories. And when composed correctly, it delivers the money shot the media is always looking for: a single iconic photo that speaks for itself, that tells the whole story on its own *see THEORY: Action Logic*.

A human banner can be spur of the moment — a milling crowd can be quickly arranged and photographed from a nearby building or lamppost — but conscientious planning can produce staggering works of aerial art.

Here are some things to keep in mind when planning your human banner:

The slogan/image: Your image needs to communicate your message concisely and powerfully. Words and symbols are easiest to lay out, pictures trickier. You want viewers to *get* your message on first blink, and gasp at its beauty, audacity, and clarity.

The site: An iconic background anchors your photo to a place. Murals can be created on sand (etch the outlines before the crowd arrives), on grass (mark it with ropes or string), on pavement (chalk). A football field-sized area works well. My preferred font size for lettering is 100 feet tall, ten feet wide.

Photography: Video is nice, but getting at least one great photo is your goal. A helicopter gives optimal photographic maneuverability, but other possibilities include small planes, tall buildings, cranes and camera-balloons.

Crowd: You'll definitely want enough folks to fill in your lettering, plus a cadre of event volunteers. Pre-registration prevents last-minute scrambling — or, worse, a "thin," scraggly image. Focus on designing an event you'd be excited to attend. Nail the details.

POTENTIAL PITFALLS: It's easy to get grandiose in your plans, but complexity doesn't scale well. Keep it simple. Or if you do want to get complicated, test drive a smaller version first, then plan meticulously.

KEY PRINCIPLE
at work

DO THE MEDIA'S WORK FOR THEM: A human banner allows you to tell an entire story in one stunning image, but you'll likely have to deliver that image yourself. Invite the media along, but don't expect them to bring a helicopter. After the event, with aerial photo and press release in hand, you'll have a ready-for-prime-time package.

OTHER PRINCIPLES AT WORK:

Play to the audience that isn't there p. 160

This ain't the Sistine Chapel p. 188

Show, don't tell p. 174

Make new folks welcome p. 150

Balance art and message p. 100

Da Vinci's Vitruvian Man on Arctic Sea Ice. Artist John Quigley in coordination with Greenpeace. Photo by Nick Cobbing. (Copper and Arctic Sea ice)

TACTIC:
Identity correction

When trying to understand how a machine works, it helps to expose its guts. The same can be said of powerful people or corporations who enrich themselves at the expense of everyone else. By catching powerful entities off-guard — say, by speaking on their behalf about wonderful things they should do (but in reality won't) — you can momentarily expose them to public scrutiny. In this way, everyone gets to see how they work and can figure out how better to oppose them.

"By catching powerful entities off-guard, you can momentarily expose them to public scrutiny."

This is identity correction: exposing an entity's inner workings to public scrutiny. To practice it, find a target — some entity running amok — and think of something true they could say but never would — something that's also lots of fun. What you say can either be something your target would say if its PR department went absent or berserk (*modest proposal*), or things they *would say* if by some miracle they decided to do the right thing (*honest proposal*). Instead of speaking truth to power, as the Quakers suggest, you assume the mask of power to speak a little lie that tells a greater truth.

The *modest proposal* approach — which the Yes Men and others have used on many occasions to impersonate companies and parody them — can be a hit-or-miss affair. It usually involves an absurd and extreme — but logical — extension of the entity's current practices, like when the Billionaires for Bush put Social Security up for sale on eBay, or when the Yes Men suggested that CEOs in the West would want to remotely monitor and control workers in factories in Africa via a control panel mounted on a huge golden phallus.

In spite of the emotionally satisfying payoff of antics like those, it's the *honest proposal* approach — assuming the identity of a big evildoer and announcing they're doing something wonderful — that has proven to be the more effective way to embarrass a target. When the Yes Men impersonated Dow Chemical on the twentieth anniversary of the Bhopal catastrophe and announced on Dow's behalf that it was finally taking responsibility for the disaster *see CASE: Dow Chemical apologizes for Bhopal*; or when U.S. Uncut activists announced that GE was paying its 2010 taxes after all *see TACTIC: Hoax*; or when activists impersonating French officials announced that Haiti's debt — imposed when Haiti won independence from France, to compensate French slaveowners for their lost "property" — would at long last be forgiven; or when environmental activists impersonated Canada (in one case) or the U.S. Chamber of Commerce (in another) and announced surprising and wonderful things... In all these cases, the consequences were immediate: voluminous news reports about the unlikely turn of events (and, in the Dow and GE cases, giant temporary drops in each company's stock value). These in turn provided fodder for a wave of other articles about the whole hoax, providing a media platform for the reform programs of campaigners working on these issues.

POTENTIAL PITFALLS: Getting caught by the real folks you are impersonating. Not really a pitfall, just a plot twist.

. . . .

THE REAL ACTION IS YOUR TARGET'S REACTION: Often the most revealing moment in a successful identity correction is the reaction of the target. When you identity-correct a major corporation, you force them to react. They can't let the lie that tells the truth stand in the media. GE had to tell the press it was NOT returning its questionable tax refund to stand in solidarity with struggling Americans. Dow Chemical had to issue a statement indicating it had NOT apologized for the Bhopal disaster and would NOT be compensating the victims.

KEY PRINCIPLE
at work

TACTIC:
Image theater

COMMON USES

To foster dialogue and develop action strategies; to create a compelling public image in a direct action.

PRACTITIONERS

Julian Boal
Brent Blair
Cheryl Harrison
Mark Weinburg
Mark Weinblatt
Rosa Gonzales
Melina Bobadilla
Jiwon Chung
Practicing Freedom

FURTHER INSIGHT

Boal, Augusto. Games for Actors and Non-Actors. London: Routledge, 1992.

Boal, Augusto. Theater of the Oppressed. New York: Theater Communications Group, 1993.

CONTRIBUTED BY

Levana Saxon

Image theater, a social change tool developed by Augusto Boal, is one of the more widely used forms of Theater of the Oppressed, in which activists, students or any group are invited to form statues that represent a moment in time of an oppressive situation. The image can then serve as a springboard for critical group reflection in order to both understand the situation better and to try out possible "solutions." Through the process of creating and working with the image, participants can decode the situation, dissecting each character's personality, motivation and range of possible actions. Insofar as the participants identify with the characters, they can explore possible actions that they themselves can take in their lives.

Image theater is similar to forum theater in every way, except that everyone is holding still. This allows for both faster development and use of the process: whereas forum theater often involves a small team that develops and rehearses a skit for months, image theater can be created on the spot, collaboratively. In this way, image theater is an incredibly accessible tool to use in trainings, strategy development and direct actions.

For example, at a 2005 rally to support a disruption of a Chevron shareholder meeting in San Rafael, California, all demonstrators present were invited to form an image to depict the entire oil industry, including the characters who benefit from it, are oppressed by it, or are bystanders of it. Portrayed in the image were drivers, oil tycoons, media, and impacted communities (people from Nigeria and Ecuador were present to represent themselves). Even water and the Earth were included as characters. Once people were satisfied that the image represented reality, they shared their character's thoughts and motivations. The few people left in the rally who were not part of the image were then asked to take ten seconds each to intervene in the image in an attempt to transform the oil industry by reshaping the characters whom they believed were the critical agents of change. Everyone could see plainly what actions could or could not get us to the "ideal image." Within twenty-five minutes, the group had arrived at goals, possible tactics and next steps.

While image theater starts with a frozen image, it quickly moves toward interventions by participants, acting in character, to collaboratively and spontaneously name their oppression and its source, and then explore courses of action. The final stage is to reflect on what happened with participants and, if appropriate, write up the actions that seem most viable.

Related:

TACTICS
Forum theater *p. 48*
Invisible theater *p. 66*

PRINCIPLES
Praxis makes perfect *p. 162*
Anyone can act *p. 98*
Don't just brainstorm, art-
storm! *p. 128*

THEORIES
Theater of the Oppressed *p. 272*
Pedagogy of the Oppressed *p. 246*

Image theater is an incredibly accessible tool to use in trainings, strategy development and direct actions. Theater games like the one pictured above, by theater of the Oppressed in Paris, 1975, can help to warm participants up to make full use of the form. Photo by Cedoc-Funarte.

POTENTIAL PITFALLS: When creating an image that involves representing people who are not present, stereotypes of those people commonly surface. This can be problematic when participants begin manipulating the image and the actor tries to imagine what is going on in that person's head. With oppressor characters, this makes for an unrealistic laboratory in which to experiment with actions. With oppressed characters, it can perpetuate the dehumanizing stereotypes that fuel their oppression in the first place. This pitfall can be avoided by directing the action toward the people in the room, which image theater is specifically designed to do.

TACTIC:
Infiltration

Cops and other agents of the state are always infiltrating our get-togethers, both for intelligence-gathering and in order to disrupt our work. Given how successful this tactic has proven when used against us, it only makes sense that we would respond in kind.

Why sneak into a meeting or conference? Maybe simply to see what's going on, or to play a trick of some sort. You might not even know in advance what the trick will be. In 2004, Mike Bonnano and I snuck into the Heritage Foundation luncheon for conservative think tanks just to get acquainted with that world, and on the spur of the moment, seeing Ed Meese sitting next to the podium, I stepped up to the unguarded microphone and proceeded to nominate him for President. His reaction on camera is priceless.

Again and again, the Yes Men have successfully impersonated corporate presenters at conferences and pulled off some very revealing stunts *see CASE STUDY: The Yes Men Pose as Exxon*.

A completely different approach is to stage a guerrilla musical in the middle of the keynote speech of an evil lobbyist. That's what health care activists did at a major insurance industry conference in 2009 *see CASE STUDY: Public Option Annie*.

Always make sure that one or more of your team is filming your action. Remember: it's not the audience there in the room that you're most concerned with, but the audience who will see your footage, read the press release, or benefit from the secrets you've liberated from behind closed doors *see: PRINCIPLE: Play to the audience that isn't there*.

In many cases, at least for run-of-the-mill conferences, the actual sneaking-in is so easy it's almost an afterthought. Simply walk up to the table near the entrance that's full of name badges; choose one, and

> *"It's not the audience in the room that you're most concerned with, but the audience who will see your footage, read the press release, or benefit from the secrets you've liberated."*

say it's yours (and, if asked, say you've forgotten your business cards). Take the conference materials you'll be graciously offered along with the badge, and proceed inside, or, if you like, to your nearest copy shop to make a bunch of other badges with other names for your pals. Alternately, come to the table after the initial registration rush is over, perhaps midday (when only a few tags are left, probably belonging to no-shows), observe a tag, and then run out and print a few business cards (a sheet of pre-perforated cards and a copy shop will do the trick). Return and claim your badge.

. . . .

DO THE MEDIA'S WORK FOR THEM: No matter what you do when you're inside the conference — whether impersonating your enemy or singing at them — it's not likely to be perfect in the actual space and moment. A fake speech might go on too long, some singing voices may not be loud enough to hear, etc. That's why you'll want to document it yourself. By the same token, you'll want to set up the action not for maximum impact in the moment, but for how you want it to be seen and heard via the photos and videos that you take and later supply to the press.

Related:

TACTICS
Media-jacking p. 72
Creative disruption p. 18
Hoax p. 54

KEY PRINCIPLE
at work

OTHER PRINCIPLES AT WORK:
Anyone can act p. 98
Everyone has balls/
ovaries of steel p. 136
Play to the audience that
isn't there p. 160
Do the media's work for them p. 124
The real action is in your tar-
get's reaction web
Make it funny web

THEORIES
Acton logic p. 208
Points of intervention p. 250
The tactics of everyday life p. 268

CASE STUDIES
Bidder 70 p. 290
Public Option Annie p. 346
Yes Men pose as Exxon web

TACTIC:
Invisible theater

COMMON USES

To pose a moral dilemma in the midst of everyday life — this can be particularly useful on a topic that people might normally be "too polite" to bring up, such as poverty, racism or homophobia.

PRACTITIONERS

Augusto Boal
David Diamond
Improv Everywhere

FURTHER INSIGHT

Video: "Primetime from ABC News: Gay Parents Bashed"
http://trb.la/zt3L7P

Burstow, Bonnie. "Invisible theater, Ethics, and the Adult Educator." International Journal of Life-long Education 27, no. 3 (May-June 2008): 273-88.

CONTRIBUTED BY

Tracey Mitchell

You're dining in a restaurant when suddenly a lesbian couple and their two children, dining nearby, are accosted by a homophobic server. "These children need a father," she says. "You're making everyone else here uncomfortable." Other customers chime-in in agreement, while still others leap to the defense of the family. Some of these people are actors, the rest, including you, are unwittingly participating in an invisible theater performance.[1]

Invisible theater is theater that seeks never to be recognized as theater, performed in a public place. The goal is to make the intervention as realistic as possible so that it provokes spontaneous responses. The scene must be loud enough to be heard and noticed by people, but not so loud or conspicuous that it appears staged. Bystanders can and will engage with the scene as if it were real life, because for them it *is* real life. Invisible theater can thus achieve things that most other theater cannot, removing barriers between performer and spectator and creating very accessible conflictual situations in which people can rethink their assumptions and engage with sensitive issues they might otherwise avoid.

> "Your invisible theater performance is only as strong as the reaction or thought process it provokes in your audience."

Invisible theater is one of Augusto Boal's Theater of the Oppressed techniques, and has been used around the world in many different settings. In New York City in 2003, actors posing as tourists made loud comments about the potential terrorist threat posed by two Muslim women in hijab (also actors) who were taking photos of the Empire State Building. This scene sparked important dialogue about racial profiling and the "War on Terror." In other instances, actors posing as customers in restaurants and grocery stores have claimed not to be able to afford their bill, sparking a dialogue with the cashier and nearby customers (some of them also actors) about questions of economic justice.

Invisible theater requires a significant amount of preparation and rehearsal. The form requires actors to remain in character even when the action goes in unexpected and challenging directions. In its pure form, invisible theater never lets on that it is theater. Unlike other stealth theater forms like guerrilla theater, Yes Men-style hoaxes or Improv Everywhere pranks, there is never "a reveal." People who encounter an invisible theater performance should experience it as reality and forever after think it was real.

POTENTIAL PITFALLS: Invisible theater carries with it significant ethical and safety considerations, which should be explored carefully before choosing this tactic. Actors should rehearse a range of observer reactions, including aggression and abuse, and should be prepared to roll with the punches (sometimes literally!). Having an escape plan or distress signal, and discussing ahead of time if or when to break character, is also advisable *see PRINCIPLE: Take risks, but take care.*

Related:

TACTICS
Guerrilla musical web
Guerrilla theater web
Street theater web
Forum theater p. 48
Image theater p. 62

THEORIES
Theater of the Oppressed p. 272

CASE STUDIES
The Big Donor Show p. 294
Santa Claus army p. 358
Operation First Casualty web

- -

THE REAL ACTION IS YOUR TARGET'S REACTION: While part of the beauty of invisible theater is its spontaneity, it is also important to anticipate and rehearse potential audience responses. It is a good idea to test out your scene with people who did not participate in its creation to see what responses it provokes. Your invisible theater performance is only as strong as the reaction or thought process it provokes in your audience.

KEY PRINCIPLE
at work

OTHER PRINCIPLES AT WORK:
Make the invisible visible p. 152
Think narratively p. 186
Anyone can act p. 98
Lead with sympathetic characters p. 146
Take risks, but take care p. 182

¹ This scenario was played out on the ABC News Show What Would You Do? which uses a version of invisible theater to generate discussion. While the show breaks the usual rules of invisible theater by surreptitiously filming the scene and eventually telling those present that the scene is not real, it is nevertheless a good introduction to the power and possibility of invisible theater.

TACTIC: Mass Street Action

COMMON USES

To pressure a corporate or government target with a mass of people in the street telling a unified story.

PRACTITIONERS

Egypt's April 6 Youth Movement
Direct Action Network
The Other 98%
Alliance of Community Trainers
United for Peace and Justice
SEIU
ACT-UP
Lesbian Avengers
Washington Action Group

FURTHER INSIGHT

Crespo, Al. Protest In The Land Of Plenty: A View of Democracy from the Streets of America As We Enter the 21st Century. USA: Center Lane Press, 2002.

Wikipedia entry on Feb 15, 2003: Largest anti-war global action http://en.wikipedia.org/wiki/February_15,_2003_anti-war_protest

This Is What Democracy Looks Like. Directed by Jill Friedberg and Rick Rowley. Big Noise Films, 2000. http://www.imdb.com/title/tt0265871/

CONTRIBUTED BY

John Sellers
Andrew Boyd

Everyone's felt the irresistible people-power of a large march or rally. When a crowd is fired up by great musicians or fiery speakers it can rock. There is *real* strength in numbers. Most of us have also been inspired by a great nonviolent direct action. When individuals or small teams decide to creatively throw themselves upon the gears of the machine, it can detonate powerful mind bombs in our psyches.

But when you bring the two together, and thousands of folks from all walks of life collaborate in a mass street action, that's when magic and movements happen. Movements do mass actions. And you need a highly functioning and energized movement in order to repeatedly pull off smart mass actions in an escalating struggle for change.

"A mass street action is simply too big to direct by shouting through a megaphone; you can't tango with a battleship."

In the spring of 2011, a million Egyptians took to the streets, occupied Tahrir Square, fought off wave after wave of security forces, and after eighteen eventful and often bloody days, forced President Hosni Mubarak from office. In 1999, 70,000 took to the streets of Seattle and nonviolently shut down the WTO Ministerial meeting, the world's largest business meeting. In 2010, 3,000 trade unionists and their allies formed a "Citizens' Posse" and encircled a downtown D.C. hotel full of insurance industry lobbyists for a day in a show of force during the closing weeks of America's epic health care reform fight.

In spite of the differences here in scale, duration, political importance, targets and tactics, all three of these mass street actions succeeded in their goals because they all shared a few key ingredients:

- they disrupted business as usual;
- they had a clear motive and story;
- they used disciplined nonviolence and focused militancy;
- and they offered an easy way for individuals to participate.

Related:

TACTICS
Strategic nonviolence p. 88
Carnival protest web
Blockade p. 14
Occupation p. 78
Sit-in web

THEORIES
Action logic p. 208
Hamoq & hamas p. 236

CASE STUDIES
Battle in Seattle p. 286
Citizens' Posse p. 300
Reclaim the Streets p. 350
The salt march p. 354
Occupy Wall Street web
Critical Mass web
Koch Guerrilla Drive-In web

Top: Photo by Rezik Teebi.
Bottom: To succeed, mass actions need to provide a self-evident and organic way for individuals like these flag-wavers in Tahrir Square to participate.

A mass street action can't really be choreographed; it's too big to direct by shouting through a megaphone — instead, it needs to be largely self-organizing. To work, though, it needs a shared framework, mode of action or rough script to both facilitate self-organizing and maintain the coherence of the overall action *see PRINCIPLE: Simple rules can lead to grand results.*

Tahrir didn't need a script. It needed a call to congregate in public spaces.

The movement that shut down the WTO was built around a loose coalition, held together by a horizontally democratic spokescouncil. It agreed on a broad messaging frame and laid down some tactical ground rules (e.g. an agreement on nonviolence, specific responsibilities for each cluster of affinity groups, etc.). It was not choreographed, it was chaotic; decentralized but connected.

The Citizens' Posse action *was* tightly scripted. Coalition partners designed and agreed on the action frame up front. It needed a tighter script because the action relied more on theater and story than on an actual shutdown of the target. Even though it was primarily a communicative action, it *felt* like a concrete one because the theater itself was militant, and participants were given a powerful role to play in it *see PRINCIPLE: Make your actions both concrete and communicative.*

POTENTIAL PITFALLS: At their best, mass street actions make for beautiful organized chaos. But provocateurs (theirs or ours) can easily tip the fragile balance toward a nightmarish battle between cops and protesters. Unless this is your agreed-upon goal, you have to have strong agreements, principles, and preparation to ensure the safety of those who have picked up your call to action.

. . . .

KEY PRINCIPLE
at work

OTHER PRINCIPLES AT WORK:
Escalate strategically p. 134
Maintain nonviolent dis-
cipline p. 148
Enable, don't command p. 132
Simple rules can have
grand results p. 176
Don't dress like a protester p. 126
When the people are
with you, act! web

SHOW, DON'T TELL: Actions speak louder than words. The best mass street actions put a problem on the map by mobilizing thousands of people from all walks of life to congregate and confront a shared injustice. Hopefully you can gather right at the scene of the crime or an iconic location of symbolic power and literally show your adversaries (and yourselves) that the people united will never be defeated.

Police resorted to pepper spray and other harsh tactics after 70,000 protesters swarmed Seattle in late 1999, successfully shutting down the WTO Ministerial Conference with a combination of human blockades and mass street protests.

TACTIC: Media-jacking

U.S. athletes Tommie Smith and John Carlos capture global attention with a Black Power salute on the medal stand at the 1968 Olympics in Mexico City. This famous image subverted the spectacle of the medal ceremony to make a powerful statement rejecting racism and oppression.

Media-jacking is when you subvert your opponent's spectacle for your own purposes. Politicians, corporations and lobbyists have much bigger PR budgets and name-brand draw to attract press to their staged media events. Through well-planned creative interventions, however, you can refocus things and highlight a different side the story.

There are a few different ways to design a successful media-jacking. The first is simply commandeering the media. One of the most literal (and bold) examples of this occurred in 1991 during the first Gulf War, when the anti-AIDS organization ACT UP burst into a CBS TV studio during a live primetime news broadcast and took over the set, chanting "Fight AIDS, not Arabs."

Another option is to use your *opposition's platform* to tell your own story. In 2007, Kleenex ran an expensive PR stunt where they interviewed people on the street for a commercial they were making, getting participants to cry and say, "I need a Kleenex." Greenpeace activists stealthily lined up to be interviewed, crying instead because Kleenex was clear-cutting old growth forests to make their tissues. They successfully shut down the shoot for the rest of the day, and a video of the action went viral.

> "Sophisticated media-jacking uses your target's own story against them."

Sophisticated media-jacking uses your target's own story against them, undermining them at the point of assumption *see THEORY: Points of intervention*. For example, when activists from United for a Fair Economy hijacked the Republican stunt on Tax Day 1998 *see CASE: Whose Tea Party?*, they turned the message "taxes = oppression" on its head, to show instead that tax breaks for the rich are destroying working families *see PRINCIPLE: Reframe*.

Similarly, in 2006, activists with the Rainforest Action Network made fake press passes, put on suits and snuck into the Los Angeles Auto Show. Rick Wagoner, the CEO of General Motors, was giving a keynote address about how "environmentally friendly" GM's cars are. The speech was bullshit, but rather than *saying* it was bullshit, RAN activists stepped on to the stage and up to the mic, pretending to be the emcees *see PRINCIPLE: Use the Jedi mind trick*. They congratulated Wagoner, then told the audience that they were pleased to announce that GM was prepared to *commit in writing* to the promises he'd just made, and unfurled an oversized "pledge" that they asked him to sign. He had two options: 1) sign it, and give the campaigners something in writing to hold him to, or 2) refuse, demonstrating his dishonesty *see PRINCIPLE: Put your target in a decision dilemma*. He chose the second option, and the media went nuts. Over 700 media outlets ran stories about GM's greenwashing exposed.

Related:

TACTICS
Creative disruption *p. 18*
Infiltration *p. 64*
Hoax *p. 54*
Identity correction *p. 60*

THEORIES
Action logic *p. 208*
Ethical spectacle *p. 230*
Narrative power analysis *p. 244*

CASE STUDIES
Whose Tea Party? *p. 392*
Public Option Annie *p. 346*
Battle in Seattle *p. 286*
Dow Chemical apologizes for Bhopal *p. 318*
Billionaires for Bush *p. 296*
Colbert roasts Bush *p. 308*

POTENTIAL PITFALLS: Media is an extremely uneven terrain of struggle. Accurate and sympathetic media coverage is often based on having good relationships with journalists, so be careful your action doesn't alienate the very media professionals you need to be covering the story.

KEY PRINCIPLE
at work

SHOW, DON'T TELL: Media-jacking offers activists the unique opportunity to not just engage opponents on their playing field, but to actually call the shots and reframe the discussion. By putting their targets on the spot in front of the media, they can reshape how the public perceives the "good guys" and "bad guys" and flip their opponents' story on its head.

HOPE IS NOT A FEELING OF CERTAINTY THAT EVERYTHING ENDS WELL.

HOPE

HOPE

HOPE

HOPE IS JUST A FEELING THAT LIFE AND WORK HAVE MEANING

HOPE

—*Václav Havel*

TACTIC:
Nonviolent search and seizure

COMMON USES

Does the government or a polluting corporation have hidden documents or secret plans? Liberate them!

PRACTITIONERS

Casino-Free Philadelphia
Operation SalAMI
Canadian Union of Postal Workers

FURTHER INSIGHT

Guide New Tactics in Human Rights: "Tactical Transferability: The Nonviolent Raid as Case Study" http://trb.la/wnJnkL

Canadian Union of Postal Workers, "Operation Transparency: Their Secret Documents, Our Right to Know" http://trb.la/A8Csk2

Casino-Free Philadelphia, "Operation Transparency" http://trb.la/xr3stB

Video: "Operation Transparency Direct Action at Pennsylvania Gaming Control Board" http://trb.la/yiIu3m

CONTRIBUTED BY

Daniel Hunter

The tactic of *nonviolent search and seizure* rests on the idea that any information that impacts the public but is being hidden from them should be liberated. It's a direct action tactic that involves taking matters into our own hands by showing up with a "citizens' search warrant" and attempting, nonviolently, to liberate the documents in question. Even though the tactic is unlikely to succeed directly, the ensuing controversy (and possible arrests) can nonetheless bring the secret documents to the public's attention. In several high-profile cases, the successful application of the tactic has created enough outcry that the target has been forced to make the documents public.

The tactic originated in 2001, when Philippe Duhamel, a trainer and organizer based in Montréal, Canada, thought back to Gandhi's strategy of *nonviolent raids* on colonial salt deposits. Duhamel was working with Operation SalAMI's campaign to expose the secretive Free Trade Area of Americas (FTAA) trade agreement being negotiated. Even senators and members of parliament could not see the negotiating texts — only key CEOs and the leaders of participating nations. Decrying the anti-democratic nature of the negotiations, Duhamel decided to reinvent Gandhi's open, transparent raids.

Weeks ahead of the Québec City summit, Operation SalAMI announced it would attempt to "liberate" the texts for public scrutiny. On the day of the action, wave

> "This action places the opponent in a quandary: if they release the documents, your direct action brings meaningful information to light and scores political points. If they don't, it raises the public's interest, and ultimately suspicion, over what is being hidden from them."

after wave of participants approached the police barricades erected (for their benefit) around the Department
of Foreign Affairs and International Trade. Each wave
read aloud a citizens' search warrant: "Hello, my name
is ____. Access to information is basic to democracy.
Without that information we cannot have a meaningful
public debate. We ask the police to do their job and help
us search for the texts. Please let me through."

The first wave went over and was promptly arrested.
Over several hours, eighty people — some dressed as
Robin Hood — climbed over the fence and attempted
to liberate the documents. Their action was their message *see THEORY: Action logic*.

As the public saw the lengths the government and
corporations were going to hide the texts, public outrage
mounted until eventually the Canadian government
broke down and released the texts. Exposed to public
scrutiny as the corporate coup d'état it was, the FTAA
never moved forward.

Nonviolent search and seizure has since been used
successfully by other groups and campaigns, including
the Canadian Union of Postal Workers and Casino-
Free Philadelphia, which won the release of 95% of
the documents they had sought to liberate with only
fourteen arrests, showing the tactic can be effective on
a small scale.

Related:

TACTICS
Direct action p. 32
Mass street action p. 68
Prefigurative intervention p. 82

THEORIES
Action logic p. 208
Points of intervention p. 250
The commons p. 220

PUT YOUR TARGET IN A DECISION DILEMMA: This action
places the opponent in a quandary: if they release the
documents, your direct action brings meaningful information to light and scores political points. If they don't, it
raises the public's interest, and ultimately suspicion, over
what is being hidden from them. Heads you win, tails
they lose.

KEY PRINCIPLE
at work

OTHER PRINCIPLES AT WORK:
Maintain nonviolent
discipline p. 148
Get arrested in an
intelligent way web
Create a theatrical motivation
that keeps the action going web
Be an ethical prankster web

TACTIC:
Occupation

COMMON USES

To hold public space; to pressure a target; to reclaim or squat property; to defend against "development"; to assert Indigenous sovereignty.

EPIGRAPH

"Lost a job, found an occupation"

– Occupy Wall Street

PRACTITIONERS

Take Back The Land
Landless Workers Movement (MST)
La Via Campesina
Occupy Wall Street
Los Indignados
April 6 Youth Movement

FURTHER INSIGHT

Twin Cities Indymedia, "Ten Year Anniversary of Minnehaha Free State"
http://trb.la/xirh70

Occupy USA Today, "7 Occupations that changed U.S. History"
http://trb.la/ArEnhs

Take Back The Land
www.takebacktheland.org

CONTRIBUTED BY

Joshua Kahn Russell
Arun Gupta

The first recorded labor strike was a form of occupation: over 3,000 years ago, ancient Egyptian tomb builders from the desert village of Deir el-Medina repeatedly occupied temples following the failure of Pharaoh Ramses III to provide adequate provisions. We see other examples of public occupations that have propelled history forward ever since.

United Auto Workers' strike in Flint, Michigan.

In seventeenth-century England, for instance, the Diggers formed a utopian agrarian community on common land. Workers, soldiers and citizens established the Paris Commune in 1871. In the United States, in the Great Upheaval of 1877, striking railway workers and their supporters occupied train yards across the land. A wave of plant occupations in the mid-1930s led to the justly famous Flint sit-down strikes of 1936, which won union recognition for hundreds of thousands of auto workers.

Occupations are a popular tactic employed by social movements to hold and defend space. Other direct action tactics may also be deployed to support the occupation *see TACTICS: Sit in, Blockade, Banner drop*; or in some circumstances full-blown occupations have been known to *grow* out of a smaller tactic, such as a sit-in.

While the term can refer to an oppressor who has invaded or annexed land from a population ("occupied North America/Turtle Island" or "occupied Palestine"), the tactic of occupation is often used by those same groups to assert their right to that land: for example, the occupation of Alcatraz Island in 1969 by Indians of All Tribes, or when the Mendota Mdewakanton Dakota community, American Indian Movement, and Earth First! held a sixteen-month occupation to defend Minnehaha State Park from highway construction slated to desecrate sacred land.

The action logic *see PRINCIPLE* of many of these occupations is that people are reclaiming space that they are entitled to, thereby highlighting a greater theft. This same action logic can be applied to students taking over a building that should be serving them (for instance, in the late 1960s when African-American students occupied university buildings across the U.S., leading to the creation of many African American/Ethnic Studies departments), or environmentalists defending land that should be held in common, or workers occupying the factory in which they labor.

Related:

TACTICS
Direct action p. 32
Eviction blockade p. 44
Blockade p. 14
Sit-in web
Encampment web

PRINCIPLES
Choose tactics that support your strategy p. 112
Put your target in a decision dilemma p. 166
Escalate strategically p. 134
Choose your target wisely p. 114
Use the law, don't be afraid of it p. 196
Play to the audience that isn't there p. 160
Kill them with kindness p. 140
Be both concrete and communicative web
Take risks, but take care p. 182
Maintain nonviolent discipline p. 148
When the people are with you, act! web

CASE STUDIES
Occupy Wall Street web
Wisconsin Capitol Occupation p. 396

The "indignados" encampments inspired occupy movements worldwide. Puerta del Sol, Madrid. May 18, 2011. (Reuters/ Paul Hanna)

While occupations can range in style and form, they generally have two key components: 1) a focus on the logistics of maintaining an encampment, semi-permanent rally, or sit-in, which requires meeting needs around food, shelter, defense from police raids, etc., and which can often be a profoundly politicizing experience in its own right, and 2) a public pressure campaign that seeks to put the target in a decision dilemma *see PRINCIPLE*.

The location chosen for an occupation site often determines its success. A number of considerations may factor into the decision, such as symbolic significance, ability to concretely disrupt a target *see PRINCIPLE: Make your actions both concrete and communicative*, a logistical ability to maintain the occupation, as well as public visibility and technicalities of legal ownership. Historically, occupations have lent themselves to spontaneity, but the enduring ones tend to be well-planned.

Occupation of Wall Street 2011.

Groups like the Landless Workers Movement (MST) and La Via Campesina support communities of peasants in occupying fallow private land and reclaiming it for common use or basic subsistence. In the United States, groups like Take Back the Land apply this same principle to foreclosures, defending housing as a human right *see TACTIC: Eviction blockade*. In the environmental movement, tree-sits are a common example of occupations being used to defend forests from logging. Squatters movements across Europe have "taken back" abandoned buildings and repurposed them as homes and social centers with the intention of flying under the radar of authorities until they can lay legal claim to the space.

Occupations inherently threaten the legitimacy of a target by demonstrating the power-holder's inability to enforce the status quo. They also serve to expose the arbitrary, and often unjust, nature of private property regimes *see THEORY: The commons*.

POTENTIAL PITFALLS: Occupations are difficult to sustain indefinitely. Have a plan — including an exit plan.

. . . .

POINTS OF INTERVENTION: Different points of intervention will yield different sorts of occupations. An occupation of a factory is an intervention at the point of production that seeks to physically interrupt (or restart [1]) economic activity. Other occupations, say of the Wisconsin State Capitol (see CASE), occur at the point of decision. Occupy Wall Street (see CASE) began as an intervention at the point of assumption: occupying Zuccotti Park didn't physically inconvenience anyone on Wall Street — at first. Until the tents went up, it was just a park near some banks. Then it became a rallying point, a place from which to undermine the assumptions of unaccountable economic power and begin organizing against specific targets (banks, the stock exchange, courthouses, etc.) at other points of intervention.

KEY THEORY
at work

OTHER RELATED THEORIES:

Action logic p. 208
Points of intervention p. 250
The commons p. 220
Pillars of support p. 248
Hamoq & hamas p. 236
Temporary Autonomous
Zone (TAZ) p. 270
Revolutionary nonviolence p. 260

---

[1] During the 1999–2002 economic crisis, Argentinian workers occupied their shuttered workplaces in an effort to recover unpaid wages, keep their jobs, and ultimately run the factories for themselves. See The Take, directed by Avi Lewis (2004).

TACTIC:
Prefigurative Intervention

COMMON USES

To give a glimpse of the Utopia we're working for; to show how the world could be; to make such a world feel not just possible, but irresistible.

EPIGRAPH

"You never change things by fighting the existing reality. To change something, build a new model that makes the existing model obsolete."
–Buckminster Fuller

PRACTITIONERS

Steve Lambert
The Yes Men
The Provos
The (new) Diggers

FURTHER INSIGHT

Provo Images, "White Plans"
http://provo-images.info/
WhitePlans.html

Burning Man, "Ten Principles"
http://trb.la/weruXo

L. M. Bogad, "Radical Simula-crum, Regulation By Prank: The Oil Enforcement Agency," in Contemporary theater Review, Vol. 17(2), 2007, p261.
http://trb.la/wgzZKU

Artists Against Cuts, "A User's Guide to Demanding the Impossible"
http://trb.la/yExE89

PARK(ing) Day
http://parkingday.org/

CONTRIBUTED BY

Andrew Boyd

Many of us spend so much time trying to stop bad things from happening that we rarely take the time to sketch out how things could be better, let alone actually go out and create a little slice of the future we want to live in. Prefigurative interventions seek to address that imbalance.

The lunch counter sit-ins of the U.S. civil rights movement are frequently referenced as defiant, courageous and ultimately successful acts of resistance against America's Jim Crow-era apartheid. They were certainly that, but they were also profoundly prefigurative. The students' actions — mixed-race groups of people violating the law by sitting at lunch counters and demanding to be served — *foreshadowed victory* and prefigured the world they wanted to live in: they were enacting the integration they wanted.

"We can't create a world we haven't yet imagined. Better if we've already tasted it."

Pranks, art interventions, tactical media, alternative festivals and temporary communities, even electoral guerrilla theater, can also be effective ways to prefigure the world we want to live in.

Prefigurative interventions are direct actions sited at the *point of assumption* — where beliefs are made and unmade, and the limits of the possible can be stretched *see THEORY: Points of intervention*. The goal of a prefigurative intervention is twofold: to offer a compelling glimpse of a possible, and better, future, and also — slyly or baldly — to point up the poverty of imagination of the world we actually do live in.

Like the occupation of Tahrir Square in Egypt and the encampments in public squares across Spain by the *Indignados* movement, the Occupy encampments across the world are crucibles of prefigurative intervention, providing a space for people to create in microcosm the communitarian and democratic world they want to bring into being. Likewise, the Burning Man art festival works as a temporary autonomous zone where people can live out values, test out ideas and experiment with the future in real time *see THEORY: Temporary Autonomous Zones.*

PARK(ing) Day. An annual worldwide event where artists, designers and citizens transform metered parking spots into temporary public parks.

Related:

TACTICS
Electoral guerrilla theater p. 40
Occupation p. 78
Direct action p. 32
Guerrilla theater web
Art intervention web
Encampment web

THEORIES
Action logic p. 208
Points of intervention p. 250
The commons p. 220

CASE STUDIES
The salt march p. 354
Occupy Wall Street web
Daycare center sit-in p. 316
Small Gifts p. 360
New York Times "Special Edition" web
Critical Mass web
Burning Man web
The Oil Enforcement Agency web

Monthly Critical Mass bike rides prefigure future cities in which bicycles actually hold their own as traffic. Or PARK(ing) Day, in which people in cities across the country put a day's worth of coins into a parking meter and transform their parking space into a mini-park or jazz lounge or tiny public swimming pool, prefigure a greening of urban space and a reclaimed commons.

The Oil Enforcement Agency was a 2006 theatrical action campaign in which environmental activists — complete with SWAT-team-like caps and badges, posed as agents of a government agency — one that didn't exist, but should have. Agents ticketed SUVs, impounded fuel-inefficient vehicles at auto shows and generally modelled a future in which government took climate change seriously.

If hope truly is a muscle that we build by exercising, then interventions that prefigure the world we want to live in — whether by prophetic acts of civil disobedience, the formation of alternative communities or the staging of prankish provocations — are one of the best ways to work that muscle.

POTENTIAL PITFALLS: When playing with utopian visions, it's easy to get all squishy-Kumbaya or run off into esoteric fantasy-land. The idea is not to paint a pretty picture full of rainbows and unicorns, but to put forward a fragment of something visionary, desirable, and just beyond the realm of the possible — and in such a way that your action calls out the vested interests making it impossible.

Banksy says: every day is park(ing) day.

In sum, it has got to make sense. Don't go proposing replacing a cash-and-credit economy with a hug-and-kiss economy and think that'll demonstrate how the CEOs are keeping us all from being happy.

KEY PRINCIPLE
at work

OTHER PRINCIPLES AT WORK:

Use your radical fringe to slide
the Overton window p. 200
Kill them with kindness p. 140
Show, don't tell p. 174
Reframe p. 168
Team up with experts p. 184
Be the change you want to see web
Hope is a muscle web
All power to the imagination web
The price of a successful attack is
a constructive alternative web
Have an inside/outside
strategy web

SHOW, DON'T TELL: You can go on about Utopia, about the better world you dream of, about how things *could* be different, til you're blue in the face, and it might not sink in. *You* might not even believe it. But creating a lived experience of the change you seek — whether it's a prophetic headline that for fifteen seconds you believe to be true *see CASE: New York Times "Special Edition"*, or an unlocked white bicycle leaning against a building that is free for anyone to use — is the best way to break through cynicism, stimulate our political imaginations and affirm that, "Yes, another world *is* possible." After all, we can't create a world we haven't yet imagined. Better if we've already tasted it.

These bicycle enthusiasts show us what our world could look like if more people challenged the dominant reality of car culture. Internationally dispersed, uncoordinated actions such as this operate under the name Critical Mass.

TACTIC:
Public filibuster

COMMON USES

Interrupting or shutting
down a hearing or
government vote.

PRACTITIONERS

Casino-Free Philadelphia
Delaware Riverkeeper Network

FURTHER INSIGHT

Casino-Free Philadelphia, "How
to Do a Public Filibuster"
http://trb.la/y1COgt

CONTRIBUTED BY

Daniel Hunter

Many people know about the U.S. Senate's procedural filibusters, in which a dissenting senator holds the floor to keep a vote from happening. The people's version, the *public filibuster*, is no different. When activists face hostile government agencies or hearings that exclude the public, this relatively low-risk tactic injects the public's voice into an otherwise closed-off process. Confrontational but constructive, it has been adapted by a range of citizen groups.

In 2007, for example, a dozen members of Casino-Free Philadelphia decided to use the public filibuster at a Pennsylvania Gaming Control Board (PGCB) meeting. For two years, the PGCB had refused to let members of the public testify at so-called public hearings, but this time the public was going to have its say. One at a time, members stood up and began testifying. Each one was told to be quiet by the chairwoman. A recess was quickly called, and the members who had spoken were escorted out of the building by police and told they would not be allowed to return.

When the board reconvened, the chairwoman warned the remaining members of the group not to interrupt. Naturally, one after another of the members immediately stood up and continued the filibuster. They spoke over the banging gavel of the distressed chairwoman and over the "official" testifiers as they coolly tried to continue. Another recess was called, and then another, as the public filibuster continued. Finally, the PGCB shut down the entire meeting. The result: rather than risk another such engagement, the PGCB changed its policy to allow the public to speak at hearings.

> "The power of the public filibuster depends on carrying out the action in a dignified manner, as well as framing the tactic properly."

To an unsympathetic eye, disrupting a meeting can come across as mob rule, especially when poorly done *see TACTIC: Creative disruption*. The power of the public filibuster depends on carrying out the action in a dignified manner, as well as framing the tactic properly. Calling the action a "public filibuster" helps lend the kind of legitimacy recognized by reporters and the broader public.

When planning a public filibuster, be sure to stay positive and respectful. Your tone matters a great deal, and your bearing and presentation should be above reproach. Be honest, expressive, polite and on-message. Focus on the issue at hand, not the person trying to run the meeting. Also, show some compassion for the chairperson, who is used to being in control. This action threatens their power and puts them in an awkward and uncomfortable position. Be gentle with them.

· ·

MAKE THE INVISIBLE VISIBLE: Our opponents use bureaucratic delays and restrictions on public hearings to keep their dealings in the shadows. Such delays and restrictions are boring procedural issues that happen quietly and can easily go unnoticed. The public filibuster puts a spotlight on these practices by creating conflict and drama where there was none before, flushing into the open the undemocratic nature of the current process. Then everyone can see the problem for themselves and make up their own mind.

Related:

TACTICS
Infiltration p. 64
Creative disruption p. 18
Eviction blockade p. 44
Sit-in web
Direct action p. 32

KEY PRINCIPLE
at work

OTHER PRINCIPLES AT WORK:
Everyone has balls/ovaries of steel p. 136
If protest is made illegal, make daily life a protest p. 138
Maintain nonviolent discipline p. 148
Don't dress like a protester p. 126
Turn the tables p. 190
Show, don't tell p. 174
Kill them with kindness p. 140

THEORIES
Acton logic p. 208
Hamoq & hamas p. 236
Points of intervention p. 250
The tactics of everyday life p. 268

CASE STUDIES
Bidder 70 p. 290

TACTIC:
Strategic nonviolence

COMMON USES

To create a framework for broad-based direct action conducive to building large, inclusive, diverse and effective movements.

FURTHER INSIGHT

Alliance of Community Trainers, "An Open Letter to the Occupy Movement: Why We Need Agreements" http://trainersalliance.org/?p=221

CONTRIBUTED BY

Starhawk & the Association of Community Trainers

For over a decade, questions of violence, property destruction and confrontational tactics generally have tended to be debated under the frame *diversity of tactics*, but the time has come to seek a new frame. Diversity of tactics becomes an easy way to avoid wrestling with questions of strategy and accountability. It lets us off the hook from doing the hard work of debating positions and coming to agreements about how we want to act together. It becomes a code for "anything goes," and makes it impossible for our movements to hold anyone accountable for their actions.

A framework that might better serve our purposes is one of strategic nonviolent direct action. Within a strategic nonviolence framework, groups make clear agreements about which tactics to use for a given action. This frame is strategic — it makes no moral judgments about whether or not violence is ever appropriate, it does not demand we commit ourselves

"Diversity of tactics becomes code for 'anything goes.'"

to a lifetime of Gandhian pacifism, but it says, "This is how we agree to act together at this time." It is active, not passive. It seeks to create a dilemma for the opposition *see PRINCIPLE: Put your target in a decision dilemma*, and to dramatize the difference between our values and theirs.

Strategic nonviolent direct action has powerful advantages:

> *We make agreements about what types of action we will take, and hold one another accountable for keeping them.* Making agreements is empowering. If I know what to expect in an action, I can make a choice about whether or not to participate. We don't place unwilling people in the position of being held responsible for acts they did not commit and do not support.

> *In the process of coming to agreements, we listen to each other's differing viewpoints.* We don't avoid disagreements within our group, but learn to debate freely, passionately and respectfully.

We organize openly, without fear, because we stand behind our actions. We may break laws in service to the higher laws of conscience. We don't seek punishment, nor admit the right of the system to punish us, but we face the potential consequences for our actions with courage and pride.

Because we organize openly, we can invite new people into our movements and they can continue to grow. As soon as we institute a security culture in the midst of a mass movement, the movement begins to close in upon itself and to shrink.

Though a framework of nonviolent direct action does not make us "safe," it does let us make clear decisions about what kinds of actions we put ourselves at risk for. That said, we can't control what the police do and they need no direct provocation to attack us *see PRINCIPLE: Take risks but take care.*

A framework of strategic nonviolent direct action makes it easy to reject provocation. We know what we've agreed to — and anyone urging other courses of action can be reminded of those agreements or rejected.

There's plenty of room in this struggle for a diversity of movements and a diversity of organizing and actions. Some may choose strict Gandhian nonviolence, others may choose emphatic resistance. But for movements that embrace it, strategicnonviolent direct action is a framework that will allow broad-based movements to grow in diversity and power.

Related:

TACTICS
Mass street action p. 68
Occupation p. 78
Direct action p. 32
Prefigurative intervention p.82
Carnival protest web

THEORIES
Hamoq & hamas p. 236
Revolutionary nonviolence p. 260
Points of intervention p. 250
Pillars of support p. 248
Action logic p. 208
The tactics of everyday life p. 268
Cycles of social movements web

CASE STUDIES
Occupy Wall Street web

· ·

ESCALATE STRATEGICALLY: Activists tend to become increasingly radicalized through greater exposure to repression and injustice. Young activists, especially, will increasingly seek more "hardcore" ways to challenge the structures they oppose. These tendencies are valuable and should be honored and supported, but not all "hardcore" actions are equally effective. By charting a course of strategic escalation, we make space for the more radical among us to grow, without leaving behind the more cautious in our midst.

KEY PRINCIPLE
at work

OTHER PRINCIPLES AT WORK:
Put your target in a decision dilemma p. 166
The real action is your target's reaction web
One no, many yesses web

TACTIC:
Trek

COMMON USES

To link disparate locations that seek to have impact on a common issue; to model alternative community; to demonstrate commitment to a cause through endurance; to physically embody a pathway to an alternative.

EPIGRAPH

"The path is made by walking."
—Antonio Machado

PRACTITIONERS

Zapatistas
Greenpeace
Sojourner Truth
Peace Pilgrim
Hudson River Sloop Clearwater, New York

FURTHER INSIGHT

On-to-Ottawa Trek
http://www.ontoottawa.
ca/trek/trek.html

New York Times, "Soviet-American Group Plans Voyage for Peace"
http://trb.la/Ad9ANo

Trail of Dreams
http://trail2010.org/

CONTRIBUTED BY

Nadine Bloch

We learn to walk at a very early age, and almost simultaneously, we learn the power of being able to move ourselves toward places we want to go (that pile of toys) or away from places we want to leave (that plate of smashed peas). Each step of our path embodies the message.

People's resistance stories are full of walks, treks, sea voyagesand even flights. Over the millennia of human existence, entire communities have packed up and voted with their feet, moving away from untenable situaions to more fertile lands. In the last century, extended marches have been used broadly and strategically as a platform for outreach and mobilization, and as a visible expression of issues.

India's Salt March of 1932 is likely the best-known example of a mass, many-day trek *see CASE: The salt march*. Gandhi conceived of this march as a living lesson for India, creating a community, literally one step at a time, that both supported and embodied an independent India.

Many other treks have followed suit, usually with a commitment to demonstrate an ideal or alternative way of living. The 1986 Great Peace March for Global Nuclear Disarmamentflourished during its cross-continental trek, arriving in Washington, D.C., with 1,500 marchers and thousands more supporters. In the course of the 3,700 logged miles, the marchers not only educated and agitated for action on nuclear disarmament, but also built a participatory mobile city.

Not all treks model alternative social or living structures; some focus on specific strategic functions of the tactic itself. In 2010, four immigrant students embarked on a 1,500-mile march to Washington, D.C., to support immediate passage of the DREAM (Development, Relief and Education of Alien Minors) Act and a moratorium on deportations of eligible students. The Trail of Dreams *see CASE: The Trail of Dreams* embodied the impossible hurdles placed on the path to success of immigrants in the USA.

Many forms of transportation, from bicycles to trains and even sailboats, have been used in treks. In the 1935 On-to-Ottawa trek, hundreds of unemployed Canadian workers boarded boxcars in Vancouver to take their grievances to the national capital. Their basic demands proved so threatening to the government that they were physically stopped from reaching Ottawa, but the unrest that fueled their trek soon brought down the conservative government. In 1989, a citizen diplomatic venture, the Soviet American Sail, navigated a 156' schooner from NYC to Leningrad to bring home the counter-Cold War and environmental message, "We're all in the same boat." The trek tactic can prove a potent tool in focusing attention on an issue.

Schooner Te Vega's crew prepares for departure to Leningrad on the Soviet American Sail. Success comes from pulling together.

POTENTIAL PITFALLS: All of these mobile protests require immense amounts of logistical support before, during, and after the action itself. Sometimes this burden can prove too heavy and the logistics can overwhelm the organizers, leaving the strategy unrealized. When things go badly, the physical requirements of the trek or ride can exhaust members and burn out the broader support network. Make sure to allow adequate preparation time and gather appropriate resources to ensure success.

MAKE THE INVISIBLE VISIBLE: The routes of treks are often strategically chosen to make the invisible visible, bringing issues that are currently under the radar into the public dialogue.

Related:

TACTICS
Prefigurative intervention p. 82
Artistic vigil p. 10
Creative petition delivery p. 22

THEORIES
Action logic p. 208
Points of intervention p. 250
Pillars of support p. 248
Ethical spectacle p. 230

CASE STUDIES
The salt march p. 354
Trail of Dreams p. 384

KEY PRINCIPLE
at work

OTHER PRINCIPLES AT WORK:
Know your cultural terrain p. 142
Pace yourself p. 158
Use the power of ritual p. 198

TACTIC:
Write your own TACTIC

COMMON USES   *How does it work?*

EPIGRAPH

PRACTITIONERS

FURTHER INSIGHT

CONTRIBUTED BY

KEY PRINCIPLE
at work

**OTHER PRINCIPLES
AT WORK:**

Related:

POTENTIAL PITFALLS:

TACTICS

THEORIES

CASES

. . . .

The modular format of *Beautiful Trouble* allows the collection to expand endlessly to reflect new tactical breakthroughs, underrepresented areas of struggle and overlooked pearls of wisdom.

Become part of *Beautiful Trouble*. Use this template to write up your own creative-activism insights. Submit your own module for publication on the *Beautiful Trouble* website here: http://beautifultrouble.org.

PRINCIPLES

- - - - - - - - - - - -

DESIGN GUIDELINES

- - - - - - - - - - - -

Hard-won insights that can inform creative action design.

- - - - - - - - - - - -

"*Knowledge emerges only through invention and re-invention, through the restless, impatient, continuing, hopeful inquiry human beings pursue in the world, with the world, and with each other.*"

—*Paulo Freire*

- - - - - - - - - - - -

After decades of making foolish mistakes, veteran creative activists tend to acquire a set of mental short-cuts. Whether they're conscious of them or not, they bring these operating principles to bear on each new action or campaign they cook up. After a string of late-night truth serum injections and fugue-state urban vagabonding, we managed to pry a bunch of them loose. Enjoy.

PRINCIPLE:
Anger works best when you have the moral high ground

IN SUM

Anger is potent. Use it wisely. If you have the moral higher ground, it is compelling and people will join you. If you don't, you'll look like a cranky wing-nut.

EPIGRAPH

"The truth will set you free, but first it will piss you off."
—*Gloria Steinem*

PRACTITIONERS

Malcolm X
SNCC
Occupy Wall Street

FURTHER INSIGHT

Elephant Journal.
"Buddhism and the Occupy Movement: Taking Care of Our Anger," by Michael Stone
http://trb.la/xuhdo8

Video: "You're Doing It Right: UC Davis Students Respond with Silent, Powerful Protest of Pepper Spraying"
http://trb.la/yhOk5z

Video: "Occupy Wall Street: Chris Hedges Shuts Down CBC's Kevin O'Leary"
http://trb.la/y61Rrm

CONTRIBUTED BY

Joshua Kahn Russell

Anger is a double-edged sword. Or perhaps it's more like a water hose: it's full of force, it's hard to control, and it's important where you aim it.

There is a crucial distinction to be made between moral indignation and self-righteousness. Moral indignation channels anger into resolve, courage and powerful assertions of dignity. Think: the civil rights movement. *Self-righteousness*, on the other hand, is predictable and easily dismissed. Think: masked 16-year-olds holding a banner that says "SMASH CAPITALISM AND EAT THE RICH."

Have you seen the scene of the "Malcolm X" movie where an army of outraged people gather and stand in perfect formation, with perfect posture, outside a prison to demand the release of their friend? It was so bad-ass! They were all wearing suits, they stood as one, and their discipline clearly communicated: *we're mad as hell, we're right, you're wrong, and you're going to give us what we want.*

Integrity gives deep meaning and moral force to anger. We should never come off as mad-for-the-sake-of-being-mad, but rather as reluctantly, genuinely angry in the face of outrageous circumstances. Rather than reacting, we respond. Rather than lashing out, we stand our ground.

Of course, suppressng legitimate anger can be as debilitating as hair-trigger reactions. Parts of the Left have been held back because we are afraid to express or channel popular outrage. Unable to tap into large-scale disaffection, we remain marginal. By contrast, many youth movements self-marginalize precisely because

> "*Integrity gives deep meaning and moral force to anger. We should never come off as mad-for-the-sake-of-being-mad, but rather as reluctantly, genuinely angry in the face of outrageous circumstances.*"

Malcolm X's anger was earned by a life of oppression, and he wielded it with discipline and dignity.

Related:

TACTICS
Creative disruption p. 18
Infiltration p. 64
Public filibuster p. 86
Strategic nonviolence p. 88
Nonviolent search and seizure p. 76
Blockade p. 14

PRINCIPLES
Reframe p. 168
Maintain nonviolent
discipline p. 148
Escalate strategically p. 134
Use the law, don't be
afraid of it p. 196
Play to the audience that
isn't there p. 160
Pace yourself p. 158
Take leadership from the most
impacted p. 180
Take risks, but take care p. 182
Seek common ground p. 170

THEORIES
Hamoq & hamas p. 236
Revolutionary nonviolence p. 260
The tactics of everyday life p. 268
Anti-oppression p. 212
Points of intervention p. 250

CASE STUDIES
Occupy Wall Street web

their anger doesn't resonate. Find the sweet spot between the two.

PRINCIPLE:
Anyone can act

IN SUM

Don't worry about being a lousy actor – you're a great one.

EPIGRAPH

"Acting is the least mysterious of all crafts. Whenever we want something from somebody or when we want to hide something or pretend, we're acting. Most people do it all day long."

—Marlon Brando

PRACTITIONERS

The Yes Men
Sascha Baron Cohen
Improv Everywhere

FURTHER INSIGHT

Improv can be an excellent tool for overcoming your instincts to shy away or duck out. Find a local improv class in your community if one's available, or check out these seminal texts:

Halpern, Charna, Del Close, and Kim Johnson. Truth in Comedy: The Manual of Improvisation. Colorado Springs, CO: Meriwether, 1994.

Madison, Patricia Ryan. Improv Wisdom: Don't Prepare, Just Show Up. New York: Bell Tower, 2005.

Boal, Augusto. Games for Actors and Non-Actors. New York: Routledge, 2002.

CONTRIBUTED BY

Andy Bichlbaum

If you want to pose as someone you're not — for example, while infiltrating a conference — you *don't* need to worry about being a lousy actor.

The Yes Men scrutinizing their fake business cards.

Andy from the Yes Men, for example, is a terrible actor. In college he got kicked out of a play. In high school he did really well in an audition, once, and got a part — but then was atrocious in the actual performance, as he couldn't stay interested in the role. Yes Man Mike, for his part, once played the role of a dinosaur in an elementary school play. He was good at it, but only because you couldn't actually see his expression, which was most likely not the least bit credible.

OK, you'll say, but Andy looks very convincing when he appears on the BBC, posing as a spokesperson for Dow Chemical. Actually, look closely: he's terrified. The whole time *see PRINCIPLE: Everyone has balls/ovaries of steel.* But after a week of solid rehearsals, he managed to pretty much memorize everything he had to say and spit it out. His terrified look became the look of a nervous PR flak, which is exactly what he'd turned himself into. Professional PR people are probably terrified too, but they're very, very rehearsed.

Rehearsing is one of the two keys to successful "acting," which in this context is basically synonymous with "keeping your shit together." (Incidentally, here's how you can become an excellent PR flak yourself: just memorize the five answers you want to give, and recite them in response to whatever question you're asked, with appropriate hemming and hawing, which, in the biz is called "bridging" *see PRINCIPLE: Stay on message*. That's all there is to it! And it works whether you're pretending to be Dow Chemical on TV, posing at a conference as the CIA or speaking as yourself to a reporter about your latest action.)

> *"You'll quickly find that when everyone in the room believes that you're a particular person, a magical thing happens: you start to believe it as well."*

The second key to keeping your shit together (AKA acting) is to realize that once you're up there, pretty much *anything* you do is going to be fine. After all, you're the most important person in the room!

You'll quickly find that when everyone in the room believes that you're a particular person, a magical thing happens: you start to believe it as well. That's what makes "identity correction" *see PRINCIPLE* so much easier than regular acting. When you're a regular actor, everyone in the room knows you're not actually Hamlet, or Sweeney Todd's wife, or an elementary-school dinosaur — and they have to work plenty hard to "suspend disbelief." In hoax-like acting, the audience already believes you are who you're billed as. It's suspension of disbelief in reverse: under the influence of your audience, you end up believing it as well, and acting just right.

A quick way to test the principle: just put on a suit or business dress, and notice how you act differently. See?

Related:

TACTICS

Identity correction p. 60
Hoax p. 54
Infiltration p. 64
Invisible theater p. 66

PRINCIPLES

Use the Jedi mind trick p. 194
Do the media's work for them p. 124
Everyone has balls/
ovaries of steel p. 136
Use other people's
prejudices against them p. 192
Stay on message p. 178
Play to the audience that
isn't there p. 160

CASE STUDIES

Bidder 70 p. 290
Dow Chemical
apologizes for Bhopal p. 318
Public Option Annie p. 346
Insurgent Rebel Clown Army web
Billionaires for Bush p. 296

PRINCIPLE:
Balance art and message

IN SUM

Effective creative interventions require a judicious balance of art and message. It's not just what you say, it's how you say it. If the role of the artist is to "deepen the mystery," what is the role of the political artist?

EPIGRAPH

"Art is not a mirror held up to reality, but a hammer with which to shape it."
—Bertolt Brecht

PRACTITIONERS

Bread and Puppet Theater
Art and Revolution Collective
ACT-UP
Gran Fury
I Dream Your Dream
Suzanne Lacy
Reverend Billy & the
Church of Earthalujah
El Teatro Campesino
Coco Fusco
Living Theater

CONTRIBUTED BY

Kevin Buckland
Andrew Boyd
Nadine Bloch

"Political art." Easily said, harder to do. Art seeks to explore the deep questions. Politics demands a clear direction and message. That's a tough tension to manage. Sometimes quick gimmicks are called for; sometimes it pays to dig deeper — in our craft and in ourselves — to mobilize the unique powers of art.

"If I could tell you what it meant," Martha Graham once said, "there would be no point in dancing it." Unlike politics, which tends toward plain prose in endless repetition, art goes beyond explicit meanings to connect with that more elusive, soulful dimension of being human — a realm which must be engaged if we are to truly change the world *see THEORY: Ethical Spectacle.*

Song has its own special powers. Singing together builds emotional ties and harmonies — literally and figuratively. Song makes us feel powerful and united in a way nothing else can. During the breakup of the Soviet Union in 1989, the Estonian liberation movement used the country's traditional songs in resistance work. At one juncture, a full quarter of the country's population sang together in the streets, facing down Soviet tanks.

Consider the power of Picasso's *Guernica.* A striking and visceral canvas painted in protest of the first aerial bombing of civilians, its aura as a global symbol of the senseless devastation of war was still strong enough seventy years later that the Bush Administration felt compelled to throw a cloth over a tapestry copy of it when Colin Powell spoke at the UN pushing for war with Iraq. Images from Guernica continue to resurface in anti-war marches the world over.

Advertising is the dominant art form of capitalism, as well as a science of messaging. In the late 1980's Gran Fury, an AIDS activist art collective *see PRACTITIONERS,* used the artistic and messaging power of graphics to bring the AIDS epidemic front and center and move a critical social conversation in a direction it had never gone before. Their "Kissing Doesn't Kill: Greed and Indifference Do" bus ads featuring same- and mixed-sex couples kissing were not only explicit in their visual content, but beautiful, hip, emotive and evocative.

Art invites us to think rather than telling us what to think. This is one of its great powers, and if you make

FURTHER INSIGHT

Marc O'Brien and Craig Little,
Reimaging America: The
Arts of Social Change.
Philadelphia: New Society, 1990.

Queer Arts, "AIDS: Making
Art & Raising Hell"
http://trb.la/w28Uab

Douglas Crimp with Adam Rolston.
AIDS DEMOGRAPHICS.
Seattle: Bay Press, 1990.

Documentary: The Singing
Revolution http://www.
singingrevolution.com

Video: Amandla! A revolution in
Four Part Harmony
http://trb.la/yc1pzt

Video: Amnesty International,
"Making the invisible visible"
http://trb.la/x3XU4n

Related:

your art accessible and beautiful enough, people will want to follow where the thought goes. And because *they're* deciding where to go with it, they'll more easily connect it to their own experience.

The right balance of art and message can move both hearts and minds. Striking this balance, however, can be difficult. Think about your audience and your goals. What do you want your art to achieve? Do you want to evoke sympathy? Provoke deep soul-searching on a given issue? Get people to call their Senator? Art can help you do all of these things, but only when art and message are in balance. You know you've struck gold when you're able to say something so clearly that it hardly needs to be said at all, but is instead embodied in the *way* you say it.

POTENTIAL PITFALLS: Creative communication can get lots of attention — so make sure to connect that attention to your desired action. Give people the tools to act on your issue, even if it's just a URL or a phone number.

PRINCIPLE:
Beware the tyranny of structurelessness

IN SUM

Sometimes the least structured group can be the most tyrannical. Counter by promoting accountability within the group.

FURTHER INSIGHT

Jo Freeman, "The Tyranny of Strucureless"
http://trb.la/ywAM7u

How to organize and facilitate meetings effectively
http://trb.la/y8EE5S

CONTRIBUTED BY

Josh Bolotsky

Have you ever sat through an interminable meeting where everyone is theoretically on equal grounding, and yet only one or two people are doing eighty percent of the talking? Where there's no facilitator, for fear of introducing hierarchy, and so the discussion goes in endless circles, never quite sure when it's finished? Where new members lose patience because their suggestions are ignored and their ideas left to float in the ether?

Welcome to the tyranny of structurelessness.

Jo Freeman's seminal 1970 essay "The Tyranny of Structurelessness" put a name to the persistent problem that plagues decision makers in non-hierarchical groupings, organizations or collectives.[1] Freeman argued that by claiming to eschew hierarchy, or even leadership, activists are really unilaterally disarming themselves when it comes to identifying and correcting impediments to effective collective action. As she points out, "there is no such thing as a structureless group."

"Accountability is what gives democracy its bite, distinguishing it from a rote exercise in communicating preferences."

This means that to strive for a structureless group is as useful, and as deceptive, as to aim at an "objective" news story, "value-free" social science, or a "free" economy. A "laissez-faire" group is about as realistic as a "laissez faire" society; the idea becomes a smokescreen for the strong or the lucky to establish unquestioned hegemony over others… Thus structurelessness becomes a way of masking power.

It would be bad enough if structurelessness merely led to bruised feelings and longer meetings, but there is a further problem: it simply doesn't work for long. If you're engaging in any kind of long-term campaign, a lack of accountability and organized incorporation of feedback will often prove fatal.

So what's the way out of a structureless organization that is not working properly? The best cure is prevention: establish clear processes from the start. But if you're stuck in such an arrangement, and wish to change the culture to something more democratic and participatory, the key concept to introduce and press for isn't *hierarchy* per se, but *accountability*.

Accountability is what gives democracy its bite, distinguishing it from a rote exercise in communicating preferences. It involves the establishment of real consequences when the expressed will of the people is not implemented as promised. (By contrast, structurelessness provides plenty of ways to note collective preferences, but precious few equitable or effective ways to ensure they're acted upon.) Hierarchy is a particular vision of how accountability is carried out, but for the hierarchy-adverse it's by no means the only one.

There are as many organizational structures as there are philosophies of collective action. But they virtually all share one thing in common: for better or worse, they *acknowledge* their own structure, instead of hiding behind unlikely and obfuscating assertions of structurelessness. That acknowledgment, and the accountability it fosters, is the only way to ensure effective and equitable decision-making.

Related:

PRINCIPLES

Consensus is a means, not an end p. 116
Take leadership from the most impacted p. 102
Don't mistake your group for society p. 130
Make new folks welcome p. 150
Delegate p. 122
We are all leaders p. 202
Enable, don't command p. 132

THEORIES

Movement as network web
Cycles of social movements web

---

[1] Structurelessness is often mistakenly conflated with *absence of hierarchy*, when in fact, effective non-hierarchical forms of organizing actually require a great deal of structure. Anyone who has participated in an effectively facilitated general assembly or spokescouncil meeting will well understand this distinction.

PRINCIPLE: Beware the tyranny of structurelessness

PRINCIPLE :
Brand or be branded

IN SUM

Branding is one of the more misunderstood communication concepts, especially among anti-corporate activists, who can and should use branding to their advantage.

EPIGRAPH

"Success means never letting the competition define you. Instead you have to define yourself based on a point of view you care deeply about."

—Tom Chappell, Tom's of Maine

PRACTITIONERS

Adbusters
ACT-UP
Gran Fury
Otpor!
Greenpeace
The Yes Men

FURTHER INSIGHT

Adbusters
www.adbusters.org
AIDS: Making Art &
Raising Hell
http://trb.la/w28Uab
Center for Applied Nonviolent
Action & Strategies (CANVAS/
Otpor!), "Protest and Persuasion"
http://trb.la/AxZcyP

CONTRIBUTED BY

Cristian Fleming

Branding is a dirty word for many activists, but it really just means "the set of expectations, memories, stories, and relationships that, taken together, account for a consumer's decision to choose one product or service over another."[1] If we take branding out of the realm of consumption and into the interplay of ideas in the public sphere, then we see that the tools of branding can be used for more than just selling soap.

Three important points to keep in mind about branding:

Branding isn't inherently "corporate." Branding is really nothing more than a set of proven principles for associating, in the collective imagination, a certain word, phrase or image with a set of emotions or ideas. There's nothing inherently capitalist about that. Corporations use branding because it works. Anti-corporate activists can use it, too.

Branding can make the difference between success and failure. Every movement wants its message to be heard, but simply being right won't sell your ideas. The human mind needs to be persuaded.

There are copious examples of movements using branding effectively. In the '90s, for instance, an adherence to a certain aesthetic helped unify the Otpor! youth movement that swept Serbia and ousted Slobodan Miloševic.

Whatever the context, if you craft your message for your intended audience, then that audience will want to know more. It's as simple as engaging people in a dialogue that appeals to them. If they feel you aren't talking to them, they'll ignore you — or worse, work against you.

You'll be branded whether you like it or not, so be proactive. Even conspicuously "unbranded" campaigns have a brand. Despite its efforts to avoid defining itself, the Occupy movement ended up with an effective brand when the "99%" meme organically emerged as the touchstone for people within and outside the movement.

Even AdBusters' famous anti-branding philosophy uses strong branding conventions. Here's a sneaker from their "black-spot" campaign, also known as the "unswoosh."

If you decline to brand yourself, you leave an opening for other people — including enemies — to brand you instead. Operating within someone else's frame is always more difficult than operating within a frame that you yourself have set. Think of your group's brand as water spewing out of a hose. You can either leave the hose on the ground, or you can pick it up and direct its flow. Either way, the water continues to flow — and if you don't pick up the hose, someone else will!

Branding is an opportunity to shape your message and ultimately use the power of that message, its meaning, and its delivery to win the war of ideas. There's no such thing as an unbranded campaign or movement — though there are plenty of examples of poorly branded ones. Brand or be branded.

POTENTIAL PITFALLS: Branding, like anything, can be overdone. If people feel like something is being "sold" to them, they'll respond negatively.

---

[1] Seth Godin, "define: Brand," *Seth's Blog*, December 13, 2009, *http://sethgodin. typepad.com/seths_blog/2009/12/define-brand.html.*

PRINCIPLE:
Bring the issue home

IN SUM

Creative activists can make an otherwise abstract, far-away issue relevant by making it personal, visceral and local.

EPIGRAPH

"If facts are the seeds that later produce knowledge and wisdom, then the emotions and the impressions of the senses are the fertile soil in which the seeds must grow."
—Rachel Carson

PRACTITIONERS

CODEPINK Women for Peace
(www.codepink.org)
American Friends
Service Committee
Iraq Veterans Against the War
Veterans for Peace
Amazon Watch
National People's Action Network
Occupy Together

FURTHER INSIGHT

Walk in Their Shoes action guide
www.codepink.org/shoes
Peace Ribbon Project (useful for making a quilt on any issue)
www.codepink.org/peaceribbon
Bring Our War $$ Home
National Campaign
www.wardollarshome.org
Video: Rethink
Afghanistan: Cost of War
http://trb.la/xLxf8b

CONTRIBUTED BY

Rae Abileah
Jodie Evans

The destruction of a far-off rainforest. The carnage of war thousands of miles away. People care, but usually not enough to act on that concern, at least until they understand viscerally what's at stake. Here are a few ways to bring the issue home to people with creative visuals, powerful personal narratives and by highlighting localized costs.

Show the human cost

When the Iraq War was raging, mainstream media didn't show the stream of flag-draped caskets coming off planes or images of bombed buildings and dead Iraqis. Most Americans, with the exception of military families, didn't viscerally feel the war's impact. To bring the human cost of war home, Nancy Kricorian, a CODEPINK activist in New York City, stood outside her senator's office and arranged a row of shoes of all sizes tagged with the names of Iraqi civilians who had been killed, and asked passersby to "walk in their shoes." Her gesture was picked up and repeated across the country. In a similar spirit, veterans have met on the beach in Santa Monica, California, every Sunday since the start of the Iraq War, to set up a field of white crosses in neat rows across the beach — one for each soldier who has died. A powerful reminder of the human cost of war, at once intimate and horrific.

Make it personal

Los Angeles-based Occidental Petroleum was recently planning to expand its operations in the Peruvian Amazon jungle. Well-researched pleas to halt the drilling got nowhere. That all changed when a delegation of native Achuar people (who would have been displaced by the drilling, their ancestral lands ravaged) traveled to the U.S. to share their story. The issue shifted from stopping an oil project to defending the homes of these people. Occidental had to cancel the project, and the Achuar are pursuing legal claims against Occidental for environmental damage already done. Bringing forward the names, faces and stories of your far-away issue makes the consequences of inaction far more real and relevant.

Put a price tag on it

If people don't connect to the human cost of an issue, reaching their pocketbooks is another route. In 2005, when the historic Steinbeck Library in Salinas, California, was threatened with closure due to drastic budget cuts, farm workers and peace advocates joined forces and held a twenty-four-hour read-in to keep the library open, drawing attention to the money spent on waging wars rather than other priorities. Before the read-in, few in Salinas cared enough about the Iraq war to protest it; twenty-four hours later, the entire community understood how the high price of occupation affected them. When the local consequences of global policies are highlighted, people's circle of concern often widens.

Related:

TACTICS
Creative disruption p. 18
Advanced leafleting p. 8
Invisible theater p. 66
Occupation p. 78
Art intervention web

PRINCIPLES
Make the invisible visible p. 152
Know your cultural terrain p. 142
Think narratively p. 186

THEORIES
Cultural hegemony p. 222
Action logic p. 208
Environmental justice p. 228
Narrative power analysis p. 244

CASE STUDIES
Stolen Beauty boycott campaign p. 364
Taco Bell boycott p. 372
Occupy Wall Street web

"Daughter of Hussein al Tarish, Age 3." A pair of shoes from CODEPINK's "Walk in Their Shoes" anti-war action.

POTENTIAL PITFALLS: Be careful not to focus solely on the financial cost of the issue. Imagine if peace advocates only held up signs about the amount of money spent on war, with no mention of the lives lost. Use dollar figures only when it makes sense.

PRINCIPLE:
Challenge patriarchy as you organize

IN SUM

Like all other unjust and arbitrary systems of authority and power, patriarchy must be actively challenged in political organizing if we are to achieve collective liberation.

EPIGRAPH

"Patriarchy is a political-social system that insists that males are inherently dominating, superior to everything and everyone deemed weak, especially females, and endowed with the right to dominate and rule over the weak and to maintain that dominance through various forms of psychological terrorism and violence."

–bell hooks

PRACTITIONERS

Guerrilla Girls
Mothers of the Plaza de Mayo
Eve Ensler
CODEPINK: Women for Peace

CONTRIBUTED BY

Harsha Walia

(Left to right) 'I think she made the whole thing up.' 'She's just a crazy bitch.' 'Look, SWEETIE: class should come first. The rest is just divisive.' 'It's not really as bad as you say it is.' In order to be an effective comrade/ally you have to challenge patriarchy within yourself, and within the group. Art by Suzy Exposito.

Patriarchy is a system of unequal power relations that gives men privileges in all areas of our lives — social, economic, institutional, cultural, political, and spiritual — while women and gender non-conforming people are systemically disadvantaged. *Feminism* is not about "man-hating"; it is about transforming the socially constructed and hierarchical ideology of patriarchy. Since patriarchy pervades society, it is no surprise that it pervades social movements as well. So a commitment to feminist praxis that challenges the toxic impact of patriarchy in organizing efforts is essential to building inclusive movements.[1]

Given the urgency of confronting "big issues" like corporate power, militarization and environmental destruction, patriarchy and sexism within our groups often remain unaddressed. Some male allies feel they are not capable of sexism; but simply believing in gender equality does not erase male privilege. If we want to challenge patriarchy, we must understand how our actions and assumptions are influenced by the prevalence of sexism in our consciousness and social relations.

There are five key ways in which sexism manifests itself in our social movements:

1 Women face an uphill battle to prove their intelligence and commitment as political activists.

2 Political meetings are dominated by male speakers and leaders, while secretarial work, cooking, childcare, and the emotional labor of supporting community well-being are largely borne by women. This gendered division of labor is a frequently reproduced patriarchal pattern.

3 Women continue to be sexually objectified. Women of color and femme women in particular are fetishized, obscuring the dynamics of racism, fatphobia, ability and hetero-patriarchy behind "personal preferences."

4 Women are more likely to challenge men on sexist comments than men are. Given the particular socialization of women under patriarchy, seemingly minor comments or incidents can leave women and gender non-conforming people feeling humiliated, angry or upset; yet such comments are often dismissed as harmless. Women discussing sexism are often characterized as "divisive" or "over-ractive" and women's concerns are belittled unless validated by other men. This highlights disrspect for women's voices in discussing their own oppression.

"Transforming gender roles is not about guilt or blame; it is about a lifelong learning process to effectively and humbly confront oppression."

5 Feminism is not seen as central to revolutionary or collective struggle; instead it is relegated to a special-interest issue. This results in the trivialization of women's issues, particularly violence against women and reproductive justice.

Transforming gender roles is not about guilt or blame; it is about a lifelong learning process to effectively and humbly confront oppression. Some ways to build pro-feminist communities include: a shared division of labor;

FURTHER INSIGHT

Alas!, "The Male Privilege Checklist," Barry Deutsch
http://trb.la/yo1Smp

Colours of Resistance Archive, "Tools for White Guys who are Working for Social Change and other people socialized in a society based on domination," Chris Crass
http://trb.la/zlz2ml

Cherríe Moraga and Gloria E. Anzaldúa, eds. This Bridge Called My Back: Writings by Radical Women of Color, (Berkeley, CA: Third Woman Press, 2002)

Silvia Federici, Caliban and the Witch: Women, The Body, and Primitive Accumulation, (Brooklyn, NY: Autonomedia, 2004)

Chandra Talpade Mohanty, Feminism without Borders: Decolonizing Theory, Practicing Solidarity, (Duke University Press, 2003)

Jessica Yee, ed. Feminism FOR REAL: Deconstructing the academic industrial complex of feminism, (Ottawa: Canadian Centre for Policy Alternatives, 2011)

Video: Shit MANarchists Say (YouTube, Jan 25, 2012)
http://trb.la/zpgVWF

Related:

TACTICS
Prefigurative intervention p. 82

PRINCIPLES
Make the invisible visible p. 152
Take leadership from the most impacted p. 180
Shift the spectrum of allies p. 172

THEORIES
Pedagogy of the Oppressed p. 246
Environmental justice p. 228
Capitalism p. 244

CASE STUDIES
Barbie Liberation Organization p. 282

encouraging women's voices and leadership in non-tokenizing ways; respecting self-identification by using preferred names and pronouns; being pro-active in breaking the silence around sexual violence within broader society and activist communities; making our groups safe spaces in which to raise and address issues; and not marginalizing women's issues or placing the sole responsibility for fighting oppression on the oppressed.

We must also realize that we do not just want "more" women's representation; rather, we must actively facilitate and highlight women's *own* analysis and experiences of capitalism and oppression, especially those of women of color. Though patriarchy affects women much more severely, it distorts the humanity of all genders and reduces our ability to be in kinship with one another. Smashing patriarchy is not just a collective responsibility — it is ultimately about personal and interpersonal growth and collective liberation.

---

[1] This is an abridged version of a lengthier piece available on the *Colours of Resistance* website.

PRINCIPLE: Challenge patriarchy as you organize

DURING TIMES OF
UNIVERSAL DECEIT
TELLING THE TRUTH
BECOMES A
revolutionary
ACT

—*George Orwell*

PRINCIPLE: Choose tactics that support your strategy

IN SUM

Don't let an individual tactic distract from a larger strategy. Strategy is your overall plan, and tactics are those things you do to implement the plan — a distinction critical for structuring effective campaigns.

EPIGRAPH

"If you don't have a strategy, you're part of someone else's strategy."

–Alvin Toffler

PRACTITIONERS

National organizations:
ACORN
Industrial Areas Foundation
Midwest Academy
USAction
Center for Third World Organizing
National Peoples Action
PICO
Dart
Gamaliel
Center for Community Change

Issue groups, including:
Sierra Club
National Organiza-
tion of Women (NOW)

Many local commu-
nity organizations
and worker centers

CONTRIBUTED BY

Janice Fine

Strategy involves identifying your group's power and then finding specific ways to concentrate it in order to achieve your goals.[1] Organizing a rally, for example, should never be thought of as a strategy. It's a tactic. Before you can identify appropriate tactics, you need to identify your target *see PRINCIPLE: Choose your target wisely* and figure out what power you can bring to bear against it.

Developing a strategy requires:

* analyzing the problem;
* identifying your goal (formulation of demands);
* understanding your target[2] — who holds the power to
  meet your demands;
* identifying specific forms of power you have over your
  target and how to concentrate that power to max-
  imal
  effect.

If your target is a city councilor whose vote you need in order to pass a living wage ordinance, tactics that concentrate your power must involve or influence voters in her district in some way.

If your target is a bank that is carrying out foreclosures, tactics that concentrate your power must involve or influence their customers or regulators.

Within that framework, *tactics* are specific activities that:

* mobilize a specific type and amount of power;
* are directed at a specific target;
* are intended to achieve a specific objective.

In choosing a tactic you must always be able to answer the question: "What is the power behind the tactic?" In other words, how does the tactic give you leverage over your target?

We use tactics to demonstrate (or imply) a certain form of power. For example, when we carry out an action against a particular company, our underlying power *is economic* — it must cost them time or customers. That's why disruption matters. If we target an elected official, our underlying power is *political* — our tactic must cost them contributions or votes. (The power to "embarrass" is only effective if embarrassing your target costs them money or votes by making voters or donors question their moral legitimacy. Embarrassment in and of itself isn't a form of power.)

In community organizing, power can be broken down into two broad categories:

Strategic power
Power that is sufficiently strong to win the issue.

Tactical power
Power that can move you along toward a goal and help you gain ground, but is itself not decisive.

Once we understand the forms of power we can deploy, we are ready to develop our *campaign plan*.

A campaign is a series of tactics deployed over a specified period of time, each of which builds the strength of the organization and puts increasing pressure on the target until it gives in on your specific demands. A campaign is not a series of events on a common theme; it is a series of tactics, each one carefully selected for its power to ratchet up pressure on a target over time. All tactics are connected, and each one is chosen on the basis of how much work it requires to pull off and how much pressure it will bring to bear.

A campaign is not endless; it has a beginning, middle and end. It ends, ideally, in a specific victory: people get something they wanted or needed, and/or the target agrees to do something they previously refused to do.

FURTHER INSIGHT

Saul Alinsky, Rules for Radicals: A Pragmatic Primer for Realistic Radicals (New York: Random House, 1971)

Saul Alinsky, Reveille for Radicals (New York: Random House, 1989)

John Atlas, Seeds of Change (Nashville, Tennessee: Vanderbilt University Press, 2010)

Gary Delgado, Organizing the Movement: The Roots and Growth of ACORN (Philadelphia, PA: Temple University Press, 1986)

Michael Gecan, Going Public: An Organizer's Guide to Citizen Action (New York: Anchor Books, 2004)

Rogers, Mary Beth, Cold Anger (Austin, TX: University of North Texas Press, 1990)

Mark Warren, Dry Bones Rattling: Community Building to Revitalize American Democracy (Princeton, NJ: Princeton University Press, 2001)

Related:

---

[1] The author wishes to acknowledge Midwest Academy and Northeast Action, both of whom assisted in developing the curriculum that this module is based on.

[2] Often it's important to identify "secondary targets." These are individuals who have significant power over your target and over whom you may have more power than you have over your primary target (see CASE: Taco Bell Boycott).

PRINCIPLE: Choose your target wisely

IN SUM

We increase our chances of victory when our actions target the person or entity with the institutional power to meet our demands.

EPIGRAPH

"Power concedes nothing without a demand. It never did and it never will."

—Frederick Douglass

PRACTITIONERS

Ontario Coalition Against Poverty
Coalition of Immokalee Workers
Saul Alinsky & Midwest Academy
Industrial Workers of the World
UK Uncut

FURTHER INSIGHT

Dirks, Yutaka. "From the Jaws of Defeat: Four Thoughts on Social Change Strategy." Briarpatch Magazine (Nov.-Dec. 2011). http://trb.la/AAb568

Alinksy, Saul. Rules for Radicals: A Pragmatic Primer for Realistic Radicals. New York: Vintage, 1989.

CONTRIBUTED BY

Yutaka Dirks

Victories don't come by throwing fists in all directions at once, hoping to land a knockout punch by chance alone. Winning takes training, preparation and strategic thinking in order to land blows where they will have the greatest impact. Choosing the right target and figuring out how to effectively apply pressure is essential.

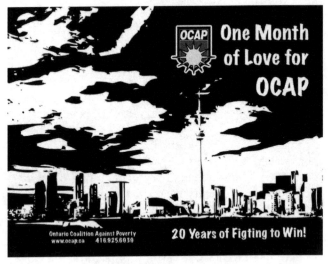

The Ontario Coalition Against Poverty (OCAP) chooses their targets wisely—they "Fight to Win."

Since the early 2000s, the Ontario Coalition Against Poverty (OCAP), a radical anti-poverty organization based in Toronto, Canada, has organized under the slogan "Fight to Win." It's a simple slogan packed with meaning: to win, you've got to fight. But the point isn't to fight; the point is to win.

An organization run by and for the poor, OCAP has proven extremely effective in compelling politicians, welfare workers and employers to grant the concrete gains they seek. In one of many successful actions, for example, OCAP prevented a gas station from pumping gas until the employer came out with money owed to a former employee. Similarly, mass delegations by OCAP to welfare offices have led to the reinstatement of benefits for low-income members. OCAP has been effective because it recognizes that social change comes through struggle, which involves articulating clear demands and applying targeted pressure on those in power to comply with those demands.

Nothing is more demoralizing to folks who have put many long hours into a fun and creative action than to hear the target of the action say: "I don't have the power to do that for you, even if I wanted to. The guy you want is next door." (And actually have that be a true statement rather than a blow-off line.) When we plan our actions and campaigns, we have to understand our targets and what makes them tick, taking care to focus on the person with the power to meet our demands: to sign the check, to introduce the legislation or to cancel the contract.

> "To win, you've got to fight. But the point isn't to fight; the point is to win."

Not every target is vulnerable in the same way. A blockade, occupation or creative disruption may be effective against one target but not against another. What works once may not work a second time. We need to figure out where our target is weakest, and where we are strongest. What actions can we take that are outside their experience? Nothing rattles a target more than something they aren't prepared to deal with.

You might not have enough power to push your primary target at first, but your actions may help you identify a *secondary target* — an individual or group that can be pressured to leverage their influence on the primary target. The Coalition of Immokalee Workers, for instance, won their battle by identifying and pressuring a secondary target (fast-food corporations) when their primary target (tomato growers) proved immovable *see CASE: Taco Bell boycott.*

We are creative folks. If we're smart about where and how we apply pressure, there's nothing we can't accomplish.

Related:

TACTICS
Direct action p. 32
Blockade p. 14
Sit-in web
General Strike p. 50

PRINCIPLES
Choose tactics that support your strategy p. 112
Make your actions concrete and communicative p. 154
Put your target in a decision dilemma p. 166
Pick battles big enough to matter, small enough to win web

THEORIES
Points of intervention p. 250
Pedagogy of the Oppressed p. 272
Pillars of support p. 248
Activist realpolitik web

CASE STUDIES
Taco Bell boycott p. 372

PRINCIPLE:
Consensus is a means, not an end

IN SUM

The two foundational values of consensus decision making are empowering every person's full participation in decision making, and respecting and accommodating diverse opinions. These values are more important than the form itself, which activists should modify as needed to uphold these values.

EPIGRAPH

"The problem is not that of taking power, but rather who exercises it."

–Subcomandante Marcos

PRACTITIONERS

Occupy General Assemblies
Spain's Indignados
Zapatistas (EZLN)
Anti-nuclear movements of the '70s and '80s

FURTHER INSIGHT

Starhawk. *The Empowerment Manual. A Guide for Collaborative Groups. Canada, New Society Publishers. 2011.*

Butler, C. T., and Amy Rothstein. *On Conflict and Consensus: A Handbook on Formal Consensus Decisionmaking.* http://www.ic.org/pnp/ocac/

Speck, Andreas. "Consensus Decision Making." *War Resisters International, October 14, 2008.* http://www.wri-irg.org/node/5165

CONTRIBUTED BY

Harsha Walia

Consensus decision making is an egalitarian and inclusive method of reaching agreement based on the active participation and consent of group members to collectively reach a decision. Consensus decision making focuses as much on the underlying processes and values as the decision itself. The word consensus has its roots in the Latin word *consentire*, meaning "to experience or feel together."

Consensus is rooted in many decentralized models of direct democracy practiced across the world — from village *panchayats* in India to the indigenous Haudenosaunee Confederacy (aka Iroquois), from Quaker meetings to anarchist spokescouncils.

Consensus stands in stark contrast to simple voting procedures or Robert's Rules of Order, in which proposals are debated and then voted on, with majority rule. Consensus, on the other hand, is a prefigurative affirmation of our power to organize ourselves in accordance with the principles of direct democracy: horizontal, participatory, inclusive, cooperative and non-coercive. As author David Graeber has written of consensus, "Ultimately it aspires to reinvent daily life as whole."

A common abuse of consensus, however, is a dogmatic attachment to the structures and forms with which it is associated, which can sometimes be as exclusive and alienating as the systems it seeks to replace. If this is happening, the response should not be "Well this is how consensus works!" Instead, it is our collective responsibility to delve into the dynamics that might be creating these negative reactions.

There are five common problems with consensus that can create frustration. First, consensus often reproduces majoritarian rule by creating sectarian camps of *those in agreement* versus *those who are blocking*. Contrary to popular belief, consensus does not necessarily mean unanimous agreement. This misconception causes us to wrongly view dissent as a distraction or obstacle, and increases the pressure toward homogenizing opinions. Second, a few voices can dominate the discussion, a problem that tends to perpetuate power imbalances around race, class, gender, and education level. Third, there is often a faulty assumption that silence implies consent, which can end up stifling broader discussion and the consideration of alternative proposals. Fourth, facilitators have an unfortunate tendency to exercise covert forms of *power-over* rather than *power-with* by steering the conversation based on their own biases.

The fifth problem with consensus is more fundamental and structural. Ironically, the seemingly benign notion that *all voices are equal* can hide the uncomfortable truth of systemic inequality. Almost inherently, the consensus process can absolve us of actively examining how privilege and oppression shape our spaces.

> "A dogmatic attachment to the structures and forms of consensus can sometimes be as exclusive and alienating as the systems it seeks to replace."

In an effort to address these problems, many communities and collectives use modified forms of consensus — for example, prioritizing and taking leadership from women, people of color and those directly affected by decisions being made; facilitating small break-out groups to ensure more engaged participation; encouraging more debate and discussion rather than just asking for blocks; and actively incorporating anti-oppression principles to prevent harmful opinions from further marginalizing historically disadvantaged peoples.

Consensus can be beautiful and transformative, but only when the structures and processes are meeting the needs and desires of those engaging in it. Otherwise, it can be just as shackling as more conventionally authoritative decision-making systems. Remember, consensus is a means to an end, not an end unto itself.

PRINCIPLE:
Consider your audience

IN SUM

If a banner drops in the forest and your target audience isn't around to see it, will it make a difference? Probably not.

FURTHER INSIGHT

War Resisters International, "Working with media resources" http://wri-irg.org/node/5246

CONTRIBUTED BY

Sally Kohn

When evaluating the success of a particular action, it doesn't matter what *you* think about your creative poster or press release or civil disobedience. All that matters is what your audience thinks. Protesting solely for the sake of self-expression and self-gratification? That's the political equivalent of masturbation. Political action that is carefully and thoughtfully designed and executed to cause a reaction or response from a targeted audience? Now *that* is making love!

If you've already thought up some awesome, off-the-wall action and are now trying to figure out who you want to reach with it, you're doing it backwards. The point of creative political action isn't simply to be creative, but to have a desired impact on a particular audience. First identify your target audience and then brainstorm actions to effectively convey your message. A guerrilla musical performance of the latest Justin Bieber hit would be awesome — unless you're trying to influence the members of the American Association of Retired Persons.

Remember that there is no right audience, just the audience that is right for your particular goals. Try this basic formula: we can get A to do B if they believe C. A is your audience, B is your objective and C is your message. Design your action or actions toward getting A to believe C.

If your core tactics and actions aren't explicitly and strategically designed to get the desired impact on your target audience, you're not being strategic. That Bieber number may be fun and the hits on YouTube astronomical, but will it reach your senior citizen target audience? *Baby, quit playin'.*

Traditional artists don't necessarily worry about their audience's experience. For them, creative self-expression may suffice. But for political artists, the audience is everything. The purpose of political art is the reaction of those who experience it. When you push over your tree in a grand act of theatrics, make sure the right people are watching, and that they hear one heckuva loud noise.

"If you've already thought up some awesome, off-the-wall action and are now trying to figure out who you want to reach with it, you're doing it backwards."

Related:

TACTICS

PRINCIPLES

THEORIES

CASE STUDIES

PRINCIPLE:
Debtors of the world, unite!

IN SUM

Today the burden of debt unites millions in common struggle, providing the basis of a new mass movement and new forms of large-scale organizing.

PRACTITIONERS

Take Back the Land

FURTHER INSIGHT

John Ralston Saul, *"Unsustainable levels of debt."* The Doubter's Companion http://trb.la/xaulP2

Deena Stryker, *"Why Iceland Should Be in the News, But Is Not."* Truthout, August 15, 2011. http://trb.la/wdUrvm

CONTRIBUTED BY

Dmytri Kleiner

From 2009 to the present, countries from the UK to Chile have seen an upsurge of student strikes and school occupationsto protest raising tuition fees. The 2011 Spanish *indignados* uprising began under the slogan "we are not goods in the hands of politicians and bankers." A few months later, encampment protests began in Tel Aviv's Rothschild Boulevard demanding public housing. Student debt and housing debt are central themes in the Occupy movement, which from a few tents in New York City spread worldwide.

These movements were able to build popular support because they focused on specific conditions. Many people are unable to afford education, health care, housing and child care. These conditions all reflect the growing debt burden that many carry. Essential goods like housing, education and health care have relatively inelastic demand, which means the limit to their price is basically *everything you have plus everything you can borrow.* Meanwhile, consumer spending, the engine of the economy, is increasingly fuelled not by rising wages, but by cheap credit, resulting in greater and greater levels of consumer debt. Today the issue of debt unites millions in a common struggle.

Building a mass movement around debt, like building any mass movement, is a consciousness-raising process. For the people to be united in a movement, they must possess a consciousness of their common interests and their common enemies. There must be a consciousness of class, and a willingness to understand that the only way to change class conditions is to unite and fight. Major social changes occur when people unite around a common cause.

Debt is at the core of the market system itself, and the solution is not better terms alone, but alternatives to that system. Instead of the conservative motto "fair financial terms from honest bankers," we must paint our banners with the words "Abolition of the debt system." Debtors of the world, unite!

New forms of struggle require new forms of organization to directly fight for changes. Debtors' unions are one such form: organizing debtors to collectively bargain for favorable terms for existing debtors. Just as labor unions bargain for improved wages and working

San Precario, the Patron Saint of Precarious Workers, emerged as an iconographic figure within Italy in 2004. Dedicated to critiquing casual employment contracts and the burden of debt, San Precario spread by playing off of the many rituals of saint idolisation, as in the saint card pictured here.

Related:

TACTICS
Debt strike p. 24
Eviction blockade p. 44

PRINCIPLES
Choose your target wisely p. 114
Take leadership from the
most impacted p. 180
Shift the spectrum of allies p. 172

THEORIES
Debt revolt p. 226
The commons p. 220
Capitalism p. 216

conditions through the threat of refusal to work, debtors unions could use organized refusals to pay debts to bargain.

Drawing on mass support from millions of people struggling to pay their bills, we can build a movement that aspires to far more than small reforms to banking and bankruptcy rules, but that challenges the entire capitalist system and its drive to profit from imposing scarcity on essential goods like education, housing, child care and health care. As we find our way across this new terrain, we must keep our eyes on the big prize: not better terms alone, but alternatives to the market system.

PRINCIPLE:
Delegate

IN SUM

In the final analysis, groups don't get things done, people do. Delegate!

EPIGRAPH

"Leadership is getting people to want to do what you want them to do."

–Dwight D. Eisenhower

FURTHER INSIGHT

David Allen, Getting Things Done: The Art of Stress-Free Productivity. Penguin, 2002.

Merlin Mann, "Getting started with 'Getting Things Done,'" 43 Folders http://trb.la/zKXViR

The principles of democratic structuring outlined by Jo Freeman in "The Tyranny of Structurelessness" http://trb.la/ywAM7u

Francesca Polletta, Freedom Is an Endless Meeting: Democracy in American Social Movements. University of Chicago Press, 2004.

Art Intervention: San Precario, Patron Saint of Precarious Workers http://temporaryculture. wordpress.com/san-precario2/

CONTRIBUTED BY

Josh Bolotsky
Andrew Boyd

One flaw of group work is that it's easy to walk out of a meeting with no assigned tasks, thinking "someone else is going to do that." Obviously, if everyone thinks that, nothing gets done. Just because the group comes to consensus on the need for something to get done doesn't mean anyone is

"Things get done only when the task is clearly defined and on someone's to-do list."

necessarily going to do it. Things get done only when the task is clearly defined and on someone's to-do list.

This principle may sound simple and obvious, but you'd be shocked how often we forget it.

Make sure every group meeting has a note-taker who records all tasks and who's agreed to do them, and then emails or otherwise shares that task list with the whole group soon after the meeting (same day, if possible). To ensure effective follow-through, have people explicitly commit to their tasks in front of the group, and begin each meeting by reviewing the last meeting's task list.

Some responsibilities are limited to a single action item, such as, "reserve a room for next week's meeting." But other responsibilities — say, "organize a press conference" — often involve a whole complex of tasks and the contributions of a number of people over many days. That's when you may need someone to "bottom-line." A bottom-liner doesn't do everything herself, but takes responsibility for ensuring everything gets done. If people on her team don't come through, it's her responsibility to find someone else, triage, or do it herself. It doesn't ultimately matter how the job gets done, just that she is accountable to the larger group for ensuring that it does, or explaining why it didn't.

Proper delegation and sharing of tasks is also one of the best ways to prevent burn-out *see PRINCIPLE: Pace yourself*.

Regardless of whether your group has a more vertical or horizontal leadership structure, delegation is key. Good leaders know how to delegate tasks, how to choose and support bottom-liners (some of the best people won't step up unless they're asked), and how to make sure everyone knows their role. Be explicit. People don't want vague responsibilities. They want to know what their role is and why it's important.

Volunteer and grassroots groups often struggle with participants who commit to doing something but then never follow through. You have to factor that in upfront. Be careful when giving critical tasks to an untested volunteer. Here's the standard conversation one of the authors has with new volunteers:

> "Do you know the most important word in a volunteer's vocabulary?"
>
> "Um, no."
>
> "Exactly."
>
> "Huh?"
>
> "'No' is the most important word you can say. Use it. A lot. If you say 'yes I can do it' out of guilt or an over-enthusiasm that you can't follow through on, then we're screwed. I'd much prefer a 'No.' Then we can assign the task to someone whose 'Yes' means yes."

Far from being onerous, this is actually empowering — and honoring. You're saying: your work is valuable enough that we need to have a solid commitment and the specifics nailed down. That's a principle, by the way, that's not just true for volunteers but for the whole team.

Related:

PRINCIPLES
Beware the tyranny of structurelessness p. 102
Don't mistake your group for society p. 130
Enable, don't command p. 132
We are all leaders p. 202

THEORIES
Dunbar's Number web
Anarchism web

PRINCIPLE:
Do the media's work for them

IN SUM

Often journalists want to cover an important issue, but can't for editorial reasons. The right creative action (that you photograph or film yourself) can give them the excuse or materials they need.

EPIGRAPH

"Don't hate the media, become the media."

–Jello Biafra

PRACTITIONERS

The Yes Men
Agit-Pop Communications
Code Pink
Greenpeace

FURTHER INSIGHT

Salzman, Jason. Making the News: A Guide For Activists And Nonprofits : Revised And Updated. U.S.A. Basic Books 2003
National Media Conference for Progressives: http://www.truespinconference.com

CONTRIBUTED BY

Andy Bichlbaum

If you want media coverage of your event, give them a story they can't refuse: one that makes your point very clearly, with great visuals, an unexpected twist or a lot of humor. If a journalist already wants to cover an issue, this assist will give them the excuse or extra ammunition they need to sell their editor on it.

Don't worry about squeezing all the relevant information into the stunt or hoax itself. If you can, great, but most of the key info can be conveyed via an accompanying press release. The action itself just needs to provide a hook or entry point by lifting the veil on a black-and-white situation and pointing out obvious but seldom discussed truths. If your action does this well, journalists will enjoy writing about it and public opinion (along with a well-orchestrated activist campaign) can do the rest.

When the Yes Men announced that the Chamber of Commerce was supporting climate change legislation, or that Dow was going to accept its responsibility for Bhopal, or that General Electric was giving back its $3.2 billion tax credit, these were just funny actions pointing to simple, undeniable realities: the Chamber was mad to *not* support climate-change legislation, Dow *should* clean up Bhopal, GE *should* pay its taxes. Many journalists want to write about these obvious truths, but for editorial reasons, cannot. Creating a funny, spectacular action that's all about an issue allows them to cover it.

Make the journalists' job as simple as possible. Provide them with what they need: a concise press release, photo with clear permissions, or a good video news release, replete with the facts, figures and soundbites that illustrate your point.

It's imperative to document your action yourself and make your photos and footage available. The glitter-bombing of Newt Gingrich *see: TACTIC: Creative Disruption* wouldn't have gone viral if there hadn't been an accomplice videotaping it. When Brad Newsham organizes human banners, he hires a helicopter and professional photographer to fly overhead, then passes those photos to interested media outlets that couldn't make it out there themselves.

Knowing their 1969 marriage would be widely publicised, John and Yoko decided to do the media's work for them. Spending their honeymoon in bed, talking about peace, they directed their own media event through their actions, words, and the signs they posted behind them: "Hair peace, bed peace".

Related:

TACTICS

Creative disruption p. 18
Flash mob p. 46
Hoax p. 54
Human banner p. 56

PRINCIPLES

Keep it simple web
Play to the audience that isn't there p.160
Make it funny web
Show, don't tell p. 174
Team up with experts p. 184

THEORIES

The propaganda model p. 256

CASE STUDIES

Survivaballs take the UN by storm web
Public Option Annie p. 346
Yes Men pose as Exxon web
Dollar bills on stock exchange floor web

The stealthier the action, the more important it is to document it yourself. Nobody but the organizers of flash mobs or guerrilla musicals know when and where they're going to occur, so you have to integrate photographers and videographers into those actions. But afterwards, don't just post your stuff on Flickr and YouTube and hope for the best. Instead, have a plan for getting those visuals out to the media. When Agit-Pop carried out the Public Option Annie guerrilla musical, they did a lightning edit of their footage immediately after the action and got it out to key outlets within the day's news cycle. MSNBC, CNN, and Comedy Central all built stories around the footage.

POTENTIAL PITFALLS: Many journalists will be loath to directly use footage that has a strong editorial slant, but it might still prompt them to do their own story.

PRINCIPLE:
Don't dress like a protester

IN SUM

If you look like a stereotypical protester, it's easy for people to write you off. If you look like someone who doesn't usually hit the streets (the guy next door or an airline pilot in full uniform), people can more easily identify with you. Therefore, don't dress like a protester.

EPIGRAPH

"Dress like a Republican so you can talk like an anarchist."

—Colman McCarthy

PRACTITIONERS

ArTmani
*Prêt a Revolter - http://leodecerca.
net/proyectos/pret-a-revolter/
Masquerade Project
Billionaires for Bush
Tute Bianche - http://en.wikipedia.
org/wiki/Tute_Bianche
Ladies Against Women
The Orange Alternative
The Ya Basta Association*

FURTHER INSIGHT

*Subversive Business Outfits
as Tactical Camouflage :
http://www.suitsforwallstreet.org/*

CONTRIBUTED BY

Andrew Boyd

People don't care about protesters. *Oh, there go those silly protesters again. What are they protesting this time? Look: the police are hitting them over the head! Well, they must have done something to deserve it.*

It's not quite that bad, but you get the idea. Based on what they see in the media, folks get a fairly fixed idea of what "protesters" look like — and the stereotype doesn't usually lend itself to immediate sympathy for your cause. If you're planning a mass street action and want to reach out to people who may not already agree with you, think about how you can undermine their stereotypes about "protesters" *see PRINCIPLE: Use others' prejudices against them.* Remember: protest is what you are *doing;* it is not your *identity see THEORY: Political identity paradox.*

If you want schoolteachers, seniors and office workers to get angry that a cop is hitting you over the head, dress like you're on your way over to their house for Sunday dinner. Make it easy for them to imagine themselves, or their kids, in your position.

Consider the aura conveyed by what you wear, whether that's the civility and seriousness of civil rights marchers in suit and tie or the calculated absurdity of "Billionaires" in tuxedos. In all ten years that Billionaires for Bush *see CASE* protested in the streets, including in the midst of some running street battles with police, never did a single one of us get arrested. It undoubtedly helped that most of us were white, but it also helped that most of us were wearing tuxedos. In New York, we had a one-liner: "New York's Finest would never arrest New York's finest dressed." And it was true. They never did.   Of course, the action you're involved in may not afford the luxury of tuxedos, or generally leave you a lot of room to not dress like a protester. It may require protective gear: bandannas or gas masks to protect from tear gas; heavy clothing or even shields to protect yourself from billy clubs and rubber bullets. Even then, creativity can show the human and beautiful side of dissent. At the Battle in Seattle, many blockades were works of art, and many blockaders were creatively costumed. Or consider the Masquerade Project in New York, decorating gas masks with multicolored sequins and feathers, or the Tute Bianche in Italy or the Prêt à

Over 700 Continental and United pilots, demonstrate in front of the New York Stock Exchange, September, 2011. Their sharp pilot uniforms and military marching pattern are a far cry from the standard protester stereotype.

Related:

TACTICS
Mass street action p. 68
Strategic nonviolence p. 88
Street theater web

PRINCIPLES
Maintain nonviolent
discipline p. 148
Show, don't tell p. 174
Consider your audience p.118
Lead with sympathet-
ic characters p. 146
Use others' prejudices
against them p. 192

THEORIES
Political Identity Paradox p. 254

CASE STUDIES
Battle in Seattle p. 286
Billionaires for Bush p. 296
Occupy Wall Street web

Révolter collective in Spain, or the "Book Bloc" in the UK, all of which wore creative yet protective protest gear into battle, thereby subverting the official media narrative that protesters are violent, scary and (worst of all!) humorless.

Often the most effective protests are those that don't look like protests. Perhaps to be effective — to quote a character in Peter Carey's novel *The Unusual Life of Tristan Smith* — "you will have to make yourself into something beyond anyone's capacity to imagine you."

PRINCIPLE:
Don't just brainstorm, artstorm!

IN SUM

When seeking to awaken collective intelligence, brainstorming can only get you so far. "Artstorming" invites participants to jump directly into the unmediated experience of creation, engaging the full spectrum of our creative intelligence. Better ideas, and often amazing creations, result.

EPIGRAPH

"Often such little small cultural experiments open up space and possibility for the bigger changes to happen. The real seeds for revolutionary changes can grow in artistic practices."

–John Jordan

PRACTITIONERS

Art in Action
Bread and Puppet Theater
Practicing Freedom

FURTHER INSIGHT

Bronson, Po, and Ashley Merryman, "Forget Brainstorming," Newsweek, July 12, 2010.

Kevin Buckland, on line pamphlet, How to Organize an Art Build, 350. org, http://trb.la/xz4ITY

CONTRIBUTED BY

Levana Saxon

Brainstorm sessions should be a great way for groups to arrive at an idea that is better than an idea that an individual could have come up with alone, but they often don't work that way. In a big group, the ideas of a few people who feel confident enough to share their half-baked musings tend to drown out the rest. Yale researchers actually found that brainstorming can *reduce* a group's creativity. So when collectively designing an arts action, instead of brainstorming, try artstorming!

When artstorming, instead of a blank wall where people write up ideas from the group, everyone stands up and starts improvising together with all the tools at hand. Instead of theorizing about what would look or sound good, they try it out. It starts with physical movement (proven to enhance creative output), then some form of improvisation (word association, or improv theater games) which prepares the brain to take risks.

Artstorming is useful because it:

Makes space for multiple intelligences and fluencies: Artstorming creates space for the spatially, kinesthetically and musically gifted folks who might be alienated from a verbal brainstorm.

Invites people to be fully present: By engaging the full spectrum of our creative intelligence, artstorming taps into parts of us that might be snoozing most of the time. These parts will be badly needed in an arts action.

Supports creativity: In an artstorm, people's honest expression of the feelings and ideas that brought the group together in the first place are safe to come out and play, so more expression happens.

> *"Artstorming creates space for the spatially, kinesthetically and musically gifted folks who might be alienated from a verbal brainstorm."*

Is anti-capitalist: That's right. Hakim Bey asserts that under capitalism we have become increasingly alienated from our direct experiences with each other and with our art. Artstorming is an opportunity to reconnect with ourselves, our art, and each other.

To design an artstorm, begin with the simple question, "What art could we use to effectively tell X message to Y audience to achieve Z result?" (X, Y and Z are figured out prior). Use a brainstorm (not all brainstorms are bad) to list all of the different art media possible, including both visual and performance arts. Next, break up the room into groups that will artstorm using one to three media of their choice to develop their message. After ten minutes, have each group report back and give each other feedback so each can arrive at a focus for the next stage. Allow people to switch groups at this time if they'd like. Now the *real* artstorm begins, focusing on a single idea from the first round with a group of people who all want to make it happen. Invite people to take turns experimenting, with minimal verbal feedback. Eventually, groups will hit on an idea that works and morph into a group-led process of artistic co-creation.

POTENTIAL PITFALLS: Some people may find an artstorm terrifying. Don't force people to do it or assume everyone is comfortable working this way. For those who declare discomfort with spontaneous creative work, give them a different role: say, offering verbal feedback to ensure that the groups are staying on-message.

Related:

TACTICS
Forum theater p. 48
Image theater p. 62

PRINCIPLES
Praxis makes perfect p. 162
Take leadership from the
most impacted p. 180
Consider your audience p. 118
Don't confuse your
strategy and your tactic web
Balance art and message p. 100

THEORIES
Temporary Autonomous
Zone (TAZ) p. 270
Theater of the Oppressed p. 272

PRINCIPLE:
Don't mistake your group for society

IN SUM

Don't get too caught up in trying to make your little activist group "inclusive," "democratic," or other qualities that we all want for society. Why? Because your group *isn't* society.

PRACTITIONERS

The Yes Men
Earth First!

CONTRIBUTED BY

Andy Bichlbaum

Sure, we should all try to be the change we want to see in the world *see: PRINCIPLE*. We should also think hard about who we are, what we're fighting for and why we're fighting for it. We should mull over the future society we want and how we can best model it in the here and now. We should even read books about it. But no matter how much we get absorbed in thinking about society, we should never mistake our activist groups *for* society.

For example, we want society to be democratic, but our bands *cannot* be models of the sort of democracy we're fighting for. Like families and rebel units, affinity groups aren't models for how society should be. Even a well-functioning, happy group may have unelected leaders. Decisions may be taken without fully consulting all members — or even any members. These would be odious practices if extended to society as a whole, but can be perfectly acceptable in a small group, where formal mechanisms are unnecessary because all members share a basic level of trust.

We obviously don't want society to be a place where everyone must fulfill their duty punctually and without complaint; we want real freedom, which is why turbo-capitalism is anathema to many of us. Yet to operate effectively, a small group may need to operate like an army battalion, or, more poetically, like the crew of a sailboat, with clear divisions of roles and responsibilities. And there may be dictators: while one or two people can't usually do all the work, it may be that one or two people must make all the decisions, especially in the heat of action, so that things happen quickly.

"To operate effectively, a small group may need to operate like an army battalion or the crew of a sailboat, with clear divisions of roles and responsibilities."

If you're in a group that works, at some point you may figure out the hidden interpersonal rules that enable the whole thing to crank along. Don't be appalled when you do. Those rules probably have nothing to do with democratic principles or consensus, but are based on intuitive navigation of face-to-face relationships. Often, whoever has the most energy simply makes things happen, and ends up making most of the decisions. Even when the starting model is consensus, the formal consensus process often gets jettisoned and the active members simply coordinate informally to get it all done. Why not take a shortcut and skip the formal consensus step, period?

If your group *was* working well and then ceases to, could it be that you've complicated the decision making process through "openness," and, to put it brutally, the wrong people have taken control?

HOW THE OPPOSITE IS EQUALLY TRUE: This is a case in which the opposite is *often* equally true, especially in larger groups! See almost any of the related principles.

Related:

PRINCIPLES

Consensus is a means, not an end p. 116
We are all leaders p. 202
Enable, don't command p. 132
Delegate p. 122
Beware the tyranny of structurelessness p. 102
Challenge patriarchy as you organize p. 108
Take leadership from the most impacted p. 180
Be the change you want to see web
Be an ethical prankster web

CASE STUDIES

New York Times "Special Edition" web
Billionaires for Bush p. 296

PRINCIPLE:
Enable, don't command

There's one style of leadership in which a charismatic, commanding leader serves as the public face of a project, sets up a vertical organizational structure, and then brings a whole lot of people along for the ride. The job of everyone else is to serve, support, and follow the commands of the charismatic, commanding leader. It's a very top-down approach.

Conversely, there's a style of leadership which is far more bottom-up, in which the job of the supportive, enabling leader is to set up a lateral organizational structure with a compelling, inspiring vision, and then spend his/her time encouraging others to participate and assisting them in maximizing their creative contributions.

The value of the "supportive, enabling leader" approach is that it unlocks the creativity, ingenuity, and innovation of everyone involved in the project or cause. Participants are inspired to engage because of the positive vision, and then encouraged to learn new skills, take on new challenges, and become supportive, enabling leaders in their own right. The long-term success of the project or cause isn't dependent on one person's energy and presence. Rather, it's a combination of the beautiful juiciness of the vision and the creative synergy of large numbers of people working together to realize that vision.

> "The value of the 'supportive, enabling leader' approach is that it unlocks the creativity, ingenuity, and innovation of everyone involved in the project or cause."

NOT ONLY MUST
GREAT *ideas* HAVE

INGS

THEY MUST ALSO HAVE
LANDING GEARS.

—*Unknown*

PRINCIPLE:
Escalate strategically

IN SUM

If dissident political groups tend to become more extreme over time, then good leaders should help define that 'extreme' in constructive ways.

PRACTITIONERS

Earth First!

FURTHER INSIGHT

Canvas Core Curriculum: A Guide to Effective Nonviolent Action, available on line: http://trb.la/yTS9mF

Helvey, Robert L. *On Strategic Nonviolent Conflict: Thinking about the Fundamentals.* *Boston:The Albert Einstein Institution, 2004. Avail on line:* http://trb.la/wrZ0tw

Beyond the Choir, "Activists Caught in the Filter Bubble" http://trb.la/AasOwe

Beyond the Choir, "What Prevents Radicals from Acting Strategically? (Part 2: Encapsulation)" http://trb.la/wDgKch

CONTRIBUTED BY

Jonathan Matthew Smucker

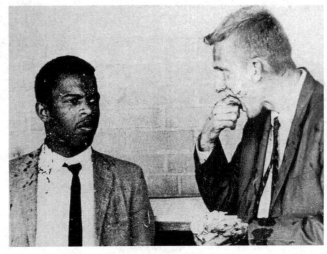

John Lewis and Jim Zwerg of the Student Nonviolent Coordination Committee after being beaten during the Freedom Rides. Photo of a museum exhibit.

There is a tendency within highly cohesive political groups to want to turn up the heat. It seems to be written into the social DNA of oppositional political groups: when group members' level of commitment increases, *they want to go further.* They want to be a little more hardcore. This tendency toward escalation and increased militancy can be a good thing — but not inevitably. It all depends on how hardcore is defined within the culture of the group. It can either move a cause forward — or send it into a dangerous or dysfunctional downward spiral.

Compare the trajectories of Students for a Democratic Society (SDS) and the Student Nonviolent Coordinating Committee (SNCC) — two of the most important radical youth organizations of the 1960s. Students for a Democratic Society imploded in 1969 and the Weather Underground was born because some leaders succeeded in defining hardcore to mean *immediate armed guerrilla struggle against the U.S. government* — an absurd prospect for their context. In the case of the Student Nonviolent Coordinating Committee (SNCC), on the other hand, some very astute leaders defined hardcore to mean acts such as going into the most segregated areas in the south and organizing some of the poorest, least educated, and most disenfranchised people in the entire country. SNCC engaged in other more visible "hardcore" tactics as well.

In both cases, hardcore really was *HARDCORE*. (You can't satiate the desire for hardcore with anything less!) Members of both groups demonstrated overwhelming levels of commitment to the values of the groups they belonged to. Members of both groups risked their lives, were imprisoned and brutalized, and some lost their lives. But hardcore was defined *strategically* in the case of SNCC, and *tragically* in the case of the Weather Underground.

Good leaders anticipate the emergent desire for hardcore—for escalation—and they own it. They model it themselves. And they make sure that the expression of hardcore is designed to strengthen bonds between the group's core members and its broader political base. It should *feel hardcore* to the participants, and it should *look like moral leadership* to the political base and to a broader public.

> "A tendency toward increased militancy ... can either move a cause forward or send it in a dangerous and dysfunctional direction."

Related:

PRINCIPLE:
Everyone has balls/ovaries of steel

IN SUM

Courage is in the eye of the beholder.

PRACTITIONERS

Abbie Hoffman

CONTRIBUTED BY

Andy Bichlbaum

Many people over the years have said to the Yes Men (and many other activists) that they have "balls of steel," an impolite way of saying that they are courageous. This is simply not so.

Watch any pre-conference moment of *The Yes Men Fix the World* and you will see a great deal of nervousness. It has even been said that Andy is a good bit more nervous than the average bear. "He's a real nervous nellie," says long-time friend-of-Andy, Joseph R. Wolin. This is even more remarkable because the contexts in which the Yes Men operate are entirely without threat, populated mainly by timid, polite men in suits who would never endanger their reputation by hitting someone.

What the Yes Men have, which is mistaken for courage, is a need to follow through on crazy ideas (single-mindedness), and an ability to goad each other on to do so (peer pressure). Really, this formula can be reproduced by anyone.

"What the Yes Men have, which is mistaken for courage, is a need to follow through on crazy ideas (single-mindedness), and an ability to goad each other on to do so (peer pressure)."

Andy Bichlbaum of The Yes Men appears live from the the BBC's Paris studio on the 20th anniversary of the Bhopal Disaster. Posing as a representative of Dow, he announced his corporation would take full responsibility and compensate the victims. This news story, and the later retraction, remained the top news story on Google that day.

Related:

TACTICS

Banner hang p. 12
Infiltration p. 64
Identity correction p. 60
Creative disruption p. 18

PRINCIPLES

Use the Jedi mind trick p. 194
This ain't the Sistine Chapel p. 188

THEORIES

The social cure p. 264
The tactics of everyday life p. 268

CASE STUDIES

Dow Chemical apologizes
for Bhopal p. 318
Bidder 70 p. 290

If protest is made illegal, make daily life a protest

IN SUM

When standard dissent is made impossible by overwhelming state repression, find ways to make ordinary acts subversive.

PRACTITIONERS

Orange Alternative
Dance Liberation Front
SNCC
Otpor!
ACT UP

FURTHER INSIGHT

T.V. Reed. The Art of Protest: Culture and Activism from the Civil Rights Movement to the Streets of Seattle. University of Minnesota Press, 2005.

Lester Kurtz. "Chile: Struggle Against A Military Dictator". 2009. http://trb.la/zdrpX0

CONTRIBUTED BY

Nadine Bloch

In July 2011, public frustration in Belarus over a deepening economic crisis reached a boiling point. The authoritarian regime of President Alexander Lukashenko had outlawed any political protest, and police were cracking down on any vocal expression of dissent. In response, organizers calling themselves "Revolution Through Social Networks" began calling on people to gather in public and clap their hands, or set their cell phones to ring all at once, thereby turning these simple everyday actions into profound public expressions of dissent.

As the non-protests spread, the police cracked down hard. The regime rightly recognized that the clapping was serving to undermine their authority. If they did nothing and continued to allow people to gather and clap without punishment, then the population could openly oppose the regime in other ways. Instead, the world saw the absurd sight of large numbers of Belarus citizens arrested for clapping. The crackdown exposed the government's deep irrationality, a perception only strengthened when it submitted to Parliament a bill to make "the organized inaction" of silent protesters illegal.

Many years earlier, in 1983, organized labor in Chile planned to kick off new resistance to the ten-year-old Pinochet dictatorship with a massive strike in the copper mines, the backbone of Chile's economy. Before the strike could occur, the mines were surrounded by the military and it seemed a bloodbath was certain to follow if the miners went through with this plan. Instead, the leadership brilliantly switched gears to a National Day of Protest made of decentralized actions, calling on those who supported them to drive slowly, turn their lights on and off at night, and at 8 pm to bang pots and pans. Many participated, and these mini-protests helped to rebuild the confidence of the brutalized opposition movement as people overcame their fear of acting.

As both of these actions dramatize, when mass gatherings and public protests become too dangerous, everyday actions can be used to signal dissent, gather crowds, get the word out, illustrate the ridiculous nature of repressive authority, and set up decision dilemmas, all the while avoiding or deferring violent repression *see PRINCIPLE: Put your target in a decision dilemma*.

This principle doesn't only apply to repressive third-world dictatorships, but to situations in supposedly more open societies where daily life has been criminalized for certain segments of the population. Think of the two queer women who kissed in front of the Mormon Church in Salt Lake City until they were hurriedly pushed off the grounds by security. Or the Dance Liberation Front, which organized dances in the streets and unlicensed spaces of Giuliani's New York to flout repressive 1920s era "cabaret laws" still on the books.

POTENTIAL PITFALLS: When it's time to escalate, don't miss the boat. From the beginning, it is important to have a strategic trajectory in mind for your campaign: focus on activities that build toward bigger and bolder actions.

Related:

TACTICS
Flash mob p. 46
Strategic nonviolence p. 88
Invisible theater p. 66

PRINCIPLES
Put your target in a
decision dilemma p. 166
Escalate strategically p. 134
Know your cultural terrain p. 142
Anyone can act p. 98
Use the Jedi mind trick p. 194

THEORIES
Hamoq & Hamas p. 236
Action logic p. 208
Points of intervention p. 250
Pillars of support p. 248
Temporary Autonomous
Zone (TAZ) p. 270

CASE STUDIES
Trail of Dreams p. 384
The salt march p. 354
Occupy Wall Street web

PRINCIPLE:
Kill them with kindness

IN SUM

Kindness, smiles, gifts and unicorns (well, maybe not unicorns) can be potent weapons in the struggle against evil-doers.

EPIGRAPH

"Above all, be kind."

–Kurt Vonnegut

FURTHER INSIGHT

Video: "Auctioneer: Stop All the Sales Right Now!" http://www.youtube.com/ watch?v=u3X89iViAlw

Occupy the Boardroom http://www.occupythe-boardroom.org/

CONTRIBUTED BY

Andrew Boyd

There's a time to be angry *see PRINCIPLE: Anger works best when you have the moral high ground*. There's a time to be reverent *see PRINCIPLE: Use the power of ritual*. There's a time to be funny *see PRINCIPLE: Make it funny*. And there's also a time to be sweet, charming and generous. In fact, that time is often.

A 2011 foreclosure auction in Brooklyn, U.S.A., for instance, was movingly disrupted by protesters breaking into song. The song wasn't angry, it wasn't agitated; it was sweet, beautiful, compassionate — even toward the auctioneer. That's what made it so powerful: the protesters were grounded and determined. They kept singing their sweet song even as the cops led them away.

When you lead with kindness, you're more likely to be seen as the sympathetic character in the story *see PRINCIPLE: Lead with sympathetic characters*. You've come in good faith. You're trying to make things better. You come with smiles, gifts and an open heart, and you are met with stony-faced indifference, scorn or abuse. In the eyes of the public and the media, you are the good guys. You are the reasonable

"It's a core element of nonviolent philosophy to recognize the humanity in everyone and seek to connect with it."

ones. This is not only good tactics, it's an assertion of your basic humanity against unjust and inhuman structures.

Just think of the iconic '60s moment: the anti-war protester putting a flower in the soldier's gun-barrel. Or more recently, the "99%ers" from Occupy the Boardroom who set up online "pen pal" relationships with the country's top bankers. When they were stopped by security from delivering their heartfelt stories in person, they folded up their letters into paper airplanes and sailed them over the heads of the cops toward the bank HQ. For some, cars parked in bike lanes would be reason enough to slash some tires, but not for the Bike Lane Liberation Clowns, who instead will approach

Bogotá, Colombia: A demonstrator embraces a riot police officer during a student protest against government plans to reform higher education. When our opponents' aggression is met with kindness, aggressors and observers alike are forced to look at their actions critically. Photo by William Fernando Martinez/AP.

drivers and kindly implore them to leave. Those who remain are given fake "this could have been a real ticket" tickets warning them they're in violation of NYC parking rules.

It's naïve to think that power will change its ways because of a sweet appeal or a considerate gesture or a paper airplane. But at the same time, it's a core element of nonviolent philosophy to recognize the humanity in everyone and seek to connect with it. The more we humanize politics, the more likely we are to win. The bureaucrat who secretly agrees with you is more likely to quit, and lend his skills to the revolution. The cop who's been given cupcakes and coffee by a Granny Against the War is that much closer to refusing an order to pepper spray a group of college students linking arms. The foreclosure auctioneer, touched by song, isn't going to slam that gavel down quite so hard the next time. And the public, witnessing all of these actions, is more likely to be moved to action themselves. All of these things don't interrupt the workings of power on their own, but at a human level they matter, and over time they add up, sowing seeds of beautiful trouble, and creating allies in the most unexpected places.

PRINCIPLE:
Know your cultural terrain
(and use it to your advantage)

IN SUM

The first rule of guerrilla warfare is to know your terrain and use it to your advantage. This holds true whether you are fighting in an actual jungle or in the metaphoric wasteland of mass culture.

EPIGRAPH

"What the world's governments should really fear is an expert in communication technologies."
–Subcomandante Marcos

PRACTITIONERS

Center for Tactical Magic
Robbie Conal
El Teatro Campesino

FURTHER INSIGHT

Duncombe, Stephen. Cultural Resistance Reader. London: Verso, 2002.

Duncombe, Stephen. Dream. New York: The New Press, 2007.

CONTRIBUTED BY

Stephen Duncombe

Those of us engaged in creative activism need to be able to navigate the broader cultural landscape in which we wage our campaigns, and use it to our advantage. In the twenty-first century, this terrain includes viral video sensations, Twitter hashtags, guerrilla advertising, celebrity gossip, sports spectacles, religious iconography, and other cultural detritus.

But how is an activist supposed to survive, much less thrive, in a cultural environment created expressly for the purposes of commodifying everything of value or fostering obedience to authority?

All cultural artifacts contain contradictions. Marketing campaigns, for instance, are developed to exploit emotion in order to sell product, but to do this they need to tap into the deep-seated dreams and nightmares of large numbers of people. Sometimes these desires are scary and reactionary (brush with Pepsodent or you will die a spinster), but they also tap into positive, often Utopian dreams (drink this beer and you will be surrounded by a beloved, albeit tipsy, community).

Or consider religion: progressive activists often think of religion as an institution designed to enforce the status quo. There's certainly much

> "All cultural artifacts contain contradictions."

to condemn in religion, but it's also a system of ethics and a code of behavior that can be used to critique the norms and ideals of consumer capitalism. The world's great religions extol such virtues as love, community and responsibility for others — surely good material for an astute organizer to work with. Moses was a spectacular leader, Mohammed a master poet, and Jesus, chasing the money-changers out of the Temple and spinning engaging parables, was a crackerjack creative activist.

In 1906, the great philosopher, psychologist and pacifist William James told a group of American students that if they wanted to reach a wider public with their pacifist message, they needed to understand that war, no matter how bloody and barbaric, also tapped into worthy sentiments like honor and sacrifice, and that these values

The more you
TIGHTEN YOUR GRIP
BLOOMBERG
The more
THE 99%
will slip through
YOUR FINGERS

#OccupyWallStreet

Design: Andy Menconi.

needed to first be recognized and then redirected. In-stead of rejecting war outright, he concluded, the activists needed to articulate a "moral equivalent of war" to take its place in the culture's value system. The trick, according to James' insight, is to tap into what's potentially positive in the surrounding culture and then redirect those dreams, desires, images and impulses into more progressive and creative social ends.

Today's cultural terrain is multilayered and ex-tremely varied. Unlike the guerrilla in the jungle, who pretty much only needs to know his own local terrain, we twenty-first century cultural guerrillas need to range far and wide. You may not like or be familiar with Nas-car, professional sports, reality TV and superheroes, but they are all fertile arenas of culture to work with. It may take an open mind and a bit of personal courage, but it behooves us to immerse ourselves in, learn about and respect the world of the cultural "Other" — which, for many of us counter-culture types, ironically, is mass culture.

In 2003 activists from Katuah Earth First! in Knoxville, TN won popular support and massive media coverage for their anti-war action by tapping into the popular narrative of the Lord of the Rings movies

POTENTIAL PITFALLS: The mass culture we seek to appropriate and repurpose is often rooted in deeply regressive ideas and ideologies. Use it carefully and creatively, or its original purpose might prevail.

IF I REPENT

OF ANYTHING IT IS LIKELY TO BE

my good behavior.

—Henry David Thoreau

PRINCIPLE:
Lead with sympathetic characters

IN SUM

Good actions tell a good story; good stories revolve around sympathetic characters.

PRACTITIONERS

Coalition of Immokalee Workers
Cindy Sheehan
Mothers of the Plaza de Mayo
Los Angeles Poverty Department (LAPD)

FURTHER INSIGHT

smartMeme, "Resources"
http://smartmeme.org/
section.php?id=86

CONTRIBUTED BY

Doyle Canning
Patrick Reinsborough

Assembling a compelling cast of characters is a critical strategic consideration for any action designer. Actions tend to be strong on identifying and vilifying the *antagonists* of the narrative, but an audience will care much more about injustice if they can relate to the people who are being affected. Successful actions are often those that present strong protagonists and other sympathetic characters.

The role of the messenger who delivers the story of an action is key. Messengers embody the message by putting a human face on conflict and placing the action within a larger context. Those most impacted by the issue tend to make for more sympathetic and compelling messengers. For instance, if the action is about farm workers, it can be more effective to amplify the voices of a small group of farm workers who are taking action than to have a larger group of non-farm workers to speak up on their behalf. (Of course, solidarity actions certainly have their place: *see CASE: Taco Bell boycott.*)

Power holders understand the importance of deploying sympathetic characters. For instance, welfare cuts get presented as benefiting working mothers, or corporate tax cuts sold as job-creation tools to help the unemployed. Time and again, the powerful play one group of sympathetic characters off another, or argue with Orwellian duplicity that the victims of a policy will actually benefit from it.

In these cases, a campaign becomes a contest over who gets to speak for those suffering. With whom do we sympathize, and are those characters actually given space to speak for themselves? A showdown results between messengers jockeying to represent themselves as the authentic representatives of the impacted constituencies.

In recent years, we have seen several uprisings against repressive governments framed explicitly around sympathetic characters. In Myanmar, monks became the new face of the pro-democracy movement, replacing the students of the 1988 mobilizations as the primary messengers. Obviously, many factions of society supported the movement, but with the monks at the front of the marches it was clear that the pro-democracy movement spoke for the conscience of the nation. Similarly, in Pakistan lawyers became the face of the fight against government impunity. Who better to embody the message of a need to respect the rule of law than lawyers?

It's important to ensure that the faces of the action are not just representative of the relevant impacted community, but also are easily recognizable to outsiders as key characters in the story. This can come down to the crude but important dynamics of costuming: a single religious leader wearing religious sacraments will communicate that people of faith are involved in the action better than twenty religious leaders wearing jeans and sweatshirts *see PRINCIPLE: Don't dress like a protester.*

Indigenous Ecuadorean leader Emergildo Criollo travels from Amazon rainforest to California to deliver 325,000+ letters urging Chevron CEO John Watson to clean up the oil giant's toxic legacy. Photo by Jonathan McIntosh / Rainforest Action Network.

POTENTIAL PITFALLS: The dynamics of who gets to speak, how the characters are portrayed, and who is cast as the heroes, victims, and villains, are deeply entwined in the dynamics of power and privilege. Activists should take care not to play into narratives of victimization that plague marginalized communities. Navigating these dynamics skillfully and authentically is essential to successful actions and campaigns.

PRINCIPLE: Maintain nonviolent discipline

IN SUM

Nonviolent action works best when you stay nonviolent.

EPIGRAPH

"We must forever conduct our struggle on the high plane of dignity and discipline. We must not allow our creative protests to degenerate into physical violence. Again and again we must rise to the majestic heights of meeting physical force with soul force."

—Dr. Martin Luther King, Jr.

PRACTITIONERS

*Jesus of Nazareth
Gandhi
Civil Rights Movement
Otpor
Greenpeace
Peaceful Uprising
Gene Sharpe
The Ya Basta Association*

FURTHER INSIGHT

Erica Chenoweth and Maria Stephan, Why Civil Resistance Works *(Columbia UP, 2011).*

Hardy Merriman, "The Trifecta of Civil Resistance: Unity, Planning, Discipline." http://trb.la/AOH8NI

CONTRIBUTED BY

Nathan Schneider

It's amazing to think that unarmed masses of people have defeated armed-to-the-teeth forces using humble techniques as strikes, occupations, boycotts and sit-ins. One way of understanding why this can happen is that nonviolent methods put the oppressor in a decision dilemma: either rain pain on a bunch of unarmed resisters, or capitulate. The former can turn public opinion toward the protesters and undermine the legitimacy upon which the oppressor's power rests. If the resistance persists, escalating crackdowns can start to backfire, even to the point that the police or military refuse to participate. Eventually the sovereign has no choice but to capitulate.

By maintaining nonviolent discipline in the face of police dogs, this civil rights demonstrator in Birmingham, Alabama, put his oppressor in a decision dilemma, May 3, 1963.

This basic logic frays, however, as soon as the resisters start meeting violence with violence. If the opponent succeeds in portraying resisters as a threat to peace and order, it escapes the decision dilemma, reasserting its legitimacy by playing the part of protector, of securer, of stabilizer. Unless you can scrounge up enough guns to match the military's firepower, your movement is toast.

PRINCIPLE: Maintain nonviolent discipline

Political scientist Erica Chenoweth and sociologist Kurt Schock examined the data of past resistance movements and found that having an armed flank dramatically reduces the ability of an uprising to attract widespread participation. Most people aren't interested in getting martyred in a firefight, so they'll stay home. Rather than merely representing one wing of a "diversity of tactics," therefore, undisciplined violence in a movement tends to lessen the effectiveness of nonviolent mass movements *see: TACTIC: Strategic nonviolence.* That's why oppressors love to insert provocateurs into resistance movements to push them into violence and then discredit them.

Many people keep nonviolent discipline for mainly strategic reasons: they do it because it's effective, rather than as a matter of principle. In practice, though, maintaining nonviolent discipline in the face of provocation can be difficult if you don't consider it at least partly as an end in itself. Fortunately, almost everybody aspires to build the least violent society possible. To the extent that we build our movements as models of the world we'd like to see, nonviolent discipline should come naturally.

The practice of maintaining nonviolent discipline should never be confused with passivity or acquiescence in the face of injustice.

POTENTIAL PITFALLS: When a given nonviolent tactic doesn't work, it's tempting to conclude that nonviolence has failed and the only recourse is violence. That's incredibly hasty. There is an enormous range of nonviolent tactics — Gene Sharp famously listed 198 of them,[1] and that's just for starters — varying from purely symbolic acts to direct action designed to disrupt the smooth operation of oppressive systems. There is no one-tactic-fits-all solution: when one nonviolent tactic isn't doing the trick, try another, or more than one at once!

"Nonviolent methods put the oppressor in a decision dilemma: either rain down pain on a bunch of unarmed resisters, or capitulate."

---

[1] Gene Sharp, *The Politics of Nonviolent Action, Vols 1-3* (Boston: Porter Sargent, 1973). http://aeinstein.org/organizations/org/198_methods.pdf

PRINCIPLE:
Make new folks welcome

IN SUM

Recruitment and retention go hand in hand. A few simple procedures for orienting new participants can go a long way to ensuring their ongoing involvement.

EPIGRAPH

"You are invited. By anyone, to do anything. You are invited, for all time. You are so needed, by everyone, to do everything. You are invited, for all time."

–The Dismemberment Plan, You Are Invited

PRACTITIONERS

Iraq Veterans Against the War

FURTHER INSIGHT

Jonathan Matthew Smucker, "Three Tips for Plugging People In," Beyond the Choir, February 28, 2011

CONTRIBUTED BY

Jonathan Matthew Smucker

Bringing in new participants is essential to any activist group that wants to grow in size and capacity — but recruiting is only the first step. Integrating people into an established group can be a much bigger challenge, and it helps to be intentional about it. Getting good at involving people requires some deliberate attention and probably the establishment of some basic procedures to make new folks welcome.

For starters, when someone says they're interested in finding out more or getting involved in your group, don't just invite them to come to your next meeting and leave it at that. Even the most welcoming and inclusive groups tend to develop their own meeting culture that can unintentionally make new folks feel like outsiders. To increase your new member retention rates, schedule one-on-one intake interviews with new folks before they come to a group meeting. Get to know the person. Find out what attracted them to the group, what kinds of tasks they enjoy or are good at, and how much time they have. Then tell them more about the group and discuss what their involvement could look like. While this level of orientation requires more time up front, it saves time in the long run: people tend to plug into the work faster and stick around longer. It may make sense for one or two members of your group to take on this responsibility as an ongoing role.

> "Even the most welcoming and inclusive groups tend to develop their own meeting culture that can unintentionally make new folks feel like outsiders."

Secondly, if you want to inspire people to stay involved, you need to make them feel valued and appreciated. People like to be around people who treat them well. Most of us have no shortage of things we can do with a finite amount of free time: if you expect people to prioritize your group over aikido classes, contra dancing or advanced origami, you gotta treat 'em right. Notice and acknowledge new folks' contributions, however small. Make time to check in with them outside of meetings.

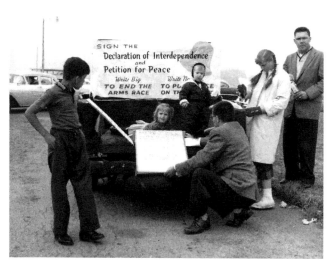

Even a toddler can hold a petition on the back of a truck. Get people involved at their level. (Protesting the nuclear arms race in San Francisco, California in 1960. Photo by Pip R. Lagenta/Flickr.)

Related:

PRINCIPLES
Don't mistake your group
for society p. 130
Enable, don't command p. 132
We are all leaders p. 202
Challenge patriarchy as
you organize p. 108
Shift the spectrum of allies p. 172

THEORIES
Political identity paradox p. 254
Anti-oppression p. 212

CASE STUDIES
Lysistrata project p. 330

Ask their opinions often: What did they think about the meeting? the event? the action? Bounce your ideas off of them and ask for their feedback.

PRINCIPLE:
Make the invisible visible

IN SUM

Many injustices are invisible to the mainstream. When you bring these wrongs into full view, you change the game, making the need to take action palpable.

EPIGRAPH

"We who in engage in nonviolent direct action are not the creators of tension. We merely bring to the surface the hidden tension that is already alive."

–Dr. Martin Luther King, Jr

PRACTITIONERS

Greenpeace
ACT-UP & Gran Fury
Coalition of Immokalee Workers
Guerrilla Girls
Eve Ensler
United Farm Workers
SNCC
Rainforest Action Network
Coco Fusco
Lesbian Avengers
Mothers of the Plaza de Mayo
Operation SalAMI
Preemptive Media

CONTRIBUTED BY

Nadine Bloch

Social problems are often obscured by *distance, ideology,* or *simple chemistry* (when was the last time you noticed PCBs in your drinking water?). If you can't see it, you can't change it: the first task of an activist is often to *make the invisible visible.*

There are several kinds of "invisibility." Which one you're dealing with will shape the approach you take.

Distance

Climate chaos might be stranding polar bears in the Arctic or submerging small island nations in the Pacific, but for most people in the global north it's out of sight, out of mind. Countless artful interventions have sought to make accelerating climate changes more visible, whether by painting anticipated future sea levels on city streets and buildings or mock-drowning a polar bear in the fountain outside the Department of the Interior in D.C., as Greenpeace did in 2009.

People with privilege often have the luxury of putting distance between themselves and the consequences of their actions. When tackling an issue that seems distant, it helps to bring the issue home *see PRINCIPLE: Bring the issue home* by highlighting the human cost.

Ideology

People who have the luxury of not seeing an uncomfortable truth often simply won't, even if it's in front of their faces. Privileged whites easily ignored the everyday injustices inflicted during the Jim Crow era until blacks organized and took action, sitting in the "wrong" seats in diners and on buses, marching in the streets, and so on.

Injustices made invisible by ideology can be brought to light by judicious reframing *see PRINCIPLE: Reframe.* A frame defines what is part of the story and, more importantly, what is not. Actions that target the *point of assumption* (the simple question of who can sit where on a bus, for instance) can focus attention on what was previously "outside the frame."

Chemistry, and other easily overlooked facts of life
Many pollutants cannot be seen by the naked eye, yet cause great harm. The key is to bring that harm into public view. Consider the makers of the movie *Gasland*, who lit some Pennsylvania tap water on fire, powerfully refuting years of industry denial with a single powerful visual demonstration. Or the forest activists who filled several city intersections with the stumps of cut-down trees. When Kodak was caught discharging toxins from its manufacturing plant in upstate New York, Greenpeace created a public fountain that brought the effluent from the pipe — normally out of site below the water surface — cascading into public view. These kind of actions are particularly effective when the corporation has worked hard to hide or deny the damage, or simply done it far away from consumers.

A still from the movie Gasland by documentary filmmaker Josh Fox exposes the effects of fracking.

The role of the activist often resembles that of the child in the Hans Christian Andersen story: even if everyone knows the emperor has no clothes, saying as much in public can have revolutionary consequences. Exposing previously hidden problems can be the first and most important step in resolving them.

FURTHER INSIGHT

Video: Amnesty International, "Making the invisible visible" http://trb.la/xJNGDV

New Tactics in Human Rights. Resources and Tools/Building Awareness http://trb.la/z2HFML

Hudson River Sloop Clearwater http://www.clearwater.org/about/history/

Slavoj Zizek, "Good Manners in the Age of Wikileaks," London Review of Books, January 20, 2011.

Greenpeace, "Giant Melting da Vinci Artwork Recreated on Arctic Sea Ice" http://trb.la/wRJEgi

Related:

PRINCIPLE:
Make your actions both concrete and communicative (but don't confuse the two)

IN SUM

Concrete tactics have measurable goals and are designed to have a direct physical impact. Communicative ones can be more symbolic. Knowing the difference and planning accordingly is important.

PRACTITIONERS

The Diggers (1960s)
The Ya Basta Association
The Zapatista Army of National Liberation
Greenpeace
Art and Revolution Collective

CONTRIBUTED BY

Joshua Kahn Russell

To varying degrees, all tactics might be *concrete* and *communicative*. When activists confuse the two, the results can be counter-productive.

A tactic is *concrete* to the degree that it seeks to achieve a specific, quantifiable objective. For example, anti-war organizers may seek to blockade a port to keep a shipment of weapons from passing through. There is a specific goal, a tangible cost for the port and the companies that use it, and a way to evaluate success: either we stop the weapons or we don't.

A tactic is *communicative* insomuch as it communicates a political position, set of values or worldview. A mass march in response to an injustice can fall into this category. *Communicative* tactics can be useful for exciting our base, building networks, seeking to sway public opinion, or scaring a target, but often do not have a *specific, measurable, activating, realistic, time-bound* (S.M.A.R.T.) goal. Success is more qualitative.

To succeed, concrete tactics must force a response from the target *see PRINCIPLE: Put your target in a decision dilemma*. Communicative tactics might have a target, but can also work without one.

While some actions can be both communicative and concrete, it is important to understand the difference. People often get discouraged by direct action because they take part in a communicative action and expect a concrete outcome. It's better to be clear from the beginning about the difference, so that everyone knows how to measure, and contribute to, the action's impact.[1]

Consider an Occupy Wall Street effort to blockade the entrance to Goldman Sachs. At the action planning meeting, because there was no clarity about whether the action was communicative or concrete, at first the discussion was circular and unproductive. Some wanted people to lock arms in a simple human blockade *see TACTIC: Blockade*, others wanted to up the ante by using chains and other "hard gear." Using gear has the benefit of *staying power* (it's more difficult for the police to remove you), but it carries much greater risk and is more difficult to deploy. It became clear the group had neither time nor numbers to blockade every single exit. Therefore, if the action was conceived as concrete (trying to shut down Goldman Sachs), it would fail because it could not achieve a realistic *instrumental outcome*. If it was *communicative*, however — a symbolic act to amplify a message — it could be successful. Furthermore, a communicative action might have a powerful *expressive* outcome by building the resolve, connection and commitment of participants by offering them a cathartic, transformative experience. When participants agreed to carry out a communicative action, the staying power of the blockade gear was no longer needed: there was no tactical advantage to holding the space longer. Instead, the group decided to go with a human blockade, which played better in the media (a main indicator of success for them in this action). If activists hadn't assessed the purpose of their action and understood their goals, they likely would have made less strategic choices.

> "People often get discouraged by direct action because they take part in a communicative action and expect a concrete outcome."

Related:

TACTICS

Direct action p. 32
Blockade p. 14
Occupation web
Sit-in web

PRINCIPLES

Put your target in a decision dilemma p. 166
Praxis makes perfect p. 162
Escalate strategically p. 134
Consider your audience p. 118
Shift the spectrum of allies p. 172

THEORIES

Expressive and instrumental actions p. 232
Points of intervention p. 250
Action logic p. 208
Activist realpolitik web
Narrative power analysis p. 244
Ethical spectacle p. 230

CASE STUDIES

Battle in Seattle p. 286
Whose tea party? p. 392
Taco Bell boycott p. 372
Tar sands action p. 376
Wisconsin Capitol Occupation p. 396

The categories "concrete" and "communicative" are ways to measure the instrumental outcome of an action, as opposed to its expressive dimension. The expressive part of your action is focused on the self-expression of participants, while the instrumental outcome of an action is concerned with your action's more direct impacts (see THEORY: Expressive and instrumental actions).

PRINCIPLE:
No one wants to watch a drum circle

IN SUM

Participating in a drum circle is amazing, transformative and fun. Watching a drum circle, on the other hand, is torture. Don't ask people to watch you have fun: get them involved!

FURTHER INSIGHT

Weapons Lab Conversion Proposal
http://trb.la/zUOYwt

Video: "Say Something Nice."
ImprovEverywhere. August 22, 2011
http://youtu.be/RwEYYI-AGWs

PRACTITIONERS

Improv Everywhere
Otpor!
The (new) Diggers
"I Dream Your Dream"

CONTRIBUTED BY

Steve Lambert

Drum circles are incredible! Hanging out in the park with a mix of friends and strangers, making rhythms together, communicating intuitively, adding your own rhythm, and making a big and beautiful sound that fills the park. It's an amazing thing.

Or so I've heard.

My *actual* experiences with drum circles are entirely different. At best, they're tolerable, but more often they're torture. I'm trying to hang out in the park with my friends and these self-indulgent dipshits won't stop banging on their goat skins. No one else cares except someone in a tie-dyed sarong who will apparently jump at any opportunity to sway with her arms in the air.

Being part of a drum circle is one thing. Experiencing it from the outside, quite another.

Way too often, activism is like a drum circle. Viewed from the outside, it can be painfully unimaginative, solipsistic and quite simply annoying. For the people involved in the creation of an action, however, the experience can be rewarding and transformative — even if everyone else walks away confused or annoyed. If that happens and it doesn't bother you, you may have fallen prey to the *political identity paradox see THEORY.*

One way to reach your audience is to entice them to become participants by expanding the creative part of the action to include as many as possible. Come up with ways for observers to meaningfully involve themselves, instead of expecting them to stand mute before your expressive outbursts of creativity.

Instead of strictly planning an action, think of creating rules to a game — one that is rewarding and fun to play *see PRINCIPLE: Simple rules can have grand results.* How can you create parameters within which large numbers of participants can meaningfully contribute, act, and create? An open framework that allows participants the freedom to bring in their own ideas and solutions?

The call to occupy Wall Street operated in this way, offering only a date, a core slogan, and the instruction *Bring tent.*[1] Flash mobs are no different: set a time, location, and a few basic rules, and let things take their course. These actions have simple rules that can expand to include thousands of participants and still deliver a provocative experience to participant and observer alike.

In any case, whatever the nature of your action, it's worth looking for ways to make passersby feel that it's more about them than about you. No matter how good a drummer you are.

While those inside this drum circle seem to be reaching new levels of existential bliss, those watching aren't likely to get much out of the event. We should strive to make our actions transparent and inclusive.

---

[1] Of course, Occupy Wall Street went on to attract its share
of drum circles: http://yeslab.org/drumcircle

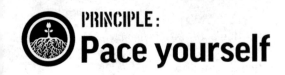

PRINCIPLE:
Pace yourself

IN SUM

Taking care of ourselves and having fun in our work for social change are essential to building stronger, larger, more effective movements.

EPIGRAPH

"Let's treat each other as if we plan to work side by side in struggle for many, many years to come. Because the task before us will demand nothing less."

–Naomi Klein, address to Occupy Wall Street

FURTHER INSIGHT

Weber, Cheyenna. "A Love Letter to the Overcommitted." Shareable.net. November 23, 2011.

Macy, Joanna, and Molly Young Brown. Coming Back to Life. Gabriola Island, BC: New Society Publishers, 1998.

Albert, Michael. The Trajectory of Change: Activist Strategies for Social Transformation. Boston: South End Press, 2002.

CONTRIBUTED BY

Tracey Mitchell

Too often, the people doing the most to take care of the world do the least to take care of themselves. It happens far too frequently that a dedicated activist suddenly (or not so suddenly, for those who know them best) burns out and disappears from public view. This scenario is common enough, and represents a large enough threat to our collective success, that it warrants serious discussion and soul-searching within our movements. Specifically, we need to talk about how to take care of ourselves and each other so we can stay involved for the long haul.

Whether we like it or not, activists are walking advertisements for our movements. If we are exhausted, frustrated, overwhelmed or unhappy most of the time, we make a life of activism look extremely unattractive to the average person. Virtually every activist has struggled with the question of how to get beyond "preaching to the choir." A first step is to make "the choir" the sort of place lots of people will want to join.

It is also important to ensure that pragmatic self-care is not seen as selfish or bourgeois. If we don't take time to focus on our physical, mental, emotional and spiritual selves, we will burn out sooner or later. It's almost guaranteed. Wouldn't it be better to take regular breaks to nurture yourself, rather than get to the point where you have to take months or years off because you are too sick or depressed to be involved?

Activists are frequently motivated by guilt, and will unconsciously use guilt to motivate others. Guilt is a dangerous motivator because it will never be satisfied, and is rooted in a sense of external obligation rather than internal passion. A better motivator, for those who have some degree of privilege and feel guilty about that, is gratitude. Coming to this work from gratitude gives us energy without sucking us into despair and self-judgment.

These are deadly serious questions. Long-time Canadian activist Tooker Gomberg took his own life in 2004 after a long battle with depression and burn-out. Before he died, he wrote a letter to social change activists. Do the activism, he said, but don't *overdo* it:

It's honorable to work to change the world, but do it in balance with other things. Explore and embrace the things you love to do, and you'll be energetic and enthusiastic about the activism. Don't drop hobbies or enjoyments. Be sure to hike and dance and sing. Keeping your spirit alive and healthy is fundamental if you are to keep going.[1]

It is important to take a long view of activism, to remember those who came before us and those who will come after. This can help us build on the work of previous generations and learn from their mistakes and triumphs, so that we are not always starting from scratch. We cannot carry all of the weight of the world's problems on our shoulders; we must simply accept, with gratitude, the opportunity to do what we can today.

"It's better to sit out a game or two than to drop the ball mid-game."

Related:

PRINCIPLES
Make new folks welcome p. 150
Delegate p. 122
Beware the tyranny of
structurelessness p. 102
Create levels of participation web
Take risks but take care p. 182
Make it funny web

THEORIES
The social cure p. 264
Hamoq & hamas p. 236

POTENTIAL PITFALLS: Don't be a flake. Often, when people suddenly realize that they need to take better care of themselves or need a break, they flake out on existing commitments and leave comrades in the lurch. Learning to anticipate breaks, plan for them and not overcommit is a really important part of pacing. It's better to sit out a game or two than to drop the ball mid-game.

---

[1] Tooker Gomberg, "Letter to an Activist, Earth Day 2002" (Greenspiration.org)

PRINCIPLE:
Play to the audience that isn't there

IN SUM

In a hyper-mediated world, often the audience you care about is not the one in the room with you, but the one you'll reach through mass and social media. Design your action with them in mind.

PRACTITIONERS

The Yes Men
Agit-Pop
CANVAS
Greenpeace
Joey Skaggs

CONTRIBUTED BY

Andy Bichlbaum
Andrew Boyd

When you're pulling off a prank or staging some kind of media spectacle, it's important to keep in mind that those you're directly confronting are often not your main audience. When Occupy Wall Street activists swarm Manhattan's financial district or Bhopal activists camp out on the lawn of the CEO of Union Carbide, there's no reason to think that the *immediate* audience will change their minds based on what they're observing. Rather, the idea is to use the immediate audience as unwitting actors in a theater piece that is being performed for a secondary audience. That *secondary* audience is comprised of film-goers or Youtube viewers or TV watchers or press-release readers — and they're the ones you care most about. Design your intervention with them in mind.

If reporters are going to be present, consider how things will look through their eyes. Regardless, however, make sure to document your own action *see PRINCIPLE: Do the media's work for them.* Choreograph the action so you create and capture the moments you need to tell the story you want to tell. When Agit-Pop pulled off their Public Option Annie guerrilla musical *see CASE,* they snuck more videographers into the conference than singers.

Obviously, the secondary audience is not always your focus. At a rally, say, the key audience might actually be the participants themselves. With most strikes or sit-ins, the key audience is the actual target — a CEO or public official — and your aim is to disrupt business as usual and exact a cost that will pressure your target to accede to your demands.

But even with some of these more disruptive actions, the key audience is not in the room. When Tim DeChristopher disrupted a Utah oil and gas auction in 2008 *see CASE: Bidder 70*, he was not tempted to address the other bidders directly. His action was for a much larger audience — as well as for the land itself that he helped to save.

Sometimes activists think they're out to change the minds of the bankers, CEOs, or others they're ostensibly targeting. It's one thing to *pretend* you're out to change their minds — in order to stage a theatrically effective action, that is often necessary — but it's another thing to believe it yourself. The idea that you can change evildoers' minds by gathering en masse outside their stronghold is not exactly supported by the historical record. Instead, think of your target and your immediate audience as unwitting actors in the theater piece you're concocting for another audience they're not even aware of.

"Think of your immediate audience as unwitting actors in the theater piece you're concocting for another audience they're not even aware of."

Related:

TACTICS
Hoax p. 54
Identity correction p. 60
Infiltration p. 64
Public filibuster p. 86
Creative disruption p. 18
Human banner p. 56
Electoral guerrilla theater p. 40
Nonviolent search and seizure p. 76
Media-jacking p. 72
Creative petition delivery p. 22

PRINCIPLES
Do the media's work for them p. 124
Stay on message p. 178
Show, don't tell p. 174
Lead with sympathetic characters p. 146
Anger works best when you have the moral high ground p. 96
Put your target in a decision dilemma p. 166
Don't look like a protester p. 126
Kill them with kindness p. 140

THEORIES
Society of the spectacle p. 266
Ethical spectacle p. 230
The propaganda model p. 256

CASE STUDIES
Public Option Annie p. 346
Bidder 70 p. 290

HOW THE OPPOSITE IS EQUALLY TRUE: Sometimes this principle is absolutely wrong. Sometimes the media and the public will see right through an action that is too heavy-handedly crafted for TV. Sometimes the best way to connect with the indirect audience is just to be your unvarnished, authentic self, warts and all *see CASE: Occupy Wall Street*.

PRINCIPLE:
Praxis makes perfect

IN SUM

Theory without action produces armchair revolutionaries. Action without reflection produces ineffective or counterproductive activism. That's why we have praxis: a cycle of theory, action and reflection that helps us analyze our efforts in order to improve our ideas.

FURTHER INSIGHT

Moore, Hillary, and Joshua Kahn Russell. Organizing Cools the Planet: Tools and Reflections to Navigate the Climate Crisis. Oakland, CA: PM Press, 2011.

Praxis Makes Perfect: Joshua Kahn Russell's blog www.praxismakesperfect.org

Beyond the Choir: A forum for grassroots mobilization www.beyondthechoir.org

CONTRIBUTED BY

Joshua Kahn Russell

Effective activism follows a cycle. We start with our theory of how change happens. Then we take action based on our theory. Then we take a step back and reflect on how the action went, which re-shapes our theory. Basically, praxis means "learning." It may seem simple, but few activists actually *do* it.

Praxis requires us to be students of our own experience and context. It's not just about being smart and reflecting. It's also about building specific *behaviors* and *group norms* that promote habits of strategy, debrief and revision. It's about your group's meeting style, organizational structure and leadership dynamics.

> "Praxis requires us to be students of our own experience and context."

Here's the difference that praxis can make:

Let's say we're in a student group at a college. If our group lacks praxis, we may say: "Let's bring Radical Thinker X to speak at our campus!" We affirm that the event will be "good." Then we have the event. It's somewhat well-attended, but afterwards our group has mixed feelings about it. We decide to keep moving forward and host another event.

That's a bit directionless. There was no actual theory, and no basis for reflection.

Instead, let's start with a theory. We start our group meeting by saying "Bringing Radical Thinker X to campus will help our campaign. They can talk about why activism is powerful, and it will reach a new audience of people who are not yet engaged in our campaign. Let's post fliers in our favorite coffee shops. Three hundred people will attend, fifty will sign up, and five of those people will show up at our next meeting."

Now that's a real theory. It has an explicit logic, a process of *how* you will do your action, and concrete measurable *outcomes* that you expect.

The event happens. Only one hundred people attend and most of them already work with your group, so only a few sign your list, and nobody new comes to your next meeting.

The Praxis Wheel. Art by Joshua Kahn Russell.

You now have a real *basis for reflection*. You can de-brief your event, and instead of subjectively talking about whether you thought it was "good" or not, you can have a conversation about why it didn't measure up to your success indicators, and what to do next time. These lessons shape how you do your next event.

Organizers should have the praxis cycle spinning in their heads all the time. We are always learning from what's going on around us. The point of building a *culture of praxis* in your group, however, is so your *whole group* can learn, not just a couple of organizers. When you develop your theory (your plan and your goals) with your group, and then have a real debrief after, the lessons are available to all. If you don't take real time out to name your theories, and then reflect, revise, and learn lessons, you will be left spinning your wheels, with fewer and fewer people understanding how to do the work of your group.

PRINCIPLE:
Put movies in the hands of movements

IN SUM

By telling a personal story, documentary film can make an otherwise difficult-to-approach issue accessible. Filmmakers and activists, working together, can collaborate to make a film a story-driven lever for change.

EPIGRAPH

"Making the movie and getting it to screen is only 50% of the job. What to do when the lights come up – how to harness that energy in the room... well that's the other 50%."

–George Stoney

PRACTITIONERS

Working Films
http://www.workingfilms.org

Active Voice
www.activevoice.net

Film Sprout
www.filmsprout.org

Films That Change the World
www.filmsthatchangetheworld.com

Hybrid Foundation/Practitioner
www.thefledglingfund.org

GOOD PITCH Channel 4
Brit-Docs Foundation's
http://britdoc.org/real_good/pitch

CONTRIBUTED BY

Judith Helfand
Anna Lee

Story-driven documentaries change minds, attitudes and policies. But they reach their fullest potential when tightly woven into the campaigns and events of organizers working on the issues. As activist filmmakers, here are a couple of key rules my colleagues and I have learned:

Create mutually beneficial relationships between filmmakers and organizers. Authentic partnerships start with the filmmaker asking the movement, "What can my film do for you?" Not, "what can you do for my film?" Certainly, the movement has much to offer the filmmaker in return (and we'll get to that) but it's important to begin with this frame.

"We create a cycle by which we build momentum for both the film and the movement."

Look for five to ten organizations to partner with — some might be small and scrappy, others may have national reach. *Ask them* for the strategy; don't guess. Effective conversations start with questions like: "What are your current programs and priorities and how could our film support them?" "What do you want audiences to do when the lights come up?" Partner organizations have resources to offer in return: online tools that can be embedded into a film's website, information that can be added to a film's screening guide or curriculum, constituents and allies eager to spread the word, and actions that audience members can take. All of this creates a cycle which builds momentum for both the film *and* the movement.

Move from "film timeline" to "organizing timeline." The first year or so of a film's life is driven by the film timeline: you take it around the festival circuit, bring it to theaters or community events and, if you're lucky, broadcast it. This is a great time to experiment together. For example, you might try out a mobile app where you ask festival audiences to sign a petition while they are still in their seats.

But at a certain point, a filmmaker shifts to "organizing time" — especially when there is a timely, urgent ongoing campaign that needs the film. Community screenings, house parties, online streaming: all these traditional venues for distribution can be utilized strategically by organizations and individual activists on the ground. They might use screening events to get more folks to sign up for an upcoming national day of action and then use clips to energize the crowd on the day of the action. Or they might use house party screenings and discussions to mobilize their constituents around a pending piece of legislation that needs that extra push. At this stage, a campaign's needs and timeline inform when and how the film is used and catalyze the long-term change everyone is working toward.

POTENTIAL PITFALLS: The most important part of being an "independent" storyteller is just that: your independence. While you have to balance the needs of your organizing partners with the needs of your narrative, the story has to come first. You might be making a film *with* Greenpeace, but you are not making it *for* them. It's critical that this relationship is understood by all parties — the organizers, the press, as well as opponents who, given half the chance, will cry, "Propaganda!" The key to this synergy is not just the perception of independence, but its reality.

FURTHER INSIGHT

Working Films, "Impact: A Series of Stories about Films Making Change" www.workingfilms.org/impact

Video: "Everything's Cool at Sundance: Leveraging a Film Fest" Part 1: http://youtu.be/zJfjv7t6Z2Q Part 2: http://youtu.be/CVvAGAPY6ik

Video: "Everything's Cool: Step It Up" http://youtu.be/kx_Pu9-TLn4

Independent Documentary Association, "DOC 'U' on the ROAD" http://trb.la/ycoowO

Related:

TACTICS
Guerrilla projection p. 52

PRINCIPLES
Think narratively p. 186
Stay on message p. 178
Balance art and message p. 100
Think nationally, screen locally web
Do the media's work for them p. 124
Know your cultural terrain p. 142
Make the invisible visible p. 152
Show, don't tell p. 174

THEORIES
Narrative power analysis p. 244
Points of intervention p. 250
Pedagogy of the oppressed p. 246
Cultural hegemony p. 222
Intellectuals and power p. 240

PRINCIPLE:
Put your target in a decision dilemma

IN SUM

Design your action so that your target is forced to make a decision, and all their available options play to your advantage.

PRACTITIONERS

Cindy Sheehan
United for a Fair Economy
Saul Alinsky
Otpor

The ProvosFURTHER INSIGHT

Philippe Duhamel, "The Dilemma Demonstration: Using nonviolent civil disobedience to put the government between a rock and a hard place" (2004).
http://trb.la/Aq6iwp

Srdja Popovic, "On Otpor's strategy." Centre for Applied Nonviolent Action and Strategies.
http://trb.la/A1kUAr

CONTRIBUTED BY

Andrew Boyd
Joshua Kahn Russell

Cindy Sheehan.

If you design your action well, you can force your target into a situation where they have to respond, but have no good options — where they're damned if they do, damned if they don't. In fact, many actions with concrete goals (such as blockades, sit-ins, tree-sits, etc) *require* such a "decision dilemma" in order to be successful.

Consider the blockade of a building. A tactically effective blockade leaves your target with only two options: 1) negotiate with you / meet your demands, or 2) react with force (violence against you or arrest). That's a decision dilemma. Don't let your target walk out the back door, and don't put yourself in a situation where they can wait you out with impunity. You must force a clear decision dilemma. Without it, you let your target and/or the police determine the success of your action, rather than calling the shots yourself. Be sure to cover all the exits — literally or figuratively.

Creative activists can adapt this tactical insight to force their target into a similar dilemma on the symbolic level.

Take Cindy Sheehan. In the summer of 2005, after the death of her son, Army Spc. Casey Sheehan, in the Iraq War, she camped out in front of President Bush's Texas ranch where he had just begun a three-week vacation. Quoting Bush's own words back to him, she vowed not to leave until he met with her to explain for what "noble cause" her son had died.

Once the media started covering the stand-off, Bush was trapped in a decision dilemma: he was damned if he did meet with her, damned if he didn't. Meeting with her would've been a media fiasco. Not meeting with her con-

PRINCIPLE: Put your target in a decision dilemma

ceded her point. Either way he lost. In the end, he never met with Sheehan, and "Camp Casey" became one of the key watershed moments that turned American public opinion against the war.

Or consider the Whose Tea Party? action *see CASE*. GOP Congressmen gathered on the Boston Tea Party ship for a set-piece media stunt: tossing a trunk labelled "tax code" into the harbor. But they were suddenly confronted by a dingy of activists — "the Working Family Life Raft" — in the water beneath them, pleading not to be swamped by the proposed flat tax. With cameras rolling, the target had two choices: either toss the tax code in and sink the raft (as they did) or back down on their declared intention to dispose of the tax code. By throwing it in and capsizing the raft, they played into the activists' story that the GOP's proposed tax reform would "sink the working family." Backing down would also have undermined the GOP argument by symbolically conceding that the tax would be harmful to working families. As with Camp Casey, this decision dilemma was not a happy accident, but a key design element of the action.

Often, for this principle to work, you have to be prepared to wait out your opponent. Cindy Sheehan committed to camping outside Bush's ranch for the duration of his vacation. She wasn't going anywhere. It was his move, and he didn't have one. Similarly, the Working Family Life Raft bobbed in the water, pleading

> "Don't let your target walk out the back door, and don't put yourself in a situation where they can wait you out with impunity."

for the GOP to spare working families while the media documented the event. Unlike a lot of actions, there were no security guards to clear them out. They could just wait, and the more the GOPers hesitated, the more they reinforced the protesters' message.

POTENTIAL PITFALLS: As with bear safety, so with activism: forcing someone into a corner can sometimes provoke a violent response. If your intention is to eliminate the *flight* option in a *fight-or-flight* scenario, then you need to take all necessary precautions to minimize the risk to you and your allies, should the target choose to lash out *see PRINCIPLE: Take risks, but take care.*

Related:

TACTICS
Identity Correction p. 60
Direct action p. 32
Blockade p. 14
Sit-in web

PRINCIPLES
Take risks but take care p. 182
The real action is your target's reaction web
Turn the tables p. 190
Get arrested in an intelligent way web
Be both expressive and instrumental web

THEORIES
Action logic p. 208
Narrative power analysis p. 244
Points of intervention p. 250
Activist realpolitik web

CASE STUDIES
Whose tea party? p. 392
Camp Casey web
Dow Chemical apologizes for Bhopal p. 318

PRINCIPLE:
Reframe

IN SUM

The easiest way to win an argument is to redefine the terms of the debate.

EPIGRAPH

"There is a basic truth about framing. If you accept the other guy's frame, you lose."

—George Lakoff

PRACTITIONERS

Design Studio for Social Intervention

Voina

CONTRIBUTED BY

Doyle Canning
Patrick Reinsborough

The United Workers and Public Justice Center on the National Day of Action Against Wage Theft — an act of radical reframing.

Reframing is a process of replacing an old story with a new one by widening the frame, narrowing the frame, or shifting the frame to another scene entirely.

The powers-that-be usually go to great lengths to frame their agenda in a way that is favorable for their interests — think *nanny state, tax relief, death panels*. Like a camera's viewfinder, the frame of a narrative focuses the public on specific information that reflects the interests of the framers.

How do you reframe an issue? The first step is to conduct a *narrative power analysis see THEORY*— a study of how the issue is currently framed, which seeks to identify its underlying assumptions — for example, "there is no alternative," or "a rising tide lifts all boats," or "the U.S. brings democracy to the Third World."

Following from your narrative power analysis, come up with another story that exposes the faulty assumptions of the status quo. For instance, cast new characters who previously haven't been heard from, or redefine the problem by introducing a different set of values, or pose a new solution that is more compelling than what is currently on offer. Reframing often involves *making the invisible visible see PRINCIPLE* by highlighting aspects of the story that have been left out of the dominant story.

Next, design a reframing action that seeks to relocate the story. Redirect the public's focus to the scene of the crime to reveal a villain, whether it's a corporate boardroom or a CEO's seventh home. Use an emblematic location tied to an historical narrative, like a monument or a park with a name that is significant in the story (Liberty Plaza Park or a Christopher Columbus statue for instance). Tie your action to high-profile events or dates that are soon to follow, framing and foreshadowing the public conversation around those celebrations. For instance, on Tax Day posing as tax collectors at the HQs of the Big Banks and trying to get them to pay their proper share might reframe the public discussion of tax evasion.

If you expand your reframing action into a campaign, you might succeed in injecting powerful new memes into the media and policy discourse. Adam Kader of the Arise Workers Center in Chicago offers this example:

> Institutions like the Department of Labor and the mainstream media referred to the phenomena of worker exploitation as "non-payment of wages." Then, several years ago, worker centers designed the "wage theft" meme. This meme overthrows the dominant assumption that wages are the property of the boss, to be shared with workers. Rather, in this new narrative, wages are the property of workers, and have been stolen by the boss. . . . The media has begun to use the meme when they report on our campaigns and legislators have incorporated the phrase "wage theft" in the names of bills.[1]

Effective creative action should serve the larger strategic goal of provoking a shift in the public conversation. Reframing is often a critical step to winning a campaign and making real change.

Drew Westen, The Political Brain: The Role of Emotion in Deciding the Fate of the Nation. Philadelphia, PA: Public Affairs, 2008.

Doyle Canning and Patrick Reinsborough. Re: Imagining Change: An Introduction to Story-Based Strategy. smartMeme, 2009. smartmeme.org/downloads/smartMeme.ReImaginingChange.pdf

ThinkProgress. "Thanks to the 99 Percent Movement, Media Finally Covering Jobs Crisis and Marginalizing Deficit Hysteria," October 18, 2011. http://thinkprogress.org/special/2011/10/18/346892/chart-media-jobs-wall-street-ignoring-deficit-hysteria/

Charlotte Ryan. Prime Time Activism: Media Strategies for Grassroots Organizing. Boston: South End Press, 1991.

The Centre for Media Justice, "Toolbox" http://centerformedia-justice.org/toolbox/

The Praxis Project. Fair Game: A Strategy for Racial Justice Communications in the Obama Era. Oakland, CA: AK Press 2011.

George Lakoff. Don't think of an Elephant! Know Your Values and Frame the Debate. White River Jct, VT: Chelsea Green, 2004.

Related:

TACTICS
Prefigurative intervention p. 82
Direct action p. 32
Identity correction p. 60
Electoral guerrilla theater p. 40

PRINCIPLES
Think narratively p. 186
Make the invisible visible p. 152

THEORIES
Memes p. 242
Narrative power analysis p. 244

CASE STUDIES
Public Option Annie p. 346
The battle in Seattle p. 286
Streets into gardens p. 368
Wisconsin Capitol Occupation p. 396

---

[1] Adam Kader, "Storytelling as Organizing: How to Rescue the Left from its Crisis of Imagination," In These Times, January 10, 2011, http://www.inthesetimes.com/working/entry/6824/

PRINCIPLE: Reframe   169

PRINCIPLE:
Seek common ground

IN SUM

In search of allies and points of agreement, we must grow comfortable adopting the rhetoric of worldviews we might otherwise oppose.

PRACTITIONERS

Evangelical Climate Initiative
smartMeme

FURTHER INSIGHT

Beyond the Choir, "Narrative Insurgency: Grassroots Communication Tips, Part 3," by Jonathan Matthew Smucker http://trb.la/wUvwRJ

Beyond the Choir, "Speak the Truth, Tell a Story: Building a Successful Antiwar Movement," by Jonathan Matthew Smucker http://trb.la/AAPfNy

CONTRIBUTED BY

Jonathan Matthew Smucker

When disagreeing with someone else's ideas, it can be tempting to engage in *narrative* attack; to make a direct attack on one narrative from the vantage point, and in the language, of your opposing narrative. For example, when someone wraps climate change–denial views in the rhetoric of creationist beliefs, it is tempting to directly attack the climate change denier's whole belief system. Once a narrative attack is made, persuasion becomes nearly impossible because the attacked person feels that their whole belief system is under siege. Change becomes impossible.

A *narrative insurgency approach*, on the other hand, examines the other's narrative framework, learning the component parts and looking for points of connection. Rather than directly attack a creationist's whole belief system, for instance, a "narrative insurgent" looks to foment home-grown insurgency against the most problematic beliefs by identifying *ally beliefs* and seeking to reinforce them. When speaking to creationists about environmental issues, for example, emphasizing humanity's mandate to care for God's creation can be an effective point of entry.

If we are to transform the political culture, we need to think not in terms of attacking opponents' views head-on, but rather in terms of fomenting homegrown insurgency. The root of the word insurgency is "rise up." Insurgencies rise up from within. *Narrative insurgency* rises up from within a cultural narrative, transforming that culture from the inside out.

The narrative insurgent's approach, well executed, can be very effective for identifying and drawing out allies: in this case, creationists who care about the environment and are uneasy seeing it ravaged for the sake of private profit. By repeating and positively reinforcing this message in the context of ongoing engagement, the belief that *we should care for the earth* can be strengthened within the given community's complex collective belief system.

Narrative insurgents do not reject problematic narratives wholesale, but distinguish between those components that are allied, hostile or neutral to their cause. They embrace as much of a cultural narrative as possible — the allied and neutral components — and encourage

Narrative insurgents seek common ground with allies by branding their eco-friendly product with the slogan "God is green."

the further development of the allied components, using these as the foundations for their organizing efforts with and within the given community.

This approach doesn't mean *always* avoiding direct confrontation with harmful narratives and beliefs. It's more like a *preference* for finding common ground and utilizing positive reinforcement whenever possible. Ultimately there comes a time when a destructive narrative becomes untenable to a critical mass of people, and when a new *polarization* will be useful (e.g. during a revolutionary moment). The strategy here is to lay the groundwork that necessarily precedes such a moment: to feed the allied components within a narrative until they are strong enough to burst out of the old framework.

Narrative insurgency only works if applied in the context of accountable relationships with reliable feedback loops. A change agent learns the intricacies of cultural narratives not to deceive people, but to communicate common values in a language that holds meaning for large numbers of people. While she may often disagree with others, she still values and even empathizes with their perspectives. She is forgiving toward shortcomings, always rooting for people, always finding something worthy of praise. Over time, narrative insurgency becomes second nature: we don't feign identification with the allied and neutral components within another community's narrative or culture, because our orientation is to connect with people wherever and whenever possible.

PRINCIPLE:
Shift the spectrum of allies

IN SUM

Movements seldom win by overpowering the opposition; they win by shifting the support out from under them. Determine the social blocs at play on a given issue, and work to shift them closer to your position.

PRACTITIONERS

April 6 Youth Movement
Cindy Sheehan

FURTHER INSIGHT

Explanation of the "Spectrum of Allies," from NewTactics
http://trb.la/AnSvdW

Training for Change (tactics for strategic nonviolence)
www.trainingforchange.org

Doug McAdam, Freedom Summer. Oxford Univ. Press, 1988.

CONTRIBUTED BY

Joshua Kahn Russell

Activists are often good at analyzing systemic social problems, but less good at thinking systemically about *organizing.*

Activism is about using your power and voice to make change. Organizing is about that, too, but it's also about activating and empowering others. It helps to think in terms of groups. Successful movement-building hinges on being able to see a society in terms of specific blocs or networks, some of which are institutions (unions, churches, schools), others of which are less visible or cohesive, like youth subcultures or demographic groupings.

Analyzing your spectrum of allies can help you to identify and mobilize the networks around you. A spectrum-of-allies analysis can be used to map out a campaign or to strategize for a whole social movement.

> "Movements win not by overpowering their active opposition, but by shifting the support out from under them."

Here's how a spectrum-of-allies analysis works: in each wedge you can place different individuals (be specific: name them!), groups, or institutions. Moving from left to right, identify your *active allies*: people who agree with you and are fighting alongside you; your *passive allies*: folks who agree with you but aren't doing anything about it; *neutrals*: fence-sitters, the unengaged; *passive opposition*: people who disagree with you but aren't trying to stop you; and finally your *active opposition.*

Some activist groups only speak or work with those in the first wedge (active allies), building insular, self-referential, marginal subcultures that are incomprehensible to everyone else. Others behave as if everyone is in the last wedge (active opposition), playing out the "story of the righteous few," acting as if the whole world is against them. Both of these approaches virtually guarantee failure. Movements win not by overpowering their active opposition, but by shifting the support out from under them.

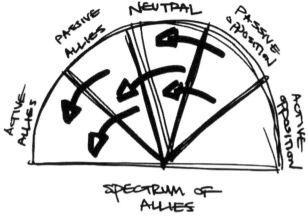

Spectrum of Allies. Art by Joshua Kahn Russell.

Related:

TACTICS
Direct action p. 32

PRINCIPLES
Use your radical fringe to slide
the Overton window p. 200
Choose tactics that support
your strategy p. 112
Escalate strategically p. 134
Reframe p. 168
Make new folks welcome p. 150
Think narratively p. 186
Consider your audience p. 118

THEORIES
Points of intervention p. 250
Cycles of social movements web

CASE STUDIES
Occupy Wall Street web
Taco Bell boycott p. 372
Bidder 70 p. 290
Trail of Dreams p. 384
Wisconsin Capitol occupation p. 396
Justice for Janitors p. 326

For example, in 1964, the Student Nonviolent Co-ordinating Committee (SNCC), a major driver of the civil rights movement in the U.S. South, conducted a "spectrum-of-allies style" analysis. They determined that they had a lot of passive allies who were students in the North: these students were sympathetic, but had no entry point into the movement. They didn't need to be "educated" or convinced, they needed an invitation to enter.

To shift these allies from "passive" to "active," SNCC sent buses north to bring folks down to participate in the struggle under the banner "Freedom Summer." Students came in droves, and many were deeply radicalized in the process, witnessing lynching, violent police abuse, and angry white mobs, all simply as a result of black activists trying to vote.

Many wrote letters home to their parents, who suddenly had a personal connection to the struggle. This triggered another shift: their families became *passive allies*, often bringing their workplaces and social networks with them. The students, meanwhile, went back to school in the fall and proceeded to organize their campuses. *More shifts.* The result: a profound transformation of the political landscape of the U.S. This cascading shift of support, it's important to emphasize, wasn't spontaneous; it was part of a deliberate movement strategy that, to this day, carries profound lessons for other movements.

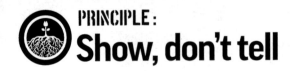

PRINCIPLE:
Show, don't tell

IN SUM

Use metaphor, visuals and action to show your message rather than falling into preaching, hectoring or otherwise telling your audience what to think.

FURTHER INSIGHT

Stephen Duncombe, Dream: Re-Imagining Progressive Politics in an age of Fantasy. New York: New Press, 2007.
Video: The Sound of Wealth Inequality http://www.youtube.com/watch?v=_AhucAN6GO0

CONTRIBUTED BY

Doyle Canning
Patrick Reinsborough
Kevin Buckland

A picture is worth a thousand words. In today's image-driven news cycle and mass media culture, this is truer than ever. Effective creative campaigns must be image-driven, too. In other words, *show, don't tell.* And there are lot of ways to do it:

Lead with story, not facts. Facts rarely speak for themselves. While the factual accuracy of your message is essential, facts should only serve as the supporting details for the story, not the hook that makes the story compelling.

If you want to convey the devastation of unemployment, don't lead with statistics. Tell us a compelling story about one person. Then tell us there are ten million more like her out there.

Make it visual. A lot of important stuff is hard to talk about — it's too big, far away, abstract or complex. Props, visuals and concrete language can

> "Showing not telling means emphasizing narrative over data and creating a story that puts the facts in perspective."

help bring things down to human scale. Take economic inequality, for example. You can easily get lost in the finer points of the tax code, but when billionaire Warren Buffet says that his secretary pays more taxes than he does, and that that's wrong, it's hard to argue with. To draw attention to the increasing disparity between CEO and worker pay, one group unveiled a tiny replica of the Washington Monument that was 419 times smaller than the actual one they were holding their press conference in front of.

Use powerful metaphors. With metaphor you can show something for what it is, rather than have to explain it. To find your compelling metaphor, look for something that embodies what you are trying to communicate. Recently, the immigration debate in the U.S. has been usefully engaged via the metaphor of migratory

PRINCIPLE: Show, don't tell

birds ("Do migrating birds need passports too?"), neatly pointing up the absurdity of the situation, without focusing on any specific policy or piece of legislation.

Speak with actions. Instead of telling, act out what it is that you want to say. At protests, whenever there are lines of police protecting a bank, a metaphor is being enacted that reflects the reality of the situation: the state defends the wealthy

Putting on makeup shouldn't be like playing with matches.

Which cosmetics company do you trust with your daughter ?

When it comes to cosmetics, we shouldn't be forced to choose between health and beauty. Personal care products should be free of chemicals linked to cancer and birth defects.

Thankfully, the hot new trend in cosmetics is a real lifesaver. This month the European Union enacted a new law to make cosmetics safer; they banned chemicals known or highly suspected of causing cancer, impaired fertility or birth defects – chemicals used in nail polish, hair spray, hair dye and other products.

Industry leaders L'Oréal, Revlon and Unilever have yet to respond to requests to remove these same toxic chemicals from all the products they sell in the United States. Ask them to join the growing number of toxin-free cosmetic companies and regain the trust of American women.

Visit www.SafeCosmetics.org to see if your favorite brand has gone toxin-free because safety shouldn't need to be imported.

Read our lips:
No More Toxic Chemicals in Cosmetics.

Paid for by the Safe Cosmetics Coalition   www.SafeCosmetics.org

This ad created by smartMeme in 2004 (designed by J Cookson) used show-don't-tell to help the Safe Cosmetics campaign successfully pressure cosmetic executives.

from the rest of us. Sometimes it's enough to just point that out — or you can ham it up *see CASE: Teddy bear catapult.*

A well-designed action explains itself, and ideally offers multiple ways into the issue. You want your audience to reach their own conclusion, rather than feeling like they are being told what to think.

Preachy isn't persuasive. Whether we're telling a story, conjuring a scene, offering up a metaphor, leading by example, or letting our actions speak volumes, there are millions of ways to convey our message and values without launching into a political diatribe. Let's do ourselves and our audience a favor: *Show, don't tell.*

PRINCIPLE:
Simple rules can have grand results

IN SUM

Movements, viral campaigns and large-scale actions can't be scripted from the top down. An invitation to participate and the right set of simple rules are often all the starter-structure you need.

EPIGRAPH

"Sept 17. Wall Street. Bring tent."

–Adbusters

PRACTITIONERS

Improv Everywhere
Adbusters
350.org
Otpor!
UK Uncut
Ze Frank
Allan Kaprow
Women in Black

FURTHER INSIGHT

"We are the 99 Percent" tumblr
http://wearethe99percent.
tumblr.com/submit

Otpor!
http://en.wikipedia.org/wiki/Otpor!

CONTRIBUTED BY

Andrew Boyd

In 1986, computer scientists did an experiment on *"emergence* — where complex global behavior can arise" unplanned and unprogrammed "from the interaction of simple local rules."[1] They created virtual birds called "boids." (The computer scientists must have been from Brooklyn.) They put these boids in a virtual environment and threw in a few virtual obstacles. They assigned every boid the same three simple rules: fly forwards, stay a certain distance from any other boids near you and don't bang into obstacles. Then they threw the switch. The birds flocked together. As the flock approached a cloud, it would break up into smaller flocks to either side, and then reform — all without the idea of flocking ever being programmed into the system.

This experiment was a stripped-down demonstration of something we experience in nature and society all the time — and something activists can put to good use.

If you're trying to organize a participatory art piece, a mass action or a viral campaign, you don't need to script it all out — even if you could. All you need are a few simple rules that participants can sign on to. If you hit on the right rules, they can lead to a surprisingly robust, effective and beautiful happening.

Think of Critical Mass, the monthly mass bike rides that take place in cities across the world. The rules are simple: Gather after work on the last Friday of the month. Stick together. If you're at the front, you decide where the mass goes next. If you're at the back, help stragglers keep up. If

> "If you hit on the right rules, they can lead to a surprisingly robust, effective and beautiful happening."

you're in the middle, just ride, or, if you want, protect other bikers from cross-traffic. No one and everyone is in charge. It's an "organized coincidence." And it works.

Flash mobs operate by the same logic. The call for a 2008 flash mob pillow fight on Wall Street consisted of two rules: *Bring a pillow, and don't hit anybody who doesn't also have a pillow.* Enough said!

These kind of efforts work well on the Internet as well. Think of the "we are the 99%" tumblr. The invitation was simple: take a picture of yourself holding a sign that describes your situation — for example, "I am a student with $25,000 in debt." Below that, write "I am the 99 percent." The resulting tapestry of voices became an eloquent statement of solidarity.

A carnival protest might succeed with an "anything goes" rule set, because, well, it's a carnival. A more politically focused mass street action *see CASE: Citizen's Posse* or viral campaign of distributed actions *see CASE: Billionaires for Bush*, however, often needs a stronger framework. The nature of your action, its complexity, and the degree of risk will determine the exact rules required.

HOW THE OPPOSITE IS EQUALLY TRUE: Simple rules, no matter how well chosen, won't magically do all the work on their own. Often, conveners (folks who make the invitation and set the rules) have to stage manage all along the way to keep the seemingly organic process going. The right set of simple rules can get you most of the way there, though, and the "there" might be somewhere you never could have planned or imagined.

---

¹ Boids, Background and update, Craig Reynolds, 1986 - http://www.red3d.com/cwr/boids

PRINCIPLE :
Stay on message

IN SUM

When we stay on message, we communicate exactly what we want our audience to know. We create harmony between our words, visuals and actions and we deliver a clear, powerful and irresistible call to action.

EPIGRAPH

"What you do speaks so loudly I can't hear what you are saying."

—Ralph Waldo Emerson

PRACTITIONERS

smartMeme
SPIN Project
Beyond the Choir
Ripple Strategies
Artist Network of Refuse & Resist

FURTHER INSIGHT

Beyond the Choir, "Grassroots Communications Tips"
http://trb.la/y7Baux

smartMeme, "Resources"
http://www.smartmeme.org/section.php?id=86

The Spin Project, "Spin Works! A Media Guidebook for the Rest of Us"
http://www.spinproject.org/article.php?id=172

Ritchie, Paul. Stay on Message. Vivid Publishing, 2010.

CONTRIBUTED BY

Celia Alario

Message discipline is the art of communicating what you set out to communicate, clearly, memorably and consistently. Everything from your talking points for an interview to the slogans on your banner to the visuals you create for an event should all align to support your core message.

> "Message discipline is not the enemy of creativity. Far from it."

WHY MESSAGE DISCIPLINE MATTERS:

It works: When you're on message, you're more likely to reach your audience and move them to action.

It honors your group process: You've worked hard with your group to determine what needs to be communicated. Staying on message honors that hard work and strategic thinking, communicating only what all of you have agreed is the right message.

Make it stick: Say one thing and say it well. The average person needs exposure to *multiple sensory impressions* of a message before it sinks in. When you practice message discipline, the consistency of your message helps make it stick.

Avoid static in the channel: Anything you say or do can be used against you in the court of public opinion, so make sure your words and actions are in sync with your group's message. Strip away any of the clutter that could be static in the channel. Remember: less is more.

HOW TO ACHIEVE IT:

In interviews: Spokesfolks should practice the ABC's: *acknowledge* the question, *build a bridge* from the question to your talking points; and *communicate* your message.

Example:

A "That's a great question" or "I'm glad you asked that."

B "I think the important issue is..." or "The real question is..."

C Insert your clear, concise, powerfully worded message.

In our visuals and actions: When designing your action, imagine a photo of it — image only, no caption. Could that photo communicate your message? If your audience could see you from afar but not hear you, would they get your message? How can you increase that possibility? *See THEORY: Action logic.*

Inventory your event: Everything your audience sees or hears at your action is inevitably a part of your message, so pay attention to details. What are your spokesfolks wearing? Are they drinking out of a Styrofoam cup? A bit of mindfulness as your event unfolds can ensure the impact you desire.

Message discipline is not the enemy of creativity. Far from it. Placards can have different messages. Each spokesperson can share a sound bite that reflects their own unique experience. But when you are "on message," all elements reinforce your core message. Each action element or interview response stands on its own, successfully delivering a strong message to your audience with clarity, consistency and credibility.

POTENTIAL PITFALLS: A sound bite will never cover everything you want to say. It may be true that decades of financial irresponsibility or hundreds of years of colonial oppression got us into this mess, but part of the art of message discipline is taming the urge to unpack all those details each time you speak. Keep your core message simple and crisp, and recognize that it's just the opening volley in your work on this issue.

Related:

PRINCIPLES
Consider your audience p. 118
Do the media's work for them p. 124
Show, don't tell p. 174
Think narratively p. 186
Lead with sympathet-
ic characters p. 146
Balance art and message p. 100

THEORIES
Memes p. 242
The propaganda model p. 256

PRINCIPLE:
Take leadership from the most impacted

IN SUM

Effective activism requires providing appropriate support to, and taking direction from, those who have the most at stake.

PRACTITIONERS

The Ruckus Society
Indigenous Environmental Network
Movement Generation
Peace Brigades International
Design Studio for Social Intervention
Iraq Veterans Against the War
Los Angeles Poverty Department
Mitch Snyder

FURTHER INSIGHT

Caron Atlas, ed. Arts & Democracy Project. People Who Live and Work in Multiple Worlds. Full Circle Color. 2011 Available on line: http://www.statevoices.org/system/files/A%2526DBridgeBook.pdf

Sheila Wilmot, Taking Responsibility, Taking Direction: White Anti-Racism in Canada. Arbeiter Ring, 2006.

CONTRIBUTED BY

Joshua Kahn Russell

The Accountability Cycle. Artist: Joshua Kahn Russell.

We're all familiar with liberal do-gooder arrogance — the kind that stems from having the luxury of choosing from a salad bar of causes because none are immediately constraining their lives, or assuming that because you studied an issue in a university, you're an expert. Avoid being that person: cultivate humility and take direction and leadership from those most affected by an issue.

Because people on the receiving end of great injustices have to live with the consequences of campaigns that seek to address those injustices, they have the most to gain from victory — and the most to lose if something goes wrong. They're also the best equipped to know, and to articulate, workable solutions to their problems. A campaign that ignores or minimizes their knowledge and voices could easily do more harm than good.

Accepting guidance from another isn't always easy for people who themselves identify as leaders. Self-identified "leaders" sometimes rush in too quickly, confident they've got the answer while their preconceptions and prejudices blind them to the organic answers all around them. We can mitigate these blind-spots by being intentional about respecting the process and cultivating *accountability*.

Accountability can be a scary concept for activists, but it's best to think of it as a *proactive process* that we walk together, rather than a standard that is either achieved or not.

The booklet *Organizing Cools the Planet* outlines four basic principles for cultivating accountability:[1]

Transparency means being clear about your politics, organizational structure, goals, desires and weaknesses. The point here is to be as open as possible about your perspectives and motivations.

Participation is about actively and equitably engaging with folks about the decisions that affect them.

Reflection and deliberation means that we actively open up conversation to re-evaluate where we're headed. It happens after participation, but once it's begun, it is a continuous thread that is woven throughout the experience.

Response is the ability to make amendments and adjustments to issues raised by *Reflection and deliberation*.

However, accountability is not our goal; collaboration is our goal. Accountability is the pathway we walk. The cycle above moves us toward increasingly successful collaborations. Don't be discouraged if collaboration is difficult at first. Trust takes time. Be forgiving of yourself and others; we all make mistakes *see THEORY: Anti-oppression.*

The Ruckus Society's experience with this principle is instructive. Ruckus is a network of direct action trainers and coordinators. After years of grappling with the problematic dynamic of "parachuters" coming into people's communities from the outside, Ruckus has developed a protocol where they only go where they're asked and prioritize long-term relationship building. Their "Ruckus Action Framework" is a great reference tool to use when building a similar protocol within your group.[2]

Taking leadership from the most impacted is a great opportunity to learn from and support impacted groups in their struggles. It can be one of the most profound and rewarding experiences of activism.

Related:

TACTICS
Boycott web
Trek p. 90
Eviction blockade p. 44
Direct action p. 32
Strategic nonviolence p. 88

PRINCIPLES
Challenge patriarchy as you organize p. 108
Praxis makes perfect p.162
Consider your audience p. 118
We are all leaders p. 202

THEORIES
Environmental justice p. 228
Pedagogy of the oppressed p. 246
Narrative power analysis p. 244

CASE STUDIES
Taco Bell boycott p. 372
Trail of Dreams p. 384

---

[1] Hilary Moore and Joshua Kahn Russell, *Organizing Cools the Planet* (Oakland, CA: PM Press, 2011).
[2] The framework is reproduced on page 54 of Organizing Cools the Planet, available for download at http://organizingcoolstheplanet.wordpress.com/get-copies-of-ocp/.

PRINCIPLE:
Take risks, but take care

IN SUM

Needlessly endangering the safety of you or the people around you hurts the movement. Don't sacrifice care of self or others for the sake of being "hardcore."

EPIGRAPH

"Martyrdom is a fascist tendency."

–Gopal Dayanenni

PRACTITIONERS

The Ya Basta Association

FURTHER INSIGHT

RANT Trainers Collective, "Resources"
http://rantcollective.net/article.php?list=type&type=17

Ruckus Society, "Training & Action Support"
http://ruckus.org/article.php?list=type&type=64

War Resisters League, "Nonviolence Training: Non-violent Action Preparation"
http://www.warresisters.org/node/1277

Alliance of Community Trainers, "Nonviolent Direct Action Training and Support"
http://trainersalliance.org

Destructables, "Copwatch: Know Your Rights!"
http://destructables.org/node/85

Destructables, "Affinity Groups"
http://destructables.org/node/54

CONTRIBUTED BY

Joshua Kahn Russell

Trainers Daniel Hunter and Joshua Kahn Russell facilitate a nonviolent direct action training for the anti-fracking movement in Nov 2011.

Direct action is a tool that oppressed people have used to build their power throughout history. When communities don't have billions of dollars to spend, they leverage *risk*. They put their bodies, freedom, and safety on the line.

Direct action carries some inherent risk. That's the whole idea. Designing an action is therefore about *minimizing* that risk in a way that is *accountable* to participants, the community, yourself, and the movement. When activists let the romance of confrontation overshadow meticulous care in action planning, they may put others in harm's way, or may leave the movement to deal with the consequences of their risky behavior.

A good action planner distinguishes between the risks she can (and should) control and the ones she cannot, and clarifies to all participants what the potential consequences may be. Thorough action planning is a responsibility you have to the people around you. Even if you plan well, if action-day comes and the situation is not what you expected, don't be afraid to call it off. Better to hold off and execute the action well another day than get into something your group is unprepared for.

The Ruckus Society pamphlet, *A Tiny Blockades Book*, outlines a number of key considerations you should keep in mind in planning your action:

- Not everyone is taking the same risks. Race, class, gender identity (real and perceived), age, appearance, immigration status, physical ability, being perceived as a "leader," all change your relationship to the action; i.e. the risks of violence and arrest by the police and the potential legal and economic consequences of the action. Also remember that there are power dynamics within your action group. Pretending that they do not exist or ignoring them "for the good of the action," can compromise your ability to execute well, increasing risks...

* Some devices increase the risk of injury simply by design: U-locking your neck to a fifty-five gallon drum filled with concrete means that any attempt to move the drum could snap your neck. *That is the point — you create this situation on purpose, or not at all...*

* This kind of gear increases the "staying power" of your action by creating a deep decision dilemma *see PRINCIPLE* for the opposition... But if you are lying down in front of a truck and the driver is not aware that you are there, then there is no decision dilemma, and no action logic *see PRINCIPLE: Action logic*. That is not direct action, it is an accident waiting to happen.

* ...The best actions are the ones where we get to stay as long as we want and the action *ends on our terms* — not in arrest or injury.

* Practice. Practice. Practice. The more you practice, the safer you will be and the more effective your action will be.

Some tactics should *never* be attempted without a thorough safety plan and skill-level assessment, such as a technical (climbing) banner hang where a fall can often prove fatal. Direct action is not a game.

Be humble. Understand that *Beautiful Trouble* is intended to be a broad toolkit, *not a direct action training manual.* If you want to design a direct action, get the proper training (see the attached list of groups).

POTENTIAL PITFALLS: Some schools of civil disobedience (for example, Gandhian civil disobedience) emphasize that "our suffering can touch the hearts of our adversaries," and therefore build prolonged jail sentences or physical harm into their action logic. This is a planned orientation to the action, and not a license for recklessness or martyrdom.

Related:

TACTICS
Direct action p. 32
Blockade p. 14
Banner hang p. 12
Occupation p. 78
Sit-in web
Eviction blockade p. 44
Nonviolent search and seizure p. 76
Infiltration p. 64
Creative disruption p. 18
Public filibuster p. 86

PRINCIPLES
Anyone can act p. 98
We are all leaders p. 202
Pace yourself p. 158

THEORIES
Anti-oppression p. 212
Points of intervention p. 250

CASE STUDIES
Battle in Seattle p. 286
Occupy Wall Street web

PRINCIPLE:
Team up with experts
(but don't become "the expert")

Experts can be terribly helpful co-conspirators and there are plenty of them out there to befriend. So go ask one for help. Why? An expert can be a great source of powerful, actionable information or can save you much embarrassment by pointing out flaws in your approach. An expert can help you do something you don't know how to do or gain access to something that requires credentials. An expert can put you in contact with even more experts. And an expert can introduce new audiences to your work.

Choose an expert whose work is aligned with your mission to increase your chance of a positive response. If the response is *no*, then simply move on to the next. (Remember: there are many experts in this world!). Experts often respond favorably because they secretly wish they could act like independent artists and activists like you. Experts tend to work within established institutions and are beholden to power structures that typically limit speech and action. For that reason, it's important to be respectful of the limits of what they can say, do, or sign their name to.

As you continue to work on your project or campaign, you might find that people start treating you like the expert. People, you notice, are really listening to what you have to say. You might be invited to give a talk or a journalist calls for a quote. A "mediagenic" project propels your cause, bringing your message to the widest possible audience. Fantastic! Use the attention to your advantage.

But beware of getting too comfortable in the role of expert. Remain tactical. Construct your environment and apply pressure as needed. If your job is done or the project has run its course, then don't linger at the mic. Reap the benefits of acting fast and freely, then disappear. Experts have made a long-term commitment and are good at sustainability; they choose their territory and stick it out, for better or worse. Activists and experts are simpatico but not interchangeable.

As a tactician, your job is to take risks. Generate a lot of ideas, prototypes or situations to see what works. Don't worry, good ideas have the tendency to stick, whether you see them through or others pick up where you left off.

EVERY TOOL IS A
WEAPON
if you hold it right.

—Ani DiFranco

PRINCIPLE: Think narratively

IN SUM

Sometimes the best response to a powerful enemy is a powerful story.

PRACTITIONERS

Iraq Veterans Against the War (IVAW)
Mitch Snyder
Cindy Sheehan
Eve Ensler
Los Angeles Poverty Department

FURTHER INSIGHT

smartMeme, "The Battle of the Story Worksheet"
http://www.smartmeme.org/downloads/sMbattleofthestoryworksheet.pdf

CONTRIBUTED BY

Doyle Canning
Patrick Reinsborough

As much as we'd like to believe that human beings are rational actors making decisions based on a sober weighing of the facts, cognitive science reminds us that we are narrative animals that apprehend the world through stories. We make decisions more with our guts than our heads, and the facts alone are seldom enough to move public opinion. Therefore, social actors are constantly waging a "battle of the story" to shape public perception.

Fairy tale repurposed. Art by Kip Lyall.

The unequal nature of our media and communications systems *see THEORY: The propaganda model* means that moneyed interests will always have more access to the airwaves — but that doesn't mean their story will be more creative or compelling. We can make up some of that difference, not just by becoming master storytellers, but by *thinking* narratively. By paying attention to how story and power are always interwoven, we can better understanding how political power operates, and also how we can contest it.

Thinking narratively means we're also strategizing narratively and listening narratively. When designing our actions and campaigns we need to step outside our own perspective to analyze how the issue is perceived by others who don't share our assumptions. (Remember, people respond to a story not so much because it is true, but because they find it meaningful.) We need to consider our audience *see PRINCIPLE*, and build our campaign narrative out of the core building blocks that make for a good story. Here are five to keep in mind:

Conflict
What is the problem or conflict being addressed? How is it framed, and what does that frame leave out?

Characters
This can be a profound organizing question: Who are "we"? Who are the other characters in the story? Do the characters speak for themselves or is someone speaking on their behalf *see PRINCIPLE: Lead with sympathetic characters*?

Imagery
What powerful images can help convey the story? Is there a metaphor or analogy that could describe the issue? A good story uses imagery and evocative language to *show us* what's at stake rather than tell the audience what to think *see PRINCIPLE: Show, don't tell*.

Foreshadowing
What is our vision of resolution to the conflict? What is our solution to the problem? How do we evoke that desired resolution without, as it were, giving the end away? *see TACTIC: Prefigurative intervention*.

Assumptions
Every story is built on unstated assumptions. Sometimes the best way to challenge a competing story is to expose and challenge its unstated assumptions *see PRINCIPLE: Make the invisible visible*.

These five elements of story can be used together to conduct a *narrative power analysis* on a dominant narrative or as scaffolding to construct a narrative of change *see THEORY: Narrative power analysis*. Fleshing out these elements as we plan out our campaigns can also give us insights into strategic opportunities for action or intervention.

PRINCIPLE:
This ain't the Sistine Chapel

IN SUM

Sky-high artistic
expectations can not
only slow you down,
but can also critically
impair execution of your
tactic and strategy.

EPIGRAPH

"We have no art. We do
everything as
well we can."

—Balinese saying

PRACTITIONERS

Bread and Puppet Theater
Art and Revolution
Women's Action Coalition (WAC)
Teatro Campesino
Washington Action Group

FURTHER INSIGHT

Kershaw, Baz and Coult, Tony.
Engineers of the Imagination. *UK:*
Welfare State International, 1990.

Ruckus Society, "Creative Direct
Action Visuals Manual"
http://www.ruckus.org/
article.php?id=305

Ruby, K. Wise Fool Basics:
A Handbook of Our Core Tech-
niques.
San Francisco, 1992.

CONTRIBUTED BY

Nadine Bloch

Semi-anonymous internationally renowned street artist JR is famous for his wheat-pastings of his photographs. This work is often done haphazardly and illegally, but the faces he pastes help to put a human face on the walls of ghetto areas — and, even for the short time before they are taken down, provide a source of community empowerment and unity.

As artists, we often have the desire to produce the most beautiful, provocative and breathtaking piece of art we can. This can be a wonderful thing — sometimes. Other times, it's more important to get something out into the world that's just beautiful enough to do the job, and then move on to strategic necessities.

Here are a few cases when seeking perfection could backfire on you:

- When building community is a key goal of your project, creating a high bar of perfection can discourage broad participation.

- When you have that *Oh shit, it has to be done in 24 hrs!* or *We need a small army to get all this done!* moment of panic, it might be better to wrap it up and move on to other tasks.

- When you are out of money or other resources, or on the verge of depriving other essential parts of your action of being funded or resourced.

- When the banner or prop will be viewed from hundreds of feet away or is not the centerpiece of the action.

- When the prop will be smashed as part of the action or taken into custody by the cops.

In short, if it's in your strategic interest to spend all your time and/or money on the "artfulness" of your action, then go right ahead and do it. But if painting the Sistine Chapel undermines your effectiveness, then do only what is strategically warranted and save your sanity and energy.

The Cheap Art campaign of the Bread and Puppet Theater Company, housed in (and exemplified by) this repurposed broken-down bus, promotes a populist DIY approach to art-making.

HOW THE OPPOSITE IS EQUALLY TRUE: There are times when quality really does matter, and an appropriate attention to detail will get you the respect and the response you desire.

PRINCIPLE :
Turn the tables

IN SUM

Sometimes the most compelling way to expose an injustice is to flip it around and visit it upon the powerful.

EPIGRAPH

"Make the enemy live up to their own book of rules."

–Saul Alinsky

PRACTITIONERS

Greenpeace
Reclaim the Streets
More Gardens! Coalition
Erin Brockovich

FURTHER INSIGHT

Briarpatch Magazine. "Ten straight questions: Learning about the Heterosexuals Among Us." March/April 2007. http://briarpatchmagazine.com/articles/view/10-straight-questions

CONTRIBUTED BY

Mark Read

Remember the great scene from "Erin Brockovich" where the hero brings a glass of contaminated water to a meeting with the companies her clients have accused of contaminating their drinking water. "You claim this water is perfectly safe to drink?" she says. "Okay, drink this," and she places the glass of water before them. When they refuse, the injustice of the situation is laid bare for all to see. She has "turned the tables."

A young girl turns the tables on an Israeli border guard in this iconic West Bank barrier mural by Banksy.

People have an innate sense of fairness, but don't always see the injustices happening around them. By taking an existing unjust situation and dramatically flipping it back upon its source, you can highlight the inherent asymmetry and activate people's sense of fairness. Turning the tables like this can be an effective means of garnering public support as well as undercutting the moral authority of your target.

Consider the "turning streets into gardens" action *see CASE*. New York Mayor Rudy Giuliani was attempting to sell off community gardens to developers, an action that would have displaced community groups and left the city with fewer places for children to play. Community members were rightly outraged, though initially they had a hard time gaining public support. To turn the tables, the activists took over a city block in Manhattan's Lower East Side and turned it into a vibrant civic space for conversation, education, and celebration. Their message was "Okay, if you can kick us out of our gardens, then we can kick you off your streets."

Greenpeace has consistently made use of this tactic to shed light on toxic dumping. In 2003 they partnered with families and victims of the massive chemical plant disaster in Bhopal, India and attempted, unsuccessfully, to deliver seven barrels of that toxic waste to the Dow Chemical company HQ in Amsterdam. The action spoke directly to basic questions of fairness and power: "If you can dump this toxic sludge on the people of India, then we can dump it back on you." Why is one act illegal while its analogue goes unpunished?

Turning the tables poses this question in a pointed, common-sense way, exposing hypocrisy and injustice for all to see. It's an easy frame for mainstream media to grasp, and difficult for them to distort. For all these reasons, it has the potential to generate support for your cause, increase pressure on your target, and enable you to win concessions.

POTENTIAL PITFALLS: An attempt to turn the tables can backfire on you if your analogy is inaccurate, indirect or insincere. Sometimes even a clear analogy may be undermined by powerful cultural assumptions. For instance, police have broad cultural legitimacy as ethical agents of authority. Whether it's deserved or not, this is the reality within which we operate. Trying to turn the tables by building an equation around police violence vs. protester violence is going to be an uphill climb. Turning the tables must always take into account cultural context and existing frames of understanding.

Related:

TACTICS
Prefigurative intervention p. 82
Identity correction p. 60
Détournement/Culture jamming p. 28
Direct action p. 32
Hoax p. 54
Carnival protest web

PRINCIPLES
Make the invisible visible p. 152
Put your target in a decision dilemma p. 166
The real action is your target's reaction web
Show, don't tell p. 174
Reframe p. 168
Know your cultural terrain p. 142
Make your actions both concrete and communicative p. 154

THEORIES
Action logic p. 208
Points of intervention p. 250
Ethical spectacle p. 230

CASE STUDIES
Streets into gardens p. 368
Daycare center sit-in p. 316
Whose tea party? p. 392

PRINCIPLE:
Use others' prejudices against them

IN SUM

Your enemy's prejudices about you are a weakness that you can exploit to your advantage.

PRACTITIONERS

Greenpeace
ACT UP
Justice for Janitors
SNCC

FURTHER INSIGHT

The Salt of The Earth. Directed by Herbert J. Biberman. 1954.

Mary Elizabeth King. A Quiet Revolution: The First Palestinian Intifada and Nonviolent Resistance. New York: Nation Books, 2007

CONTRIBUTED BY

Nadine Bloch

A prejudice is a mental shortcut that leads a person to make assumptions about others — assumptions that are often false in predictable, and therefore useful, ways. Sexism, racism, homophobia, ageism — all the -isms and the stereotypes associated with them — can be used in one way or another.

For example:

Sexism 1

Want to know when that shipment of nuclear waste is going to be docking so you can shut down the port at the right time? Maybe someone posing as a distraught, pregnant girlfriend whose guy is on the ship could make some calls and get the info.

Sexism 2

Need to distract a security guard so you can complete your action? Activists in D.C. planned to dump a ton of bloodied scallop shells on the doorstep of Shell Oil to commemorate the anniversary of Ken Saro-Wiwa's death and pressure the company to withdraw from Ogoniland, Nigeria. One cute young woman posing as a lost tourist was all it took to distract the guard and provide enough time for the truck to position itself, dump its load and drive off.

Ageism

Need to get information through enemy lines? During the First Intifada or uprising in Palestine, 1987–1993, Israel tried to quash the non-violent resistance in many ways, including cutting communication and limiting travel between Palestinian cities. In order to get the word out to coordinate strikes, boycotts, and other actions, youth were enlisted to carry memorized information between cities. The Israeli soldiers let the kids through, never imagining they were doing the real work of connecting the resistance.

Racism

Need to put more pressure on a target from unexpected directions? Saul Alinsky relates a classic example of using racism to win in Chicago in the 1950s: In a campaign to improve slum conditions in an organized black ghetto, organizers took the fight beyond their neighborhoods into the lily-white suburb where the slumlord lived. The presence of black men and women picketing outside his house led to a flood of phone calls from the neighbors who didn't care at all about the slums and would not have gotten involved otherwise, but wanted to keep their own neighborhood segregated, and so pressured the slumlord into capitulating.[1]

Classism

Need to find your way into a corporate office or exclusive event? Many a time the most radical, hairy and scruffily adorned activists have shaved, ironed and primped their way into a situation that would have been off limits to those in scrappy activist garb. You know you are hardcore when you will cut your hair, or wear pantyhose, to insure the success of an action!

> "Only deploy stereotypes in situations where the bigot eventually realizes that it was his own prejudices that put him in a compromised position."

POTENTIAL PITFALLS: Beware of simply reinforcing negative stereotypes. Try to only deploy stereotypes in situations where the bigot eventually realizes that it was his own prejudices that put him in a compromised position. Also, try to be transparent within your own work group about what forces are at play.

---

[1] Saul Alinsky, *Rules for Radicals* (Vintage Books, 1971), 144.

PRINCIPLE:
Use the Jedi mind trick
(a.k.a Confidence is contagious)

IN SUM

The Jedi mind trick worked for Luke Skywalker, and it can work for you, too. You just have to believe in yourself, and others will, too.

EPIGRAPH

"Whether you think you can, or you think you can't — you're right."

– Henry Ford

PRACTITIONERS

Abbie Hoffman

FURTHER INSIGHT

Wookieepedia, "Mind Trick"
http://starwars.wikia.com/wiki/Mind_trick

Video: "Kid Gives Inspiring Speech to All Children Learning to Ride a Bike"
http://www.youtube.com/watch?v=c47otcg13Z8

Destructables, "Evasion"
http://destructables.org/node/62

CONTRIBUTED BY

Samantha Corbin

Aside from being able to move objects with your mind and having a retractable sword made out of freaking light (how cool is that??), the best thing about being a Jedi has got to be the mind trick. The ability to persuade with a calm voice and a finger wave, "These aren't the droids you're looking for," could prove indispensable in any number of beautiful trouble-making situations.

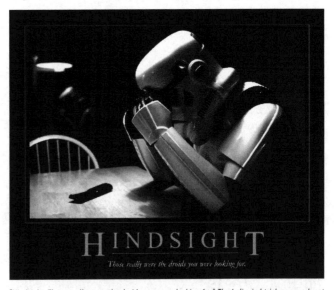

"Hindsight: Those really were the droids you were looking for." The Jedi mind trick can work not just on the Empire's storm troopers, but also on security guards, journalists and yourself.

Good news: this hypnotic power of persuasion is actually within your reach. It springs from an innate authority, an irrational confidence that mystically bends the world to your will. Though this may not work on your bill collector ("I'm not the deadbeat you're looking for"), it may work in convincing the mainstream media to cover your event or the police to leave you alone. You might even pass unchallenged through the front gate of a nuclear power plant, or take charge of a closed-door meeting to which you weren't invited. With the right attitude, much more becomes possible than you might have thought.

With nothing more than confidence, an activist adept at the Jedi mind trick can make a security guard look the other way, or convince thousands of people, including a BBC news anchor, that he is a DOW chemical spokesperson, or that it's perfectly normal to wear a climbing helmet in the middle of a convention center and start climbing the scaffolding.

Here are a couple of things to keep in mind as you prepare to break out the Jedi mind trick on an unsuspecting low-level functionary:

Know the rules, suspend the rules. The ability to transgress, trespass, or otherwise do what you shouldn't with complete self-assurance, especially if challenged, carries its own power.

Act like you belong (a.k.a. fake it 'till you get kicked out). Authority is more performed than innate. We constantly interact with, and respond to, coded indicators of status and authority, making assumptions based on attitude, manner, dress, accent, friendliness, sexiness, and other cues. By understanding and playing on these indicators we can also co-opt the authority attached to them.

POTENTIAL PITFALLS: *Beware the backlash.* The Jedi mind trick wears off quickly, and tends to leave the unsuspecting dupe it was used on angry and embarrassed. No one likes to feel like they got tricked. Use this tactic only with people you're unlikely to see again. To avoid unnecessary backlash, tell the truth as much as possible and let other people fill in their own assumptions.

"With nothing more than confidence, an activist adept at the Jedi mind trick can make a security guard look the other way, or convince thousands of people, including a BBC news anchor, that he is a DOW chemical spokesperson."

Related:

TACTICS
Infiltration p. 64
Creative disruption p. 18
Banner hang p. 12
Hoax p. 54
Direct action p. 32

PRINCIPLES
Use other people's prejudices against them p. 192
Anyone can act p. 98
Everyone has balls/ ovaries of steel p. 136
Use the law, don't be afraid of it p. 196
Don't dress like a protester p. 126

THEORIES
The tactics of everyday life p. 268

CASE STUDIES
Bidder 70 p. 290
Streets into gardens p. 368
Barbie Liberation Organization p. 282
Dow Chemical apologizes for Bhopal p. 318

PRINCIPLE:
Use the law, don't be afraid of it

IN SUM

Talk to more than one lawyer and pick the one whose advice you want to follow.

PRACTITIONERS

The Yes Men

CONTRIBUTED BY

Andy Bichlbaum

The law is a funny thing. Sometimes the Yes Men ask lawyers before we do anything particularly dangerous. We get one of two answers: "Don't do it! It's illegal. You'll get sued!" or "Awesome! It's probably legal, and besides, you're righteous in the court of public opinion." The "awesomes," are almost always right for two reasons: 1) In the U.S. at least, the law does in fact protect freedom of speech to a very high degree (not always a good thing: corporate lobbying is also considered free speech), and 2) corporations don't sue you because they know how it can blow back on them and they want to avoid having yet *more* egg on their big, blank, mechanical faces. In the Yes Men's twelve years of activism, we've only been sued once.

> "We subsequently received three more cease-and-desist letters, which we also ignored."

Corporations won't sue you, but they may send you a cease-and-desist letter. Rather than a cause to worry, this can be a great boon. C&D letters are letters from lawyers that threaten you with a lawsuit, usually in high-falutin' legal language. They carry absolutely no legal weight and can be ignored — though of course you then take the risk that the lawyers will follow through. Almost always, however, the C&D letter, while not exactly a bluff, is a formality. For example, companies have trademarks, and in order to keep them they have to demonstrate that they're making efforts to defend them — and a C&D letter qualifies as evidence of such an effort.

If you receive a C&D letter, it's a tremendous opportunity to stretch out the story and get an additional wave of news coverage for your action. First thing we do when we receive a C&D letter is reach out to a lawyer we trust and see what she thinks — though we're always prepared to ignore her advice. Then, we consider whether there's anything funny we can do with the letter. For example, after we put up the coalcares.org site, we received a C&D

letter from Peabody Energy, America's largest coal producer. Instead of taking down the site, we responded in a way that enlarged the issue. It's not just Peabody that's giving kids asthma, we noted, but all American coal companies. So we removed Peabody's name from the site and added the names of all the other coal companies. We subsequently received three more C&D letters, which we also ignored.

Lawyers are not to be feared, though the same can't always be said for the law. If you are, for example, pretending to be Exxon-Mobil at a petroleum conference, there is no need to break character when the conference's private security lock you in a small room and cross-examine you (trust us on this one). But when the real police arrive, you may as well tell them honestly what you are up to. They may even turn out to be on your side, especially if you seem reasonable in contrast to the exasperated conference organizer or private security goon. In general, you should avoid lying to the police unless you have a *really really* good reason.

Remember: Don't be afraid of suits, law- or otherwise.

HOW THE OPPOSITE IS EQUALLY TRUE: Sometimes corporations do sue activists, especially those with limited resources to defend themselves. That's called a SLAPP (Strategic Litigation Against Public Participation) suit. However, usually, all you really need to do to avoid any such corporate shenanigans is be ready to widely publicize the brouhaha, and hurl the aforementioned egg smack dab onto the corporate forehead.

Related:

TACTICS
Hoax p. 54
Infiltration p. 64
Identity correction p. 60

PRINCIPLES
Take risks but take care p. 182
The real action is your
target's reaction web
Everyone has balls/
ovaries of steel p. 136
Put your target in a
decision dilemma p. 166
Make it funny web

THEORIES
Action logic p. 208
Ethical spectacle p. 230
Points of interventions p. 250

CASE STUDIES
Dow Chemical apologizes
for Bhopal p. 318
McLibel web
Yes Men pose as Exxon web

PRINCIPLE:
Use the power of ritual

IN SUM

Rituals like weddings, funerals, baptisms, exorcisms and vigils are powerful experiences for participants. By adapting sacred and symbolic elements you can use the power of ritual to give your actions greater depth and power.

EPIGRAPH

"Ritual and ceremony in their due times kept the world under the sky and the stars in their courses."

–Terry Pratchett

PRACTITIONERS

Living Theater
Women In Black
Mothers of the Plaza de Mayo
Suzanne Lacy
Artists Network of Refuse & Resist
Rivane Neuenschwander
Billionaires for Bush
Abbie Hoffman
Reverend Billy
Arlington West
"I Dream Your Dream"

FURTHER INSIGHT

I Wish Your Wish @ The New Museum
http://www.newmuseum.org/rivane-

Memorial Ritual and Art @ MICA
http://trb.la/zgnZFF

CONTRIBUTED BY

Andrew Boyd

The power of ritual, as in the candlelight vigil above, provides an outlet for both individual catharsis and collective expression.

Rituals can connect us to the deepest truths of why politics matters. As anyone who has participated in a candlelight vigil will know, sometimes the act of quietly bearing witness to an injustice can carry more moral force than railing against it. A ritual can also give an otherwise mundane political gathering a stronger storyline, such as the 2011 protest of mortgage fraud at Chase Bank in New York City, where hundreds of members of faith communities and several ministers performed an exorcism on a bank "possessed by the demons of selfishness and avarice."

The ritual you choose need not be elaborate for it to have a powerful impact. You can imbue your political street theater with some of the power of ritual just by borrowing its rhythms. Imagine two characters on the street: a military general and a politician, slowly tossing a huge sack of money back and forth across a wide expanse. In between, a regular Joe, sitting forlornly, watches the sack sail back and forth. Nearby, a spokesperson hands out a fact sheet that tells the rest of the story. Often this kind of nonverbal, ritual-like performance, which repeats a simple but visually arresting motion, can be more powerful and effective than a full-length skit crammed with facts and figures.

Ghost Bike shrines — old bikes whitewashed and decked with flowers stationed as memorials at urban crossroads where cyclists have been killed — are a haunting presence, protest sculpture and fitting memorial all rolled into one.

"At its best, a ritual is a cathartic, transformative experience."

Because they are such well-worn forms, rituals are ripe for mockery and comic adaptation, whether it's the Billionaires for Bush doing a vigil for corporate welfare, or Reverend Billy brandishing a stuffed Mickey Mouse on a cross while doing an exorcism inside the Times Square Disney Store. In 1967, antiwar prankster Abbie Hoffman led 20,000 protesters in an attempt to levitate the Pentagon — the National Guard was under strict orders to never allow an unbroken chain of hands around the building.

Our familiarity with ritual makes it a great format for self-organizing. A ritual provides a natural script and symbolism. Even complete strangers naturally fall into a rhythm around it. This is even true for recently invented rituals such as monthly Critical Mass bike rides or the yearly ritual of Buy Nothing Day. In more repressive environments, the sacredness of a ritual offers protection, or at least courage. Think of Catholic Mass in Stalinist Poland or death squad-era El Salvador. In the Iranian Revolution (of 1979, as well as the revolts in 2010), the funerals of martyrs killed at the last protest fueled the next round of protests in an accelerating cycle.

At its best, a ritual is a cathartic, transformative experience. At a bat mitzvah, a child crosses over into adulthood. At a funeral, mourners grieve and find closure. A ritual harnessed to a political purpose should have an equally powerful effect, whether it is recommitting to a cause, finding courage, voicing dissent, or building trust.

PRINCIPLE:
Use your radical fringe to shift the Overton window

IN SUM

The Overton window is the limit of what is considered reasonable or acceptable within a range of public policy options. Slide the window of acceptable debate by focusing attention on a position that is more radical than your own.

PRACTITIONERS

The Yes Men
Greenpeace
ACT UP
Occupy Wall Street
Paul Krassner
Voina

FURTHER INSIGHT

Jimmy McMillan of The Rent is Too Damn High Party in action http://www.youtube.com/watch?v=x4o-TeMHys0&feature=related

Alinsky, Saul. Rules for Radicals: a practical primer for realistic radicals. USA. Vintage Books, 1971.

Grist, "Occupy Wall Street can shake up a city–but can it create lasting change?," Greg Hanscom, November 18, 2011 http://trb.la/xsK7HI

The Oberlin Review, "Wall Street Demonstrators Challenge Centrist Consensus," Will Rubenstein, November 20, 2011 http://trb.la/yOJKbU

CONTRIBUTED BY

Josh Bolotsky

The various policy options available on a given issue can be roughly plotted on a spectrum of public acceptability, from unthinkable, to fringe, to acceptable, to common sense, to policy. The Overton window, named after Joseph Overton, a staffer for the center-right Mackinac Center for Public Policy, designates the range of points on the spectrum that are considered part of a "sensible" conversation within public opinion and/or traditional mass media.

The most important thing about the Overton window, however, is that it can be shifted to the left or the right, with the once merely "acceptable" becoming "popular" or even imminent policy, and formerly "unthinkable" positions becoming the open position of a partisan base. The challenge for activists and advocates is to move the window in the direction of their preferred outcomes, so their desired outcome moves closer and closer to "common sense."

There are two ways to do this: the long, hard way and the short, easy way. The long, hard way is to continue making your actual case persistently and persuasively until your position becomes more politically mainstream, whether it be due to the strength of your rhetoric or a long-term shift in societal values. By contrast, the short, easy way is to amplify and echo the voices of those who take a position a few notches more radical than what you really want.

For example, if what you actually want is a public health care option in the United States, coordinate with and promote those pushing for single-payer, universal health care. If the single-payer approach constitutes the "acceptable left" flank of the discourse, then the public option looks, by comparison, like the conservative option it was once considered back when it was first proposed by Orrin Hatch in 1994.

This is Negotiating 101. Unfortunately, the right has been far ahead of the left in moving the Overton window in their desired direction for a long time. If anything, the left often plays it in the exact wrong way, actively policing and seeking to silence its radicals for fear that

Jimmy McMillan, by running for governor of New York in 2010 on the "The Rent is Too Damn High" Party, effectively shifted the Overton window leftwards, thereby making it easier for more moderate candidates to address economic inequality.

strong left positions will serve to discredit moderate left positions. The irony is that the Overton window should actually be easier for progressives to play: if you look at the polling on issue after issue, from education to jobs to foreign policy, the actual majority stances tend to be to the left of the range of policy proposals on offer.

POTENTIAL PITFALLS: Not *all* radical positions are effective in shifting the Overton window, so don't just reach for any old radical idea. Ideally, the position you promote should carry logical and moral force, and must include some common ground with your own position — it needs to be along the same continuum of belief if it is to be effective. It also must not be so far out of the mainstream that it becomes toxic for anyone vaguely associated with it, or the backlash will in fact push the Window in the opposite of the desired direction.

PRINCIPLE:
We are all leaders

IN SUM

An otherwise healthy distrust of hierarchy can lead to a negative attitude toward all forms of leadership. Actually, we want more leadership, not less.

EPIGRAPH

"They surrounded the boat, and when they lowered the gangplank, Sheriff McGray walked to the end of it and said, 'Who are your leaders here?' And they shouted back with one voice: 'We are all leaders here!' Well, that scared the tar out of the law, you know..."

–Utah Phillips, "Fellow workers"[1]

PRACTITIONERS

Alliance of Community Trainers

FURTHER INSIGHT

Starhawk. The Empowerment Manual. A Guide for Collaborative Groups. Canada, New Society Publishers. 2011.

Lakey, Lakey, Napier and Robinson. Grassroots and Nonprofit Leadership. A Guide for Organizations in Changing Times. Philadephia, New Society, 1995.

Coover, Deacon, Esser, Moore. Resource Manual for a Living Revolution. Movement for a New Society. Philadephia, New Society, 1978.

CONTRIBUTED BY

Jonathan Matthew Smucker with help from Han Shan @ #Occupy

What is the difference between saying "none of us is a leader" and saying "we are all leaders"? At first glance these two phrases may seem like two ways of saying the same thing, which is essentially, "We believe in organizing in a way that is more horizontal than vertical. We believe in equalizing participation and resisting social hierarchies." But the word leadership can mean a lot of things, and not all involve the creation of hierarchies. *Taking leadership* can mean *taking initiative* on moving a project or task forward, or *taking responsibility* for recognizing what is needed, and stepping up individually or collectively to do that thing.

"It is important to distinguish between horizontal organization and disorganization."

It is important, in other words, to distinguish between *horizontal* organization and *dis*organization, and to foster models of dispersed leadership that promote responsibility, accountability and effectiveness.

This is not just a matter of semantics. If we are part of a group that boasts of having *no* leaders, participants may be overly hesitant about stepping up to take initiative for fear of being seen as a "leader," which would be a bad thing. If we really want to change the world, we need *more* people stepping up to take initiative, not less. The more initiative we each take in our work together, the greater our collective capacity will be. Building our collective power is one of the most important challenges of grassroots organizing.

We need to build a culture where we're all invited to step up. This means stepping up in ways that make space for others to step up — where others feel invited to step up and take initiative, too. "Stepping up" can mean actively listening to and learning from others. It can mean taking time to recognize and value many different forms of leadership in the group. And it can mean looking for and nurturing leadership potential in others, who may not feel entitled to step forward uninvited or unsupported.

A culture that values healthy leadership is one that also prizes accountability, in which we are responsible for and accountable to one another. But this focus on accountability must go hand-in-hand with a group culture that values leadership. Otherwise we may develop a "circular firing squad" mentality in which we waste our energy cutting each other down for taking initiative.

We need a movement where we are constantly encouraging each other to step into our full potential and shine as a collective of leaders working together for a better world. Let's all be leaders. Let's be leaderful, not leaderless.

Related:

TACTICS
Distributed action p. 26
General strike p. 50

PRINCIPLES
Enable, don't command p. 132
Challenge patriarchy as
you organize p. 108
Beware the tyranny of
structurelessness p. 102
Delegate p. 122
Take leadership from the
most impacted p. 180

THEORIES
Anti-oppression p. 212
Intellectuals and power p. 240
Pedagogy of the Oppressed p. 246

CASE STUDIES
Occupy Wall Street web
Lysistrata project p. 330
Justice for Janitors p. 326

Occupy together.

[1] Utah Phillips and Ani DiFranco, 1999 Fellow Workers [Audio CD]. Righteous Babe records: Buffalo, NY.

PRINCIPLE:
Write your own PRINCIPLE

IN SUM   *What's the secret?*

EPIGRAPH

PRACTITIONERS

FURTHER INSIGHT

CONTRIBUTED BY

Related:

TACTICS

POTENTIAL PITFALLS:

THEORIES

CASES

. . . .

The modular format of *Beautiful Trouble* allows the collection to expand endlessly to reflect new tactical breakthroughs, underrepresented areas of struggle and overlooked pearls of wisdom.

Become part of *Beautiful Trouble*. Use this template to write up your own creative-activism insights. Submit your own module for publication on the *Beautiful Trouble* website here: http://beautifultrouble.org.

THEORIES

CONCEPTUAL FRAMEWORKS

Big-picture ideas that help us understand how the world works and how we might go about changing it.

"Without revolutionary theory, there can be no revolutionary movement, comrade."
—V.I. Lenin (though he didn't actually say the "comrade" part)

Ever wish someone would take the most complex ideas from the likes of Brecht, Gramsci, Marx, Foucault & Co. and cook them down into fierce, accessible little nuggets of theory tailored to the pragmatic needs of the working revolutionary? Well, somebody did. Have at it.

THEORY:
Action logic

IN SUM

Your actions should speak for themselves. They should make immediate, natural sense to onlookers. They should have an obvious logic to the outside eye.

EPIGRAPH

"Actions speak louder than words."
—Ruckus Society motto

ORIGINS

Civil rights movement, USA

PRACTITIONERS

SNCC
Ruckus Society
Greenpeace
Design Studio for Social Intervention
Mitch Snyder

FURTHER INSIGHT

Canning, Doyle, and Patrick Reinsborough.

Re:Imagining Change: An Introduction to Story-Based Strategy. (PM Press, 2010).
http://trb.la/zOcslF

CONTRIBUTED BY

Andrew Boyd
Joshua Kahn Russell

Have you ever looked at a protest and wondered what the heck these people were so angry about? Perhaps it was a bunch of kids blockading an intersection. Who are they? What do they *want*?

With good action logic, nobody needs to ask those questions; an outsider can look at what you're doing and immediately understand why you're doing it. For example, people doing a tree-sit so the forest cannot be cut down — the logic is clear and obvious. The action speaks for itself.

Action logic creates powerful stories that move hearts and change minds. Not only is it true that actions speak louder than words, but, particularly in a hostile media climate where activists are often flagrantly misrepresented, it's important that our actions speak for themselves. It may sound paradoxical, but it often requires lots of thought and care to design actions that make intuitive sense.

Civil disobedience actions — for example the lunch counter sit-ins of the American civil rights movement — tend to have inherent action logic because their purpose is to violate an unjust law in order to highlight exactly that injustice. However, other forms of direct action, which sometimes break laws unrelated to their goal, often need to do some extra work to achieve clear action logic.

Communicative actions *See PRINCIPLE: Be both expressive and instrumental* also need to foster action logic. Camp Casey, where Cindy Sheehan camped outside Bush's vacation ranch until he came out and explained for what "noble cause" her Iraq veteran son Casey had died, had powerful action logic. So did the single moms in Rhode Island who pressured a public housing official for a day care center by not just sitting-in at his office, but bringing their kids with them and, for a few hours, turning his office into the day care center they needed *see CASE: Daycare sit-in*.

Most successful actions have this kind of inherent, transparent logic. They speak for themselves. When your action has this kind of clarity at its core, then no matter how the target responds or how things play out, the action will continue to make your point and make sense to observers.

THEORY: Action logic

In a perfect demonstration of action logic, mixed-race students in Jackson, Mississippi sit in at a segregated lunch-counter in 1960. Photo by Fred Blackwell. Image courtesy Library of Congress.

MOST FAMOUS APPLICATION: The lunch counter sit-ins during the civil rights movement had remarkable action logic. When legal segregation was enforced, black and white students violated the law by sitting at lunch counters and waiting to be served. Any outsider looking at the act immediately knew why they were there. They didn't need to carry signs. In fact, their action *foreshadowed victory* and prefigured the world they wanted to live in: they were living the integration they wanted.

THEORY:
Alienation effect

IN SUM

The alienation effect was Brecht's principle of using innovative theatrical techniques to "make the familiar strange" in order to provoke a social-critical audience response.

EPIGRAPH

"Sometimes it's more important to be human than to have good taste."

—Bertolt Brecht

ORIGINS

Bertolt Brecht, 1920-1930s Germany

PRACTITIONERS

Augusto Boal
Peter Schumann
Lars Von Trier
Allan Kaprow

FURTHER INSIGHT

Bertolt Brecht (Author), John Willett (Translator), Brecht on theater: The Development of an Aesthetic (New York: Hill and Wang; 13th edition, 1977)

L. M. Bogad, Tactical Performance: On the Theory and Practice of Serious Play. (forthcoming from NYU Press 2012).

CONTRIBUTED BY

L.M. Bogad

Bertolt Brecht, German leftist playwright and director, had nothing but disdain for the conventional, commercial "bourgeois" theater of his time. He considered it a "branch of the narcotics business." Why? The theater of his time, like most Hollywood movies now, relied on emotional manipulation to bring about a suspension of disbelief for the audience, along with an emotional identification with the main character. Audience members were taken on an uncritical emotional roller coaster ride, crying when the main character cried, laughing when s/he laughed — identifying with him/her even when the character had nothing in common with them or their interests (working-class audiences swooningly identifying with a Prince of Denmark, for example).

Bertolt Brecht developed a set of theatrical techniques to subvert the emotional manipulations of bourgeois theater.

Brecht saw that these audiences were manipulated by theater technology — beautiful, realistic sets, cleverly naturalistic lighting, the imaginary fourth wall, and most importantly, emotionally effusive acting techniques. He soon watched with horror as the Nazi movement gained popular support in his country with its racist, xenophobic demagoguery, relying on similar emotional manipulation. Emotional manipulation was, to him, Enemy Number One of human decency.

It was in this context that Brecht developed his theory of *Verfremdungseffekt*, also known as V-effekt, alienation effect, or distantiation effect. (Important disclaimer: there is compelling evidence that many of Brecht's greatest ideas were developed in uncredited cooperation with his artistic partners).

The alienation effect attempts to combat emotional manipulation in the theater, replacing it with an entertaining or surprising jolt. For instance, rather than investing in or "becoming" their characters, they might emotionally step away and demonstrate them with cool, witty, and skillful self-critique. The director could "break the fourth wall" and expose the technology of the theater to the audience in amusing ways. Or a technique known as the *social gest* could be used to expose unjust social power relationships so the audience sees these relationships in a new way. The *social gest* is an exaggerated gesture or action that is not to be taken literally but which critically demonstrates a social relationship or power imbalance. For example, workers in a corporate office may suddenly and quickly drop to the floor and kowtow to the CEO, or the women in a household may suddenly start to move in fast-motion, cleaning the house, while the men slowly yawn and loaf around.

By showing the instruments of theater and how they can be manipulative — for example, the actor calling out "Cue the angry red spotlight!" before he shrieks with rage, or "Time for the gleeful violin" before dancing happily as the violinist joins him on stage, or visibly dabbing water on his eyes when he is supposed to cry... the audience can be entertained without being manipulated. Many of Brecht's techniques have been co-opted and incorporated into contemporary bourgeois theater and film, though his challenge remains relevant: how to confront the problem of emotional manipulation while creating a stimulating, surprising, entertaining, radically critical, popularly appealing and accessible social art practice.

Related:

TACTICS
Détournement/Culture jamming p. 28
Identity correction p. 60
Electoral guerrilla theater p. 40

PRINCIPLES
Make the invisible visible p. 152
Use the power of ritual p. 198
Reframe p. 168
Balance art and message p. 100

THEORIES
Ethical spectacle p. 230
Society of the Spectacle p. 266
Theater of the Oppressed p. 272
Capitalism p. 216

THEORY:
Anti-oppression

IN SUM

Anti-oppression practice provides a framework for constructively addressing and changing oppressive dynamics as they play out in our organizing.

EPIGRAPH

"If you have come to help me, you are wasting your time. But if you have come because your liberation is bound up in mine, then let us work together."

–Lila Watson

ORIGINS

As long as there has been oppression, people have been working to end it. In recent decades, the Highlander Center and the People's Institute for Survival and Beyond have worked to undo racism and build collective liberation. After Seattle, a whole new wave of work began, deepening each year with new collectives emerging and new practices evolving. The work outlined here has been learned over time from many teachers.

PRACTITIONERS

People's Institute for Survival and Beyond
Alliance of Community Trainers
No One is Illegal
People of Color Organize!
Rinku Sen & Applied Research Center
The Ruckus Society

CONTRIBUTED BY

Lisa Fithian
Dave Oswald Mitchell

Activist groups sometimes make the mistake of assuming that *oppression* (the unjust exercise of power or authority) is only what *they* do; that *we* are inherently anti-oppressive purely because of our intention to do away with oppressive struc-tures. Unfortunately the situation is much more complex, and we ig-nore that complexity at our peril.[1]

We have been social-ized in cultures founded upon multiple, overlapping forms of oppression, often leading us to inadvertently perpetuate dehumanizing behaviors, situations and structures. Our oppressive actions diminish us, divide us and inhibit our ability to organize broad-based, eman-cipatory movements.

> "Our oppressive actions diminish us, divide us and inhibit our ability to organize broad-based, emancipatory movements."

In order to build a world free from domination, we offer up for discussion the following tenets and practices in the hopes they can provide a solid foundation for advancing our work and deepening our interpersonal relationships.

Tenets

* Power and privilege can play out in our group dynamics in destructive ways. For the good of all, we must challenge words and actions that marginalize, exclude or dehumanize others.

* We can only identify the ways that power and privilege play out when we are conscious and com-mitted to understanding how white supremacy, patriarchy, classism, heterosexism and other systems of oppression affect us all.

* Until we are clearly committed to anti-oppression practice, all forms of oppression will continue to divide and weaken our movements.

* Developing anti-oppression practices is life-long work. No single workshop is sufficient for

unlearning our socialization within a culture built on multiple forms of oppression.

- Dialogue, discussion and reflection are some of the tools through which we overcome oppressive attitudes, behaviors and situations in our groups. Anti-oppression work requires active listening, non-defensiveness and respectful communication.

Personal practices

- Challenge yourself to be courageously honest and open, willing to take risks and make yourself vulnerable in order to address racism, sexism, homophobia, transphobia and other oppressive dynamics head-on.

- When you witness, experience, or commit an abuse of power or oppression, address it as proactively as the situation permits, either one-on-one or with a few allies, keeping in mind that the goal is to encourage positive change.

- Challenge the behavior, not the person. Be sensitive and promote open dialogue.

- When someone offers criticism in an oppressive framework, treat it as a gift rather than an attack. Give people the benefit of the doubt.

- Be willing to lose a friend, but try not to "throw away" people who fuck up. Help them take responsibility for making reparations for their behavior, and be willing to extend forgiveness in return.

- Take on the "grunt" work that often falls on women, especially women of color. This includes the work of cooking, cleaning, set up, clean up, phone calls, e-mail, taking notes, doing support work, sending mailings.

- Understand that you will feel discomfort as you face your part in oppression, and realize that this is a necessary part of the process. We must support each other and be gentle with each other in this process.

- Don't feel guilty, feel responsible. Being part of the

FURTHER INSIGHT

Colour of Resistance archive
http://www.coloursofresistance.org/

Applied Research Center, "Toolbox for Racial Justice"
http://www.arc.org/content/blogcategory/77/214/

Peggy McIntosh, "White Privilege: Unpacking the invisible knapsack"
http://trb.la/xtbAqG

Audre Lorde, "There Is No Hierarchy of Oppressions"
http://trb.la/zBbOrc

bell hooks, Teaching to Transgress: Education as the Practice of Freedom (New York, NY: Routledge, 1994)

Tim Wise, White Like Me: Reflections on race from a privileged son. (Berkeley, CA: Soft Skull Press, 2011)

Paul Kivel, Men's Work: How to Stop the Violence that Tears Our Lives Apart (Center City, MN: Hazeldon Press, 1992)

Alliance of Community Trainers, Anti-Oppression Resources:
http://organizingforpower.wordpress.com/power/anti-oppression-resources-exercises/

Global Exchange, Anti-Oppression Reader
http://www.seac.org/wp-content/uploads/2011/07/AO_Reader_2007.pdf

Related:

TACTICS

Forum theater p. 48
Image theater p. 62

PRINCIPLES

Consensus is a means, not an end p. 116
Take leadership from the most impacted p. 180
Challenge patriarchy as you organize p. 108
Make the invisible visible p. 152
Take risks, but take care p. 182
We are all leaders web
Make new folks welcome p. 114

problem doesn't mean you can't be an active part of the solution.

- Contribute time and energy to building healthy relationships, both personal and political.

Organizational practices

- Commit time to facilitated discussions on discrimination and oppression.

- Set anti-oppression goals and continually evaluate whether or not you are meeting them.

- Create opportunities for people to develop anti-oppression skills and practices.

- Promote egalitarian group development by prioritizing skill shares and an equitable division of roles, responsibilities and recognition.

- Respect different styles of leadership and communication.

- Don't push historically marginalized people to do things because of their oppressed group (tokenism); base it on their work, experience and skills.

- Make a collective commitment to hold everyone accountable for their behavior so that the organization can be a safe and nurturing place for all.

---

[1] This article is adapted from "Anti-Oppression Principles & Practices" by Lisa Fithian, itself compiled from the "Anti-Racism Principles and Practices" by RiseUp DAN-LA, Overcoming Masculine Oppression by Bill Moyers and the FEMMAFESTO by a women's affinity group in Philadelphia.

THEORY: Anti-oppression

TO LOVE.

TO BE LOVED.

TO NEVER FORGET YOUR OWN INSIGNIFICANCE.

TO NEVER GET USED TO THE UNSPEAKABLE VIOLENCE AND VULGAR DISPARITY OF LIFE AROUND YOU.

TO SEEK JOY IN THE SADDEST PLACES.

TO PURSUE BEAUTY TO ITS LAIR.

TO NEVER SIMPLIFY WHAT IS COMPLICATED OR TO COMPLICATE WHAT IS SIMPLE.

TO RESPECT STRENGTH, NEVER POWER.

Above all,

TO WATCH.

TO TRY AND UNDERSTAND.

TO NEVER LOOK AWAY

AND
NEVER,
NEVER,
TO FORGET.

—Arundhati Roy

THEORY:
Capitalism

IN SUM

Capitalism is a profit-driven economic system rooted in inequality, exploitation, dispossession and environmental destruction.

EPIGRAPH

"Capitalism turns men and women into economic cannibals, and having done so, mistakes economic cannibalism for human nature."

–Edward Hyman

"Capitalists don't control capital; capital controls capitalists."

–Unknown

ORIGINS

The transition to capitalism took place in northwestern Europe between the sixteenth and nineteenth century, and expanded from this region to the rest of the world through colonialism and imperialism.

CONTRIBUTED BY

Jeffery Webber

The cause of the economic crisis that began in 2008 is not inadequate regulation of the free market, but runs far deeper. The global slump we are living through is the predictable manifestation of a crisis-prone economic system rooted in production for profit rather than for human need. That economic system is called *capitalism*, and for the sake of human development and ecological sanity it needs to be overthrown. But to be overthrown, it must first be understood.

Capitalism Works For Me! True/False. Original public art by Steve Lambert.

Capitalism is an economic system in which almost anything we need or want must be bought on the market, and in which most of us have nothing to sell but our labor. Capitalism is not a thing, but a social relation between capital and labor that divides humanity into two principal social classes: the capitalist class, or bourgeoisie, which owns the means of production (tools, resources, land), and the working class, or proletariat, which does not have access to the means of production and therefore must sell its own labor power, or ability to work.

The laws of competition and profit-maximization govern the capitalist market. Each enterprise exists alongside many others that are all producing similar products or services. Each needs to outperform the others, minimizing costs and maximizing profit, or they will be driven into bankruptcy. Technological innovation is one way to cut costs. Compelling em-ployees to work harder and longer for less is another.

Capitalists' drive to expand propels economic growth, but at a certain point, production exceeds demand, and there are too many factories and mills producing the same thing for every firm to be profitable. This is the recurring crisis of over-accumulation and profitability into which capitalism enters. While profits during the expansive phase are privatized in the pockets of owners, the costs of crisis are socialized through austerity measures, unemployment, and poverty.

Capitalists are indifferent to the commodities they produce so long as the need to generate profit is fulfilled *see THEORY: Commodity fetishism*. Solar energy or tar sands oil, cluster bombs or malaria medication, it does not matter what is produced or what purpose it serves, so long as it is profitable. Capitalism in this sense means production for *exchange* (profit) instead of production for *use* (human need and ecological sustainability). The moral perversity of this dynamic is played out daily in an economy that produces luxury cars and gourmet pet food for a few, while allowing the reproduction of almost unthinkable levels of global hunger and poverty, with more than one billion people living on less that $1 per day, and another billion and a half on under $2.

In sum, capitalism means waste, poverty, ecological degradation, dispossession, inequality, exploitation, imperialism, war and violence. We need to build mass movements to replace it with an economic system based on production for human need and ecological sustainability, with participatory and democratic planning, worker and community self-management, and international solidarity.

> "For the sake of human development and ecological sanity, capitalism needs to be overthrown. But to be overthrown, it must first be understood."

FURTHER INSIGHT

Ha-Joon Chang, 23 Things They Don't Tell You About Capitalism (Bloomsbury Press, 2011).

Video: Crises of Capitalism (animated lecture by David Harvey) http://trb.la/xS91HD

David McNally, Another World is Possible: Globalization and Anti-Capitalism, (Winnipeg: Arbeiter-Ring Publishing, 2005)

Ellen Meiksins Wood, The Origin of Capitalism: A Longer View (London: Verso, 2002)

Selma James, Sex, Race and Class (1975) http://trb.la/xrfB7D

Naomi Klein, "Capitalism vs the Climate," November 28, 2011 http://trb.la/xNKuPLe

THEORY:
Commodity fetishism

Commodity fetishism is the collective belief that it is natural and inevitable to measure the value of useful things with money. Marx coined the term to mock political economists who believed that carefully studying economic systems would eventually yield a set of natural laws comparable to those found in physics or chemistry.

In a regrettably racist outburst in *Capital*, Marx compared the political economists of his day to "primitive" people who attributed magical powers to ordinary objects — stones, wood carvings, weapons or, in the case of the economists, physical currency. Their theories, Marx fumed, amounted to little more than a superstitious belief that animal spirits lurked in commodities, and moved markets by magic.

Marx was convinced that most economists barely scratch the surface of economic reality because they were entranced by its elaborate symbolism: money, debt, property rights, prices and, in our time, ever more complicated methods for computing risk. For Marx, the important truths of economics could all be found in the gritty process of production, in the places where people actually worked and lived. From the roaring machinery of the factory to the rat-infested hovels of the urban proletariat, from the collapse of rural social life to the actual distribution of natural resources, the most important aspects of capitalist society were all traceable back to political domination by a small class of property owners. What really mattered about the economy, in Marx's view, was that the ruling class could rely on its military and police forces to resolve conflicts over ownership with violence.

Marx's point remains relevant. By the middle of the twentieth century, orthodox economics had become a heavily quantitative discipline that took pride in its

"For Marx, the important truths of economics could all be found in the gritty process of production, in the places where people actually worked and lived."

Reverend Billy and The Stop Shopping Gospel Choir preach the repudiation of commodity fetishism.

alleged scientific objectivity. At the heart of modern economics is the desire to devise models capable of making accurate predictions about economic reality. Consequently, economists are still dissecting the commodity market and studying it under a microscope to discern its secrets. They tend to be skeptical of collective decision-making and favorably disposed toward markets because they mistakenly attribute agency to money and markets, in effect believing that the market is moved by mysterious forces that, whether they are natural laws or animal spirits, humans simply cannot control.

The challenge for anyone who wants to radically change the world is to dispel the magical aura of the market and the attendant myth of human impotence. Markets don't have power or agency, people do. Think of what happens during a revolutionary general strike. People refuse to work or perform even basic social rituals. The state dissolves overnight and, for a miraculous instant, anything is possible. Banks could be public property, roads could be pedestrian thoroughfares, shopping districts could be spaces for political deliberation and the government could really be for the people.

Anyone who asserts that there is something inevitable in the historical process has not studied the subject. The beginning of radical hope is the recognition that social relationships are arbitrary and mutable — and need not be mediated through monetary transactions.

THEORY: The commons

IN SUM

Our common wealth – the shared bounty that we inherit and create together – precedes and surrounds our private wealth. By building a system that protects and expands our common wealth rather than one that exploits it, we can address both our ecological and social imbalances.

EPIGRAPH

"Even an entire society, a nation, or all simultaneously existing societies taken together, are not the owners of the earth. They are simply its possessors, its beneficiaries, and have to bequeath it in an improved state to succeeding generations as *boni patres familias* [good heads of the household]."

–Karl Marx

ORIGINS

The concept of the commons dates back to Roman times, with emperor Justinian (530 AD) declaring, "By the law of nature these things are common to mankind: the air, running water, the sea, and consequently the shores of the sea." The Magna Carta (1215) established forests and fisheries as commons open to all. John Locke (1689) declared that private property is appropriate only if "there is enough, and as good, left in common for others."

CONTRIBUTED BY

Peter Barnes

In pre-capitalist times, shared commons were the source of sustenance for most people. Though corporations have enclosed and diminished much of the commons, it lives on in three portfolios: *natural wealth* (air, water, seeds, ecosystems, other species); *community wealth* (streets, parks, the Internet, money, social insurance); *and cultural wealth* (music, art, science, open-source software). All of these are gifts we share and are obliged to preserve for others and for future generations.

The trouble is that, under capitalism, common wealth is increasingly appropriated by private corporations and wealthy individuals for profit. To counter this, we need to expand and strengthen both the commons and the institutions that sustain them.

Several doctrines flow from the idea of the commons:

Public trust doctrine: The state must act as the trustee of common wealth for the benefit of all, or designate accountable trustees.

We're all in this together: The capitalist-era risks of unemployment, disability, illness, climate change and unfunded retirement are best shared collectively rather than borne individually.

Polluter pays: Polluters should pay to dump wastes in shared ecosystems.

Precautionary principle: Ecosystems should be Zmanaged for long-term health, not short-term profit.

One person, one share: Rent from common assets belongs to everyone equally.

"A twenty-first-century commons sector wouldn't replace the market or the state, but would rather serve as a necessary balance to them."

Usufruct: Our right to make use of a given resource is contingent upon our responsibility to preserve and enrich that resource for future generations.

Photo by twoblueday

It's important to note that, though the commons sector needs state support (just as the private sector does), it's *not identical to the state.* One can imagine a vibrant commons sector built around the Internet and the airwaves; trusts that protect key essential resources like clean air, water, forests and topsoil; universal health care; dividends paid from common wealth to everyone and local arts funds based on copyright fees. One can also imagine fees on private transactions that profit from the financial commons.

An important function of the commons sector would be to charge corporations for costs (such as bank bailouts and pollution) that they currently impose on the rest of us. If this were done, businesses would speculate less and invest more in clean technologies, and rent from commons use could provide non-labor income to all.

In short, a twenty-first-century commons sector wouldn't replace the market or the state, but would rather serve as a necessary balance to them. While such a sector won't emerge all at once, we can build it piece by piece over time.

MOST FAMOUS APPLICATION: Parks and wilderness areas, the Internet, Wikipedia, Social Security, the Alaska Permanent Fund (pays equal dividends to all Alaskans with revenue from oil leases).

MOST INFAMOUS BETRAYAL: Free gifts of air to polluters, money to banks and airwaves to broadcasters.

PRACTITIONERS

Creative Commons
OnTheCommons
Electronic Frontier Foundation
Greenpeace

FURTHER INSIGHT

On the Commons, "All That We Share: A Field Guide to the Commons"
http://onthecommons.org/all-we-share-field-guide-commons

Capitalism 3.0: A Guide to Reclaiming the Commons
www.capitalism3.com

David Bollier: News and Perspectives on the Commons
www.bollier.org

The Commoner: A Web Journal for Other Values
http://www.commoner.org.uk/

Related:

TACTICS

THEORIES

CASE STUDIES

THEORY:
Cultural hegemony

IN SUM

Politics is not only fought out in state houses, workplaces or on battlefields, but also in the language we use, the stories we tell, and the images we conjure — in short, in the ways we make sense of the world.

EPIGRAPH

"The most obvious, important realities are often the ones that are hardest to see and talk about. Stated as an English sentence, of course, this is just a banal platitude, but the fact is that in the day to day trenches of adult existence, banal platitudes can have a life or death importance."
—David Foster Wallace

ORIGINS

Antonio Gramsci; further developed by Stuart Hall

PRACTITIONERS

Guillermo Gómez-Peña
Guerrilla Girls

CONTRIBUTED BY

Stephen Duncombe

Antonio Gramsci.

Cultural hegemony is a term developed by Antonio Gramsci, activist, theorist, and founder of the Italian Communist party. Writing while imprisoned in a Fascist jail, Gramsci was concerned with how power works: how it is wielded by those in power and how it is won by those who want to change the system. The dominant idea at the time amongst Marxist radicals like himself was that in order to attain power you needed to seize the means of production and administration — that is, take over the factories and the state. But Gramsci recognized that this was not sufficient. In his youth, he had witnessed workers take over factories in Turin, only to hand them back within weeks because they were unsure what to do with the factories, or themselves. Gramsci had also observed the skill of the Catholic Church in exercising its power and retaining the population's allegiance. Gramsci realized that in order to create and maintain a new society, you also needed to create and maintain a new consciousness.

The repository of consciousness is culture. This includes both big-C Culture, culture in an aesthetic sense, and small-c culture, culture in an anthropological sense: the norms and mores and discourses that make up our everyday lives. Culture, in this sense, is what allows us to navigate our world, guiding our ideas of right and wrong, beautiful and ugly, just and unjust, possible and impossible. You may be able to seize a factory or storm a palace, but unless this material power is backed up by a culture that reinforces the notion that what you are doing is good and beautiful and just and possible, then any gains on the economic, military and political fronts are likely to be short-lived.

The power of cultural hegemony lies in its invisibility. Unlike a soldier with a gun or a political system backed up by a written constitution, culture resides within us. It doesn't seem "political," it's just what we like, or what we think is beautiful, or what feels comfortable. Wrapped in stories and images and figures of speech, culture is a politics that doesn't look like politics and is therefore a lot harder to notice, much less resist. When a culture becomes *hegemonic*, it becomes "common sense" for the majority of the population.

No culture, however, is completely hegemonic. Even under the most complete systems of control, there are pockets of what Gramsci, and later Hall, called "counter-hegemonic" cultures: ways of thinking and doing that have revolutionary potential because they run counter to the dominant power. For Gramsci, these cultures might be located in traditional peasant beliefs or the shop-floor culture of industrial workers; for Hall they might be found in youth subcultures like Rastafarians and punks, and even in commercial entertainment. The activist's job, according to Hall, is to identify and exploit these cultural pockets, build a radical counter-culture within the shell of the old society, and wage the struggle for a new cultural hegemony.

An important caveat: Gramsci never believed that cultural power alone was enough. The fight for cultural hegemony had to be part of an overall strategy that also incorporated struggles for political and economic power.

"*The power of cultural hegemony lies in its invisibility. Unlike a soldier with a gun or a political system backed up by a written constitution, culture resides within us.* "

FURTHER INSIGHT

Gramsci, Antonio. *The Antonio Gramsci Reader: Selected Writings 1916-1935*. New York: NYU Press, 2000.

Morton, Adam. *Unravelling Gramsci: Hegemony and Passive Revolution in the Global Economy*. London: Pluto Press, 2007.

Related:

TACTICS

Invisible theater p. 66
Détournement/Culture jamming p. 28
General strike p. 50
Prefigurative intervention p. 82

PRINCIPLES

Escalate strategically p. 134
Balance art and message p. 100
Seek common ground p. 170

THEORIES

Political identity paradox p. 254
Environmental justice p. 228
Pillars of support p. 248

CASE STUDIES

Wisconsin Capitol occupation p. 396
Occupy Wall Street web

THE ROLE OF THE ARTIST IS TO MAKE THE REVOLUTION

IRRESISTIBLE

—Toni Cade Bambara

IN SUM

Today's class consciousness falls increasingly along debtor-creditor lines rather than worker-capitalist lines.

EPIGRAPH

"I ain't a Communist necessarily, but I been in the red all my life."

–Woody Guthrie

FURTHER INSIGHT

David Graeber. Debt: The First 5,000 Years. New York: Melville House, 2011.

Michael Hudson. "The New Road to Serfdom: An Illustrated Guide to the Coming Real Estate Collapse." Harper's (May 2006).

CONTRIBUTED BY

Dmytri Kleiner

Many activist communiqués employ the classical language of class struggle. This language not only often fails to engage, it may even alienate people who might otherwise be sympathetic. The majority of people in the global north do not identify as *workers*, and thus any appeal addressed to *workers* is unlikely to achieve results in these societies. As the industrial base of the economy has moved east and south, the language of class politics in the global north has gotten much murkier and more complicated. I propose that debt-centered organizing offers the potential to reinvigorate radical struggle in the twenty-first century.

The language of the labor movement emerged in an era when the power loom was the driving force of industry, nobility controlled the land and the state, and being a worker in early industry was torturous and inhumane. Most working people were direct producers. Today, most people in developed nations are non-direct producers, working in customer service, finance, and other administrative or technical fields. They are, therefore, no longer direct witnesses to the fruits of their labor being stolen from them and hoarded by capitalists, but rather are divided and subdivided in increasingly insidious ways.

"People are broke because the system is broken. We have no moral obligation to keep paying into a system that is not working."

People today don't conceive of the "product of their labor" as the actual goods sold by their employers; in their minds, the product of their labor is their paycheck. That is what they produce, that is what is taken from their hands, not by their boss, but by their bills, their debts, their taxes. This is one reason the right has been so successful at channelling populist rage away from big business and toward *big government*.

Two decades of easy credit and bubble economics have left most people deeply in debt, often as a result of having to pay for essentials like education, childcare, housing and health care. This is a real opportunity for activists to

Related:

TACTICS
Debt strike p. 24
Prefigurative intervention p. 82
Eviction-blocking p. 44

PRINCIPLES
Debtors of the world, unite! p. 120
Take leadership from the
most impacted p. 180

THEORIES
Capitalism p. 216
Commodity fetishism p. 218
Points of intervention p. 250
The commons p. 220

make the case that capitalism simply can't provide essential goods fairly and efficiently, that their debts are unjust and were forced on to them. People are broke because the system is broken. We have no moral obligation to keep paying into a system that is not working.

The labor movement transformed the working conditions in developed nations and built the welfare state, and did so by championing the demands of the organized working class. Today, we have a debtors' consciousness, united by financial stress and economic precarity, with debt its measure.

Realizing our collective power to withdraw our willingness to pay debts *see: TACTIC: Debt strike* is potentially as system-shaking today as the power of the industrial working class to withdraw its labor power a century ago. Debt is a uniting condition that can mobilize the masses to fight for change.

The debtors of the world have nothing to lose but their chains. Debtors of the world, unite!

THEORY: Environmental justice

IN SUM

By exposing the connections between social justice and environmental issues we can most effectively challenge abuses of power that disproportionately target indigenous and other economically and politically disenfranchised communities.

EPIGRAPH

"As a black person in America I am twice as likely to live in an area where air pollution poses the greatest risk to my health. I am five times more likely to live within walking distance of a power plant or chemical facility, which I do. Fortunately there are people like me who are fighting for solutions that won't compromise the lives of low-income communities of color in the short term – and won't destroy us all in the long term."

—*Majora Carter*

ORIGINS

Hazel Johnson, Dr. Benjamin Chavis, Charles Lee, Robert D. Bullard, the self-organization of impacted communities.

CONTRIBUTED BY

Margaret Campbell

In the United States today, race and class composition are the most reliable indicators of where the wastes that industrial society creates are dumped. Invariably, they have been shown to accumulate in and around poor and racialized communities. *Environmental racism* refers to this tendency to burden marginalized groups with environmental problems. The movement for *environmental justice* is the organized response, seeking to redress the inequitable distribution of waste through both community development (greening) and political empowerment (petitioning for development and enforcement of environmental law and policies) in poor communities and communities of color.

After four little girls in from the South Side Chicago Altgeld Gardens housing community died from cancer in the early 1980s, Hazel Johnson, longtime resident and founder of People for Community Recovery, put two and two together: their 190-acre community was home to over fifty documented landfills, and also to the highest incidence of cancer in the city. Her organization went on to win many grassroots struggles for environmental justice on behalf of their predominantly poor, predominantly black community, and then began networking with other organizations across the country. By the mid 1990s, the environmental justice movement had made significant strides in publicizing such issues, with organizations such as the United Church of Christ Commission for Racial Justice staging numerous acts of civil disobedience.

Globally, powerful corporations have been able to spread the practice of exploiting politically vulnerable communities. As Lawrence Summers, Secretary of the Treasury under Clinton and director of

> "What is at work here is not only racism, but a widespread and devastating ethic that withholds compassion from the environment, and denies the humanity of ninety-nine percent of the world's people."

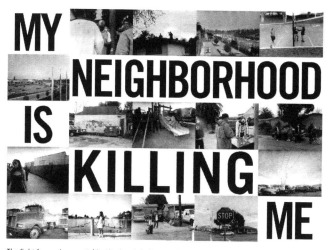

MY NEIGHBORHOOD IS KILLING ME

The fight for environmental justice is a fight for your life. Image by Wake Forest University.

the National Economic Council under Obama, argued in a 1991 memo while employed at the World Bank, "the economic logic behind dumping a load of toxic waste in the lowest wage country is impeccable and we should face up to that... I've always thought that under populated countries in Africa are vastly underpolluted." A Summers aide later claimed that the memo was intended sarcastically. Sarcasm or no, the statement accurately reflects the way waste is handled under capitalism.

What is at work here is not only racism, but a widespread and devastating ethic that withholds compassion from the environment and denies the humanity of ninety-nine percent of the world's people, treating them as resources to be exploited at best, or as entirely external to the economic calculations at worst.

It is not by chance that the civil rights movement sparked a process that, in recent decades, has culminated in a veritable explosion of environmental activism. It is because of the insidious form that racism takes under the geographical development of capitalism that an utterly unsustainable way of life was allowed to evolve to the point of global climate catastrophe. Only by confronting as one the environmental and social manifestations of the crisis can we hope to replace this system with something more equitable for all.

THEORY:
Ethical spectacle

IN SUM

To be politically effective, activists need to engage in spectacle. By keeping to certain principles, our spectacles can be ethical, emancipatory, and faithful to reality.

EPIGRAPH

"Boredom is always counter-revolutionary. Always."

—Guy Debord

ORIGINS

Andrew Boyd
Stephen Duncombe

PRACTITIONERS

The Situationists
Abbie Hoffman/Yippies
The Zapatistas Insurgent
Rebel Clown Army
Yes Men Greenpeace
Billionaires for Bush
Deconstructionist Institute
for Surreal Topology Iraq
Veterans Against the War

FURTHER INSIGHT

Duncombe, Stephen. Dream: Re-Imagining Progressive Politics in an Age of Fantasy. New York: New Press, 2007. Boyd, Andrew, and Stephen Duncombe. "The Manufacture of Dissent: What the Left Can Learn from Las Vegas." Journal of Aesthetics and Protest 1, no. 3 (2004).

CONTRIBUTED BY

Stephen Duncombe

The concept of *ethical spectacle* offers a way of thinking about the tactical and strategic use of signs, symbols, myths, and fantasies to advance progressive, democratic goals. First introduced in a 2004 article by Andrew Boyd and Stephen Duncombe and later ex-panded in Duncombe's 2007 book *Dream*, the theory's premises are:

This mashup of two iconic images captures the tensions and contradictions of the ethical spectacle.

(1) that politics is as much an affair of desire and fantasy as it is reason and rationality, (2) that we live in an intensely mediated age (what Situationist Guy Debord called the *Society of the Spectacle*), (3) that in order to be politically effective, activists need to enter the realmww of spectacle, and (4) that spectacular interventions have the potential to be both ethical and emancipatory.

An ethical spectacle is a symbolic action that seeks to shift the political culture toward more progressive values. An ethical spectacle should strive to be:

Participatory: Seeking to empower participants and specta-tors alike, with organizers acting as facilitators.

Open: Responsive and adaptive to shifting contexts and the ideas of participants.

Transparent: Engaging the imagination of spectators with out seeking to trick or deceive.

Realistic: Using fantasy to illuminate and dramatize real-world power dynamics and social relations that otherwise tend to remain hidden in plain sight.

Utopian: Celebrating the impossible — and therefore helping to make the impossible possible.

The Yippies used the symbolic power of flowers in this emancipatory spectacle. *Flower Power*, 1967, The Washington Evening Star photo by Bernie Boston.

Related:

TACTICS
Détournement/Culture jamming p. 28
Flash mob p. 46

PRINCIPLES
Be an ethical prankster web
Make the invisible visible p. 152

THEORIES
Society of the Spectacle p. 266
Expressive and Instrumental actions p. 232

CASE STUDIES
Santa Claus army p. 358
The Big Donor Show p. 294
Dow Chemical apologizes for Bhopal p. 318

Progressives tend to distrust anything that smacks of propaganda or marketing — that's what the other side does. We tend to believe that proclaiming the naked Truth is enough: "Ye shall know the truth, and the truth shall set you free." But waiting for the truth to set us free is lazy politics. The truth does not reveal itself by virtue of being the truth: it must be told, and told well. It must have stories woven around it, works of art made about it; it must be communicated in new and compelling ways that can be passed from person to person, even if this requires flights of fancy and new mythologies. The argument here is not for a progressive movement that deceives or cheapens its message but rather for a propaganda of the truth. This is the work of ethical spectacle.

THEORY:
Expressive & instrumental actions

IN SUM

Political action tends to be driven by one of two different motivations: expressing an identity, and winning concrete changes. It's important to know the difference, and to strike a balance between the two.

EPIGRAPH

"If the real radical finds that having long hair sets up psychological barriers to communication and organization, he cuts his hair."

–Saul Alinsky

ORIGINS

Resource Mobilization Theory of the 1970's–Present

PRACTITIONERS

Otpor
The orange alternative
Gran Fury
Coalition of Immokalee Workers
Deconstructionist Institute of Surrealist Topology
Lesbian Avengers
The Zapatista Army of National Liberation (EZLN)

CONTRIBUTED BY

Jonathan Matthew Smucker
Joshua Kahn Russell
Zack Malitz

Sometimes activists will take an action without much thought to how others receive it, or what precisely the action will achieve. Many people participate in actions because it's *meaningful* to them, or simply because it *feels* good to do the right thing. We call this the *expressive* part of an action. Expressive actions come from the heart and the gut — whether or not our "heads" calculate the specific outcome.

"Taking the street" during a march is a perfect example. Sure, it feels good to march un-permitted in the street. You and your comrades bravely disobey police orders and, all together, walk out into traffic. You can practically smell the group cohesion in the air. It's intoxicating. It's also usually inconsequential in terms of broader social movement objectives. Still, how many times have you heard someone say a march was "bad" simply because it stayed on the sidewalk? When someone says this, it may be because their goals are primarily expressive; affecting social change is of secondary importance.

Most trained organizers think on another level: regardless of the self-expressive value for those involved, we ask "what is this action actually achieving for our issue, cause, movement, or campaign?" We call this the *instrumental* value of an action.

Both aspects are important, and though a well-designed action can deliver on both simultaneously, expressive and instrumental often get pitted against one another. Many hard-nosed organizers focus exclusively on tangible impacts, forgetting that the self-expressive dimension of an action plays a critical role in affirming values and building group identity. On the other hand, many groups can carry out a whole string of expressive actions *without ever winning anything*. The danger here is clear: groups that don't evaluate the success of their tactics in terms of their *instrumental* goals risk becoming narcissistic and self-referential. They can spiral into irrelevance because they aren't tuned into how their action effects anyone *outside* of the group *see PRINCIPLE: No one wants to watch a drum circle.*

While instrumental actions are often focused on an "external" outcome, say, some measurable kind of pressure you can exert on the bad guy your campaign is targeting, they can also have an "internal" focus. Consider a mass teach-in that is *designed* to build your organization's capacity, or increase the skills of participants, or shift the thinking in your movement. Here, the expressive value of the action is being

MY QUESTION IS: ARE WE REALLY MAKING AN IMPACT?

Reflective wolves consider instrumental impacts. (Image by Joshua Kahn Russell and Beatriz Carmen Mendoza, inspired by a cartoon by S. Gross. Originally printed in Organizing Cools the Planet (PM Press, 2011)).

directly translated into an instrumental outcome. Expressive and instrumental are therefore not mutually exclusive categories, but rather dynamics to which we need to pay attention.

Instrumental actions can be further subdivided into "communicative" and "concrete" *see PRINCIPLE: Make your actions both concrete and communicative*. *Communicative* actions are designed to sway opinion, express an idea, or contribute to public discourse, while *concrete* actions are designed to have a tangible impact on a target. These are two separate ways of measuring an *instrumental* outcome.

While self-expression is a necessary part of the social change process, it is not sufficient. Through our rituals of self-expression, we affirm our values and visions and build the kind of group identity and cohesion without which we'd be too weak and disorganized to change the world *see THEORY: Political identity paradox*. That said, *expressing values is not the same as engaging society and affecting system-ic change.* If we really want to change the world, we must know the difference between — and artfully balance — our instrumental goals with our desire for self-expression.

THEORY:
Floating signifier

IN SUM

An empty or "floating" signifier is a symbol or concept loose enough to mean many things to many people, yet specific enough to galvanize action in a particular direction.

EPIGRAPH

"We are...the face that hides itself to be seen."

–Subcomandante Marcos

"We are the ones we've been waiting for."

–Barack Obama

"We are the 99 percent."

–Occupy Wall Street

ORIGINS

Coined by Claude Lévi-Strauss; elaborated by Roland Barthes, Stuart Hall, Ernesto Laclau, and others.

PRACTITIONERS

The Zapatista Army of National Liberation (EZLN)
Occupy Wall Street

FURTHER INSIGHT

Subcommandante Marcos, Our Word is Our Weapon: Select-ed Writings. (New York, NY: Seven Stories Press, 2002)

CONTRIBUTED BY

Jonathan Matthew Smucker
Andrew Boyd
Dave Oswald Mitchell

The American flag inspires extreme passions . . . but what exactly does it stand for? To different people it means freedom, justice, imperialism and terror — its meaning shifts wildly depending on context and observer. This emptiness, into which observers can pour almost any meaning or desire, is a large part of the symbol's power.

For activists, a well-crafted floating signifier can be a powerful tool for catalyzing broad-based action. Sub-commandante Marcos and the Zapatistas, for example, deployed the concept of the floating signifier mas-terfully. Marcos described the masks the Zapatistas wore as a mirror in which all who struggle for a better world can see themselves. The Zapatistas' iconic black balaclava was not just a ne-cessity for personal secu-rity, but became a powerful statement of unity and uni-versality. "Behind our black mask," they declared, "we are you."[1]

What do Guy Fawkes, the "hope" campaign poster and the 99% have in common? They can be used individually, or together (as in this image), as floating signifiers to unite campaigns and movements. Original design by Shepard Fairey.

In 2008, presidential candi-date Barack Obama also made masterful use of floating signifiers. His poetic rhetoric of "hope" and "change we can believe in" inspired a population weary from eight years of misrule. He became whatever his supporters wanted him to be. Obama explicitly acknowl-edged this phenomenon in the prologue to his campaign screed, *The Audacity of Hope*: "I serve as a blank screen on which people of vastly different political stripes project their own views."

Finding the right floating signifier can make or break a social movement or campaign. When a challenger so-cial movement hits upon such a catalyzing symbol, it's like striking gold. One might even argue that broad so-cial movements are constituted in the act of finding their floating signifier. Hitherto disparate groups suddenly congeal into a powerful aligned force. Momentum is on their side, and things that seemed impossible only yesterday become visible on the horizon.[1]

Indeed, the power of a good floating signifier was perhaps nowhere more evident than in the overnight growth of Occupy Wall Street *see case*. Far eclipsing the literal physical occupation in Zucotti Park, OWS resonated so far and wide because it served as a symbol about standing up to powerful elites on their own doorstep. To many people, the "occupy" in "Occupy Wall Street" essentially stands in for the F word. Millions of Americans were waiting for someone or something to stand up to Wall Street, the big banks, the mega-corporations, and the political elite. Then one day, a relatively small crew of audacious and persistent New Yorkers became that someone or something — became the catalyzing symbol of defiance we'd been waiting for. And by having an open process, and not fixing its meaning early with a ten-point program or the like, the symbol was able to continue "floating."

> *"Finding the right floating signifier can make or break a social movement."*

It's not that the symbol is empty of meaning. Both "occupy" and "the 99%" carry content that strategically frames public thinking and pulls the political discourse in a clear direction. But a degree of ambiguity is absolutely necessary if such a symbol is to catalyze a broad alignment. If the symbol's meaning becomes too particular — too associated with any one current or group within the alignment — it risks losing its powerfully broad appeal. This is why the forces defending the status quo try to *nail it down*. Their hope is that by fixing it to particular meanings, associating it with particular "kinds of people" and to narrower frameworks, it will no longer function as a popular symbol.

Float on, beautiful signifier. Float on.

---

[1] Remarks of the General Command of the EZLN, opening ceremony of the First Intercontinental Meeting For Humanity and Against Neoliberalism.
[2] This article incorporates passages from a blog post by Jonathan Matthew Smucker, "The tactic of occupation and the movement of the 99%."

THEORY:
Hamoq & hamas

IN SUM

Turning anger into action is necessary to move the powers that be, but that anger is most effective when it is disciplined and intelligently focused (hamas). Uncontrolled, stupid anger (hamoq) mostly undermines your own cause.

ORIGINS

Hamza Yusuf, 2000s

PRACTITIONERS

Tutte Bianche
Ruckus Society
Environmental Defense Fund
Egyptian Revolution

FURTHER INSIGHT

This article was adapted from The Guardian, "Raising the Temperature: Corporate Power Will Not Be Given Up Voluntarily–Non-Violent Mass Action Is Needed," July 24, 2001.

CONTRIBUTED BY

George Monbiot

The great Islamic activist Hamza Yusuf Hanson distinguishes between two forms of political action. He defines the Arabic word *hamas* as enthusiastic, but intelligent, anger. *Hamoq* means uncontrolled, stupid anger.

The Malays could not pronounce the Arabic H, and the British acquired the second word from them. On the streets of Genoa during the 2001 G8 summit, while the white overalls movement practiced hamas, seeking to rip down the fences around Genoa's red zone but refusing to return the blows of the police, the black block ran amok.

Sufi Islamic scholar Hamza Yusuf Hanson.

The important thing about hamas is that, whether or not it is popular, it is comprehensible. People can see immediately what you are doing and why you are doing it.

Hamoq, by contrast, leaves its spectators dumbfounded. Hamas may have demolished the McDonald's in Whitehall on May Day 2000, but it would have left the Portuguese restaurant and the souvenir shop beside it intact.

Hamas explains itself. It is a demonstration in both senses of the word: a protest and an exposition of the reasons for that protest. Hamoq, by contrast, seeks no public dialogue. Hamas is radical. Hamoq is reactionary.

If, like some of the black bloc warriors I have spoken to, you cannot accept this distinction, then look at how the police responded to these two very different species of anger.

On Friday, though they were armed to the teeth and greatly outnumbered the looters, the police stood by and watched as the black bloc rampaged around Brignole station, smashing every shopfront and overturning the residents' cars. Then, on Saturday night, on the pretext of looking for the people who had caused the violence, the police raided the schools in which members of the nonviolent Genoa Social

Forum were sleeping, and started beating them to a pulp before they could get out of their sleeping bags. The police, like almost everyone else in Genoa, knew perfectly well that the black bloc were, at the time, camped in a car park miles away.

It is not hard to see which faction Italy's borderline-fascist state felt threatened by, and which faction it could accept and even encourage.

"Hamas explains itself. It is a demonstration in both senses of the word: a protest and an exposition of the reasons for that protest. Hamoq, by contrast, seeks no public dialogue."

If Carlo Giuliani did not die in vain, it was because the Genoa Social Forum had so clearly articulated the case he may have been seeking to make. His hamoq forced a response because other people were practicing hamas.

Hamas instructs us to choose our enemies carefully. Indeed, when actions are clearly focused, then violence toward human beings is far less likely to take place, as it's harder to forget what we are seeking to achieve.

MOST FAMOUS APPLICATION: Tahrir Square and the U.S. civil rights movement.

Related:

TACTICS
Strategic nonviolence p. 32
Mass street action p. 14
Prefigurative intervention web
Direct action p. 68

PRINCIPLES
Escalate strategically p. 174
The real action is your target's reaction web
Don't confuse your stratgy and your tactic p. 186
Put your target in a decision dilemma p. 152
Anger works best when you have the high moral ground web
Maintain nonviolent discipline web
Kill them with kindness p. 114

THEORIES
Revolutionary nonviolence p. 260
Action logic p. 250
Pillars of support p. 244
The tactics of everyday life

THEORY:
Hashtag politics

IN SUM

Your action or campaign doesn't just send a message, it convenes a conversation. By strategically defining the hashtag and curating the ensuing conversation, you can expand and deepen your support base.

PRACTITIONERS

UK Uncut
Adbusters
The Yes Men
The Tea Party

FURTHER INSIGHT

Russia Today, "Censored: #occupy wallstreet," November 18, 2011. http://rt.com/news/ twitter-ows-protest-censorship-653/

CONTRIBUTED BY

Duncan Meisel

Our contemporary media environment encourages absolutely everyone to participate in conversations about current events. This means your action won't just send a message, but through social media like Twitter and Facebook, it will also convene a conversation. With hundreds of millions of people around the world participating in social networks, it's become passé to try to "be the media." Increasingly, activist storytelling strategies are designed to convene the conversation by practicing what one might call *hashtag politics*.

To explain the term: the users of the microblogging socialnetwork Twitter established a convention for organizing ideas, using a label called a hashtag. Twitter hashtags combine a "#" symbol and a keyword that connect posts from different authors (e.g., #noKXL for discussion about the Keystone XL pipeline, #OWS for Occupy Wall Street). Posts that share a hashtag can be viewed together in a single place, facilitating an ongoing public conversation.

Hashtags are powerful tools for convening a conversation around a strategically chosen subject. In many cases, the hashtag is a person, place, or other concrete noun.

Like a frame, a hashtag organizes and amplifies attention. Twitter hashtags are the most literal manifestation of a broader tendency of our highly connected, socially mediated environment toward greater interactivity. Each social media network has its own method for organizing conversations, from YouTube video replies, to Facebook's *friends talking about* feature, to simple blog comments. The tendency is also manifested in cable network talk shows, which are nothing more than debates about current events, now more than ever supplemented with comments harvested from social media.

Typically, the hashtag that organizes a conversation is a highly polarizing proper noun that inspires people to pick a position in a discussion about it. For instance, in 2011, UK Uncut organizers started staging protests at Vodafone stores, organizing under the hashtag #UK Uncut, to reframe the discussion about austerity to focus on corporate tax dodgers rather than public spending.

The role of the organizer practicing hashtag politics is to polarize a discussion effectively, and then curate the conversation to make your side more compelling. The hashtag is a framing device that helps define the values associated with a particular political position. To effectively practice hashtag politics, it's important to strategically and proactively define the hashtag you wish to organize the conversation around. If your hashtag is well chosen, you will draw more people to your side of the debate.

A hashtag could be any number of things. Using narrative power analysis as one guide, you could choose to polarize a discussion around a character in your story — either a sympathetic character or a villain — or perhaps a scene of conflict that locates the problem we must face (like Wall Street, or the tar sands). In an increasingly socially mediated world, to craft a winning frame, it's critical to convene and curate an effective conversation that centers on a strategically chosen subject.

Related:

TACTICS

Media-jacking p. 72
Flash mob p. 46
Human banner p. 56
Distributed action p. 26

PRINCIPLES

Reframe p. 168
Brand or be branded p. 104
Choose your target wisely p. 114
Stay on message p. 178
Do the media's work for them p. 124
Consider your audience p. 118
Think narratively p. 186
Balance art and message p. 100

THEORIES

Narrative power analysis p. 244
The propaganda model p. 256
Memes p. 242
Floating signifier p. 234

CASE STUDIES

Tar sands action p. 376
Wisconsin Capitol Occupation p. 396
Occupy Wall St. web
Camp Casey web

THEORY:
Intellectuals and power

IN SUM

Intellectuals should use their specialized knowledge to expose the machinations of power, utilize their position in institutions to amplify the voices of people struggling against oppression, and work tirelessly to reveal the ways that they themselves are agents of power.

ORIGINS

Michel Foucault (1926-1984)

PRACTITIONERS

Michel Foucault
Arundhati Roy
Antonio Gramsci
Noam Chomsky
Vandana Shiva
James Hansen
Ricardo Dominguez
Suzanne Lacy

CONTRIBUTED BY

Zack Malitz

Michel Foucault was a French historian, social theorist and philosopher whose writings about power have had a profound impact on the humanities and the social sciences. The basic premise of Foucault's work is that power today isnot something that a small number of people possess and exert on everybody else, but rather a force that acts through every institution and relationship in society, so that our very sense of self is a product of its shaping force.

Power, according to Foucault, is diffuse, decentralized and emanates from every corner of society, not just the official seats of government. Resistance, too, is everywhere. Everywhere that people refuse to cooperate with institutional authority or to uncritically accept established patterns of social behavior, every time they attempt to re-organize social relationships according to different principles or rhythms, they resist power.

People can only resist what they can see, however, so power is most effective when it remains invisible. People perceive power dynamics as immutable facts of life rather than as a historical situation that could be re-negotiated. For this reason, intellectuals, engaged in the production of knowledge, particularly social scientific knowledge, are inextricably linked to the operation of power — but also, potentially, to its resistance.

Foucault's basic premise (apparently quite disconcerting to his audience pictured here) is that power is a force that acts through every institution and relationship in society, so that our very sense of self is a product of its shaping force.

Intellectuals, as Foucault uses the term, are people who supply other people with mental frames for understanding, interpreting and inter-acting with the world. Scientists and engineers who work for big tech companies are intellectuals, as are freelance software developers, amateur bloggers, professors and school teachers, doctors, lawyers, advertisers and bureaucrats of every stripe.

For Foucault, the proper role of an intellectual is to expose the machinations of power and the systems of know- ledge that justify, naturalize or conceal the operations of power. People who face the business end of domination and exploitation don't need intellectuals to tell them that they are oppressed — they know perfectly well. What they need from intellectuals is not leadership, but resources, technical knowledge and assistance in navigating dense webs of institutional power.

Intellectuals act as agents of social change when they translate expert discourses such as law or economics into accessible language. Intellectuals, for Foucault, are at their best when, rather than telling us how the world should be, they show us that it could easily have been otherwise and, more importantly, that it need not remain the same.

"People who face the business end of domination and exploitation don't need intellectuals to tell them that they are oppressed — they know perfectly well."

Related:

PRINCIPLES

Take leadership from the most impacted p. 180
Make the invisible visible p. 152
Show, don't tell p. 174
Team up with experts p. 184

THEORY:
Memes

IN SUM

Memes (rhymes with "dreams") are self-repli-cating units of cultural information that spread virally from mind to mind, network to network, generation to generation.

ORIGINS

Term coined by evolutionary biologist Richard Dawkins in his 1976 book The Selfish Gene. First connected to social change strategies by Kalle Lasn of Adbusters magazine.

PRACTITIONERS

Adbusters
smartMeme
Robbie Conal
Women in Black

CONTRIBUTED BY

Patrick Reinsborough
Doyle Canning

How do ideas spread? How does cultural change happen? How does a symbol become a shared point of connection for a movement? Through memes! Understanding how to introduce and spread memes is a crucial skill for anyone who seeks to shift public opinion or cultural practices.

"Although the term may be relatively new, memes have always been used by social movements to spread stories of liberation and change."

A meme is like a piece of cultural DNA that evolves as it passes from person to person. The term is derived from the ancient Greek word *mimema*, meaning, *something imitated*." Playing on the word "gene," Richard Dawkins coined the term as a way of understanding how cultural practices spread. A meme is any unit of culture that has spread beyond its creator — buzz words, catchy melodies, fashion trends, ideas, rituals, iconic images, and so on.

Unscrupulous power-holders have shown considerable skill at designing memes that spread their stories through the culture: *death panels, weapons of mass destruction, the war on terror, union bosses* and *tax relief* are all memes that have become part of the public discourse. A meme is like a viral frame that allows a story to spread, carrying a certain worldview with it.

"A good meme can spread a powerful social change message and a shared meme can serve as an organizing tool."

Although the term may be relatively new, memes have always been used by social movements to spread stories of liberation and change, from *No taxation without representation* to *Black is beautiful* to *living wage*. The incredible spread of Occupy Wall Street's meme *we are the 99%* has shown not only how a good meme can spread a powerful social change message but also how a shared meme can serve as an organizing tool.

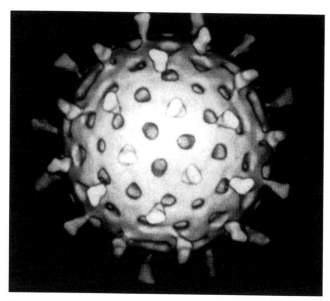

Computer assisted reconstruction of a rotavirus particle.

Effective memes are memorable, easy to spread and "sticky." In other words they linger in our consciousness, connect with our existing thinking and are easily passed on through our communications and actions. A meme that embodies a message and spreads rapidly can dramatically increase the impact of an action or campaign.

IMPORTANT CAVEAT: A potent meme alone will not win a campaign or trigger systemic change. The right meme can, however, help people-powered organizing be exponentially more effective and influential by helping a message, an idea, or a rallying cry go viral.

FURTHER INSIGHT

Adbusters Magazine
www.adbusters.org

Know Your Meme: The Internet Meme Database
http://knowyourmeme.com

Kalle Lasn. Culture Jam: How to Stop America's Suicidal Consumer Binge – And Why We Must. New York, NY: Harper Collin Publishers Inc., 2000.

Andrew Boyd. "Truth is a Virus: Meme Warfare and the Billionaires for Bush (or Gore)." In Cultural Resistance Reader, edited by Stephen Duncombe. Verso, 2002.

Jonah Peretti & Contagious Media Projects
http://contagiousmedia.org

Related:

THEORY:
Narrative power analysis

IN SUM

All power relations have a narrative dimension. Narrative power analysis is a systematic methodology for examining the stories that abet the powers that be in order to better challenge them.

ORIGINS

Developed by the smartMeme Strategy & Training Project

PRACTITIONERS

Abbie Hoffman
Greenpeace
ACT-UP
Mothers of the Plaza de Mayo

CONTRIBUTED BY

Patrick Reinsborough
Doyle Canning

Human beings are literally hardwired for narrative. Stories are the threads of our lives and weave together to form the fabric of human cultures. A story can inform or deceive, enlighten or entertain, or all of the above at once. We live in a world shaped by stories.

A traditional power analysis gives organizers and activists an understanding of the power relations and institutional dynamics among key target decision makers and allies. *Narrative power analysis* provides a framework to extend power analysis into narrative space — the intangible realm of stories, ideas, and assumptions that frame public perception of the situation and the players in question. Narrative helps define what is normal and what is legitimate, as well as the limits of what is politically possible. All power relations have such a narrative component.

> "What makes a story powerful is not necessarily facts, but how the story creates meaning in the hearts and minds of the listeners."

Narrative power analysis is based on the recognition that the currency of story is not *truth*, but *meaning*. That is, what makes a story powerful is not necessarily facts, but how the story creates meaning in the hearts and minds of the listeners. Therefore, the obstacle to convincing people is often not what they *don't* yet know but actually what they already *do* know. In other words, people's existing assumptions and beliefs can act as narrative filters to prevent them from hearing social change messages. A narrative power analysis seeks to unearth the hidden building blocks of these pernicious narratives, so that a narrative of liberation can better challenge them.

For example, in a traditional power analysis, a group of neighbors organizing against a proposed commercial development might determine that the mayor and the city council are the ultimate decision makers and are influenced by the developers' campaign contributions and by the opinions of voters in X precinct. Next, the group can build on that understanding with a *narrative* power analysis of the story and memes the developers are using to promote their agenda. This means carefully examining the developers' narrative on its own terms: how do they frame the problem they say they are solving? Who are their messengers? How do they portray the community? What are their unstated assumptions?

For instance, the developers may have framed their narrative around "bringing jobs to the neighborhood." Armed with clarity about the developer's narrative, the neighborhood group can now craft their own narrative and design a strategy to isolate the developer. Perhaps they decide to organize those same small business owners that the developer claims to represent. Perhaps they organize a jobs fair to show that there are other ways to create employment. If the developers are counting on a "You can't fight City Hall," attitude, organizers make sure that their campaign narrative emphasizes how people power has won victories in the past. In short, the group challenges not just the economic and political forces they face, but also the narratives that back those forces up, that legitimate them and allow those forces to threaten their community.

Current realities are often rooted in oppressive narratives. Our role as change agents is to undermine these narratives and replace them with new stories that help build a fairer, freer world.

> "The currency of story is not truth, but meaning."

FURTHER INSIGHT

smartMeme, "Narrative power analysis worksheet"
http://trb.la/xVOR4S

Doyle Canning and Patrick Reinsborough. Re:Imagining Change: An Introduction to Story-Based Strategy. smartMeme, 2009.
http://trb.la/ABaDFt

Center for Media Justice, "Toolbox"
http://centerformedia-justice.org/toolbox

Related:

THEORY:
Pedagogy of the Oppressed

IN SUM

An approach to education that aims to transform oppressive structures by engaging people who have been marginalized and de-humanized and drawing on what they already know.

EPIGRAPH

"Education either functions as an instrument which is used to facilitate inte-gration of the younger generation into the logic of the present system and bring about confor-mity or it becomes the practice of freedom, the means by which men and women deal critically and creatively with reality and discover how to participate in the trans-formation of their world."

—Paulo Freire, Pedagogy of the Oppressed

ORIGINS

Paulo Freire first outlined his widely influential theory of education in Pedagogy of the Oppressed (1968).

CONTRIBUTED BY

Levana Saxon
Virginia Vitzthum

Over a lifetime of work with revolutionary organizers and educators, radical educator Paulo Freire created an approach to emancipatory education and a lens through which to understand systems of oppression in order to transform them. He flipped mainstream pedagogy on its head by insisting that true knowledge and expertise already exist within people. They need no "deposits" of information (what Freire calls "banking education"), nor do they need leftist propaganda to convince them of their problems. What *is* required to transform the world is dialogue, critical questioning, love for humanity, and *praxis*, the synthesis of critical reflection and action.

In short, *Pedagogy of the Oppressed* is *education as a prac-tice of freedom*, which Freire contrasts with education as a practice of domination *see chart below*.

Banking education *education as the practice of domination*	Problem-posing education *education as a practice of freedom*
Goal is to adapt people to their oppressive conditions.	Goal is to transform struc-tural oppression.
Teacher attempts to control thinking and action of the students, who are treated as passive objects.	Both educator and educand (Freire's word for "student," designed to convey an equitable and reciprocal re-lationship) teach and learn from each other.
Assumes that people are merely in the world, not connected to it or each other.	Assumes the world is an unfolding historical process; everything and everyone is interrelated.
Removes students from their context; teaches reality as unchangeable.	Begins with the educands' history, present and unwrit-ten future.
Treats oppressed people as marginal to a healthy society and in need of incorporation into it.	Seeks to transform society to rehumanize both the op-pressed and their oppressors.
Fundamental to maintaining systems of oppression.	Fundamental to the revolu-tionary process.

THEORY: Pedagogy of the Oppressed

Dialogue and *participatory action research* are two practices heavily influenced by Freire that are now common in the fields of popular education, critical pedagogy, Theater of the Oppressed, and eco-pedagogy. Freire explains that what most people think of as *dialogue* is really just *debate*, a zero-sum game in which people compete to deposit ideas into one another or name the world on behalf of others as an end in itself. In dialogue, on the other hand, both parties work together to name their world by exploring their lived experiences to identify common patterns and generate action.

> "Many progressive movements today are still trapped in the 'banking' approach to education, seeing the public as a passive receptacle of their information."

Participatory action research, meanwhile, is a community-led process in which people determine solutions to their problems by gathering data from their peers, analyzing it, and then taking informed action. It's a model of community organizing that builds the capacity and expertise of those on the front lines.

Unfortunately, many progressive movements today are still trapped in the "banking" approach to education, seeing the public as a passive receptacle of their information. According to Freire, transforming the world requires flipping this model and replacing it with ground-up practices of emancipatory education, organizing and action.

MOST FAMOUS APPLICATION: In the United States, Freire has inspired the movement for "critical pedagogy," which seeks to reconstruct both schools and society. Around the world, Freire's work has been used by many revolutionary movements (such as Amílcar Cabral in Guinea Bissau, the Landless Workers' Movement in Brazil, and the Zapatistas in Mexico), by popular literacy campaigns, and in the World Social Forums.

MIS-APPLICATION: Some educators take the words "popular education" to simply mean taking complex information and dumbing it down or sloganizing it, a misguided approach rooted in the very idea that Pedagogy of the Oppressed opposes: that the educators are experts while the students are empty and passive receptacles awaiting knowledge.

PRACTITIONERS

Augusto Boal
bell hooks
Michael Apple
Henry Giroux
Maocir Gadotti
Carlos Alberto Torres
Richard Kahn
Highlander Center
Colectivo Flatlander
Project South PILA
Practicing Freedom
Data Center

FURTHER INSIGHT

Paulo Freire Institute
www.paulofreireinstitute.org

The Popular Education News
www.popednews.org

Project South: Institute for the Elimination of Poverty and Genocide
www.projectsouth.org

Green Theory and Praxis: The Journal of Ecopedagogy
www.greentheoryandpraxis.org

Related:

TACTICS

PRINCIPLES

THEORIES

CASE STUDIES

THEORY:
Pillars of support

IN SUM

Power stems not just from a ruler's ability to use force, but from the consent and cooperation of the ruled, which can be voluntarily and nonviolently withdrawn by identifying, targeting and undermining the ruler's "pillars of support" — the institutions and organizations that sustain its power.

ORIGINS

Gandhi, Gene Sharp, Robert Helvey

PRACTITIONERS

Otpor
CANVAS

FURTHER INSIGHT

Helvey, Robert. On Strategic Nonviolent Conflict: Thinking about the Fundamentals. Boston: Albert Einstein Institution, 2004.

Sharp, Gene. Waging Nonviolent Struggle: Twentieth-Century Practice and Twenty-First-Century Potential. Boston: Porter Sargent, 2005.

CONTRIBUTED BY

Eric Stoner

Conventional wisdom tells us that power resides in the hands of those at the top, and that when push comes to shove, "power grows out of the barrel of a gun," as Mao famously said. If so, then the only way to defeat a violent opponent is through the use of even greater violence.

At the root of all nonviolent action, however, is a different understanding of the nature of power — one that flips this conventional wisdom on its head. This understanding posits that power is ultimately dependent on the cooperation and obedience of large numbers of people acting through the institutions that constitute the state. These are its pillars of support.

Cesar Chavez leading a supermarket protest to boycott grapes. Mass withdrawal of consent through tactics like this United Farm Workers boycott can be extremely effective at pressuring power-holders.

Some of these pillars, such as the military, the police and the courts, are coercive in nature, compelling obedience through force or the threat thereof, while other pillars, like the media, education system and religious institutions, support the system through their influence over culture and popular opinion. Hence, the power of even the most charismatic or ruthless leader is contingent upon the support of key institutions, themselves vulnerable to popular action or withdrawal of consent from the general population.

Once people decide they no longer accept the status quo and begin to resist, the balance of power shifts. For example, when millions of Americans participated in the successful five-year national boycott of grapes led by Cesar Chavez to improve the pay and workers conditions of exploited farm workers; when tens of thousands of activists effectively shut down the World Trade Organization gathering in Seattle in 1999 by blocking the streets and entrances to the convention center; when thousands of U.S. soldiers refuse to deploy or redeploy to the wars in Iraq or Afghanistan, the power of the powerful is constrained, and can, in extreme situations, disintegrate entirely.

For activists, the key takeaway lesson of the *pillars of support* concept is to identify a ruling target's pillars of support, determine which can be won over and how *see PRINCIPLE: Shift the spectrum of allies*, and then set about working to win over, or at least neutralize, those pillars of support, so that the foundation that sustains the target begins to crumble.

Power ultimately rests not in the grip of presidents, generals and billionaires, but in the hands of millions of ordinary people who keep society running smoothly on a day-to-day basis, and who can shut it down should they so choose. This is the meaning of the slogan people power. One of the principle reasons that so many injustices persist is not that the powerful can simply do whatever they want with impunity, but because most people are ignorant of the power they can wield by withdrawing their consent *see TACTIC: General strike*.

This understanding of power has been repeatedly vindicated in recent decades, as numerous dictators and extremely repressive regimes were toppled by unarmed people with minimal violence but much courage and creativity. These successful nonviolent struggles simply cannot be explained by someone who sees violence as the only, or even the primary, mechanism of power.

> "Power ultimately rests not in the grip of presidents, generals and billionaires, but in the hands of millions of ordinary people who keep society running smoothly on a day-to-day basis, and who can shut it down should they so choose."

Related:

TACTICS
Mass street action p. 68
General strike p. 50
Occupation p. 78

PRINCIPLES
Choose your target wisely p. 114
Maintain nonviolent discipline p. 148
If protest is made illegal, make daily life a protest p. 138
Shift the spectrum of allies p. 172
One no, many yesses web

THEORIES
The propaganda model p. 256
Cultural hegemony p. 222
Points of intervention p. 250

CASE STUDIES
Otpor web
CANVAS web

THEORY:
Points of intervention

IN SUM

A point of intervention
is a physical or
conceptual place within
a system where presure
can be put to disrupt
its smooth functioning
and push for change.

ORIGINS

Patrick Reinsborough & the
smartMeme Strategy &
Training Project

PRACTITIONERS

Social movements
smartMeme
Ruckus Society
Design Studio for Social
Intervention
Operation SalAMI

FURTHER INSIGHT

smartMeme, "Resources"
http://smartmeme.org/
section.php?id=86

Patrick Reinsborough &
Doyle Canning, Re:Imagining
Change (PM Press, 2010).

Doyle Canning & Patrick
Reinsborough,
Story-based Strate-
gies for Action Design.
http://trb.la/w4DWB2

Patrick Reinsborough, "De-
Colonizing the Revolutionary
Imagination," Globalize Libera-
tion, edited by David Solnit (San
Francisco: City Lights Press, 1994).

Destructables, "How to
Hold Up a Bank"
http://destructables.org/node/47

CONTRIBUTED BY

Patrick Reinsborough
Doyle Canning

Points of intervention are specific places in a system where a targeted action can effectively interrupt the functioning of a system and open the way to change. By understanding these different points, organizers can develop a strategy that identifies the best places to intervene in order to have the greatest impact.

Social movements have traditionally intervened by taking direct action at physical points in the systems that shape our lives, but with the spread of effective labor organizing and the increasing power of media, *conceptual* points of intervention have become increasingly important.

"With the increasing power of media, conceptual points of intervention have become increasingly important. "

Truly effective interventions go beyond simply disrupting a system to pose a deeper challenge to its underlying assumptions and basic legitimacy. This holds true whether the intervention targets a physical system like a sweatshop or an ideological system like racism, sexism, or market fundamentalism.

The five types of points of intervention are points of production (for instance, a factory), points of destruction (a logging road), points of consumption (a retail store), points of decision (a corporate headquarters) and points of assumption (a foundational narrative or a place of symbolic importance).

Point of production

Action at the point of production is the foundational insight of the labor movement. Workers organize to target the economic system where it directly affects them, and where that system is most vulnerable. Strikes, picket lines, work slowdowns, and factory take-overs are all point-of-production actions.

Point of destruction

A point of destruction is the place where harm or injustice is actually occurring. It could be the place where resources are being extracted (a strip mine) or the place where the waste from the point of production is dumped (a land-fill). By design, the point of destruction is almost always far from public attention— made invisible by remoteness, oppressive assumptions, or ignorance — and tends to disproportionately impact already marginalized communities. Intervention at the point of destruction can halt an act of destruction in the moment, as well as dramatize the larger conflict.

Intervention at the point of decision. Image by Grassy Narrows Asubpeeschoseewagong Anishinabek.

Point of consumption

The point of consumption is the location of interaction with a product or service that is linked to injustice. Point-of-consumption actions are the traditional arena of consumer boycotts and storefront demonstrations. The point of consumption is often the most visible point of intervention for actions targeting commercial entities. Point-of-consumption actions can also be a good way to get the attention of corporations when lawmakers aren't listening.

Point of decision

The point of decision, where the power to act on a campaign's demands rests,' is often the most self-evident point of intervention, and therefore one of the most frequently targeted. Whether it's a slumlord's office *see CASE: Daycare center sit-in*, a corporate boardroom or state capital, or an international summit meeting *see CASE: Battle in Seattle*, many successful campaigns have used some form of action at the point of decision to put pressure on key decision-makers.

Point of assumption

Assumptions are the building blocks of ideology, the DNA of political belief systems. They operate best when they remain unexamined. If basic assumptions can be exposed as contrary to people's lived experience or core values, entire belief systems can be shifted. Actions that expose and target widely held assumptions *see CASE: Billionaires for Bush and CASE: Barbie Liberation Organization* can therefore be very effective at shifting the discourse around an issue and opening up new political space. Point-of-assumption actions can take many different forms, such as exposing hypocrisy, reframing the issue, amplifying the voices of previously silenced characters in the story, or offering an alternative vision *see TAC-TIC: Prefigurative intervention*.

Turning creative action into real change requires careful strategizing. Identifying different possible points to target is a great first step to help design actions that connect to large campaign and social change goals.

IF YOU DON'T LIKE THE NEWS... GO OUT AND MAKE SOME OF YOUR OWN.

—Wes "Scoop" Nisker

THEORY:
Political identity paradox

IN SUM

Group identity offers embattled activists a cohesive community, but also tends to foster a subculture that can be alienating to the public at large. Balancing these two tendencies is crucial to sustaining the work of an effective group, organization or movement.

ORIGINS

Formulated by Jonathan Matthew Smucker, influenced by Robert Putnam on bonding and bridging, Antonio Gramsci on hegemonic strategy and Frederick D. Miller on encapsulation.

PRACTITIONERS

Students for a Democratic Society (SDS)
Student Nonviolent Coordinating Committee (SNCC)
Situationist International

FURTHER INSIGHT

"The Political Identity Paradox | Evolutionary logic of collective action pt. III"

"Bonding & Bridging | Populism & Hegemony pt.3"

"Activists Caught in the Filter Bubble"

"What Prevents Radicals from Acting Strategically? (pt.2: Encapsulation)"

All articles by Jonathan Matthew Smucker
www.beyondthechoir.org

CONTRIBUTED BY

Jonathan Matthew Smucker

Any serious social movement needs a correspondingly serious group identity that encourages a core of members to contribute an exceptional level of commitment, sacrifice and heroics over the course of prolonged struggle. Strong group identity, however, is a double-edged sword. The stronger the identity and cohesion of the group, the more likely people are to become alienated from other groups, and from society. This is the *political identity paradox.*

The political identity paradox suggests that while political groups require a strong internal identity to foster the commitment needed for effective political struggle, this same cohesion tends to isolate the group. Isolated groups are hard-pressed to achieve political goals.

This is true of all groups, but tends to have particular consequences for a group involved in political struggle, which has not only to foster a strong internal identity: it also has to win allies.

The tendency toward isolation can escalate very quickly in political groups, as oppositional struggle can foster an oppositional psychology. Activists who meet the kind of brutal resistance that the civil cights movement endured, for example, have a tough row to hoe. On the one hand, participants need to turn to each other more than ever for strength and support. They feel a compelling cohesiveness to their group identity in these moments of escalated conflict. On the other hand, they need to keep outwardly oriented, to stay connected to a broad and growing base. This is difficult to do even when leaders are fully oriented to the task, let alone when they are unprepared, which is often the case.

Take, for example, Students for a Democratic Society (the original SDS that fell apart in dramatic fashion in 1969). At the center of the epic implosion of this massive student organization — beneath the rational arguments that leaders were slinging at each other — was the political identity paradox. Key leaders had become encapsulated in their oppositional identity and grown more and more out of touch. They lost the ability and inclination to relate to their broader membership — a *huge* number of students at the moment of the implosion — let alone to broader society. Some of the most committed would-be leaders of that generation came to see more value in holing up with a few comrades to make bombs than in organizing masses of students to take coordinated action.

This is the tendency toward isolation taken to the ex-treme. Dedicated radicals cut themselves off, like lone

Related:

PRINCIPLES

Escalate strategically p. 134
Pace yourself p. 158
No one wants to watch a
drum circle p. 156
Use your radical fringe to
slide the Overton window p. 200
Consider your audience p. 118
Enable, don't command p. 132
Consensus is a means,
not an end p. 116

THEORIES

The social cure p. 264
Cultural hegemony p. 222
Cycles of social movements web

By donning crash helmets, smashing windows and choosing to clash with the police during the Days of Rage protests that were organized in the wake of the 1969 Democratic Convention riot in Chicago, the Weatherman faction of SDS alienated many would-be supporters.

guerrilla fighters in enemy territory. It might have felt glorious, but it was a suicide mission.

The political identity paradox speaks to the need for political groups to develop both strong *bonding* and strong *bridging*. Without strong *within-group* bonding, group members will lack the level of commitment required for serious struggles. But without strong *beyond-group* bridging, the group will become too insular and isolated to forge broad alliances.

Good leaders have to perform an extraordinary balancing act between the conflicting imperatives of building a strong sense of identity *within* their groups and connecting with allies and potential allies *beyond* the group *see PRINCIPLE: Escalate strategically for ideas on how to strike this balance*.

THEORY:
The propaganda model

IN SUM

The propaganda model seeks to explain the behavior of news media operating within a capitalist economy. The model suggests that media outlets will consistently produce news content that aligns with the interests of political and economic elites.

EPIGRAPH

"Any dictator would admire the uniformity and obedience of the U.S. media."

—Noam Chomsky

ORIGINS

Edward S. Herman and Noam Chomsky

PRACTITIONERS

Media Lens
Glenn Greenwald
Jeffrey Klaehn
Andrew Mullen

CONTRIBUTED BY

Simon Enoch

The propaganda model seeks to explain media behavior by examining the institutional pressures that constrain and influence news content within a profit-driven system. In contrast to liberal theories that argue that journalism is ad-versarial to established power, the propaganda model predicts that corporate-owned news media will consistently produce news content that serves the interests of established power.

The mass media often serves as a tool to manufacture consent, operating on unchallenged premises that serve the narrow interests of political and economic elites.

First introduced in 1988 in Edward S. Herman's and Noam Chomsky's *Manufacturing Consent: The Political Economy of the Mass Media*, the propaganda model argues that "the raw material of news" passes through five filters that ultimately shape the news audiences receive. These filters determine what events are deemed newsworthy, how they are covered, where they are placed within the media and how much coverage they receive.

The five filters are as follows:

Concentrated ownership, owner wealth and profit-orientation of the dominant mass-media firms. Corporate media firms share common interests with other sectors of the economy, and therefore have a real stake in maintaining an economic and political climate that is conducive to their profitability. They are unlikely to be critical of economic or political policies that directly benefit them.

Advertising as primary source of income. To remain profitable, most media rely on advertising dollars for the bulk of their revenue. It is therefore against the interests of the news media to produce content that might antagonize advertisers.

Reliance on information provided by "expert" and official sources. Elites have the resources to routinely "facilitate" the news-gathering process by providing photo-ops, news conferences, press releases, think-tank reports and canned news pieces that take advantage of the news media's need for continuous and cheap news content. Business leaders, politicians and government officials are also typically viewed as credible and unbiased sources of information, jettisoning the need for fact-checking or other costly background research. This filter was clearly demonstrated during the run-up to the 2003 Iraq War, when the U.S. news media took official pronouncements at face value, refusing to investigate their veracity or accuracy.

> "We can develop media tactics that take advantage of the contradictions within corporate-sponsored journalism."

Flak as a means of disciplining the media. *Flak* refers to negative commentary to a news story that can work to police and discipline journalists or news organizations that stray too far outside the consensus. Flak includes complaints, lawsuits, petitions or government sanctions.

An external enemy or threat. Manifesting as "anti-communism" during the Cold War period when *Manufacturing Consent* was originally published, this filter still operates, particularly in the post-9/11 political climate. This filter mobilizes the population against a common enemy (terrorism, energy insecurity, Iran…) while demonizing opponents of state policy as insufficiently patriotic or in league with the enemy.

FURTHER INSIGHT

Herman, Edward S. "The Propaganda Model Revisited." Monthly Review (July 1996). http://trb.la/Admvz3

Klaehn, Jeffrey. "A Critical Review and Assessment of Herman and Chomsky's 'Propaganda Model.'" http://trb.la/xbuy8Y

Mullen, Andrew. "The Propaganda Model after 20 Years: Interview with Edward S. Herman and Noam Chomsky." http://trb.la/wTyBjz

Media Lens www.medialens.org

Salon, Glenn Greenwald http://www.salon.com/writer/glenn_greenwald/

Related:

TACTICS
Identity correction p. 60
Electoral guerrilla theater p. 40
Media-jacking p. 72
Détournement/Culture jamming p. 28
Guerrilla newspaper p. 52

PRINCIPLES
Do the media's work for them p. 124
Reframe p. 168
Stay on message p. 178
Know your cultural terrain p. 142
Use your radical fringe to slide the Overton window p. 200
Consider your audienece p. 118

THEORIES
Cultural hegemony p. 222
Intellectuals and power p. 240
Narrative power analysis p. 244
Pillars of support p. 248

CASE STUDIES
Colbert roasts Bush p. 308
New York Times "Special Edition" web

The propaganda model suggests that corporate media ultimately serve to "manufacture consent" for a narrow range of self-serving élitist policy options. It allows us to understand the institutional pressures that ultimately color how activists' causes and actions are covered. By understanding the limits of "objectivity" and the contradictions within corporate-sponsored journalism, we can develop media tactics that take advantage of these contradictions while also bypassing the filters of the corporate press, and directly appealing to the public through alternative forms of media. As Herman himself suggests, "we would like to think that the propaganda model can help activists understand where they might best deploy their efforts to influence mainstream media coverage of issues." [1]

---

[1] Edward S. Herman, "The Propaganda Model Revisited," *Monthly Review* (July 1996).

Banksy says it best.

THEORY:
Revolutionary nonviolence
(or "The marriage of Gandhi and Che")

IN SUM

Revolutionary nonviolence emphasizes unity among radicals and proposes a militant nonviolent praxis based on revolutionary transformation and mass civil resistance.

ORIGINS

Chicago 7 defendant Dave Dellinger; civil rights and feminist icon Barbara Deming in her essay "Revolution and Equilibrium"; the Plowshares movement.

PRACTITIONERS

The Zapatista Army of National Liberation (EZLN) Egypt's April 6 Youth Movement Situationist International Greenpeace Earth First!

CONTRIBUTED BY

Matt Meyer

For activists working for radical change, there is a useful distinction to be made between *Gandhian, strategic* and *revolutionary* nonviolence. Gandhian nonviolence is a combination of constructive, base-building programs and satyagraha, often interpreted in the Global North as a form of spiritual direct action. *Strategic nonviolence see TACTIC* takes a more tactical tack and focuses on the tactics enumerated by Gene Sharp. Meanwhile, as Gandhi himself noted, revolutionary nonviolence suggests that it is better to engage in violence than to do nothing in the face of oppression,[1] and that any popular movement must push beyond mere reformist change that leaves structures of oppression intact, even though this requires active confrontation.

Indian activist Jayaprakash (JP) Narayan made important advances in this line of thinking, calling for "total revolution" in a framework that included anti-authoritarianism, non-orthodox Marxism and self-determination for all peoples. As a campaigner at the time of the Chinese communist revolution, JP's main critique of Mao Zedong's maxim that "power grows out of the barrel of a gun" was the simple observation that those with the most destructive weapons were never the masses of the population, but rather those with the most entrenched power and authority. JP suggested that Mao's Great Proletarian Cultural Revolution (at least in its core intentions) bore striking similarities to *satyagraha*, in that both were meant to combat a profit-motivated mentality, and both sought to disarm the exploiting classes.

The greatest successes of the Chinese and Vietnamese strategy of people's war — which calls for mobile tactics and the creation of clandestine fighting units — often lay in the implementation of popular education programs, the creation of self-sufficient economic units and the formation of mass-based organizations. The military successes were more ambiguous. Even in the heat of battle, some of the leaders of Africa's liberation wars, most notably Amílcar Cabral of Guinea-Bissau, commanded his followers to be "militants, not militarists." The widely repeated South African dictum

THEORY: The propaganda model

that "nonviolence just didn't work" in the ultra-repressive context of the racist apartheid regime has been refuted in post-apartheid society, as even organizers of the armed struggle now openly question the ways in which authoritarian styles grew out of their military structures.

In the U.S. context, mainstream academics are beginning to discuss what many African American activists have quietly understood for decades: that the ideological and tactical differences between Dr. Martin Luther King, Jr. and Minister Malcolm X were never as contradictory or divergent as the popular narrative would have us believe. As each developed and matured, their analyses of the nature of the U.S. state, and the variety of approaches needed to resist it, increasingly converged.

The theory of revolutionary nonviolence demands a nuanced view of struggle, one that does not over-emphasize the dichotomy between nonviolent and armed revolutionaries — that neither celebrates passivity nor fetishizes confrontation. It embraces the contributions of Archbishop Desmond Tutu's *Ubuntu* philosophy: the notion that everyone's liberation is indelibly connected. Advocates of revolutionary nonviolence must include an adherence to strategic nonviolence, but also must maintain dialogues well beyond those who agree with that framework.

FURTHER INSIGHT

Amílcar Cabral, Revolution in Guinea (New York, NY: Monthly Review Press, 1970).

James H. Cone, Martin and Malcolm and America: A Dream or a Nightmare? (Maryknoll, NY: Orbis Books, 1992).

Barbara Deming, "On Revolution and Equilibrium," AJ Muste Memorial Institute Essay Series Pamphlet #2 (New York, NY: AJMMI, 1985), http://www.ajmuste.org/pamphlet.htm#2

Dave Dellinger, Revolutionary Nonviolence (New York, NY: Anchor Doubleday, 1971)

Frantz Fanon, The Wretched of the Earth (New York, NY: Grove Press, 2005)

Jayakapresh Narayan, Toward Total Revolution (Bombay: Brahmanand Popular Prakashan, 1978)

---

[1] "It is better to be violent, if there is violence in our hearts," Gandhi said, "than to put on the cloak of nonviolence to cover impotence." Mahadev Desai, *Day-to-Day with Gandhi (Secretary's Diary) Vol. II* (Rajghat, India: Sarva Seva Sangh Prakashan, 1968), p. 175. See also: Mark Shepard's *Mahatma Gandhi and His Myths: Civil Disobedience, Nonviolence, and Satyagraha in the Real World*, http://www.markshep.com/peace/Myths.html

THEORY:
The shock doctrine

IN SUM

Pro-corporate neoliberals treat crises such as wars, coups, natural disasters and economic downturns as prime opportunities to impose an agenda of privatization, deregulation, and cuts to social services.

EPIGRAPH

"Only a crisis – actual or perceived – produces real change."

—Neoliberal economist Milton Friedman

ORIGINS

Naomi Klein's 2007 book The Shock Doctrine: The Rise of Disaster Capitalism.

CONTRIBUTED BY

Mark Engler, with research assistance by Eric Augenbraun

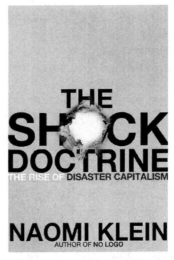

THE SHOCK DOCTRINE

THE RISE OF DISASTER CAPITALISM

NAOMI KLEIN
AUTHOR OF NO LOGO

The shock doctrine is a theory for explaining the way that force, stealth and crisis are used in implementing neoliberal economic policies such as privatization, deregulation and cuts to social services. Author Naomi Klein advanced this theory in her 2007 book, *The Shock Doctrine: The Rise of Disaster Capitalism.*

By way of metaphor, Klein recounts the history of electroshock therapy experiments conducted by Scottish psychiatrist Ewen Cameron for the CIA in the 1950s. Cameron's "shock therapy" sought to return troubled patients to a blank slate on which he could write a new personality. Klein argues that a parallel "shock therapy" process has been used at the macro level to impose neoliberal economic policies in countries around the world.

The shock doctrine posits that in periods of disorientation following wars, coups, natural disasters and economic panics, pro-corporate reformers aggressively push through unpopular "free market" measures. For more than thirty years, Klein writes, followers of Milton Friedman and other market fundamentalists have been "perfecting this very strategy: waiting for a major crisis, then selling off pieces of the state to private players while citizens were still reeling from the shock, then quickly making the 'reforms' permanent."

One of the earliest examples of the shock doctrine is the case of Chile. In 1973, Chile's democratically elected socialist President Salvador Allende was overthrown in a *coup d'état* led by army general Augusto Pinochet, with support from the United States. Amid lingering turmoil created by the coup and tensions caused by the ensuing economic downturn, Milton Friedman suggested that Pinochet implement a "shock program" of sweeping reforms including privatization of state-owned industries, elimination of trade barriers, and cuts to government spending. To implement these policies, the Pinochet regime appointed to important positions several Chilean disciples of Friedman. Additionally, to squash popular movements that opposed these changes, the regime unleashed a notorious program of torture and "disappearances," which ultimately led to the deaths of thousands of dissidents.

Klein contends that various forms of the shock doctrine have since been used to advance hyper-capitalist reforms, for example in former Eastern Bloc countries following the collapse of the Soviet Union and in South Africa after the end of apartheid. More recently, pro-corporate advocates have used the 2004 tsunami in south Asia to privatize public beaches in Sri Lanka and have worked to slash corporate taxes and public education and reshape neighborhoods in the wake of Hurricane Katrina. In each case we witness, in Klein's words, "orchestrated raids on the public sphere in the wake of catastrophic events, combined with the treatment of disasters as exciting market opportunities."

Although the shock doctrine has helped explain neoliberal attempts to take advantage of disaster situations, it cannot entirely account for the success of "free market" ideology, particularly in cases in which the market's powers of seduction play a larger role than the use of brute force. Moreover, we should remember that neoliberals are not the only ones who can capitalize on a crisis. Throughout the world, social movements are learning that political upheaval and economic downturn can create opportunities for popular movements to demand, and construct, a more just and equitable society.

"In periods of disorientation following wars, coups, natural disasters and economic panics, pro-corporate reformers aggressively push through unpopular 'free market' measures."

FURTHER INSIGHT

Naomi Klein, The Shock Doctrine: The rise of disaster capitalism. Metropolitan, 2007. http://www.naomiklein.org/shock-doctrine

Engler, Mark. "Capitalism as Catastrophe: A Review of Naomi Klein's The Shock Doctrine: The Rise of Disaster Capitalism." Dissent (Spring 2008). http://trb.la/zaqHMF

Related:

TACTICS
Mass street action p. 68

THEORIES
Intellectuals and power p. 240
The commons p. 220
Capitalism p. 216
Points of intervention p. 250
Cycles of social movements web

CASE STUDIES
Wisconsin Capitol Occupation p. 396

MOST FAMOUS APPLICATION: Chile under Pinochet (1973-1989); post-Soviet Russia; post-tsunami Sri Lanka; post-Katrina New Orleans.

THEORY:
The social cure

IN SUM

People are more likely to be motivated to action by peer groups than by information or appeals to fear. The *social cure* is a method of harnessing this power of social groups for social change.

ORIGINS

Join the Club: How Peer Pressure Can Transform the World by Tina Rosenberg (Norton, 2011)

PRACTITIONERS

Otpor & CANVAS
loveLife
Students Working Against Tobacco

FURTHER INSIGHT

Waging Nonviolence,
"How Peer Pressure Creates Social Change" (interview with Tina Rosenberg)
http://trb.la/wdxs10

A Force More Powerful, "Review of Bringing Down a Dictator"
http://trb.la/A45VtQ

Nonviolent Struggle:
50 Crucial Points
http://trb.la/xnaBVh

CANVAS Core Curriculum: A Guide to Effective Nonviolent Struggle
http://trb.la/ysF0oX

CONTRIBUTED BY

Bryan Farrell

"*Their language smelled like death. And we won because we loved life more.*"

People are rarely swayed by infor-mation alone. If they were, the tobacco industry would have collapsed when the first Surgeon General's report on smoking came out in 1964, and fossil fuels would have been phased out in 1989, when the threat of global warming reached public consciousness.

So what *does* move us? According to Tina Rosenberg, author of *Join the Club*, it's peer pressure. You know, the same thing that compels teenagers to engage in all sorts of risky behavior that drives parents crazy. But there's more to it than that.

Peer pressure is also responsible for some astounding instances of positive social change, from lowering HIV rates among South African youths (loveLife) to reducing the number of teen smokers in the United States (Students Working Against Tobacco). Both advances, Rosenberg explains, came about through targeted efforts by local NGOs to activate peer networks for positive social change.

It's a point that many are willing to accept in theory. Few, though, would believe that something so simple could topple a brutal dictator. But that's precisely what the Serbian student movement Otpor was able to achieve when it transformed a previously passive and fatalistic citizenry into the nonviolent army that overthrew Slobodan Milošević , the "Butcher of the Balkans," in 2000.

As Rosenberg explains in her book, "Traditional democracy activists create political parties. Otpor created a party. People joined the movement for the same reasons they go to the hot bar of the moment." By branding itself with hip slogans, black t-shirts, absurd humor, rock music and an iconic clenched-fist graphic, the eleven founders of Otpor — all university students at the time — reinvented resistance in Serbia by making it a desirable club to join.

They even managed to create a cult around getting arrested. For teenage boys, it was a way to be rebellious and win the respect of girls at the same time.

Eventually, getting arrested became a competition and kids would compete to rack up the most busts. As one Otpor member noted, "When someone asks me who took down Milošević , I say, 'High school kids.' "

By appealing to people's need, not just for information but for identification, Otpor showed that the social cure can be used in even the most difficult and repressive of situations as a force for rallying citizen power. Put more simply, in the words of Otpor founder Srdja Popovic, "Their language smelled like death. And we won because we loved life more."

Related:

TACTICS
Flash mob p. 46
Mass street action p. 68
Carnival-protest web

PRINCIPLES
Think narratively p. 186
Lead with sympathet-
ic characters p. 146
Create heroes, not victims web
Make new folks welcome p. 150
If protest is made illegal, make
daily life a protest p. 138
Know your cultural terrain p. 142

THEORIES
Political identity paradox p. 254
Cultural hegemony p. 222
The tactics of everyday life p. 268
Anti-oppression p. 212

"The student movement Otpor was able to galvanize a movement against Serbian president Milošovic through hip slogans and a cult of cool around getting arrested."

THEORY:
Society of the spectacle

IN SUM

Modern capitalism upholds social control through the *spectacle*, the use of mass communications to turn us into consumers and passive spectators of our own lives, history and power.

EPIGRAPH

"Politics is that dimension of social life in which things become true if enough people believe them."

–David Graeber

ORIGINS

French philosopher and activist Guy Debord

PRACTITIONERS

Adbusters
Abbie Hoffman
Situationist International

FURTHER INSIGHT

Guy Debord, The Society of the Spectacle. Paris: Bu-chet-Castel, 1967.
http://trb.la/yEMEpq

CONTRIBUTED BY

Dave Oswald Mitchell

Gil Scott Heron's famous words, embodied here at Occupy Los Angeles, October 2011, capture the disconnect between the spectacle and the political reality.

"In societies dominated by modern conditions of production, life is presented as an immense accumulation of *spectacles*," Guy Debord's *Society of the Spectacle* (1967) begins. "Everything that was directly lived has receded into a representation." The political consequence of this separation from felt experience is key to understanding both how we experience the world and how we can change it.

For example, consider how people who witness a catastrophic event often say the experience was "like a movie." Similarly, as activists we are often more concerned with the media attention our actions generate than with their end result. What we feel, what we believe, how we express desire, what we believe is possible — all are filtered through, and constrained by, the media we consume and produce. This is the *society of the spectacle* that Debord, a leading figure in the French Situationist movement, described and decried.

> "As activists we are often more concerned with the media attention our actions generate than with their end result."

Marx famously argued that under capitalism, the commodity becomes "fetishized" and reduced to its exchange value. Debord applied Marx's ideas to mass communication, showing how capitalism has penetrated not just what we produce and consume, but how we communicate. The spectacle — as manifested in mass entertainment, news, and advertising — alienates us from ourselves and our desires in order to facilitate the accumulation of capital.

Increasingly, the spectacle serves as capitalism's primary mechanism of social control. This is control by seduction and distraction, not force — but no less powerful and insidious for that fact. Debord argued that our lives have been degraded, first from *being* into *having*, then from *having* into merely *appearing*. (Think how much of our day-to-day "activist" behavior is concerned simply with maintaining our self-image as activists: too often, we don't strike, we strike poses.)

Seeking to free us from the power of the spectacle in order to mount a credible challenge to capitalism, the Situationists introduced the tactic of *détournement*: an attempt to turn the powers of the spectacle against itself *see TACTIC: Détournement/Culture jamming*.

Related:

TACTICS
Détournement/Culture jamming p. 32
Identity Correction p. 14

PRINCIPLES
Brand of be branded p. 174
Know your cultural terrain web
Do the media's work for them p. 186
No one wants to watch a drum circle p. 152
Make your actions both concrete and communicative p. 154

THEORIES
Commodity fetishism p. 236
Marxism p. 250
Ethical spectacle p. 244
The propaganda model p. 244

THEORY:
The tactics of everyday life

IN SUM

Tactics are not
a subset of strategy,
but a democratic
response to it.

ORIGINS

Michel de Certeau, The Practice
of Everyday Life (1984).

PRACTITIONERS

FURTHER INSIGHT

Stan Goff, "Strategy and
tactics," Feral Scholar, September 29, 2010, Fantasy.
http://trb.la/zXPvRC

Michel de Certeau, The Practice
of Everyday Life. (University
of California Press, 2002).

CONTRIBUTED BY

Stan Goff

Strategy and *tactics*, as the concepts are commonly under-stood, have their roots in military theory. The French Jesuit scholar Michel de Certeau, however, drew a distinction between the two terms that leaps over some of the martial history of these ideas.

In military parlance, *strategy* is the identification of key *campaigns* that are necessary to accomplish the main *objective* — in most cases, winning the war. *Operations* are the level of planning that determines key battles necessary to win campaigns. *Tactics* are those techniques that are required to win battles. So the *tactic* is subordinate to the *campaign*, which is subordinate to the *strategy*. Those who adapt the model inherit the hierarchy in which it is based.

De Certeau took a different approach, positing tactics not as *subordinate* to strategy but as opposed to it. He wrote about people in their everyday lives, not in conditions of extremity and conflict, in a book fittingly entitled *The Practice of Everyday Life* (1984).

The setting of strategy, notes de Certeau, is always the purview of power. Strategy presumes control. Strategy is self-segregating, in the same way administration and management are self-segregating, setting itself up as a barricaded insider. The strategic leaders become the Subject; the led and the enemy become the Objects. Strategy presumes an in-group that carries out campaigns.

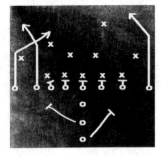

The tactics in this football play are analogous to a tactical plan for a political action or campaign. When grassroots "players" can adapt and adjust in line with a shared general goal, the resulting tactical agility gives us a one-up on the less responsive strategies of institutions.

In contrast to strategy, de Certeau characterizes tactics as the purview of the non-powerful. He understands tactics not as a subset of strategy, but as an adaptation to the environment, which has been created by the strategies of the powerful. The city planning commission may determine what streets there will be, but the local cabbie will figure out how best to navigate the lived reality of those streets. This art of making-do is what de

Certeau calls *bricolage*, a process that often implies cooperation as much as competition.

Strategy, de Certeau recognizes, makes two presumptions: *control* and an *in-group*. The inherent contradiction of strategy is that the control is never perfect and the situation upon which the strategy was constructed is always changing, which constantly makes aspects of the strategy obsolescent. The self-segregation of in-groups magnifies these myopic aspects of strategy, because the walls that keep others out also obscure their vision. Strategy becomes dangerously self-referential.

Tactics, on the other hand, are action in a constant state of reassessment and correction, based directly on observations of the actual environment. Tactical theorist John Boyd rather schematically diagrammed this process as an "OODA-loop," in which people *observe* their surroundings (O), *orient* on the most impor-

> "Tactical agility is often what sets popular uprisings apart from the institutions they seek to overthrow: they have strategy, we have tactics."

tant developments in the environment (O), decide on an immediate course of *action* (D), take that *action* (A), then revert immediately to observation of the environment to see how their last action might have changed it (orienting again, deciding again, acting again, in a perpetual adaptive loop). There is no presumption of how things will turn out, as there is in strategy. Instead, there is readiness to take advantage of unpredictable changes; this is called tactical agility, and it is often what sets popular uprisings apart from the institutions they seek to overthrow: they have strategy, we have tactics.

Strategies are undermined by unpredictability. Tactics make an ally of unpredictability.

THEORY:
Temporary autonomous zone

IN SUM

An alternative to traditional models of revolution, the T.A.Z is an uprising that creates free, ephemeral enclaves of autonomy in the here-and-now.

EPIGRAPH

"Are we who live in the present doomed never to experience autonomy, never to stand for one moment on a bit of land ruled only by freedom?"

–Hakim Bey

ORIGINS

Hakim Bey (aka Peter Lamborn Wilson)

PRACTITIONERS

The Diggers (1960s)
Improv Everywhere
The (new) Diggers

FURTHER INSIGHT

Hakim Bey, T.A.Z.: The Temporary Autonomous Zone, Ontological Anarchy, Poetic Terrorism (New York, NY: Autonomedia, 1991) Full text of book available for download here: http://hermetic.com/ bey/taz_cont.html

Video: "Improv Everywhere: Say Something Nice" http://youtu.be/RwEYYI-AGWs

CONTRIBUTED BY

John Jordan

Coined in 1990 by poet, anarcho-immediatist and Sufi scholar Hakim Bey, the term *temporary autonomous zone* (T.A.Z.) seeks to preserve the creativity, energy and enthusiasm of autonomous uprisings without replicating the inevitable betrayal and violence that has been the reaction to most revolutions throughout history. The answer, according to Bey, lies in refusing to wait for a revolutionary moment, and instead create spaces of freedom in the immediate present whilst avoiding direct confrontation with the state.

A T.A.Z. is a liberated area "of land, time or imagination" where one can be *for* something, not just *against*, and where new ways of being human together can be explored and experimented with. Locating itself in the cracks and fault lines in the global grid of control and alienation, a T.A.Z. is an eruption of free culture where life is experienced at maximum intensity. It should feel like an exceptional party where for a brief moment our desires are made manifest and we all become the creators of the art of everyday life.

> *...an eruption of free culture where life is experienced at maximum intensity."*

The key, suggests Bey, is to remain mobile, relying on stealth and the ability to melt into the darkness at a moment's notice. Before the T.A.Z is spotted and recognized by the state, whichwill inevitably seek to crush it, it dissolves and moves on, reappearing in unexpected places to celebrate once again the wonders of conviviality and life outside the law. It might last hours, days, years even, depending on how quickly it is noticed by authorities.

Bey claims that T.A.Z.s have always existed. He sees their ancestry in the numerous liberated zones that pepper history: from the secret "state" of the medieval Persian Assassins to the eighteenth century pirate utopias — islands where buccaneers, escaped slaves and convicts lived outside the law, sharing goods and property. From the radical communes of Paris and Munich to the dissatisfied colonizers of North America who deserted their enclave to join Native American communities, leaving the infamous sign behind them, "Gone to Croatan."

THEORY: Temporary autonomous zone

Burning Man – the quintessential Temporary Autonomous Zone. Photo by Dave Oswald Mitchell.

Bey maintains, however, that the T.A.Z. cannot be defined; it is simply a "suggestion…a poetic fancy," not "political dogma," and that "if the phrase became current it would be understood without difficulty…understood in action." Twenty years on, the notion of T.A.Z has inspired movements and actions across the world, from the creative play of Reclaim the Streets parties *see CASE* to the autonomy of protest encampments, the Anonymous hacker movement to the Burning Man festival and secret rainbow gatherings.

When Bey first came up with the concept, the web was in its infancy, yet he already imagined a future world where a multitude of autonomous zones could be linked by dispersed networks of communication freed from political control. The web would not be an end in itself, he wrote, but a weapon without which autonomous zones would perish. At the time, he dismissed his own theory as pure speculative science fiction, but the future always arrives faster than one can imagine.

MOST FAMOUS APPLICATION: If we wrote it down here the authorities would soon learn about it and it would have to dissolve. Keep your senses open; the nearest T.A.Z. is nearer than you think.

IMPORTANT BUT LITTLE-KNOWN APPLICATION: The 1920–24 free state of Fiume (now the city of Rijeka, Croatia), whose constitution was written by poets and anarchists.

THEORY:
Theater of the Oppressed

IN SUM

Theater of the Oppressed provides tools for people to explore collective struggles, analyze their history and present circumstances, and then experiment with inventing a new future together through theater.

EPIGRAPH

"The theater itself is not revolutionary: it is a rehearsal for the revolution."

—Augusto Boal

ORIGINS

Drawing inspiration from Freire, Brecht, and Stanislavski, Augusto Boal developed the Theater of the Oppressed in practice throughout his career, starting in the '50s in Brazil and later in Argentina, Peru, Ecuador and France while in exile from the military dictatorship.

PRACTITIONERS

Julian Boal
Brent Blair
Cheryl Harrison
Mark Weinburg
Mark Weinblatt
Rosa Gonzales
Melina Bobadilla
Jiwon Chung
Practicing Freedom
Los Angeles Poverty Department

CONTRIBUTED BY

Levana Saxon

Augusto Boal, 1975. (Cedoc/Funarte)

Theater of the Oppressed is an arsenal of theater techniques and games that seeks to motivate people, restore true dialogue, and create space for participants to rehearse taking action. It begins with the idea that everyone has the capacity to act in the "theater" of their own lives; everybody is at once an actor and a spectator. We are "spect-actors!" — a term which Boal coined.

Boal points out that when we are simply passive audience members, we transfer our desire to take action onto the characters we identify with, and then find that desire satiated as the conflict resolves itself on stage, in films or in the news. Catharsis substitutes for action.

Boal, following Brecht, calls this *bourgeois theater*, which functions to reproduce elite visions of the world and pacify spectators. He says bourgeois theater is "finished" theater; the bourgeoisie already know what the world is like and so simply present it onstage.

In contrast to bourgeois theater, "the people" do not yet know what their world will be like Their "authentic" theater is therefore unfinished, and can provide space to rehearse different possible outcomes. As Boal says: "One knows how these experiments will begin but not how they will end, because the spectator is freed from his chains, finally acts, and becomes a protagonist."[1]

Theater of the Oppressed encompasses many forms, including the following:

Image theater see TACTIC invites spect-actors to form a tableau of frozen poses to capture a moment in time dramatizing an oppressive situation. The image then becomes a source of critical reflection, facilitated by various kinds of interventions: spect-actors may be asked to depict an ideal image of liberation from that oppression, and then a sequence of transition images required to reach it, or to reshape an image to show different perspectives.

Forum theater see TACTIC is a short play or scene that dramatizes a situation, with a terribly oppressive ending that spect-actors cannot be satisfied with. After an initial performance, it is shown again, however this time the spectators become spect-actors and can at any point yell "freeze" and step on stage to replace the protagonist(s) and take the situation in different directions. Theater thus becomes rehearsal for real-world action.

Legislative theater takes forum theater to the government and asks spect-actors to not only attempt interventions on stage, but to write down the successful interventions into suggestions for legislation and hand them in to the elected officials in the room.

Invisible theater see TACTIC is a play that masquerades as reality, performed in a public space. The objective is to unsettle passive social relations and spark critical dialogue among the spect-actors, who never learn that they are part of a play. Augusto Boal said of one invisible theater intervention, "The actor became the spectator of the spectator who had become an actor, so the fiction and reality were overlapping."[2]

A final point that perhaps can't be stated enough: our movements need to be more strategic and community-led! Theater of the Oppressed offers arts-based strategy-developing exercises that foster collaboration and community-led engagement. What could be more awesome?

---

[1] Augusto Boal, *Theater of the Oppressed.* London: Pluto Press, 2000.
[2] Interview, *Democracy Now!* June 3, 2005.

FURTHER INSIGHT

International theater of the Oppressed Organization
www.theateroftheoppressed.org

Pedagogy and theater of the Oppressed
www.ptoweb.org

Boal, Augusto. Games for Actors and Non-Actors (London: Routledge, 1992).

Boal, Augusto. Theater of the Oppressed (New York: Theater Communications Group, 1993).

Friedlandm, Ellie, and Toby Emert, eds. Come Closer: Critical Perspectives on Theater of the Oppressed (New York: Peter Lang Publishing, 2011).

Related:

THEORY:
Write your own THEORY

IN SUM   *What's the big idea?*

EPIGRAPH

ORIGINS

PRACTITIONERS

FURTHER INSIGHT

CONTRIBUTED BY

Related:

TACTICS

MOST FAMOUS APPLICATION:

PRINCIPLES

MOST INFAMOUS APPLICATION:

CASES

· ·

The modular format of *Beautiful Trouble* allows the collection to expand endlessly to reflect new tactical breakthroughs, underrepresented areas of struggle and overlooked pearls of wisdom.

Become part of *Beautiful Trouble*. Use this template to write up your own creative-activism insights. Submit your own module for publication on the *Beautiful Trouble* website here: http://beautifultrouble.org.

CASE STUDIES

WHERE THE RUBBER MEETS THE ROAD

Capsule stories of successful creative actions, useful for illustrating how tactics, principles and theories can be successfully applied.

"Success means going from one failure to the next with no loss of enthusiasm."

—*Winston Churchill*

Revolutionaries practice without safety nets. Our laboratory is the world around us — the streets, the Internet, the airwaves, our own hearts, as well as the hearts and minds of our fellow citizens. We experiment, we fail, we change things up, we try again, maybe this time a little less disastrously, a little more beautifully — until we win. Always we learn. Case studies are where we learn what we've learned.

CASE STUDY:
99% bat signal

WHEN

November 17, 2011

WHERE

New York City

EPIGRAPH

"99% / MIC CHECK! /
LOOK AROUND / YOU
ARE A PART / OF A
GLOBAL UPRISING / WE
ARE A CRY / FROM THE
HEART / OF THE WORLD
/ WE ARE UNSTOPPA-
BLE / ANOTHER WORLD
IS POSSIBLE / HAPPY
BIRTHDAY / #OCCUPY
MOVEMENT / OCCUPY
WALL STREET / list of
cities, states and coun-
tries / OCCUPY EARTH /
WE ARE WINNING / IT IS
THE BEGINNING OF THE
BEGINNING / DO NOT
BE AFRAID / LOVE."

–Projection Text, Mark Read

PRACTITIONERS

Occupy Wall Street

CONTRIBUTED BY

Mark Read

A coalition of labor unions had called for a national day of action on November 17 to push back against austerity and demand infrastructure improvements and jobs. Actions were planned for seventeen bridges in seventeen cities. In New York City, a permit was obtained for a large rally in the Wall Street area, with a march over the Brooklyn Bridge to follow. November 17 also happened to be the two-month birthday celebration for #Occupy Wall Street. People wanted something spectacular to happen, something beautiful.

The November 17 action coordination working group planned to purchase ten thousand small LED lights to hand out to the crowd as they encircled City Hall and streamed over the pedestrian walkway of the bridge, creating a river of light. The metaphor of light was important, as we were celebrating Occupy Wall Street's commitment to shining a light on a corrupt and broken political and economic system. But we needed something bigger. We started talking about projections, and Hero (yes, his name is Hero) suggested a "bat signal." A big circle with "99%" in the middle. It seemed too perfect, so we got to work making that a reality.

Within spitting distance of the Brooklyn Bridge pedestrian walkway stands a thirty-two-story gray concrete slab of a building commonly known as "the Verizon building." A flat windowless expanse approximately seventy-five feet in width extends up the face, with low ambient light. City housing projects fifteen stories tall sit in its shadow. We had our projection screen. We had secured the loan of a powerful projector. We had ideas for content.

What we needed was a projection room.

We needed to project from an apartment in one of those buildings. I put up signs offering $250 for the use of an apartment for an art and film project. There were few calls at first, but eventually a call came in from one Denise Vega — a single mother of two, born and raised in those housing projects and working to keep her family fed. She had the window we needed, and more importantly a supportive and enthusiastic attitude. In the end she refused to take any money for the use of her home, declaring, "I can't charge you money, this is for the people."

In the days before the action we began to realize that we would be able to project not just the 99% symbol, but also words large enough and bright enough for people to read from the bridge. This opened up many possibilities. What if we could get the crowd to interact with the projections? We would need to project chants in the proper cadence, to get people started. After that, we imagined that we might be able to get people to use the "human microphone" to "mic check" a brief statement.

Amazingly, all went as planned, and the action was even more successful that we could have hoped for. The 20,000-strong crowd on the bridge went crazy. We could hear them shouting, cheering, and, yes, "mic-checking" from the window of Denise's bedroom. We were interacting with the crowd, mixing the projections on the fly in response to the crowd's reactions. It was the galvanizing, unifying moment of joy and celebration that we'd hoped to provide this burgeoning global movement for a more just and democratic world.

"It seemed too perfect, so we got to work making that a reality."

FURTHER INSIGHT

Video: "#Occupy Bat Signal for the 99%"
http://trb.la/A3cFFM

Xeni Jardin, "Interview with creator of Occupy Wall Street 'bat-signal' projections during Brooklyn Bridge #N17 march," Boing Boing, Nov. 17, http://trb.la/A1AydA

InterOccupy, "Occupy 'Bat Signal' Source Files"
http://interoccupy.org/occupy-bat-signal/

Related:

THEORIES

Ethical spectacle p. 230
The tactics of everyday life p. 268
Floating signifier p. 234
Points of intervention p. 250
Expressive & instrumental actions p. 232

WHY IT WORKED

The action worked because all the elements fell into place: the technology was powerful, the weather cooperated and the scale suited the occasion. Most vitally, though, the action was embedded within a movement and played on elements from movement culture — both in style and in substance. The "human mic" and "mic check" were tropes that were immediately grasped and appreciated. Most of the language came from chants or well known slogans. The "bat signal" itself required no translation. It's a part of our cultural commons, part of the "spectacular vernacular" of global pop culture, a symbol we all understand to be a call for aid and an outlaw call to arms — after all, isn't that precisely what the Occupy movement is?

Of course Batman is actually a quasi-sociopathic millionaire vigilante. A one-percenter, you might say. But by filling that symbol — by occupying it — with our own content — "99%" — we appropriated it for the rest of us. And in this reconfiguration, we were no longer waiting

KEY TACTIC
used

OTHER TACTICS USED:
Détournement/Culture
jamming p. 28
Mass street action p. 68
Prefigurative intervention p. 82
Direct action p. 32

for some superhero, be it a masked vigilante or the first black president, to swoop in and save the day. Rather, *we* were the response to our own call for aid.

GUERRILLA PROJECTION: Guerrilla projection is a visually powerful and often very beautiful method for delivering a political message. It can be used as an action in and of itself, or to enhance existing actions; to rebrand an existing structure, or to frame an action. It's versatile, carries little risk, can be done inexpensively, and only requires surprisingly less technical savvy than you might think. The success or failure of the tactic will always depend on the quality of the content: make sure that you balance the desire to do something artful with the need for clarity.

KEY PRINCIPLES
at work

OTHER PRINCIPLES AT WORK:
Balance art and message p. 100
No one wants to watch
a drum circle p. 156
Stay on message p. 178
Brand or be branded p. 104
Use the Jedi mind trick p. 194
Consider your audience p. 118
Escalate strategically p. 134
Do the media's work for them p. 124
Be both expressive and
instrumental web
Find common ground p. 170

KNOW THE CULTURAL TERRAIN: Superhero mythology is arguably one of the most prefigurative aspects of spectacular culture, and quite ripe for re-appropriation. The heroes in masks and on the screen are not just corporate cash cows; they also frequently represent values subversive to the very corporations that profit from them. Exploit these contradictions.

HOPE IS A MUSCLE: The messaging that we projected was unflaggingly inspirational and positive ("we are unstoppable," etc.). We actually had some text in the can ("Banks got bailed out, we got sold out") that we didn't end up using because it had the wrong tone. As the evening played out, it was evident that we were creating a moment of pure, celebratory optimism. It was heady and powerful.

USE THE POWER OF RITUAL: The human microphone had become the central ritual of the Occupy movement. It is itself a repeatedly performed act of solidarity and unity. With the right message and setting, it can have a powerful emotional effect on crowds. By working it into our light projection, we hit on a new incarnation of this powerful ritual.

On November 17, 2011, the 99% briefly left their imprint on the New York skyline and the world's political imagination. Photo by Brandon Neubauer.

CASE STUDY:
The Barbie Liberation Organization

WHEN

December 25, 1993

WHERE

U.S.A.

PRACTITIONERS

Barbie Liberation Organization

FURTHER INSIGHT

YouTube clip of the BLO action
http://trb.la/xaKnQw

Video Data Bank clip
of the BLO action
http://trb.la/zztsYp

David Firestone, "While Barbie
Talks Tough, G.I. Joe Goes Shopping," NY Times, Dec. 31, 1993.
http://trb.la/AyduO2

CONTRIBUTED BY

Mike Bonanno

On Christmas day in 1993, kids were finding more than they bargained for under their trees: Mattel's new talking Barbie dolls growled "Dead men tell no lies," while Hasbro's macho GI Joe's chirped "I love to shop with you."

Enter the Barbie Liberation Organization, a self-described group of "veterans against war toys" and "concerned parents" who claimed responsibility for switching the voice boxes on hundreds of the toys nationwide. A full week of news and talk radio ensued, sparking widespread discussion about gender stereotypes.

The action was a response to a very dumb PR move Mattel had made nearly a year earlier, when it released a new talking Barbie that said "Math is hard." Outraged feminists thrashed them in the press, and behind closed doors a small group of folks began plotting revenge. What else could Barbie say? One participant in the informal brainstorm sessions — an octogenarian Hungarian holocaust survivor who went by the nickname "Gyongi" — didn't care about Barbie: the problem for her was GI Joe. A quick trip to the toy store confirmed that GI Joe talked too, and a plot was hatched: all that was required to make these toys into gender-bending Trojan horses was a voice-box switcheroo. Armed with soldering irons, screwdrivers, epoxy and sweat, the Barbie Liberation Organization went to work.

The next step was to recruit other BLO members, who purchased the toys in different cities, and sent them in for surgery. Each toy was carefully removed from its packaging, "fixed," and returned. "Shop droppers" then put them right back on the store shelves they came from (without getting a refund, so nobody could call it stealing).

> "The surreptitious introduction of poetically enhanced products to store shelves is a sure-fire way of delivering subversive content to even the peskiest demographic."

Challenging the gender norms that they were designed to uphold.

Related:

THEORIES
Commodity Fetishism p. 218
Society of the Spectacle p. 266

But this wasn't to be a simple spectacle, it was to be a *media* spectacle, so an elaborate press plan was hatched. Along with each repackaged toy they included a doctored instruction sheet, complete with the numbers of local and national press, and a voicemail number for the BLO. The idea was that kids would open their toys, parents would call the numbers, and the media would cover it.

The day before Christmas, the BLO sent out a press release claiming responsibility for the action. The hope was that on Christmas day, when the media started getting phone calls from real people who'd gotten the toys, they'd put two and two together.

In case even that didn't do the trick, the BLO built additional layers of redundancy into the media plan. They recruited two kids — one in San Diego, California, and one in Albany, New York — who were willing to put on a little show for the news cameras, thereby "proving" that the action was really happening. Lastly, they kept a stash of extra dolls on hand and stood ready to scramble to the toy stores nearest to any media who called their voicemail. When the media called, the BLO located the nearest store to the caller, got there as fast as they could, and put an altered toy on the shelf. On at least one occasion, BLO members were still in the store when the journalist arrived. They watched him find the toy, test it, and triumphantly purchase it — proof-positive of the power and reach of the Barbie Liberation Organization.

The stunt worked because the altered toys were funny, surprising and revealing. There were cute kids involved, which helped make it more media-genic, as did the name recognition of two American icons: Barbie and GI Joe. The event made a huge media splash and had everyone talking about what was wrong with teaching these stereotypes to our kids.

WHY IT WORKED

WHAT DIDN'T WORK

The BLO didn't directly translate attention into action: it was an isolated prank without direct links to an on-going campaign. This kind of hit-and-run tactic has an impact, but it arguably could have been more effective with the right campaign tie-ins.

. . . .

KEY TACTIC
used

OTHER TACTICS USED:

Détournement/Culture jamming p. 28

Identity correction p. 60

Prefigurative intervention p. 82

Distributed action p. 32

SHOP-DROPPING: The surreptitious introduction of po-etically enhanced products to store shelves is a sure-fire way of delivering subversive content to even the peskiest demographic. In the BLO's case, the shop-dropping is just the foundation upon which a major media spectacle was built.

KEY PRINCIPLES
at work

OTHER PRINCIPLES AT WORK:

Make the invisible visible p. 152

Reframe p. 168

Show, don't tell p. 174

Use the materials at hand web

Consider your audience p. 118

Play to the audience that isn't there p. 160

Seek common ground p. 120

DO THE MEDIA'S WORK FOR THEM: Do the media's work for them. The BLO's success relied not just on a "sticky" prank, but on thoughtfully crafted press releases, vid-eo news releases, and having people ready to be inter-viewed. It was an artful marriage of creative storytelling and do-it-yourself publicity.

MAKE YOUR OWN MYTHS: Make your own myths: Ex-aggerate. Don't be afraid to make it sound bigger than it is. There were only about fifty dolls that made it to store shelves in three states: but the BLO said 300 in fifty states. No problem. The next Christmas, when the media came knocking, the BLO had done "thousands more" with no effort whatsoever.

MAKE IT FUNNY: A video news release showing Barbie dolls with soldering irons operating on GI Joes had TV anchors giggling like kids in between segments. With smiles like that, even conservative commentators were embracing the content.

IF
YOU
WANT
TO
TELL
PEOPLE
THE
TRUTH,
MAKE
THEM
LAUGH,
OTHERWISE
THEY'LL
KILL
YOU
:)

—*Oscar Wilde*

CASE STUDY:
Battle in Seattle

WHEN

November 30, 1999

WHERE

Seattle

PRACTITIONERS

Ruckus Society
Direct Action Network
Art & Revolution
Rainforest Action Network
AFL-CIO
Alliance of Community Trainers

FURTHER INSIGHT

This is What Democracy
Looks Like (documentary film).
Big Noise Films, 2000.
http://trb.la/Asw04E

Elizabeth Martinez, "Where was
the color in Seattle? Looking
for reasons why the Great
Battle was so white." Colorlines
Magazine. March 20, 2000.

CONTRIBUTED BY

John Sellers

Hundreds of feet in the air, four climbers from Rainforest Action Network and the Ruckus Society hang a giant banner off of a construction crane on the eve of the mass street protests against the WTO, Seattle, 1999.

In 1999, the World Trade Organization decided to hold global capitalism's board meeting in Seattle, WA. Most Americans had never heard of the WTO before, but savvy organizers across a spectrum of single-issue silos, including labor, environmental, human rights and others, decided that they would team up and act like a movement for a change. Our critiques of neoliberalism varied widely and there were both reformers and abolitionists in our ranks, but we were united in the recognition that the meeting represented a potent symbolic target for anyone challenging the juggernaut of undemocratic global corporate power.

Radicals and liberals agreed early on that a healthy inside/outside strategy was called for. A critical mass of activists began organizing, recruiting and training together to attempt a many-thousands-strong blockade of the WTO ministerial. We believed that if we could achieve the tactical victory of a mass shutdown of the WTO's coming-out party, it would strengthen the hands of everyone working against corporate globalization.

Scores of affinity groups organized themselves into thirteen "clusters" and through a highly functional (and democratic) spokescouncil, hammered out a plan to capture the key intersections around the Seattle Convention Center in a massive nonviolent blockade. And so, in the predawn darkness of November 30, 5,000 direct actionistas marched through the streets of Seattle toward their targets. Each individual action had its own logic and narrative. Each would have stood on its own as extraordinary. When connected together, they became unstoppable.

The action frame we chose was carnival-protest, equal parts communicative and concrete *see PRINCIPLE: Make your actions both concrete and communicative*. Outside the stodgy corporate meeting, a giant dance party broke out, complete with marching bands, dancers, theater troupes, giant puppets, radical cheerleaders, a phalanx of 300 turtles and even Christmas carolers. Thousands of folks joined together (with hands and chains) around key entrances and intersections, preventing delegates from entering (that was the instrumental part). It could have looked threatening, but with all the celebratory art and solidarity, we looked beautiful and human doing it. Our theme was "Another World Is Possible" and we were living it out.

"On the day of the event, we surprised everyone, even ourselves."

By morning, 5,000 more folks, inspired by the audacity and courage of these artful actions, had spontaneously joined the human wall around the WTO. Teamsters and turtles were literally dancing together in the streets. A few hours later, as the Seattle police unleashed a torrent of tear gas and pepper spray to crack the blockade, 50,000 labor marchers defied their own marshals and reinforced us with a sea of humanity. The biggest business meeting on Earth had been shut down, a tactical victory most thought impossible. And the rest, as they say, is history.

The impact of Seattle was enormous. It launched the global justice movement in the Global North. It showed that a people's victory against global capital was possible. It created a teachable moment — for the public, on the WTO and the dark side of corporate globalization, and also for the movement, showcasing direct and mass action tactics and a carnivalesque sensibility that are still influential today, as well as training a new wave of actionistas who have gone on to play critical roles across the next decade of progressive movements.

Related:

THEORIES
Hamoq & hamas p. 236
Points of intervention p. 250
Action logic p. 208
Cycles of social movements web
Revolutionary nonviolence p. 260

WHY IT WORKED

We had a great democratic process that let us hammer out agreements on both actions and messaging frameworks that thousands of people signed onto. We picked the fight early and framed it well. We planned for nine months. We started the media story months in advance. On the day of the event, we surprised everyone, even ourselves.

WHAT DIDN'T WORK

Where was the color in Seattle? When your two most popular battle cries are "This is what democracy looks like!" and "Another world is possible," and most of the people chanting them are white, then you have a serious problem. There were some amazing young organizers of color with us in the streets of Seattle, but a "global justice movement" must be inclusive and share leadership with those folks on the front lines of injustice. In Seattle we came up short.

Victim of our own tactical success. The global justice movement spent the next couple of years trying to repeat Seattle's tactical magic, trying to shut down every major summit we could reach, from Québec to Qatar. But you can't exploit the element of surprise twice.

Inability to maintain nonviolent discipline. Small groups of protesters engaging in black bloc tactics smashed the windows of banks and Starbucks and thereby gave the cops the moral authority to use violence against all of us, and the corporate media all the ammunition they needed to tell the story they wanted to tell.

. . . .

KEY TACTIC
used

OTHER TACTICS USED:

Mass street action p. 68
Direct action p. 32
Banner hang p. 12
Street theater web
Creative disruption p. 18
Strategic nonviolence p. 88

BLOCKADE: The shut-down of the WTO blended both soft and hard blockade technologies. Of the thousands who participated, all but a few hundred simply joined hands and stood shoulder to shoulder with their comrades to prevent delegates from getting through. However, several hundred people used lock-boxes, chains, barrels, and other hard blockade technology to hold key intersections where we knew our people power would be lightest. With art and costumes and good cheer, we made these gear-intensive technical "lockdowns" look beautiful, not scary.

CASE STUDY: Battle in Seattle

THINK NARATIVELY: When 50,000 lefties take the streets to confront corporate power, you're going to get 50,000 different critiques. To try to unify all that message diversity, we designed a "framing action." The day before the big protest, four climbers dropped a massive banner 300 feet above Seattle's main commuter highway that framed the action as a choice between democracy and the WTO. The photo of the banner went global on the day of the mass action, summing up in stark and simplest terms what Battle in Seattle was all about.

ONE NO, MANY YESSES: Whether your YES! was the freedom to keep making the Roquefort cheese that your great grandfather made or to continue living in an ancient rainforest unpoisoned by Big Oil or to keep your good union job and not have it outsourced to a sweatshop, you shared a NO! with billions of others. This "unity in diversity" was present on the streets with Teamsters and Turtles linking arms, and in the "movement of movements" that organized the protest.

USE YOUR RADICAL FRINGE TO SLIDE THE OVERTON WINDOW: Before the WTO uprising in Seattle, relatively few people in the Global North questioned the process of corporate globalization and so-called "free" trade. Seattle jolted the entire Overton window sharply to the left. Fair trade and other alternatives moved out of the fringe. The idea that militant mass action could stop corporate globalization in its tracks became not only thinkable, but popular. Every major summit between Seattle and 9/11 was met with mass protest.

KEY PRINCIPLES
at work

OTHER PRINCIPLES AT WORK:

Choose your target wisely p. 114
Maintain nonviolent discipline p. 48
Escalate strategically p. 134
Be both concrete and
communicative p. 154
Choose tactics that support
your strategy p. 112
If you're not uncomfortable, your
coalition is too small web

CASE STUDY:
Bidder 70
(Tim DeChristopher)

WHEN

December 2008

WHERE

Salt Lake City, Utah

PRACTITIONERS

Tim deChristopher

FURTHER INSIGHT

Tim DeChristopher, "I do not want
mercy, I want you to join me,"
Common Dreams, July 27, 2011
http://trb.la/wAqNPf

Video: "Posing as a bidder,
Utah student disrupts government auction"
http://trb.la/xx1MbW

Peaceful Uprising, "Fre-
quently Asked Questions
about Tim DeChristopher"
http://trb.la/xOIKVY

CONTRIBUTED BY

Andy Bichlbaum
Duncan Meisel

In December 2008, word got out about an illegal Bureau of Land Management auction of oil and gas leases for drilling near beautiful Arches and Canyonlands National Parks in Utah. The auction was Bush's parting gift to his good friends in industry. Student Tim DeChristopher set out with the intention of physically disrupting the event, but as he walked through the door, he was taken by surprise when an attendant asked him if he was there to bid. "Why, yes, yes I am," he answered, and the attendant gave Tim a paddle. In Tim's words:

> Once I was in there, I realized that any kind of speech or disruption wasn't going to be very effective. But I saw pretty quickly how I could have a pretty major impact on the way this worked. It took me a little bit of time to build up my courage, knowing what the consequences would be — and then I started bidding and started driving up the prices. But I knew I could be doing more. So then I started winning bids, and disrupting it as clearly as I could.[1]

Tim won about a dozen lots in a row — until the auctioneer realized something was wrong, suspended the proceedings, and had Tim arrested.

After Obama took office, his administration investigated the auction for "irregularities," and a federal judge cancelled the sales. Tim's action — which singlehandedly saved many precious acres of Utah wilderness from destruction — stands out as one of the most inspired and successful acts of civil disobedience in recent history.

At his sentencing hearing, Tim addressed the presiding judge to explain his actions. He concluded his remarks with the following words:

> I want you to join me in standing up for the right and responsibility of citizens to challenge their government. I want you to join me in valuing this country's rich history of nonviolent civil disobedience. If you share those values but think

my tactics are mistaken, you have the power to redirect them. You can sentence me to a wide range of community service efforts that would point my commitment to a healthy and just world down a different path. You can have me work with troubled teens, as I spent most of my career doing. . . . You can steer that commitment if you agree with it, but you can't kill it.

This is not going away. At this point of unimaginable threats on the horizon, this is what hope looks like. In these times of a morally bankrupt government that has sold out its principles, this is what patriotism looks like. With countless lives on the line, this is what love looks like, and it will only grow. The choice you are making today is what side are you on.[2]

> "Tim's action stands out as one of the most inspired and successful acts of civil disobedience in recent history."

After reading his statement, Tim was sentenced to two years in federal prison.

Related:

THEORIES
Points of intervention p. 250
Action logic p. 20
The commons p. 220
The tactics of everyday life p. 268

WHY IT WORKED

Tim took bold and effective action, and then used the coverage and attention his act generated as a platform to both defend his action and call for bolder action by the climate movement in general. His closing statement to the judge, excerpted above, became a rallying cry for other organizing efforts — like the Tar Sands Action against the Keystone XL Pipeline later that year — and countless other acts of civil disobedience. Tim and his allies stood strong in defense of his actions, effectively demonstrating why civil disobedience was necessary to stop the climate crisis.

· ·

KEY TACTIC
used

CREATIVE DISRUPTION: Tim intervened directly in the proceedings that would have sold off beloved public lands to the oil companies. He hit upon an effective way

---

[1] *Democracy Now!* "Posing as a bidder, Utah student disrupts government auction," December 22, 2008.

[2] Tim DeChristopher, *"I do not want mercy, I want you to join me," Common Dreams,* July 27, 2011.

to make sure the auction did not proceed (basically inventing a new kind of creative disruption on the spot), and then defended that action without compromise.

KEY PRINCIPLES
at work

GET ARRESTED IN AN INTELLIGENT WAY: The case against Tim has provided him with a very large platform to call for further civil disobedience. Tim and his allies used every step of his case to attack the political system and economic interests that allow climate change to happen. His powerful final statement to the court, and the jail time he subsequently served, are the clearest examples of this.

CONSIDER YOUR AUDIENCE: Even when given the chance, Tim did not stand up and harangue the crowd of oil men, knowing such a crude disruption would be futile. Instead, he opted to do something seemingy compliant, but ultimately deeply disruptive: he played along with the bidding process until it became clear that he had no intention of paying for all the leases he'd won. Then he turned his attention to another, more dispersed audience: activists who would be inspired by his example, and the public whose sympathies could shift toward greater support for action on climate change *see PRINCIPLE: Shift the spectrum of allies.*

CASE STUDY: Bidder 70

"... those who write the rules are those who profit from the status quo. If we want to change that status quo, we might have to work outside of those rules because the legal pathways available to us have been structured precisely to make sure we don't make any substantial change." Portrait by Robert Shetterly/ www.americanswhotellthetruth.org

CASE STUDY:
The Big Donor Show

WHEN
June 1, 2007

WHERE
Broadcast in the Netherlands by the Dutch public broadcaster BNN.

PRACTITIONERS
Dutch broadcaster BNN and Endemol
Director Paul Römer
Laurens Drillich, BNN Chairman

FURTHER INSIGHT
De Grote Donorshow website
http://sites.bnn.nl/page/donorshow

CONTRIBUTED BY
Silas Harrebye

De Grote Donorshow, a hoax TV program presented as a reality show, stands as one of the most effective and unique public awareness campaigns in recent years. The premise of the show was that a terminally ill woman would donate her kidney to the most worthy person of a group of people needing kidney transplants. She would make her selection based on how the contestants answered a series of questions, much like a dating program. Viewers were able to weigh in via text message on whom they thought should receive the life-saving kidney.

Even before it was aired, the show provoked much heated discussion. Soon media across the Netherlands and beyond were debating the ethics of waiting lists and the propriety of turning organ donation into public entertainment. On June 1, 2007, when the show finally aired, millions of viewers worldwide tuned in to watch.

The surprising twist to an already spectacular and highly controversial program was that it was all a hoax. Just before the alleged cancer patient was about to choose the lucky recipient of her kidney, the host announced that the "cancer patient" was actually a hired actor. The entire program had been staged to raise awareness about the insufficient number of organ donors in the country. He then announced that the people who were performing as competitors to receive a kidney were, however, real patients awaiting kidney donors.

Within a day, 30,000 donor registration forms were requested. A month after the show aired, 7,300 new donors were registered by the Dutch donor registration. In Denmark alone, 700 citizens registered as donors the day after the program was aired — fifteen times the average on a regular Saturday. The show won an International Emmy for non-scripted entertainment.

WHY IT WORKED

This stunt was successful because the TV network used its prestige as a broadcaster to send a powerful political message. The cautionary glimpse at how the future might look forced the viewers to reflect on their own agency as witnesses to the disgusting spectacle of people competing for organ donations.

The stunt worked by breaking the implicit contract between broadcaster and viewer to make clear distinctions between truth and fiction. What justified the prank is that while the show itself wasn't real, the issues that it addressed were. The act of deception served to expose a very real need that was not being met, with the spectators forced to confront their own agency to address the issue.

Related:

THEORIES
Ethical spectacle p. 230
Society of the Spectacle p. 266
Points of intervention p. 250

· ·

HOAX: The hoax is not only an effective tactic to get an issue on the agenda, it is also capable of causing a type of embarrassment that not only provokes reflection, but forces us to reflect on our most deeply held beliefs and take action. It lures people in and exposes them to a subversive idea when they are most vulnerable. In this case, it also pointed toward a practical way of responding to the issue it raised.

KEY TACTIC
used

THE REAL ACTION IS YOUR TARGET'S REACTION: Researchers and politicians who had been quick to denounce the show and lament its social implications were forced to revisit their initial diagnoses, thus offering useful meta-reflection on the event, their own role as commentators, and the future of reality TV. Millions of ordinary viewers were forced to do the same.

KEY PRINCIPLES
at work

OTHER PRINCIPLES AT WORK:
Bring the issue home p. 106
*Lead with sympathet-
ic characters* p. 146
Show, don't tell p. 174

BE AN ETHICAL PRANKSTER: A lot of people felt misled after the show, and the trustworthiness of the channel might have suffered, but the positive outcome cannot be denied. So a few questions remain: do the ends justify the means? and how do you weigh competing causes or principles? — both classical activist dilemmas.

DO THE MEDIA'S WORK FOR THEM: The donor show gave journalists around the world an excuse to cover the critical lack of organ donors. Many important issues have the same strategic challenge: they are chronic problems rather than acute crises, and therefore do not live up to the criteria for what makes news. If you add an unexpected twist to a good story with a clear and provocative point, as the Big Donor Show did, you provide the hook the media needs.

CASE STUDY:
Billionaires for Bush

WHEN

2000–2009
with biggest spike in 2004

WHERE

U.S.A.

EPIGRAPH

"Shut up! You are not
helping the President
get re-elected. You are
making the Republi-
can Party look like a
bunch of out of-touch-
elitists! Assholes!"

*—Email from an exasper-
ated Republican*

PRACTITIONERS

Billionaires for Bush
Billionaires for Wealthcare
United for a Fair Economy
Ladies Against Women

CONTRIBUTED BY

Jeremy Varon
Andrew Boyd
Brian Fairbanks

The "Billionaires" used wit, hijinx and great duds to sneak their radical critique of crony capitalism into the corporate media. Photo by Landon Nordeman.

"Some people call you the elite," George W. Bush joked to his wealthy funders, "I call you my base." Whether candidate Bush meant it as a joke or not, the Billionaires for Bush (B4B) campaign used humor, street theater and creative media actions to show the country how true the quip was. Working to expose how the Republican Party serves the interests of the super-rich, the Billionaires also addressed the broader issues of economic inequality and corporate greed.

An early version of the campaign in 2000, "Billionaires for Bush (or Gore)," had spread virally via the internet and mainstream media exposure. It rebranded itself for the 2004 election, taking as its crusade the defeat of Bush. The New York City chapter took the lead, assembling talented volunteers, among them professional designers, media producers, and actors. It then put the campaign pieces in place. A stylish logo swapped the Republican elephant with a piggy bank stuffed with bills. Satirical slogans — "Repeal the First Amendment," "Free the Forbes 400," "Corporations are people too" — adorned bumper stickers, buttons, and a slick website, mimicking the look of Bush-Cheney propaganda. A songwriter produced tuneful renditions of what the super-wealthy *really* think, performed by meticulously rehearsed singers. The members themselves adopted personae, with names and costumes to match, spoofing iconic versions of the .01 percent: the *Monopoly*-style robber baron (Phil T. Rich), the dim-witted heiress (Alexis Anna Rolls), the trust-fund fuck-up (Monet Oliver D'Place), and so on.

Soon, the Billionaires could be found talking down to "the little people" at Bush-Cheney campaign events, left-wing rallies, and street corners. They could also be found all over the mainstream media, garnering thousands of hits, including multiple features in the New York *Times* and on network and cable TV. Even the chant "Watch more Fox News, then you'll share our right-wing views!" made it to air... on Fox News.

Media coverage was generated by carefully planned hoaxes, such as the appearance, to a throng of adoring billionaires, of a Karl Rove impostor at a GOP fundraiser. Other times, the campaign outsmarted the authorities to attract the media glare, such as when it held a croquet match on Central Park's "Great Lawn," from which a half-million anti-Bush demonstrators had been banned by New York's mayor. The media was smitten by the Billionaires' glamour and charmed by their say-the-opposite-of-what-you-believe theatrics.

"Some observers remained fatally confused as to the group's message. Occasionally, true conservatives begged the Billionaires not to make Bush look bad by being so brazenly pro-rich."

The campaign was designed to be participatory and national. The core idea was easy both to replicate and embellish. Activists could download the materials they needed to do local actions, while a field organizer helped set up chapters in swing states like Ohio. By late July the hundreds of B4B "billionaires" from thirty states who showed up to protest at the Republican National Convention far exceeded the number of actual billionaires working hard for their President.

Deflated by Bush's victory, the B4B idea nonetheless lived on, generating spin-off campaigns such as Billionaires for Wealthcare, active in the health care debates of 2008-9. Often feeling in 2004 like a clever joke in the wilderness, the campaign in fact anticipated many of the

FURTHER INSIGHT

Billionaires for Bush
http://billionairesforbush.com

Haugerud, Angelique. The Billionaires: Satirical Political Activism in America Today. Stanford, California: Stanford University Press, 2013.

Bogad, Larry. "A Place for Protest: res for Bush Interrupt the Hegemonologue" in Performance and Place. Eds, Leslie and Helen Paris. New York: Palgrave McMillian, 2006. Full article available online at: http://trb.la/x00Zqz

Boyd, Andrew. "TRUTH IS A VIRUS: Meme Warfare and the Billionaires for Bush (or Gore)" in Cultural Resistance Reader, ed. Stephen Duncombe. New York: Verso, 2002. Full article available online at: http://trb.la/zyXyR6

Haugerud, Angelique. "Neoliberalism, Satirical Protest, and the 2004 U.S. Presidential Campaign" in Ethnographies of Neoliberalism, ed. Carol J. Greenhouse. Philadelphia: University of Pennsylvania Press, 2010.

Related:

THEORIES

CASE

core concerns of Occupy Wall Street and other "Great Recession"-era activism.

WHY IT WORKED

B4B pulled off tricky balancing acts. It was a highly disciplined media campaign that was also able to invite creative participation and grow virally. It had a scrappy, DIY feel but used high-production values, tight messaging, and sex appeal to wow the media and audiences alike. It addressed serious issues with irony, humor, and camp. The result was an entertaining and accessible vehicle for speaking about realities of American life often ignored in public discourse. The costuming and alter-ego-tripping was also empowering for the group itself: no matter one's station in life, one could become someone important and "fabulous" — it was like drag for the middle class. For all these reasons, the campaign inspired in its participants an extraordinary level of commitment — to their "characters" and to the larger struggle for justice.

WHAT DIDN'T WORK

Though dedicated to defeating Bush, the Billionaires had no hard deliverables, like voter turnout. And regardless of the media exposure, nationally and in swing states, there is no evidence that B4B messaging actually "swung" voters. The campaign therefore risked being an in-house joke, best appreciated by those already opposing Bush, or a media curiosity, ripe for fluff pieces from the campaign trail.

KEY TACTICS
used

OTHER TACTICS USED:
Infiltration p. 64
Mass street action p. 68
Media jacking p. 72
Hoax p. 54

DISTRIBUTED ACTION: Well-crafted actions, occurring simultaneously in disparate locales, amplified the campaign's sense of unity, power, and reach. The B4B repertoire of distributed actions included *Cheap* Labor Day, "Education is not for everyone Day" at the beginning of the school year, and others. "Dick Cheney is Innocent Day" began as a national day of action featuring coordinated, candle-lit vigils in front of Cheney's VP residence in D.C., state capital buildings, an official Cheney speaking engagement in Milwaukee, and outside the Fox News windows in Times Square. Flyers were produced listing all of ol' Dick's many crimes (but protesting how baseless they were, of course!) and made available for easy download, alongside a national press release

CASE STUDY: Billionaires for Bush

DÉTOURNEMENT/CULTURE JAMMING: The Billionaire spectacle was a mindbending double- or triple-take: apparent Bush supporters, spewing over-the-top pro-Bush rhetoric, were really Bush opponents, who made the Republicans appear both venal and ridiculous. Some observers remained fatally confused as to the group's message. Occasionally, true conservatives begged the Billionaires not to make Bush look bad by being so brazenly pro-rich. Most people, however, soon got the joke: that the Republicans, despite their populist rhetoric, are a party of, by, and for the wealthy. Sometimes the Billionaires "jammed" the earnest culture of the political left. Retorting "This is what plutocracy looks like!" and "Whose Street? Wall Street!" to familiar lefty chants, the Billionaires suggested that progressive advocates of We the People had little inkling of the wealth and influence they were up against. The Billionaires tried to speak truth to — and about — power.

DON'T DRESS LIKE A PROTESTER: The Billionaires were distinguished from other anti-Bush activists by their upper-crust look and ironic messaging, which denounced the Republicans through parodic expressions of reactionary principles. As something new and different, the campaign avoided the media's boredom with covering angry protesters protesting, well, angrily. The result was media exposure of B4B messaging vastly disproportionate to the group's size and resources.

MAKE THE INVISIBLE VISIBLE: Politicians often avoid any direct reference to their ultimate agenda, especially when their plan is to plunder. The activist must expose their true intent. This "unmasking" was central to B4B shtick, and was the basis for particular actions. In 2005, the Billionaires joined the fight against Bush's plan to privatize social security, which would have been the biggest shift of public capital in history. To dramatize this outcome, Billionaires for Bush auctioned off Social Security in the most public forum available: eBay. The auction limited bidding to Wall Street bankers and casino operators and broke down the numbers on exactly what was to be gained by the wealthy and lost by the rest. Though eBay quickly took down the auction, more than 25,000 people visited the sale, and bidding peaked at $99,999,999. For days, media coverage continued to spread the message: "Billionaires for Bush auctioned off Social Security on eBay."

KEY PRINCIPLES
at work

OTHER PRINCIPLES AT WORK:
Make it funny web
Brand or be branded p. 104
Know your cultural terrain p. 142
Do the media's work for them p. 124
Enable don't command p. 132
Delegate p. 122
Show, don't tell p. 174
Think narratively p. 186
Create levels of participation web
Balance art and message p. 104

CASE STUDY:
Citizens' Posse

WHEN
March 9, 2010

WHERE
Washington, D.C.

PRACTITIONERS
Agit-Pop Communications
Health Care for America
Now (HCAN)

CONTRIBUTED BY
John Sellers

In early spring of 2010, the prospects of the U.S. Congress passing comprehensive health care reform were looking bleak. The Democrats had caved on the public option, the Blue Dogs were turning red, and Democratic leaders weren't sure if they had the votes to pass anything.

Most of the mainstream players in the health care reform movement were busy on Capitol Hill "making sausage" while the reform bill grew weaker and less popular by the day. An edgier wing of health care reformers, however, were looking to expand the theater of conflict *à la* Donald Rumsfeld. We had to remind people why reform was needed and we knew that if we could expose the criminal behavior of Big Insurance, they would be convicted in the court of pubic opinion.

Luckily, a perfect target presented itself. AHIP, the top health insurance lobbying group, decided to bring their chief executives and lobbyists together at a fancy hotel in downtown Washington, D.C., for a summit. They sensed they were close to total victory. They needed to plot out their final moves, smoke their final cigars and cut their final backroom deals.

Health Care for America Now (HCAN) — an alliance of labor unions, the progressive netroots, and a host of community-based organizations — hired Agit-Pop to help them go big, creative, and militant. Our job was to stage a major street action that would finally tell the story right: Americans want affordable universal health care; insurance companies don't because they're profiting from a broken system.

We decided to cast the CEOs as organized crime bosses who bribed politicians, denied health care to the critically ill, and ran real Death Panels for profit. We cast participants in the planned rally as a "People's Posse" which would be composed of ordinary people called upon to bring these corporate criminals to justice.

WANTED BY THE AMERICAN PEOPLE

David Cordani: CIGNA CEO

CASE No. 405,942 G

Photos from various crime scenes

CRIMINAL RECORD

➡ **45,000 COUNTS OF INVOLUNTARY MANSLAUGHTER**
- deaths incurred in the process of pursuing insurance industry profit
Title 18 US Code § 1112

➡ **BREACH OF CONTRACT & FRAUD** - denial of promised coverage paid for by working Americans
Title 25 US Code § 3116

➡ **MONEY LAUNDERING** - clandestinely transferred $10-20 million dollars to fund attacks designed to deny health coverage
Title 18 US Code § 1956

➡ **BRIBERY OF PUBLIC OFFICIALS**
Title 18 US Code § 201

IF YOU HAVE ANY INFORMATION CONCERNING THIS PERSON, PLEASE NOTIFY YOUR LOCAL OFFICE OF PUBLIC ACCOUNTABILITY AT CITIZENSPOSSE.COM

Wanted Flyer 442-A
Feb 25, 2010

EXHIBIT II
TO THE AFFIDAVIT OF
THE US CITIZENS

FURTHER INSIGHT

Citizens' Posse website
http://citizensposse.com/

Video of the action
http://www.youtube.com/
watch?v=kMrFOySI8SE

Related:

THEORIES

Action logic p. 208
Ethical spectacle p. 230
Hamoq & hamas p. 236
Points of intervention p. 250
Narrative power analysis p. 244

Union leaders were skeptical about whether their folks would take to the "posse" frame. But on action day, when their members saw the "CEO Wanted" posters, Citizens' Posse badges and crime scene tape, they quickly wanted in. Our action had two marches of 1,500 people each converge on the D.C. Ritz Carlton. At that point, we surrounded the building, declared it a crime scene, and posted wanted posters of the CEOs. We had a rally with rousing speeches about corporate criminals, which culminated with William McNary deputizing the crowd by administering the Citizens' Posse Oath of Office. Then several union presidents and a VIP posse attempted to enter the hotel and make citizens' arrests. Ten VIP deputies were eventually taken into custody by D.C.'s finest.

As a result, the reform movement got a much-needed shot in the arm, and we owned the media cycle for a critical day or two in the homestretch to the vote. The bill (however flawed) eventually passed.

WHY IT WORKED

The action used a clear and powerful frame (corporate criminals brought to justice by the people) that not only made it clear who the good and bad guys were, but told a story for the media. It also gave the 3,000 angry liberals who showed up a powerful role to play and an animated narrative arc that kept them in motion. Finally, it allowed layers of creative elaboration (badges, wanted posters, oath of office, giant crime tape, etc.).

WHAT DIDN'T WORK

The posse action was designed to empower everyone in attendance across the board. However, labor insisted that their presidents play the lead roles throughout the day and be the center of attention, which led to an unnecessary, long and mostly boring rally until "The Oath" was administered. Also, we designed the Citizens' Posse frame to be easily adaptable by any organization or movement confronting criminal corporate behavior, regardless of their issue silo. Unfortunately, no one has picked it up and used it again.

. . . .

KEY TACTIC
used

OTHER TACTICS USED:

Nonviolent search and seizure p. 76
Strategic nonviolence p. 88
Blockade p. 14
Direct action p. 32

MASS STREET ACTION: Too often street actions are like dances that everyone already knows the steps to: (A) march, followed by rally, with people speechifying from the stage, or (B) set-piece acts of civil disobedience with everyone singing Kumbaya until they're arrested (or worse, ignored). The posse achieved a greater degree of militancy and dynamism by putting "We the People" in a heroic role that called for *action* throughout the action.

THINK NARRATIVELY: The "posse" framework set up clear good and bad guys and put a whole universe of iconography and story elements at our disposal. All the rally speakers hammered on the "criminal" behavior of the insurance companies and their conspiracy with crooked politicians. By deputizing the crowd, we pulled them into the story and the action in a heroic role that demanded justice and respect.

USE THE POWER OF RITUAL: The most powerful moment of the whole action was when the entire 3,000-strong crowd, in call-and-response style, ritually took the Citizen's Posse oath:

> I solemnly swear to support and defend the Constitution of the United States against all enemies, foreign and domestic. [...] In the tradition of citizen posses throughout American history who in times of need have been called to service to bring criminals — corporate or otherwise — to justice, I swear to well and faithfully discharge the duties of the office on which I am about to enter. So help me Jefferson.

SIMPLE RULES LEAD TO GRAND RESULTS: The "citizens' posse" concept provided an organic way for individuals to participate that helped the 3,000-strong mass in the streets operate as a cohesive whole. The rules were simple — take this oath, put on this badge, try to bring the corporate criminals to justice — yet the overall frame it set up for the crowd (and the media covering it) was grand and powerful.

KEY PRINCIPLES
at work

OTHER PRINCIPLES AT WORK:

Make your actions both concrete and communicative p. 154
Pick battles big enough to matter, small enough to win web
Anger works best when you have the moral high ground p. 96
Use powerful metaphors web
Lead with sympathetic characters 146
Reframe p. 168
Re-capture the flag web

CASE STUDY:
Clandestine Insurgent Rebel Clown Army
(CIRCA)

WHEN
2003–Present

WHERE
London, then global

PRACTITIONERS
Clandestine Insurgent Rebel Clown Army Deconstructionist Institute of Surreal Topology Deterritorial Support Group

CONTRIBUTED BY
John Jordan

Hoping against hope, clowns ask for their toys back from Nice Mr. Policeman

To some, the Clandestine Insurgent Rebel Clown Army (CIRCA) might appear to be but a ragged bunch of activists sporting false noses, a smudge of grease paint, camouflage pants and bad wigs. And those people may be right. But it is also a highly disciplined army of professional clowns, a militia of authentic fools, a battalion of true buffoons.

Art activist John Jordan and colleagues L.M. Bogad, Jen Verson and Matt Trevelyan founded CIRCA in late 2003 to welcome arch-clown George W. Bush on his royal visit to London. CIRCA aimed to be a new methodology of civil disobedience, merging the ancient art of clowning with contemporary tactics of nonviolent direct action. It went on to be a successful meme and international protest phenomenon, with self-organized groups taking action in the streets outside summits and military bases in dozens of countries from Colombia to New Zealand.

CIRCA worked with professional clowns to develop a methodology, *rebel clowning*, that introduced play and games into the process of political organizing. We developed a series of trainings that encouraged activists to reprogram their bodies, to develop their intuition and to "find their clown" — a childlike state of generosity and spontaneity. Rebel clown trainings attempted to peel off the activist armor and find the vulnerable human within.

Emphasizing the inner work of personal transformation that too many movements ignore, CIRCA viewed both soul and street as sites of struggle. The deep work of clowning, involving real letting go and finding the absolute spontaneous self, can have profoundly liberating psychological effects on participants. CIRCA's combatants are not meant to *pretend* to be clowns, they should be real clowns. Clowning is a state of being rather than a technique.

It's a core CIRCA premise that mocking and utterly confusing the enemy can be more powerful than direct confrontation. In one instance, a seventy-person-strong gaggle of clowns walked straight through a line of UK riot cops who, strangely, could not hold their line. When the video footage of the event was examined, it turned out that beneath their visors the cops were laughing too much to be able to concentrate. Other clowns filled their pockets with so much strange junk that it took hours and lots of paper work when stop-and-searches occurred. A favorite tactic was to walk into army recruitment agencies and, in a clownish way, try to join up, thus causing so much chaos that the agencies had to close down for the day, whereupon CIRCA would set up its own shabby recruitment stall outside.

Turn-of-the-century anarchist Emma Goldman posed this problem: "how to be one's self and yet in oneness with others, to feel deeply with all human beings and still retain one's own characteristic qualities." CIRCA bridged that divide, allowing participants to discover their own inner clown while at the same time wearing a "uniform" that made them feel part of a strongly bonded group.

Rebel clowning was a gateway for lots of people to get involved in radical politics who were otherwise put off by its seriousness. For many recruits, it was their first experience of civil disobedience, but the playfulness and mask-like make-up empowered them to be deeply disobedient, often in unexpectedly absurd and creative ways.

FURTHER INSIGHT

CIRCA website
www.clownarmy.org

Kolonel Klepto and Major Up Evil. "The Clandestine Insurgent Rebel Clown Army goes to Scotland via a few other Places." In Shut Them Down!: The G8, Gleneagles 2005 and the Movement of Movements, edited by David Harvie, David Watts, and Ben Trott. Autonomedia, 2006.

L.M. Bogad, "The Clandestine Insurgent Rebel Clown Army." Journal of Aesthetics and Protest Issue 3, June 2004. http://www.journalofaestheticsandprotest.org/3/bogad.htm

L. M. Bogad, "Carnivals Against Capital: Radical Clowning and the Global Justice Movement," Social Identities: Journal for the Study of Race, Nation and Culture 16.4 (Summer 2010): 537–557.

John Jordan, "Notes whilst walking on 'How to break the heart of empire." European Institute for Progressive Cultural Policies. August 2005. http://trb.la/z45r4E

Related:

THEORIES
Ethical Spectacle p. 230
Hamoq & hamas p. 236
Memes p. 242

WHY IT WORKED

WHAT DIDN'T WORK

There's nothing worse than a bad clown — and being a good one is hard. Anyone who has seen the great clowns of the world — Chaplin, say, or Keaton — realizes how difficult an art it is to master.

"Clowning is a state of being rather than a technique."

Less is often more. As rebel clowning became popular with activists in the mid 2000s, many wanted to join up with CIRCA but few were prepared to follow the intense training. Many bad "hippie" clowns made it onto the street. CIRCA founders also underestimated how hard it was to be a good clown, and in their rush to build mass actions of hundreds of clowns, they forgot to start small and build.

Insurgent Clowns on a stroll.

- -

KEY TACTIC
used

OTHER TACTICS USED:
Direct action p. 32
Creative disruption p. 18
Prefigurative intervention p. 82
Mass street action p. 68

CARNIVAL-PROTEST: The use of carnivalesque forms of resistance was a key tactic for the global anti-capitalist mass actions of the 1990s. CIRCA took this carnival spirit deeper into the individual mind and body of the activist. Clowning exists on the borderlines, dancing delicately on the edge of chaos, somewhere between life and art, being and pretending. Clowns are both fearsome and innocent, wise and stupid, healers and laughing stocks, scapegoats and subversives. They take this carnivalesque spirit with them wherever they go, infecting the body politic with insurrectionary dreams. When a crisis hits a culture, perhaps it is in these gray zones of creative uncertainty that we might find the answers.

USE ABSURDITY TO UNDERMINE THE AURA OF AUTHORITY: Ridicule and absurdity are powerful tools against authority. To be effective, authority has to be perceived as such, otherwise people would never obey its commands. On the other hand, who ever takes a clown seriously? Rebel clowning used this slippery dichotomy to great effect, turning the tables on authority in the street by posing in mock-serious fashion next to lines of cops, as well as at the highest levels of power, by pointing out the clownish behavior of George W. Bush and other authority figures.

GET ARRESTED IN AN INTELLIGENT WAY: Watching police handcuff and bundle clowns into police vans is always entertaining for passersby, begging the question: What did the clowns do wrong? What is this all about? An arrested clown also makes for very mediagenic images. By staying in character during the whole process of an arrest, including giving their clown army names (e.g., Private Joke) and addressees (e.g., the big top in the sky) as their real identity, rebel clowns caused much mirth and havoc in the police stations.

REFRAME: Rebel clowning helped reframe the media images of protests during the big summit mobilizations of the mid 1990s. A colorful band of disobedient clowns could easily capture the limelight and shift the narrative away from "violent clashes" and smashed windows.

KEY PRINCIPLES
at work

OTHER PRINCIPLES AT WORK:
Anyone can act p. 98
Make new folks welcome p. 150
Everyone has balls/
ovaries of steel p. 136
Escalate strategically p. 134

CASE STUDY:
Colbert roasts Bush

WHEN
April 29, 2006

WHERE
Washington, D.C.

PRACTITIONERS
Stephen Colbert

FURTHER INSIGHT
Video: Colbert Roasts Bush
- 2006 White House Cor-
respondents' Dinner
http://trb.la/xMMDiE

A full transcript of the speech is
available in the back of
Colbert's book: Stephen Colbert,
I Am America (and So Can You!)
New York: Grand Central Publish-
ing Hachette Book Group, 2007)

Salon, "The Truthiness Hurts,"
May 1, 2006
http://trb.la/yOvOvl

CONTRIBUTED BY
Elisabeth Ginsberg

Every year, a celebrity, often a comedian, is invited to roast the President at the White House Correspondents' Dinner, an annual gathering of journalists who regularly cover the White House and the President. But it isn't every year that the President has "that look that he's ready to blow,"[1] as an aide of President Bush expressed it after comedian Stephen Colbert delivered his speech in 2006.

Stephen Colbert performing at the White House correspondents' dinner, with his primary foil, President Bush, sitting nearby. The audience's uncomfortable refusal to give in and laugh at Colbert's jokes, perfectly captured in this photo, underscored the seriousness of Colbert's attack.

Colbert delivered his lines with militant irony, professing to approve of the very things about Bush he was in fact attacking. He satirized a host of topics including the typically Republican opposition to big governments by referencing the war in Iraq: "I believe the government that governs best is the government that governs least. And by these standards, we have set up a fabulous government in Iraq," he said. He then turned to Bush's decreasing popularity:

CASE STUDY: Colbert roasts Bush

Now, I know there are some polls out there saying that this man has a thirty-two percent approval rating. But guys like us, we don't pay attention to the polls... We know that polls are just a collection of statistics that reflect what people are thinking in "reality." And reality has a well-known liberal bias.

Related:

THEORIES

Ethical spectacle p. 230
Political jujitsu web

While Colbert's mock defense of Bush took up most of the sixteen minute-long speech, he didn't spare the gathered press corps either: "As excited as I am to be here with the president, I am appalled to be surrounded by the liberal media that is destroying America. With the exception of Fox News. Fox News gives you both sides of every story: the president's side, and the vice president's side," he said before reviewing "the rules":

Here's how it works. The president makes decisions. He's the decider. The press secretary announces those decisions, and you people of the press type those decisions down. Make, announce, type. Just put 'em through a spell check and go home. Get to know your family again. Make love to your wife. Write that novel you got kicking around in your head. You know, the one about the intrepid Washington reporter with the courage to stand up to the Administration? You know, fiction!

Colbert's sarcastic performance was broadcast live on the cable network C-SPAN and viewed on YouTube 2.7 million times in the first forty-eight hours after it was posted. By calling to account some of the world's most powerful people as they sat, grinning uncomfortably, in the camera's glare, he affirmed his status as someone who speaks "truthiness" to power.

If his intent was of to shame the president and the press into improvement, it'd be hard to call it a success. But judging from online discussions of the speech, a good portion of the public experienced it as an em-

---

[1] Paul Bedard, "Skewering comedy skit angers Bush and aides," *U.S. News & World Report.* http://www.usnews.com/usnews/news/articles/060501/1whwatch.htm
[2] Dan Savage, "Dan Savage Interviews Frank Rich Before Frank Rich Interviews Stephen Sondheim," *The Stranger.* http://www.thestranger.com/seattle/dan-savage-interviews-frank-rich/Content?oid=2535771

powering emperor-has-no-clothes moment. Liberal columnist Dan Savage, for example, referred to it as "one of the things that kept people like me sane during the darkest days of the Bush years."[2] For Bush's critics, the speech felt like a victory. As with all victories, it was important for morale.

WHY IT WORKED

An overall comic tension was created by the incongruity between the celebratory format — with Bush himself only a few feet from the podium — and the scathing content of Colbert's speech. To many people, especially Colbert fans, it was hilarious. However, relatively few people in the room laughed or otherwise applauded Colbert during his speech. The strength of Colbert's ironic delivery was that to laugh was to admit that you got the joke — and the joke was on Bush, the Administration and the entire press corps. The audience's uncomfortable refusal to give in and laugh at Colbert's jokes thus indirectly affirmed the seriousness of his attack.

Aware that his real audience was not the people present at the dinner *see PRINCIPLE: Play to the audience that isn't there*, Colbert managed to deliver his entire performance with a minimum amount of comforting feedback from the audience. It worked — but only because he had the confidence and professionalism to pull it off.

. . . .

KEY TACTIC
used

OTHER TACTICS USED:
Identity Correction p. 60

DÉTOURNEMENT/CULTURE JAM: For his performance, Colbert adopted the role of the character that he plays on his satirical news show, the *Colbert Report*. This same-name persona — whom Colbert has described in many interviews as a "well-intentioned, poorly informed, high-status idiot" — is carefully modeled on typical male Fox News hosts such as Bill O'Reilly or Sean Hannity. Because the artifice of Colbert's persona is obvious, there is no deception of the audience. Yet his critique remains indirect. It requires that the audience draw the conclusions.

CASE STUDY: Colbert roasts Bush

REDUCTIO AD ABSURDUM: Instead of directly challenging Bush's reasoning, Colbert ridiculed it by feigning total agreement. Enthusiastically extrapolating from Bush's statements in ways Bush would not, Colbert carried the unspoken assumptions through to their presumably logical conclusions: "The greatest thing about this man is that he's steady. You know where he stands," Colbert said about Bush. "He believes the same thing Wednesday that he believed on Monday — no matter what happened Tuesday. Events can change; this man's beliefs never will," Colbert concluded. It was the seeming logical outcome of Bush's own reasoning but at the same time, of course, it was unacceptable to Bush, as it really pointed out the il-logic of Bush's "logic."

USE CHARACTERS: Taking on a character enabled Colbert to attack and ridicule the president in ways that would not have been permitted to the outright preacher, politician, or social reformer.

KEY PRINCIPLES
at work

OTHER PRINCIPLES AT WORK:

Play to the audience that isn't there p. 160
Show, don't tell p. 174
The real action is your target's reaction web
Balance art and message p. 100
Use the Jedi mind trick p. 194
Choose your target wisely p. 114
Know your cultural terrain p. 142
Everyone has balls of steel p. 136
Use the Jedi mind trick p. 194
Kill them with kindness p. 140
Reframe p. 168

CASE STUDY:
The Couple in the Cage

WHEN
1992-1993

WHERE
Various museums across
Europe and North America

PRACTITIONERS
Coco Fusco
Guillermo Gómez-Peña

FURTHER INSIGHT
Coco Fusco's website
http://www.thing.net/~cocofusco/

Guillermo Gómez-Peña's website
http://www.pochanostra.com/

CONTRIBUTED BY
Elisabeth Ginsberg

Performance artists Guillermo Gómez-Peña and Coco Fusco started their "The Couple in the Cage" tour five hundred years after Christopher Columbus' arrival in the Americas. For two years, they travelled through various Western metropolises, presenting themselves as undiscovered Amerindians from an island in the Gulf of Mexico that had somehow been overlooked for five centuries. They called their homeland Guatinau and themselves Guatinauis.

Two undiscovered Amerindians visit Columbus Plaza, Madrid, Spain. Photo by Peter Barker.

Exhibited in a cage, the couple performed "traditional tasks," which ranged from sewing voodoo dolls to watching television. A donation box in front of the cage indicated that for a small fee, the female Guatinaui would perform a traditional dance (to rap music), the male Guatinaui would tell authentic Amerindian stories (in a made-up language), and they would both pose with visitors. At the Whitney Museum in New York, sex was added to the spectacle when visitors were offered a peek at "authentic Guatinaui male genitals" for five dollars.

Next to the cage were two official-looking guards ready to answer visitors' questions, feed the Guatinauis, and take them to the bathroom on leashes. In addition to the authority of the guards, an institutional framework was evoked by didactic panels listing highlights from the history of exhibiting non-Western peoples and a simulated Encyclopedia Britannica entry with a fake map of the Gulf of Mexico showing Guatinau.

Aside from the authority provided by the various museum venues, everything on display was blatantly theatrical and clichéed: the Guatinauis had their skulls measured, were fed bananas, and were described as "specimens," among other things.

The performances were filmed and compiled in a documentary titled *The Couple in the Cage: A Guatinaui Odyssey*. Whereas the couple was the object on display during the live performance, the audience became the object on display during the documentary. While Fusco and Gómez-Peña adopted the roles of the caged natives, they were simultaneously scrutinizing the audience's responses. And what they found was surprising: Despite their intent to create an over-the-top satirical commentary on Western concepts of the exotic, primitive Other, it turned out that a substantial portion of the audience believed in the authenticity of the Guatinauis.

In an article about the performance, Fusco argues that the audience's immediate response reveals their fundamental beliefs: "In such encounters with the unexpected, people's defense mechanisms are less likely to operate with their normal efficiency; caught off-guard, their beliefs are more likely to rise to the surface."[1]

Seemingly making the same assumption, the documentary presents the audience's reactions as indirect proof that racist beliefs — non-Western people are primitive, inferior, and essentially different from Western people — permeate our postcolonial society. Whether or not this is true, *The Couple in the Cage* persuasively argues that colonial ideas continue to influence our approach to non-Western cultures.

Related:

THEORIES
Action logic p. 250
Theater of the Oppressed p. 20

WHY IT WORKED

It was nearly impossible to respond "appropriately" to the display of the caged couple. What would have been the ideal audience reaction? To laugh? To appear indifferent and stone-faced? To turn away in disgust? Interact with (or try to free) the couple? There seemed to be no appropriate response, even if the audience caught on to the inauthenticity of the Guatinauis and got the ironic critique of similar displays from centuries past.

WHAT DIDN'T WORK

If Fusco and Gómez-Peña intended to use the audience as nothing but an instrument to argue that colonial ideas prevail, the setup was perfect. However, if they intended it as an open examination of people's beliefs (as they presented it), it is problematic that their performance offered the audience no legitimate alternative to enacting the role of the subjugating gazer and, in a way, no real agency: the audience couldn't react in a way that dismissed the colonial structure of the encounter.

. . . .

KEY TACTIC
used

HOAX: The Couple in the Cage was an ironic reenactment of the imperialist practice of displaying indigenous peoples in public venues such as taverns, museums, World Expos, and freak shows. By performing "The Couple in the Cage" in various museums, Fusco and Gómez-Peña were exposing the racism, colonialism, and voyeurism of the frame in which they appeared.

OTHER TACTICS USED:
Street theater web
Invisible theater p. 66
Fake press release web
Cognitive dissonance web
*Détournement/Culture
jamming* p. 28

KEY PRINCIPLES
at work

SHOW, DON'T TELL: The performance is an example of silent eloquence. It said it all — colonialism, primitivism, the myth of the noble savage, exoticism — without explicitly stating anything. Viewers were left to draw their own conclusions.

OTHER PRINCIPLES AT WORK:
*The real action is your
target's reaction* web
Do the media's work for them p. 124

MAKE THE AUDIENCE PART OF THE THEATER: Before the audience could fully digest and come to terms with the show, their responses (via video) were turned into a show for another audience.

RECOGNIZE AN OPENING WHEN YOU SEE IT: When the audience seemed to enjoy the same colonial exhibition practice that the performance meant to critique, it added some unintended irony. Yet Fusco and Gómez-Peña were quick to seize the audience's misinterpretation and turn it into the focal point of the performance.

CASE STUDY: The Couple in the Cage

Two undiscovered Amerindians visit the Walker Art Center, Minneapolis. Photo by Robert Sanchez.

[1] Coco Fusco, "The Other History of Intercultural Performance," *TDR: Journal of Performance Studies* 38, no. 1 (Spring 1994): 148.

CASE STUDY:
Daycare center sit-in

WHEN
1989

WHERE
Providence, Rhode Island

PRACTITIONERS
Direct Action for Rights
and Equality (DARE)

CONTRIBUTED BY
Andrew Boyd

Low-income tenants at a public housing project in Rhode Island — many of them working mothers with young children — wanted an affordable day care center in their building. With petitions, pickets, and letters to the city council, they built up a steady drumbeat of pressure on the key decision maker, the local Housing and Urban Development (HUD) director. At a certain point they decided to escalate with direct action *see PRINCIPLE: Escalate strategically*. They occupied the HUD director's office.

They didn't just take it over with signs and shouting or a simple sit-in, however. They brought their kids. They brought their kids' toys. They brought song books, a diaper changing table, and a fold-out crib. And they marched right into the HUD director's office and turned it into a day care center.

They stayed for the whole day, and invited the press. Eventually HUD caved, and a permanent day care center was set up in the housing project.

WHY IT WORKED

This action succeeded because it was very human and visual and had an underlying logic that was impossible to ignore. It was led by those most impacted by the issue: single moms with moral authority in spades.

KEY TACTIC
used

OTHER TACTICS USED:
Direct action p. 32
Occupation p. 78
Creative disruption p. 18
Sit-in web

PREFIGURATIVE ACTION: This action was, in essence, a sit-in, but it had quite a bit more going for it than your average sit-in. It wasn't just disruptive, it was also constructive. The mothers didn't just occupy the office and demand a day care center — they made their own. Their day care center may have only lasted a day, but it was a powerful and prefigurative statement. And by setting it up in the middle of the HUD office, they wielded the basic power of direct action: disrupting business-as-usual and increasing the pressure on HUD to meet their demands. It was both a barn raising and a sit-in; an act of mutual aid and a pressure tactic — and all the more powerful because of it.

MAKE YOUR GROUP COMFORTABLE AND YOUR TARGET UNCOMFORTABLE: What could be more an organic part of these parents' lives than taking care of their own kids? They were completely comfortable with it, and needed to do it anyway. By the same token, having toddlers climbing around the office furniture was quite foreign to the business-as-usual habits of the HUD staff. It was messy and chaotic and made the target uncomfortable. Both of these dynamics helped shift power in the direction of the tenants, and made the target more willing to compromise.

CREATE A THEATRICAL SITUATION THAT KEEPS THE ACTION GOING: Sometimes a protest can peter out because people don't know what to do next. You get rebuffed by your target or the police and can't figure out your next move, or you simply run out of chants, get bored, feel silly, and go home. But the set-up-your-own-day-care-center concept had a built-in theatrical logic and motivation that guided the whole action and kept it going all day. The tenants knew their roles well (they were simply playing themselves, the good parents they already were), and could respond naturally and "in character" to whatever action HUD or the police took, even if they were completely ignored.

BE THE CHANGE YOU WANT TO SEE: The tenants wanted a day care center, so they made one themselves. They were the change they wanted to see in the world. This isn't just good ethics, it's good tactics, too. By walking their talk, the tenants demonstrated an integrity and authenticity that was not only empowering for all who participated, but also earned them respect from the public and in the press.

ACTION LOGIC: Everything the tenants needed to say was embedded in the action itself. The action made all of the elements of their cause visible: the reality of their need (young children), what they wanted (the day care center they had set up), and who was standing in the way (the HUD director). The demand, the target, and the consequences of inaction were all organic parts of the action itself.

KEY PRINCIPLES
at work

OTHER PRINCIPLES AT WORK:
Deploy sympathetic characters p. 146
Pick battles big enough to matter, small enough to win web
Kill them with kindness p. 140
Take leadership from the most impacted p. 180
Everyone has balls/ovaries of steel p. 136
Think narratively p. 186
Make the invisible visible p. 152
Turn the tables p. 190
Show, don't tell p. 124

KEY THEORY
at work

OTHER THEORIES AT WORK:
Points of intervention p. 250

CASE STUDY:
Dow Chemical apologizes for Bhopal

WHEN
December 3, 2004

WHERE
BBC,
broadcast worldwide

PRACTITIONERS
The Yes Men

FURTHER INSIGHT
Video: "Bhopal Disaster
- BBC - The Yes Men"
http://trb.la/y3Gwy2

CONTRIBUTED BY
Mike Bonanno

On the twentieth anniversary of the Bhopal disaster, when an industrial gas leak killed thousands of people, a spokesperson for the company responsible appeared live on BBC World News and announces the impossible: Dow accepted full responsibility for the Bhopal disaster, and had created a $12 billion dollar plan to compensate the victims and clean up the site.

When the broadcast ended, the BBC studio technician was beaming. "What a nice thing to announce," she said.

"I wouldn't work for Dow if I didn't believe in it," he replied. He wasn't lying, but he didn't work for Dow either. In the next hour before the hoax was revealed, Dow's stock temporarily lost billions of dollars.

Red-faced, the BBC chalked it up to an "elaborate hoax," serving their need to cover up the truth: the cause of the hoax was almost too simple to believe: it all came down to a research error.

On November 29, 2004, an email from a BBC researcher came in to DowEthics.com: The network was looking for a Dow representative to discuss the company's position on the 1984 Bhopal tragedy. (The DowEthics website had been set up two years earlier by the Yes Men for a different action, so the email was totally unexpected.)

Since the Yes Men couldn't afford to go to London with their pathetic American dollars, they asked to be booked into a studio in Paris, where Andy was living. No problem. Mr. Jude (patron saint of the impossible) Finisterra (earth's end) became Dow's official spokesperson.

What to say? We settled on the impossible: Jude would announce a radical new direction for the company, one in which Dow would take full responsibility for the disaster. We would lay out a straightforward ethical path for Dow to follow to compensate the victims, clean up the plant site, and otherwise help make amends for one of the worst industrial disasters in history. It would be impossible for Dow not to react in an embarrassing way, which would generate tons of press and needed attention to the disaster *see PRINCIPLE: Put your target in a decision dilemma*).

After the announcement was made, the Yes Men helped Dow express itself more fully by mailing out a more formal retraction: "Dow's sole and unique responsibility is to its shareholders, and Dow CANNOT do anything that goes against its bottom line unless forced to by law." For a while, this statement — as picked up by *Men's News Daily,* a reactionary drivel bucket that didn't realize that the news release was also fake, and didn't object to what it said — became the top story on Google News.

The action put Bhopal and Dow front and center in the U.S. news on the twentieth anniversary of the disaster. And it forced Dow to show, by its curt refusal to do anything proactive, just what "corporate social responsibility" really means.

"When the broadcast ended, the BBC studio technician was beaming. 'What a nice thing to announce,' she said."

Related:

THEORIES
Environmental justice *p. 228*
Ethical spectacle *p. 230*
Points of intervention *p. 250*

This action got massive coverage in the United States, where most Dow shareholders live. It reminded folks of the unfinished business in Bhopal, and let people know that Dow is the company that needs to be held accountable.

WHY IT WORKED

IDENTITY CORRECTION: As fake Dow representative Jude Finisterra said in the interview, this was "the first time in history that a publicly owned company went against their bottom line simply because it was the right thing to do." And it was, of course, too good to be true: Dow quickly made clear that it would *not* do the right thing... simply because it went against their bottom line.

KEY TACTIC
used

OTHER TACTICS USED:
Prefigurative intervention *p. 82*
Hoax *p. 54*

PUT YOUR TARGET IN A DECISION DILEMMA: By announcing on live television that Dow was going to clean up the mess in Bhopal, the action forced Dow to respond. Any move they could make would make them look bad and draw further attention to their inaction on the issue.

KEY PRINCIPLES
at work

CASE STUDY: Dow Chemical apologizes for Bhopal

TAKE LEADERSHIP FROM THE MOST IMPACTED: Figuring out what Dow should say on the twentieth anniversary of the Bhopal disaster proved to be easy: the work was already done by Bhopal activists, who had very specific demands, clearly articulated on their website. It was a simple matter of putting those words in Dow's mouth.

MAKE THE INVISIBLE VISIBLE: When Dow's stock fell because the market thought the company did a good deed for the Bhopal victims, it revealed the callousness of the market in an almost clinical way.

Yes Man Andy Bichlbaum, impersonating Dow Chemical, poses with an "Acceptable Risk Golden Skeleton" that celebrates the concept of acceptable (i.e., economically profitable) human risk.

IF I COULD
TELL YOU
WHAT IT MEANT

THERE WOULD
BE NO POINT IN
DANCING IT

—*Isadora Duncan*

CASE STUDY:
Harry Potter Alliance

WHEN
2005–Present

WHERE
U.S.A.

PRACTITIONERS
Harry Potter Alliance
Nerdfighters
Harry and the Potters
The International Quid-
ditch Association

FURTHER INSIGHT
Video: "TEDxTransmedia
2011 - Andrew Slack - The
strength of a story"
http://trb.la/zUqjvX

Andrew Slack, "Cultural Acupuncture and a Future for
Social Change." The Huffington Post, July 2, 2010.
http://trb.la/xxjucy

Abby Ohlheiser, "Fans of
Action: How Harry Potter Inspired a New Generation
of Activists," The Revealer
http://therevealer.org/
archives/9074

Confessions of an Aca-Fan:
The Official Weblong of Henry
Jenkins, "How "Dumbledore's
Army" Is Transforming Our
World: An Interview with the
HP Alliance's Andrew Slack"
http://trb.la/xQGSgC

CONTRIBUTED BY
Andrew Slack

In 2005, I was amazed by the Harry Potter fan-phe-
nomenon. The franchise was the highest selling work
of fiction in the history of literature. It cut across cultures. Besides the Koran, it was the most requested
book in the Guantánamo Bay prison. Fans invested
enormous resources into conferences, wrote reams
of fan fiction, started Quidditch sports leagues and
tournaments and birthed an entire genre of music:
Wizard Rock, with literally hundreds of bands, all singing about Harry Potter.

And yet, I was frustrated.

"If Harry Potter were in our world," I realized,
"he'd do more than talk about Harry Potter. If we
really were fans of the books, we should fight injustice in our world, the way Harry did in his." In the
books, Harry starts a student activist group called
Dumbledore's Army that wakes the media and
government to Voldemort's return. I wanted to create a
Dumbledore's Army in our own world that could wake
our media and governments to stop global warming and
end genocide in Darfur. By tapping into a teenager's

narrative connection to Harry Potter, such an organization could create a fun and accessible point of entry into what could otherwise be intimidating social issues.

In mid-2005, I met up with Harry and the Potters, two brothers, both indie rock musicians who dress as Harry Potter and sing wildly popular punk songs at concerts with audiences in the hundreds and sometimes thousands. Together, we and a few others founded the Harry Potter Alliance: a "novel" approach to activism, and began using social media to organize the Harry Potter fanbase. Harry and the Potters reposted my action alerts to their 60,000 followers. Soon, other Wizard Rock bands were reposting the alerts. The biggest fan sites, like The Leaky Cauldron and Mugglenet, caught on and media coverage followed, with J. K. Rowling praising the group in *Time* magazine and on her own site. Soon the HPA was organizing amongst almost every facet of the Harry Potter fandom, and grew to seventy volunteer staff and over ninety chapters around the world.

To date, the HPA has sent five cargo planes of relief supplies to Haiti, donated 90,000 books to needy communities and schools across the world, and has made strides in advocating for human rights, LGBTQ equality, media reform and net neutrality.

> "Fan and nerd culture make up a huge section of the most active people online."

Related:

THEORIES

The social cure p. 264
Memes p. 242
Floating signifier p. 234
The tactics of everyday life p. 268
Points of intervention p. 250
Narrative power analysis p. 244
Cultural hegemony p. 222

WHY IT WORKED

J. K. Rowling once worked for Amnesty International. She believes in human rights and other core progressive values and has woven them deeply into the stories. The HPA leverages the identification that millions of young readers have with Harry's values, as well as the rich story parallels between his world and our own. Dumbledore's Army fought media consolidation by the *Daily Prophet* and Wizarding Wireless Network; the HPA fights for net neutrality. Inspired by Harry, who fought inequality facing werewolves, half-giants, and Muggleborns, HPA members have set records phone banking for Massachusetts Equality. We've advocated for indigenous rights just as Dumbledore worked for centaur rights, and just as Hermione organized for equal wages, the HPA "Not in Harry's Name" campaign is challenging Warner Brothers to make all Harry Potter chocolate Fair Trade.

The HPA Haiti Relief plane loaded and ready to go.

. . . .

KEY TACTIC
used

DISTRIBUTED ACTION: HPA has over ninety offline chapters worldwide, and relies on distributed action events as a way to act in unison. Our most successful actions have centered on the midnight releases of new Potter films. (They're simultaneous and worldwide, and people are already going, so it's a great organizing opportunity.) We ask supporters to organize a specific offline action in the movie theater line that goes with the theme of the film. Fan sites are more eager to advertise for this event, as they are already hyping the movie release. At one release night, the *New York Times* showed up at our flagship event, and we gathered thousands of petition signatures from people all over the world asking Warner Brothers to make all Harry Potter chocolate Fair Trade. Distributed actions around movie releases is a tactical approach that can be neatly put to work by other campaigns doing culture-based organizing.

CASE STUDY: Harry Potter Alliance

KNOW YOUR CULTURAL TERRAIN: Meet people where they're at, not where you want them to be. Harry Potter has tens of millions of young fans. HPA went to that fanbase as a *fan*, and *then* from there to the political issues. HPA has also hooked into another huge base of young people: nerds. Fan and nerd culture make up a huge section of the most active people online, and nerdy teenagers are using the Internet to come together in unprecedented ways (just google HP, Hunger Games, Whedon or Dr. Who). The Nerdfighters ("nerds using the power of their awesome to fight world suck") are already starting to do for nerd-dom what HPA has done for Harry Potter fans. Remember to speak your group's language and start with the values they would most readily respond to.

THINK NARRATIVELY: We need to organize through narratives on three levels: personal, collective, and mythological. The personal is your or your constituents' individual story; the collective is the story of a nation or group; the mythological is the deeper, archetypal language of the psyche. Think: Avatar fans fighting against the Sky People (aka the coal industry) to protect the Pandora for our world. History's villains — Hitler, bin Laden and mining companies — work the mythological level, the good guys must, too. In its best moments, the Harry Potter Alliance is engaging in this kind of cultural dreamwork and cultural acupuncture.

CREATE ONLINE/OFFLINE SYNERGY: People congregate online around common interests, but long for offline and real-world connection. Give it to them. Offer the big fan websites and group leaders a chance to make a difference (they normally want it) while demonstrating how it will help them engage their audience more deeply. Have a project for them with a solid ask that is authentically in the language of their site/fandom. Use social media playfully, and with a healthy balance of the three P's: patience, persistence, and pizzazz.

KEY PRINCIPLES
at work

OTHER PRINCIPLES AT WORK:

Make new folks welcome p. 150
Lead with sympathetic characters p. 146
Consider your audience p. 118
Kill them with kindness p. 140
Brand or be branded p. 104
Make your own myths web
Hope is a muscle web
By any media necessary web
Use powerful metaphors web

CASE STUDY:
Justice for Janitors (D.C.)

WHEN
1994–1995

WHERE
Washington, D.C.

PRACTITIONERS
Workers and strategic direct
action practitioners
SEIU

FURTHER INSIGHT
SEIU, "Justice for Janitors"
http://trb.la/wp7UI6
Movie :"The Corporation"
http://trb.la/xuGi1U

Dan La Botz, Troublemaker's
Handbook: How to Fight Back
Where You Work – and Win!
Detroit: Labor Notes, 1991.

CONTRIBUTED BY
Lisa Fithian

In 1994, after ten years of organizing, the Janitors Union in Washington, D.C., had only organized about twenty percent of the commercial real estate buildings downtown — not nearly enough to put upward pressure on wages in the sector. A change in strategy was required. Over the next two years, Justice for Janitors organized a series of creative escalating actions weaving together corporate campaigns, worker organizing, community support and direct actions, called Days of Rage. Within the year, 5,000 janitors — ninety percent of the D.C. market — were unionized and had won wage hikes and benefits. It was a huge victory. Justice for Janitors had hit upon one of the most successful union organizing strategies in recent U.S. history, and the Days of Rage model has been repeated in many places since then.

The model requires several key components: 1) a visibility campaign designed to permeate the collective consciousness, 2) strategic research and campaign planning to create a map and calendar of opportunities, and 3) creative and escalating direct actions focused on a clear target. Combined, these elements help create a political crisis that forces the opponent to either resolve the issues or lose standing in the community.

"D.C. Has Carr Trouble" was our main slogan in December of 1994. Oliver Carr was the biggest commercial real estate owner in D.C. and we thought our little pun creative, given how traffic was sure to be impacted by our bridge-blockading actions. We blocked buildings and parking garages of key real estate giants, took over lobbies and the streets, and got arrested throughout the week.

In March we went to the homes of real estate moguls and blocked the roads to the Capitol building by erecting mock houses in traffic lanes. Then we simultaneously took over the City Council Chambers, the office of Speaker of the House Newt Gingrich, and disrupted Congress from the House Gallery right after the morning prayer, demanding that the wealthy pay their fair share.

September culminated in a massive action shutting down a major bridge from Virginia into D.C. In the middle of the highway, hundreds of janitors erected a classroom, complete with desks and chalk boards. We also parked a school bus and a school van across all four lanes, effectively closing the bridge.

When called out for blocking the bridges, SEIU President John Sweeney replied: "I believe in building bridges whenever [we can] be a full partner with our employers and a full citizen of the communities we live in. But I believe in blocking bridges whenever those employers and those communities turn a deaf ear to the working families we represent."

The September actions had an impact beyond our expectations. Some Cabinet members couldn't commute in. Flights were delayed at Reagan National Airport and the Senate had to delay votes. Needless to say, it was soon made a felony to block a bridge in D.C. Meanwhile, though, we had captured the hearts and minds of people in D.C. for whom janitors were no longer invisible.

Related:

THEORIES

Points of intervention p. 250
The social cure p. 264
Pedagogy of the Oppressed p. 246
Pillars of support p. 248
Narrative power analysis p. 244

Rick Reinhard 1995.

The Janitors for Justice creative direct action model of organizing has been used again and again to great success, including the series of street actions in New York during the week of May 12, 2011, which to some degree set the stage for Occupy Wall Street and the growing movement against Big Banking.

Hundreds of people were willing to use their bodies to take and hold space. Mobility, flexibility and good research were critical, and so was working with allies. The escalating actions created a political crisis. The city could no longer tolerate what was happening, so they had to intervene, creating a political settlement in which the janitors won!

WHY IT WORKED

Rick Reinhard 1995.

WHAT DIDN'T WORK Our message in December 1994 that "D.C. has Carr Trouble," was too clever by half. It did not make clear to the general public who was being impacted. In March of 1995 we shifted to "Pay Your Fair Share," a much clearer message, which we carried into the September actions. It served us well.

BLOCKADE: With those risking arrest in the front, slow cars behind and blockade vehicles in the middle, we shut down numerous bridges. Mobile teams known as "flying squads" were key, as was having a committed group of people who showed up every day to be trained and participate in creative actions and social disruption. By concentrating that level of participation and commitment over a specific period in a specific geographic zone, we created the kind of sociopolitical crisis needed to effect real change.

KEY TACTIC
used

OTHER TACTICS USED:
Mass street action p. 68
Creative disruption p. 18
Direct action p. 32
General strike p. 50

. . . .

ESCALATE STRATEGICALLY: Building a campaign to win requires escalation over time, leading to a moment of compression and crisis. You have to start simply, keep training and building people's confidence so that they take yet more radical steps and courageous actions.

MAINTAIN NONVIOLENT DISCIPLINE: If you are going to build a political crisis using a committed minority, nonviolent discipline is critical.

ANGER WORKS BEST WHEN YOU HAVE THE MORAL HIGH GROUND: If you are going to block a bridge and inconvenience thousands, people must understand what's at stake. You need to illustrate the depth of your commitment and passion for a just solution. You can then channel the resulting public anger to help solve the problem: *If you are pissed about this inconvenience, we are sorry, but call the mayor and demand that he resolve these issues!*

KEY PRINCIPLES
at work

OTHER PRINCIPLES AT WORK:
Choose your target wisely p. 114
Stay on message p. 178
The real action is your target's reaction web
Shift the spectrum of allies p. 172

CASE STUDY:
Lysistrata Project

WHEN

March 3, 2003

WHERE

All over the world

PRACTITIONERS

Eve Ensler

FURTHER INSIGHT

Lysistrata Project archive
http://lysistrataprojectarchive.com/

Operation Lysistrata. Directed by Michael Patrick Kelly. Aquapio films, 2006.
http://aquapiofilms.com/
operation-lysistrata

CONTRIBUTED BY

Kathryn Blume

A publicity photo for a Lysistrata Project production in London. Photo by Nicky Dunsire.

It was early 2003. In the face of unprecedented global public opposition, the Bush Administration was moving relentlessly toward an illegal and unjustified war with Iraq. Desperate to stop the war, people all over the world were seeking creative ways to voice their opposition.

Inspired by the recently organized New York group Theaters Against War, Sharron Bower and I, both of us actors, organized an international day of theatrical action centered around a famous ancient Greek anti-war comedy, *Lysistrata*. Written by the playwright Aristophanes, *Lysistrata* tells the fictitious story of the women of Greece ending the Peloponnesian War by refusing sex until the men quit fighting. Productions traditionally involve nudity on the part of the women and excessively large phalli on the priapically crippled men — conditions which make viewing the play a highly memorable experience.

Over the course of a few days, Bower and I set up a website that served as an instruction manual for organizing a reading of the play. It contained downloadable logos, posters, fliers, a sample press release, a top-ten list of reasons for opposing the war, instructions for organizing a reading and a page listing readings by geographic area with contact information. We then sent an email to everyone we knew offering this reading as a fun, powerful means of opposing the impending war. We suggested people adapt the play to the needs of their own community, and feel free to do readings anywhere that suited them.

Everyone we knew forwarded the email to everyone *they* knew, and we started getting phone calls and emails from all over the world, including one from a college student in Texas which read:

FINALLY! SOMETHING WE CAN DO! I'M
SKIPPING CLASS TO GO ORGANIZE A
READING IN THE QUAD. THANK YOU
FOR THINKING OF THIS! PEACE, PEACE,
PEACE, PEACE, PEACE PEACE PEACE
PEACE PEACE PEACE PEACE!!!!
LOVE, KATE

Related:

THEORIES
The social cure p. 264
Action logic p. 208

Numerous playwrights offered their own transla-
tions of the play, which were posted on the website for
free, and an educational team put together a penis-free
version of the show for kids called *No Hugs, No Kisses* and
a fifty-page study guide — also posted on the site.

By March 3, the day of the event, we had 1,029 readings in fifty-nine countries on six continents (no Antarc-
tica) and in all fifty states. The readings received widespread news coverage in the U.S. and around the world.
There were two star-studded readings in New York and
LA, and smaller readings in living rooms, churches, parks,
rain forest campsites, community theaters, trailer park
diners, a Kurdish refugee camp, as well as at the foot of
the Acropolis in Athens where the play is set. There were
clandestine readings in China and Jerusalem, as well as in
Northern Iraq — undertaken by the international press
corps who had to keep it secret so they wouldn't get fired.

Lysistrata Project readings reached an estimated
200,000 people and raised over $100,000 for peace-ori-
ented charities.

WHY IT WORKED

Lysistrata Project was one of the first virally organized simultaneous events to harness the power of
the Internet to inspire and equip dispersed actions. It
worked partly because we made available an easy-to-
use guide to make participation easy. It worked partly
because the play is a comedy, so it was fun to do and
fun to watch. It worked partly because sex sells. As
playwright Ellen McLaughlin, who directed the main
New York reading at the Brooklyn Academy of Music,
pointed out, "Nobody can resist an ancient Greek dick
joke." It worked partly because the play is in the public domain and could be freely adapted for the needs
of each individual reading. It was also of a particular
moment in time. There had been a ramping-up of protests happening already — including millions turning
out all over the world on February 15, 2003 — and
there was a sense of hope and optimism that the power
of the people might actually prevent the war.

WHAT DIDN'T WORK

The readings didn't stop the war. Also, while the tactic of simultaneous events has frequently been replicated in the years since Lysistrata Project — most successfully by the environmental group 350.org — nobody has ever managed to do another day of theatrical action on such a huge scale. It did, however, inspire smaller simultaneous actions such as readings of Bury the Dead and My Name is Rachel Corrie.

. . . .

KEY TACTIC
used

DISTRIBUTED ACTION: Lysistrata Project participants took great comfort and inspiration in knowing that they were part of a global day of action, and that there were people all over the world participating.

The fact that the event was a mass distributed action also multiplied the power of what each group was doing, so there was less pressure on local organizers to have the biggest possible event — private living room readings were just as valuable as star-studded extravaganzas. The cumulative power of the collective action also made adding readings easier, because gaps became more obvious, and people living in those gaps were driven to organize a reading.

Local, national, and international media outlets were also far more inclined to cover the event because it was happening on such a large scale.

KEY PRINCIPLE
at work

OTHER PRINCIPLES AT WORK:
Balance art and message p. 100
Do the media's work for them p. 124
Create levels of participation web
Make new folks welcome p. 150
Anyone can act p. 98

MAKE IT FUNNY: By choosing a comedy about a sex strike as a form of protest, Lysistrata Project organizers made participation fun for their performers and audience members and made the event irresistible to the media.

TO THOSE WHO CALL US HYPOCRITES FOR USING CORPORATE RESOURCES IN OUR STRUGGLE—WE ARE IN

THE BELLY
OF THE BEAST

AND THERE'S NO WAY OUT THAT DOESN'T GO THROUGH. AND, AFTER ALL, WE'VE PAID FOR THE VERY TEETH THAT CHEW US.

—Occupy Regina

CASE STUDY:
Mining the Museum

WHEN

April 3, 1992 – February 28, 1993

WHERE

Baltimore

PRACTITIONERS

Fred Wilson

FURTHER INSIGHT

Fred Wilson, Mining the Museum: An Installation. (New York, NY: Folio, 1994)

Video: "A Change of Heart: Fred Wilson's Impact on Museums" http://vimeo.com/11838838

CONTRIBUTED BY

Elisabeth Ginsberg

In 1992, a huge sign was hanging from the façade of the Maryland Historical Society announcing that "another" history was now being told inside. The sign referred to African-American artist Fred Wilson's exhibition project "Mining the Museum," which presented the museum's collection in a new, critical light.

Incorporated in 1844, the Maryland Historical Society was founded to collect, preserve, and study objects related to the state's history. This mission included accounts of colonization, slavery and abolition, but the museum tended to present this history from a specific viewpoint, namely that of the its white male founding board. It was this worldview that Wilson aimed to "mine." He did so simply by assembling the museum's collection in a new and surprising way, deploying various satirical techniques, first and foremost irony.

Wilson visually argues that historical representation is as manipulative as advertising.

For instance, in the first room of the exhibit, the audience was confronted with a silver globe — an advertising industry award given at clubs in the first half of the century — bearing the single word "Truth." The trophy was flanked by, on the one side, a trio of portrait busts of prominent white men and, on the other side, three empty black pedestals. The busts were of Napoleon, Henry Clay, and Andrew Jackson. None of these worthies had ever lived in Maryland; they exemplified those deemed deserving of sculptural representation and subsequent museum acquisition. The empty busts were labeled Harriet Tubman, Benjamin Banneker, and Frederick Douglass, three important African-American Marylanders who were overlooked by the ostensibly "local" institution.

"What they put on view says a lot about a museum, but what they don't put on view says even more,"[1] Wilson said in an interview about his installations. He communicated this point by contrasting *what is* with *what should be.* By drawing attention to the overlooked black figures, his installment asked whose truth was on display at the Maryland Historical Society.

The installation "Metalwork 1793–1880" was another way that Wilson reshuffled the museum's collection to highlight the history of African Americans. The installation juxtaposed ornate silver pitchers, flacons, and teacups with a pair of iron slave shackles. Traditionally, the display of arts and craft is kept separate from the display of traumatic artifacts such as slave shackles. By displaying these artifacts side by side, Wilson created an atmosphere of unease and made apparent the link between the two kinds of metal works: The production of the one was made possible by the subjugation enforced by the other. When the audience made this connection, Wilson succeeded in creating awareness of the biases that often underlie historical exhibitions and, further, the way these biases shape the meaning we attach to what we are viewing.

Related:

THEORIES
Cultural hegemony p. 250
Alienation effect p. 210
Anti-oppression p. 220

There have been other attempts to use satirical techniques to critique museum institutions from within. Often these have caused controversies due to misinterpretations and the difficulties inherent in the ambition to destabilize one's own foundation. "Mining the Museum" worked because it was suggestive rather than didactic, provocative rather than moralizing.

WHY IT WORKED

. . . .

IDENTITY CORRECTION: Wilson's intervention was a correction of the museum's identity in the sense that it made the underlying racism apparent. Using glass cases and neat labeling, Wilson's installations mimicked the usual methods of museum display but with a twist so that

KEY TACTICS
used

a new voice or persona was created. As he said it himself: "By bringing things out of storage and shifting things already on view, I believe I created a new public persona for the historical society."[2]

DÉTOURNEMENT/CULTURE JAMMING: Wilson appropriated the museum's collection and reshuffled it so that it communicated a different message, almost antithetical to that of the original constellation. Titling his exhibition "Mining the Museum," he sowed a three-way pun: excavating the collections to extract the covert presence of racial minorities; planting emotionally explosive historical material to raise consciousness; and, finding reflections of himself within the museum (as in "making it mine" — mine-ing).

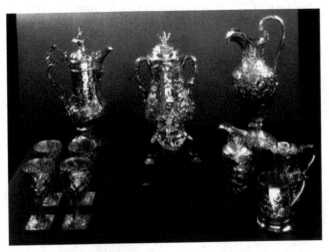

Wilson's installation "Metalwork 1793-1880."

KEY PRINCIPLES
at work

OTHER PRINCIPLES AT WORK:
Reframe p. 168
Use others' prejudices against them p. 192
Lead with sympathetic characters p. 146
Balance art and message p. 100
Seek common ground p. 120

SHOW, DON'T TELL: Wilson communicated his critique through a strategic juxtaposition of the museum's artifacts. The audience was left to draw the conclusions. For example, in an installation entitled "Modes of Transport," Wilson exhibited an old baby carriage in which a Ku Klux Klan hood substituted the usual bedding. The baby carriage was placed next to a photograph of black nannies with white babies — their future employers. Again, Wilson did not make any explicit statements, but simply provided the audience with a strong visual statement about the persistence of racial hierarchies. The suggestion that children readily absorb their parents' prejudices was clear.

MAKE THE INVISIBLE VISIBLE: One of the ways Wilson made the invisible visible was by rewriting the tags of the museum's paintings and changing the lighting to redirect viewers' attention. Further, in a series of "talking paintings," Wilson gave black child slaves voices by playing recordings asking such questions as: "Who calms me when I'm afraid? Who washes my back?" or "Am I your friend? Am I your brother? Am I your pet?" By altering the lighting and adding an audio track, Wilson drew attention to people and groups who historically have been rendered invisible and mute.

> "What they put on view says a lot about a museum, but what they don't put on view says even more."

HOPE IS A MUSCLE: In the final part of his exhibition, Wilson displayed the journal of Benjamin Banneker, a free, self-taught African-American who became a prominent mathematician, surveyor, and astronomer. Banneker was one of the figures absent from the exhibition's first installation. In this way, the exhibition ended with a solution to the problem it pointed out in the beginning. After the indictment of institutionally codified racism, Wilson offered a testament to those pioneers who had managed to resist oppression.

---

[1] Coco Fusco, "The Other History of Intercultural Performance," *TDR: Journal of Performance Studies* 38, no. 1 (Spring 1994): 148.
[2] Ibid. 258

CASE STUDY
Modern-Day Slavery Museum

WHEN
2010–Present

WHERE
Exhibit has toured from
Florida to Massachusetts

PRACTITIONERS
Coalition of Immokalee Workers
Student/Farmworker Alliance
Interfaith Action of South-
west Florida
Just Harvest USA

FURTHER INSIGHT
Modern-Day Slavery
Museum website
http://ciw-online.org/
museum/index.html

CONTRIBUTED BY
Coalition of Immokalee Workers

In December 2008, farm labor contractors Cesar and Geovanni Navarrete were each sentenced to twelve years in prison for their part in what U.S. Attorney Doug Molloy called "slavery, plain and simple." According to the Justice Department, the employers "pleaded guilty to beating, threatening, restraining, and locking workers in trucks to force them to work as agricultural laborers... [They] were accused of paying the workersminimal wages and driving the workers into debt, while simultaneously threatening physical harm if the workers left their employment before their debts had been repaid to the Navarrete family."

Although shocking in its details, the Navarrete case was simply the latest link in a long, unbroken chain of exploitation — including forced labor — in Florida's fields. It was the seventh farm labor operation to be prosecuted for servitude in the state in the past decade, cases involving well over 1,000 workers and more than a dozen employers in total. The federal government has since initiated two additional prosecutions, bringing the total to nine as of 2011.

Even setting aside forced labor, farm work in the U.S. still offers the worst combination of sub-poverty wages, dangerous, backbreaking working conditions, and lack of fundamental labor protections. In this context of structural poverty and powerlessness, extreme forms of abuse such as forced labor are able to take root and flourish. However these cases are reflective of the impunity and exploitation that is rampant throughout the agricultural sector. In other words, modern-day slavery does not take place in a vacuum, nor is it an inevitable feature of our food system.

To highlight these abuses and to identify their causes and solution, in 2010 the Coalition of Immokalee Workers — a community-based farmworker organization — decided to create the Florida Modern-Day Slavery Museum. The mobile museum consists of a cargo truck carefully outfitted as a replica of the trucks involved in the Navarrete case and a collection of displays on the history and evolution of slavery in Florida over the past four hundred years. The multimedia exhibits were developed in consultation with workers who have escaped from forced labor operations, as well as leading academic authorities on slavery and labor history in Florida.

The Florida Modern Slavery Museum is exhibited on the National Mall, Washington, D.C., June 2010. Photo by Fritz Myer

Related:

CASE STUDIES
Taco Bell boycott p. 372

With a team of farmworker and ally docents, the museum toured Florida intensively, visiting churches, schools, universities and community centers for six weeks in the lead-up to the Coalition of Immokalee Workers' three-day Farmworker Freedom March in 2010.

People's reactions to the museum were so overwhelmingly positive and such a buzz was generated that the CIW later decided to tour outside Florida to cities throughout the Southeast and Northeast, including a stop on the National Mall in Washington, D.C. In March 2011, former President Jimmy Carter visited the museum in Atlanta, Georgia. Approximately 10,000 people have toured the museum since its creation.

WHY IT WORKED

The Coalition of Immokalee Workers closely links education and action in its work. The last panel of the museum highlighted the ongoing Campaign for Fair Food as a systemic solution to the problem of farmworker exploitation. And since the Florida tour occurred during the lead-up to a major mobilization, docents were able to extend countless personal invitations for museum-goers (i.e., grocery shoppers) to join the three-day march to the corporate headquarters of Publix Super Markets, one of the CIW's main campaign targets. The museum was both an educational and an organizing tool, reminding attendees of their own capacity for social change and the indispensable role they could play alongside farmworkers in transforming the food system.

A man tours the inside of the box truck that houses the Florida Modern-Day Slavery Museum. Photo by Fritz Myer

KEY TACTIC
used

ART INTERVENTION: The museum was not a "work of art" in the conventional sense of the term, but it did transform both the public spaces it inhabited and the people who viewed it. Through a host of different media and creative displays — the highlight of which was the careful re-creation of the Naverrete operation inside the truck itself — the museum was able to reach viewers at a visceral level.

KEY PRINCIPLES
at work

OTHER PRINCIPLES AT WORK:
Take leadership from the most impacted p. 180
Make the invisible visible p. 152
Lead with sympathetic characters p. 146
Reframe p. 168

SHOW, DON'T TELL: It is often difficult for people to accept that modern-day slavery is a systemic problem facing U.S. agriculture. The thought that the tomato topping your hamburger or tossed in your salad may have been picked by a slave — and was certainly picked by someone receiving very low wages for very difficult work — can trigger a denial impulse that is difficult to break through. But the museum, by using actual historical artifacts, presented a tight and irrefutable indictment of the status quo that was able to pierce this veil and open peoples' minds to dialogue and possibly collective action.

TAKE THE SHOW ON THE ROAD: Instead of waiting for people to come to Immokalee to visit the museum, the CIW brought the museum to the people. With the museum as Exhibit A of an old-fashioned speaking tour, the museum crew toured across Florida and the Eastern U.S., often parking the exhibit right in the center of town. There's nothing like a museum on wheels to draw people's attention, not to mention a museum on wheels that addresses such a pressing and controversial topic as modern-day slavery. It was an effective conversation starter.

TEAM UP WITH EXPERT ADVISERS: A key factor that lent the museum credibility was the support garnered for the project from leading academic authorities on modern-day slavery and Florida's labor history. Several academics had the opportunity to offer crucial feedback on organizers' draft research brief. Others contributed "blurbs" similar to the advance praise you might read on the back of a book jacket, which were included in the museum booklet (which was itself a polished version of the research brief) so that attendees would know that the museum's content had been independently vetted.

CASE STUDY:
The Nihilist Democratic Party

WHEN

2009

WHERE

Denmark

PRACTITIONERS

The Nihilist Democratic Party

FURTHER INSIGHT

NDP website
http://www.nihilistisk-folkeparti.dk/

CONTRIBUTED BY

Simon Roel
Elisabeth Ginsberg

The Nihilist Democratic Party (NDP) was founded by a group of philosophy graduates and students who decided to run for public office on a nihilist platform. Fed up with the state of Danish politics, the students constructed an absurd political position, ironically claiming that the nihilism within religion and science had spread into the political sphere: "All Danes are nihilists. We have no values except our flat-screen TVs. Holding other values is considered religious extremism. The Nihilist Dem-ocratic Party, therefore, is the answer to the democratic deficit that we have witnessed up until now," the party's chairman and candidate for mayor of Copenhagen, Mads Vestergaard, explained in one of the NDP's videos.

> "The NDP's campaign was intended to galvanize opposition to the 'empty promises, cleavage, and emotional porn' that permeate contemporary politics."

The party ran a full campaign in the 2009 local elections, promising such things as psychedelically painted subway tunnels (why should a subway ride be boring?), tax exemption on drugs and alcohol (the death rate stays at 100% anyway, so we might as well have some fun), and the production of a "cuteness canon" that would list all animals deemed cute enough for state-guaranteed protection and care — a reference to a heated debate about the government's production of a "national culture canon" and to the fact that the extreme right wing in Denmark is obsessed with the needs of animals while comfortably ignoring those of immigrants.

The NDP's platform ironically addressed a number of divisive issues. For example, it promoted an aggressive international security policy — not to defend Danish democracy, but to protect the Danes from people with "actual values" (such as Muslims). They were opposed to work *per se* as it aids the government in hiding "the metaphysical fact that life is pointless and completely void of meaning." And they strongly opposed any set of cultural policies, considering culture and art an unwarranted escape from a meaningless existence. Only sports should be funded as they accurately represent the meaninglessness of life, one team or player fighting another for the sake of pointless scores.

The campaign provoked both delight and skepticism. Since the NDP always stayed in character and never admitted to being a hoax, some people, including noted intellectuals, criticized the project on its own terms. For most people, though, the party simply spiced up an otherwise predictable election period. On the popular talk show "Good morning Denmark," the NDP won a poll based on the viewers' text-messaged votes. Yet in the elections, NDP collected "only" around 4,500 votes (out of 2.8 million). Not enough to get into office — but enough to get into the spotlight. Thus, activists managed to deliver a critique of a political sphere riddled with empty pledges and spin much more effectively than had they been writing op-ed articles or otherwise made use of regular channels for citizens to present their views.

Related:

THEORIES
Ethical spectacle p. 230
Theater of the Oppressed p. 272
The propaganda model p. 256
Alienation effect p. 210

WHY IT WORKED

By officially forming a political party and running for elections—complete with banners, posters, flyers, a website, a Facebook page, public speeches, and several candidates in each key policy area—the NDP made it virtually impossible to ignore their candidacy. Because NDP candidates never broke character, voters were kept in a state of confusion. This provoked discussions about the soundness of the NDP's arguments and positions. Indirectly, these discussions invited people to see the proper political parties in a new, critical light.

. . . .

ELECTORAL GUERRILLA THEATER: The NDP's campaign was intended to galvanize opposition to the "empty promises, cleavage, and emotional porn" that permeate contemporary politics. Making fun of cynical campaign promises, their main slogans were "Everything is meaningless anyway - waste your vote on us" and "Politics is shit, and so is the NDP, but at least we admit it." Exaggerating already existing tendencies — e.g., the tendency to see Muslim immigration as a threat to Danish culture or to give priority to the well-being of animals over that of human beings — the NDP called attention to the absurdity of some of the serious campaign pledges.

KEY TACTIC
used

OTHER TACTICS USED:
Identity correction p. 60
Hoax p. 54
Media-jacking p. 72
Prefigurative intervention p. 82
Détournement/Culture jamming p. 28

The NDP wanted Danes to see themselves for what politicians make them out to be: materialists with no higher values beyond what's compatible with an easy, mediocre life demanding few personal sacrifices. Pledges such as the state protection of cute pets financed by a total elimination of foreign aid were intended to expose as false the (self) image of Danes as an idealistic people.

KEY PRINCIPLES
at work

OTHER PRINCIPLES AT WORK:

Use your radical fringe to slide the Overton window p. 200

The real action is your target's reaction web

Turn the tables p. 190

Use absurdity to undermine the aura of authority web

Anyone can act p. 98

Know your cultural terrain p. 142

Balance art and message p. 100

Seek common ground p. 120

DO THE MEDIA'S WORK FOR THEM: Nearly all major Danish newspapers wrote about the new party promoting no values, it being too good a story not to feature. In addition, chairman Mads Vestergaard, visually memorable for his combination of mohawk and business suit, made several appearances on prime-time talk shows, often accusing his political opponents of being "closet nihilists." Both the idea and the execution of a "Nihilist Democratic Party" turned out to be fun enough to make journalists laugh, which, in turn, resulted in a good amount of coverage.

MAKE IT FUNNY: Basing their campaign on pledges such as "children and young people who spend eight hours a day playing World of Warcraft will be released from all mandatory education," it was obvious that the NDP's political to-do list, if carried out, would cripple society. The NDP had no intention of making good on these pledges if elected (which they knew wouldn't happen). Although making sincere, critical statements about Danish politics, the NDP didn't give into the temptation of using the media attention to propel a serious political career.

Psychedelic colors in the metro. Stop the gray brainwashing!

CASE STUDY
Public Option Annie

WHEN
October, 2009

WHERE
Washington, D.C.

PRACTITIONERS
Agit-Pop
Billionaires for Wealthcare
Healthcare for America Now (HCAN)

FURTHER INSIGHT
Video: "Public Option Annie"
http://trb.la/zy2NxP

Video: "The Public Options Rising
Tide," Rachel Maddow Show,
MSNBC, October 23, 2009
http://trb.la/xE7XaK

Video: "Protesters Sing their
Satire," CNN, October 26, 2009
http://trb.la/x66rDw

Video: "Public Option Limited,"
Jon Stewart, October 28, 2009
http://trb.la/yi4Nzy

CONTRIBUTED BY
Andrew Boyd

By the fall of 2009, with Sarah Palin tweeting about "death panels" and town hall meetings overrun by angry teabaggers up in arms (literally) about a supposed "government takeover of healthcare," progressives had officially lost control of the healthcare debate. Could a daring creative action that brought the fight directly to the insurance industry help reframe the conversation and shift momentum back toward reform? One group of activists centered around a small "subvertising" agency called Agit-Pop, certainly thought so.

Working closely with the main healthcare reform coalition, we snuck a handful of professional singers and stealth videographers into a high-profile gathering of insurance industry lobbyists. With fake name tags and business suits, we blended in with the crowd and, just as the closing keynote began, let loose with a "guerrilla musical" complete with soloists, chorus and comic asides. Dubbed "Public Option Annie," and set to the tune of Annie's "Tomorrow," it by turn surprised,

> "Public Option Annie shows what a few determined pranksters can do when they combine moxie, military precision, fake IDs and good old musical theater."

charmed and irritated the assembled lobbyists until security escorted everyone out. Within two hours we had turned the footage and audio into a polished viral video, loaded it onto YouTube and shopped it around to media outlets.

Rachel Maddow ran a glowing segment on it that same night, calling it "the single most unexpected turn of events yet in the fight over health reform." It was then picked up by CNN's Wolf Blitzer and numerous local TV stations. The blogosphere lit up, reform supporters cheered, and Jon Stewart picked up the story, mocking the "terrible" singing for blowing out his eardrums.

That same week the public option made it into the Senate bill. Of course, it later got struck from the final legislation. "Tomorrow," indeed!

Here's what *Variety* magazine had to say about the prank:

Related:

> The stunt was worthy of something dreamed up by a Hollywood press agent of yesteryear: A group of health reform activists quietly infiltrated a D.C. meeting of health insurance executives and, one by one, added their voices to a growing chorus of a satirical version of "Tomorrow" from "Annie." The antics, from the group Billionaires for Wealthcare, was a bit of showmanship in a health care debate that has until only recently been scarce in showbiz moments.

THEORIES
Action logic p. 208
Ethical spectacle p. 230

And as one YouTube user commented:

> The right sends armed, angry and misinformed people to disrupt town halls. The left invades with clever send ups. Charm, wit and intelligence will eventually carry the day.

Public Option Annie shows what a few determined pranksters can do when they combine moxie, military precision, fake IDs and good old musical theater. It's also a great example of the synergies possible when an action has both a "real world" and online dimension. While the action itself was a surgical strike inside the belly of the insurance industry beast, the "stickiness" of the presentation ensured that millions of Americans witnessed it on the tubes.

WHY IT WORKED

. . . .

GUERRILLA MUSICAL: Who doesn't love a good song and dance number? And how much more exciting when the musical breaks out unexpectedly, right next to you, in the middle of an otherwise boring day? And, if on top of that, this "guerrilla musical" is actually singing truth to power behind enemy lines, all the while smiling and staying in key? Those insurance industry lobbyists never had a chance.

KEY TACTICS used

OTHER TACTICS USED:
Infiltration p. 64
Creative disruption p. 18
Direct action p. 32

MEDIA-JACKING: In the theater proper there's a literal stage, but in the (political) world at large, a stage is wherever the action is, whether that's Tiananmen Square or inside an insurance industry conference. By inserting your action into a contested space, you turn it into a stage. By challenging the powers that rule that space, you create the kind of real-world, conflict-laced drama that can powerfully tell your story — and, if packaged right, go viral.

KEY PRINCIPLES
at work

OTHER PRINCIPLES AT WORK:

Kill them with kindness p. 140
Play to the audience that isn't there p. 160
This ain't the Sistine Chapel p. 188
Leverage the celebrity of your target web
Plan your action with military precision web
The real action is your target's reaction web

DO THE MEDIA'S WORK FOR THEM: You cannot count on the mainstream media to tell your story for you — and in our age of cell phone cams, YouTube and instant blogging, you don't have to. The "Annie" team snuck more videographers (six) into the conference than they did singers (five). The whole action was orchestrated for expressive impact, scripted, rehearsed and performed for the camera. Our own cameras.

BALANCE ART AND MESSAGE: There's a tendency on the Left to think that if intentions are good, art doesn't have to be. This is rarely true. If your art is good, people will pay more attention to what you're trying to say. Even people who disagree with your views will still respect your effort because you showed them the respect of making as strong and beautiful an artwork as possible. The lead "Annie" soloist was a professionally trained opera singer with six years at the Met. The "Annie" team went through four scripts till they hit on the right one, and then rehearsed it as intensely as time would allow. That amount of preparation isn't always possible but, in general, if you take your art seriously, your audience is more likely to take your ideas seriously.

CASE STUDY: Public Option Annie

POLITICS

IS THAT

DIMENSION

OF SOCIAL LIFE
IN WHICH THINGS
BECOME

TRUE

IF ENOUGH PEOPLE
BELIEVE THEM

—*David Graeber*

CASE STUDY
Reclaim the Streets

WHEN
1995–2000

WHERE
London and
around the world

PRACTITIONERS
Reclaim the Streets
Situationist International

FURTHER INSIGHT
Hamm, Marion. "Reclaim the
Streets: Global Protest, Local Space"
Republicart. May, 2002.
Mckay, George (ed.). DIY
Culture: Party and Protest
in Nineties Britain. London &
New York: Verso, 1998.
Klein, Naomi. No Logo:Taking Aim
at the Brand Bullies.
New York: Picador, 2000.
Notes From Nowhere (ed.), We Are
Everywhere: The Irresistible
Rise of Global Anticapitalism.
London & New York: Verso, 2003.

CONTRIBUTED BY
John Jordan

Reclaim the Streets (RTS) began as creative activist group in London, but its tactics, blending party and protest, soon spread around the world. Merging the direct action of Britain's anti-road building movement and the carnivalesque nature of the counter-cultural rave scene, RTS became a catalyst for the global anti-capitalist movements of the late '90s.

RTS saw the streets as the urban equivalent of the commons *see THEORY: The commons*, in need of reclaiming from the enclosures of the car and commerce and transformed into truly public places to be enjoyed by all. RTS became most known for its street parties, which served not only as a protest vehicle against car culture but also as a prefigurative vision of what city streets could be in a system that prioritized people over profit and ecology over the economy *see TACTIC: Prefigurative intervention*.

The first street party took place in North London in May 1995. Using rave culture tactics, the location was kept secret until the last moment, and participants were led from a public meeting point through the subway to emerge at the party site before the police had time to gather forces.

The event began with two cars crashing into each other. The drivers jumped out in theatrical road rage and began to destroy each other's vehicles with hammers. Meanwhile, 500 people emerged from the subway station into the traffic-free street that the crashed cars had blocked, and started the party, dancing, sharing free food and meeting new friends.

From 1995-98, street parties evolved in complexity and scale. Creative techniques ranged from tons of sand dumped in the road to create a sand box, to tripods made from scaffolding erected in the middle of the street with someone sitting on top. These "intelligent" barricades blocked the road from cars and yet opened it for pedestrians.

In the summer of 1996, 8,000 participants took over a motorway while huge carnival figures with hooped skirts moved amongst them. Underneath the skirts, hidden from view, activists drilled into the tarmac with jack hammers and planting saplings into the motorway. This story took on the power of a myth as it circulated on the early threads of the world wide web. It even inspired striking longshoremen from Liverpool to make common cause with RTS, proof that imagination can break down barriers of class and political/ cultural difference.

The RTS meme soon spread across the UK and the Western world. A global street party in seventy cities occurred in May 1998, coinciding with the G8 summit. A year later, a "Carnival Against Capital" on June 18th, coordinated by RTS and the People's Global Action network, saw simultaneous actions in financial districts across the world, from Nigeria to Uruguay, Seoul to Melbourne, Belarus to Dhaka. Six months after that, a carnivalesque mass street action shut down the WTO in Seattle, an event that proved to be the coming-out party for the anti-globalization movement.

"Much political action is predictable and boring; street parties are quite the opposite."

Related:

THEORIES
Ethical spectacle p. 230
Memes p. 242
Society of the Spectacle p. 266
Temporary Autonomous Zone (TAZ) p. 270

CASE STUDIES
Streets into gardens p. 368

RTS was successful because it did not look or feel like a typical protest. Much political action is predictable and boring; street parties are quite the opposite. All sorts of people got involved because they knew it would be both a transgressive political adventure and a brilliant party. RTS's political audacity — "let's hold a mass carnival in the financial district or a rave on a motorway" — ignited hope, and hope is the catalyst for the formation of new movements. Another key reason for its popularity was that it involved a simple, adaptable formula: disseminate an invitation over the still-young Internet, get a sound system and occupy a street. Its creativity came from its diversity — from artists to anarchists, unionists to ecologists, ravers to cyclists — all came together to experiment with new forms of mass action.

WHY IT WORKED

CARNIVAL-PROTEST: With its music, wild costumes, liberated bodies, color and revelry, RTS created rebel carnivals. Unlike regular carnivals and parades, RTS never asked for permission, leaving the event open to the possible and impossible, turning the world on its head in true carnival spirit.

KEY TACTIC
used

OTHER TACTICS USED:
Direct action p. 32
Mass street action p. 68
Flash mob p. 46

Reclaim the Streets NYC logo.

CASE STUDY: Reclaim the Streets

HOPE IS A MUSCLE: While street parties were often accompanied by written propaganda explaining the ideas and theories behind them, the thing that had the greatest impact was not the theory that went into the events but the hope that emerged. The hope that unfurled from these events not only catalysed the anti-globalization movement, but many of those involved went on to work in various global justice movement groups such as Genetic Engineering Network, the Wombles, Dissent!, the Rising Tide Network, the Clandestine Insurgent Clown Army, the Climate Camp and the Occupy movement.

NO ONE WANTS TO WATCH A DRUM CIRCLE: Whilst the surprise location of the street parties was not something that could be public knowledge before the event, as the police would have shut them down, the events themselves were very participatory. RTS was an open invitation for people to come to the street party with whatever creative ideas they wanted. Unlike marches with set themes and slogans, street parties were frames for collective spontaneity. Even if you did not bring your own costume, giant prop or free feast, then simply the act of dancing with thousands of others on a road meant that you were an active participant rather than spectator or consumer.

KEY PRINCIPLES
at work

OTHER PRINCIPLES AT WORK:

Put your target in a decision dilemma p. 166
Simple rules can have grand results p. 176
Create levels of participation web
Everyone has balls/ ovaries of steel p. 136
Show, don't tell p. 174
Take risks, but take care p. 182
Change attitudes by transforming space web

CASE STUDY:
The salt march

WHEN
1930

WHERE
Gujarat, India

EPIGRAPH
"Gandhi's greatness lay in doing what everyone could do but doesn't."
–Louis Fischer, Gandhi's biographer[1]

PRACTITIONERS
Gandhi
Indian independence movement

FURTHER INSIGHT
Nonviolent Conflict, "The Indian Independence Struggle (1930-1931)"
http://trb.la/yPdPOu
Video: "Salt March"
http://trb.la/w6WuLH

CONTRIBUTED BY
Nadine Bloch

Any collection of creative actions worth its salt would include a reference to Gandhi's famous march — and the conversation would be flavored with strategic and practical lessons still resonant today.

In 1930, the Indian National Congress adopted *satyagraha* (essentially, nonviolent protest) as their main tactic in their campaign for independence. Mahatma Gandhi was appointed to develop a plan of action; he proposed marching to the sea to make salt in defiance of the Salt Act of 1882. Violation of the Salt Act, which made it illegal for anyone to collect or produce salt except for authorized British nationals, did not immediately catch the imagination of the delegates, and was reportedly met with some laughter in the Congress. The Raj (as the British empire in India was known) did not take this idea as much of a threat either. Viceroy Lord Irwin actually wrote back to London to report, "At present the prospect of a salt campaign does not keep me awake at night."[2]

This would soon change, however, as the salt march, which began with about eighty men, quickly gathered supporters on its way to the Indian Ocean. Gandhi framed the 240-mile march from his ashram to the sea within a traditional cultural practice known as the *padyatra* (a long spiritual march). Not only did this help make the whole program more understandable to the Indian public, it opened up the possibility to do outreach, gather more supporters, educate and provide training, and work the national and international press. Advance teams worked the route and followers slept out in the open in each town to be more accessible.

When he and more than 12,000 supporters finally reached the sea, the day chosen to make salt was the ten-year anniversary of the first round of national resistance actions. The British were slow to react at first, allowing more Indians to join in the protest. As salt making spread, and the British responded brutally, the empire's facade of civility slipped and then fell away entirely.

WHY IT WORKED

The salt march had profound cultural resonance for Indians across lines of caste and class because Gandhi did his strategic planning homework by travelling (always third class) all over India for a year.[3] In the process of talking

CASE STUDY: The salt march

the pulse of the country, he recognized that in order to attract unified masses across caste and religious lines, the campaign to win something as ethereal as independence needed to be linked to a tangible manifestation of that demand. The more it affected or appealed to the poor and lower classes, and the greater the benefit for the majority of Indians, the greater the chance of expanding the movement, and therefore winning.

When people could hold the physical distillation of their labor — salt — in their hands, the esoteric, long-term goal of independence became concrete and immediate. This was action design at its most brilliant.

Related:

THEORIES
Action logic p. 208
Pillars of support p. 248
Hamoq & hamas p. 236
Ethical spectacle p. 230
Points of intervention p. 250
Floating signifier p. 234
Revolutionary nonviolence p. 260

TREK: The act of marching and the culminating act of making salt by the sea's edge, while seemingly simple, actually offered the masses a chance to act courageously through both coordinated and dispersed action. As the march attracted more adherents, and as the movement grew, so the pillars of the empire's power *see THEORY: Pillars of support* were seriously undermined. The salt march set the stage for India's eventual independence as Indians and Brits alike realized that rule was not practicable without the consent of the governed. That consent had dissolved into the sea.

"As saltmaking spread, and the British responded brutally, the empire's facade of civility slipped and then fell away entirely."

KEY TACTICS
used

OTHER TACTICS USED:
Strategic nonviolence p. 88
Direct action p. 32
Distributed action p. 36

PREFIGURATIVE INTERVENTION: Making salt married an improvement in quality of life to political aspirations for independence, and provided a pattern for "constructive work" that was the backbone of a myriad of Indian resistance efforts, which included advocacy of homespun cloth, schools and gardens. In fact, the entire march was set up to prefigure an alternative way of life and social structure that modeled an ideal (and economically

[1] Life Positive, "Mahatma Gandhi - A Living Sermon," by Tom Weber.
   http://www.lifepositive.com/spirit/masters/mahatma-gandhi/dandi-march.asp
[2] Peter Ackerman and Jack Duvall, *A Force More Powerful* (New York, NY: Palgrave, 200), 84
[3] Peter Ackerman and Jack Duvall, *A Force More Powerful* (New York, NY: Palgrave, 200), 71

Gandhi during the Salt March, March 1930.

CASE STUDY: The salt march

self-reliant) Indian society and prepared Indians to assume political leadership.

PUT YOUR TARGET IN A DECISION DILEMMA: The public defiance of the salt march put the empire in a classic double bind: Each salt maker arrested would become a martyr for the movement and expose the brutal hand of the regime. Of course, by doing nothing, they also gave space for the movement to grow, and even worse, for onlookers to think that the English had either lost the will or the ability to control the situation.

CHOOSE YOUR TARGET WISELY: Challenging the British Salt Tax perfectly embodied the injustice of the British rule. The burden of this regressive tax fell disproportionately on those who could least afford it. It also provided a way for anyone with access to seawater — upper class or untouchable, Hindu or Muslim — to participate. Outreach and education events were used throughout the march to broaden its reach.

KEY PRINCIPLES
at work

OTHER PRINCIPLES AT WORK:

Know your cultural terrain p. 142
Use the power of ritual p. 198
If protest is made illegal, make daily life a protest p. 138
Maintain nonviolent discipline p. 148
Make new folks welcome p. 150
Enable, don't command p. 132
Make the invisible visible p. 152
Create levels of participation web
Reframe p. 168
When the people are with you, act web
Do your research web

CASE STUDY:
Santa Claus Army

WHEN

1974

WHERE

Denmark

PRACTITIONERS

Solvognen

FURTHER INSIGHT

Video: "Julemandshæren" (Danish
documentary on the Santa
Claus Army, English subtitles)
http://trb.la/zpgVWF

CONTRIBUTED BY

Elisabeth Ginsberg

In the lead-up to Christmas 1974, an army of about seventy Santa Clauses, male and female, paraded through the city of Copenhagen, singing carols, handing out sweets and hot chocolate, and asking everyone what they wanted for Christmas.

Members of the Santa Claus Army giving away books they just took off the shelves. Photos such as the one above, showing the Danish police harassing the Santas for being "too generous," circulated widely in the 1970s.

After spending a few days cementing the good image of good old Santa Claus, their generosity became increasingly radical. Among other things, the Santas climbed a barbed wire fence surrounding the recently shuttered General Motors assembly plant with the purpose of giving jobs back to "their rightful owners."

The week-long performance reached its crescendo inside one of Copenhagen's biggest department stores when the Santas started handing out presents to customers directly off the shelves. Before too long, security guards and shop assistants interrupted the magic, desperately tearing the presents out of people's hands. The police soon showed up and escorted the Santa Clauses out onto the street, where they were roughed up and thrown into paddy wagons in spite of the fact that it wasn't clear that a criminal act had been committed, except perhaps on the part of customers who took home the presents without paying.

The performance exposed the radical implications of the myth of Santa Claus' boundless generosity, demonstrating that true generosity is impossible within the narrow terms of capitalist society. With widely distributed photos of Santa Claus getting beaten for being too generous, the action was a hit.

The people behind Santa's beards were the Danish theater collective *Solvognen* ("The Sun Chariot," an allusion to Norse mythology). During the 1970s, the collective performed many large-scale actions intended to make bourgeois Danish society "act itself out as theater."

Related:

THEORIES
Ethical spectacle p. 230
Cultural hegemony p. 222
Action logic p. 208
The commons p. 220

Solvognen's spectacles were powerful, among other reasons because they appropriated images from popular culture and ascribed these images a new meaning: Father Christmas handing out gifts to children became a critique of hypocrisy in consumerist society. The well-known imagery drew the audience quickly into the performances and, further, equipped them with a key to interpret what was going on.

WHY IT WORKED

GUERILLA THEATER: Most of Solvognen's actions were surprise performances in unlikely public spaces to an unsuspecting audience. Through performances that were playful, bold and easy to understand, Solvognen managed to spread its political ideas beyond the circle of true believers: most Danes knew about Solvognen and its activities. Legend has it that people even started seeing them when they weren't there: at a public viewing of an American F-16 jet fighter, three *real* security guards were arrested on suspicion of being members of Solvognen!

KEY TACTIC
used

OTHER TACTICS USED:
Prefigurative intervention p. 82
Identity correction p. 60
Creative disruption p. 18
Hoax p. 54
Direct action p. 32

THE REAL ACTION IS YOUR TARGET'S REACTION: The performers made it difficult for the authorities not to become part of the theater. Doing their job, the police were obligated to intervene. Had the police for some reason ignored the performers, the theater would have been incomplete. Hence, the success of the performance was dependent on the actions of the target.

MAKE FRIENDS WITH THE POLICE (UNLESS IT IS FUNNY NOT TO): Solvognen's interaction with the police was highly strategic. Alwaysstaying in character even in the midst of violent confrontation with the police, the performers created priceless photo ops.

KEY PRINCIPLES
at work

OTHER PRINCIPLES AT WORK:
Kill them with kindness p. 140
Do the media's work for them p. 124
Know your cultural terrain p. 142
Escalate strategically p. 134
Play to the audience that isn't there p. 160
Lead with sympathetic characters p. 146
Use the power of ritual p. 198
Use your radical fringe to slide the Overton window p. 200

CASE STUDY:
Small gifts

WHEN

2006–present

WHERE

Various public locations
across the UK and Europe

EPIGRAPH

"The gift must travel."

–Anonymous

PRACTITIONERS

Rajni Shah

FURTHER INSIGHT

Small gifts, Rajni Shah
http://trb.la/wOUh8ws

Marcel Mauss, The Gift: The Form
and Reason for Exchange in Archaic
Societies.
W. W. Norton & Company, 2000.

"Everything for Everyone,
Nothing for Ourselves" by the
Lab of Insurrectionary
Imagination
http://labofii.net/experiments/psi

"Burning with Desire: At Black
Rock City, it is better to be
awesome than rich." Walrus
Blog, September 13, 2010.
http://trb.la/zkCirr

CONTRIBUTED BY

Rajni Shah

Small gifts is a series of interventions that introduces new spaces for conversation and generosity within shopping centers. The series was conceived as a way of presenting concepts of radical generosity to people who might otherwise not think of themselves as political.

Some of the questions that this series addressed include:

- What would our world look like if we exchanged gifts rather than money?
- What is the value in speaking to strangers?
- What if we focused on giving as much as we can rather than as little?

One particular intervention, called "give what you can, take what you need," invites passersby to share resources, cultivating the recognition that everyone might have something useful to bring to the table.

The intervention takes place in a busy shopping center, where three artists (Rajni Shah and two other collaborators including, at various times, Lucille Acevedo-Jones, Lucy Cash, Sheila Ghelani and Ilana Mitchell) set up a large dining table and chairs and prepare one hundred tiny envelopes, each containing a one-pound coin (US$1.50), a question to serve as a conversation starter, and an instruction to use the pound as inspiration to make, buy or find something to bring back to the table.

> "Because the interventions don't ask participants to assume any particular political position, they involve a much broader range of people than other, more targeted actions."

Passersby are approached by the artists and invited to take part in the intervention by accepting the gift contained within the small envelope. On acceptance of the envelope, they become part of the conversation, and decide for themselves whether or how they will spend the pound, and whether they will return to the table.

If they do return with something to offer, they are invited to use their conversation-starter question to meet new people, and can partake of whatever is on the table at that time.

This intervention is typical of the *small gifts* series in that it asks the participant to determine what he/she takes from the experience, guided only by a series of simple conversation starters and whatever is being shared on the table. Stated outcomes included a renewal of faith in other people and the formation of community among strangers. In addition to the people who return to the table, everyone who takes an envelope then has to decide what to do with their pound coin, provoking discussion about generosity, value and ownership.

Related:

THEORIES
Points of intervention p. 250
Temporary Autono-
mous Zone p. 270
The tactics of everyday life p. 268
The commons p. 220
Capitalism p. 216

WHY IT WORKED

Because the interventions don't ask participants to assume any particular political position, they involve a much broader range of people than other, more targeted actions. The participatory, conversation-sparking nature of the work allowed for a deeper connection with the principles of generosity and gift economy, and actively encouraged strangers to connect with one another.

WHAT DIDN'T WORK

This type of intervention only worked within a busy environment and required a lot of initiative and attention to detail. In the example described, there were always three people "hosting" and constantly engaging in unique conversations with passersby.

. . . .

KEY TACTIC
used

HAPPENING: This is an example of a gentle happening that can take on a life of its own. When the artists did this project in Manchester, they left the party in progress, and allowed conversations to continue without them. It felt important that the public had taken ownership of the concept *also see PRINCIPLE: Simple rules can lead to grand results.*

KEY PRINCIPLES
at work

KILL THEM WITH KINDNESS: The beauty of this kind of gentle, open intervention, which uses gift giving to engage with people, is that it attracts people who are not usually drawn to either "arty" or "political" interventions. *Small gifts* allowed the artists to create spaces for

'Give what you can, take what you need' gift envelope with pound coin. Photo provided by artist.

"Give what you can, take what you need" in Piccadilly Gardens, Manchester, with artists Sheila Ghelani, Ilana Mitchell and Rajni Shah. Photo provided by artist.

CASE STUDY: Small gifts

genuine conversation and then let those conversations lead where they may. It also allowed for new relationships to develop across social divides — a deeply political but almost entirely non-confrontational action.

OTHER PRINCIPLES AT WORK:
Simple rules can have grand results p. 176
Show, don't tell p. 174
Make new folks welcome p. 150

BALANCE ART AND MESSAGE: *Small gifts* aimed to bring a sense of trust and beauty into the otherwise manipulative and fully commodified world of shopping centers. The artist-originators spent a lot of time preparing their materials, so that the gifts they were handing out would feel like real gifts and not easily be dismissed. By beautifully handcrafting their initial gifts, the artists invited the same care and attention to detail from passersby.

BE THE CHANGE YOU WANT TO SEE: This action came from the artist's own sadness that most radical works of art only create a greater divide between those who already believe in a cause and those who don't — and a realization that she herself was afraid of speaking to strangers.

KNOW YOUR CULTURAL TERRAIN: Choosing to site the interventions in shopping centers only added to the message: operating within a hub of commercialism, the ideas of gift exchange and simple generosity seemed all the more radical and transgressive.

CASE STUDY
The Stolen Beauty
boycott campaign

WHEN

June 2009–present

WHERE

Global

PRACTITIONERS

Palestinian BDS (Boycott,
Divestment & Sanctions) campaign
Palestinian civil society

FURTHER INSIGHT

Stolen Beauty campaign
www.stolenbeauty.com
Boycott Soda Stream
www.codepink.org/
boycottsodastream
Boycott, Divestment &
Sanctions campaign
www.bdsmovement.net
VIDEO: BDS Brides Take LA
http://trb.la/Axwl82
VIDEO: CODEPINK Goes
to Cosmoprof
http://trb.la/yXz9sz

CONTRIBUTED BY

Kristen Ess Schurr

A group of American and Israeli women enter the Ahava cosmetics shop in the Tel Aviv Hilton. Sporting bikinis, they smear mud on their bodies, scrawling the words "Stolen Beauty" and "No Love in Ahava." Questions are asked, a dialogue begins. A few weeks later at a "Tel Aviv Beach Party" in New York, another group of women in bikinis conveys the same messages.

These actions were just the beginning of a multi-pronged international campaign against Ahava Dead Sea Laboratories, an Israeli company located in an illegal settlement in the Occupied West Bank. The message is in the mud: there is nothing beautiful about occupation.

Stolen Beauty seeks to educate consumers, store managers, CEOs, and the general public about Ahava's illegal practices. Our tactics range from guerrilla theater to online culture jamming. We target Ahava — its location in an illegal settlement, its fraudulent labeling, and its illegal pillaging of mud from the shores of occupied lands — as a poster child of the Israeli occupation of the West Bank, East Jerusalem and Gaza Strip. By drawing attention to Ahava's settlement products, we educate the American and global public on what is really happening in the occupied West Bank, contributing to the much larger international campaign of boycotts, divestment and sanctions calling on the Israeli government to respect international law and Palestinian rights.

Soon after the launch of the campaign, we discover that *Sex and the City* star Kristin Davis is both Ahava's spokes-model and an Oxfam Goodwill Ambassador. Our boycott supporters contact Oxfam, which has an explicit policy against Israeli settlement products. Oxfam suspends Davis from publicity work for the duration of her Ahava contract. The story lands in the gossip column of the New York Post; terrible publicity for

> "The Stolen Beauty campaign has proven effective because it is multipronged, strategic, global and responsive."

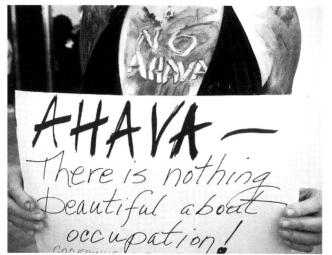

Muddy Reality: Ahava is Stolen Beauty. Photo by CODEPINK.

Related:

THEORIES
Points of intervention p. 250
Action logic p. 208

Ahava, but good for fans of justice and peace. Davis does not renew her contract with the company.

Next, Ahava announces a Twitter contest for free products. We issue a call to Tweet in messages like: "Does AHAVA offer a moisturizer to sooth my hands after so much ethnic cleansing?" We culture jam their marketing contest, turning it into a #socialmediafail.

Creative interventions continue to target points of intervention such as stores that carry Ahava's products *see THEORY: Points of intervention.* For instance, ten women don pink bathrobes with matching towels wrapped around their heads and walk into these stores, singing jingles about the ills of occupation. Protesters and other patrons ask the store to stop stocking Ahava cosmetics.

Ahava's reputation as an international brand has been tarnished by the first two years of the boycott campaign and the resulting bad press. The company lost its celebrity spokesmodel, it lost the lease on its Covent Garden store, and a number of small, independent stores stopped stocking its products. Ahava removed the store locator from its U.S. web site, and sent a letter to retailers filled with false claims about our campaign and where they source their materials. In 2010, Ahavawas condemned as being complicit in Israeli government crimes at the Russell Tribunal on Palestine, London Session, and its production and labeling practices have come under extensive scrutiny in Europe.

The Stolen Beauty campaign has proven effective because it is multipronged, strategic, global and responsive. It provides space for engagement at all levels of activism,

WHY IT WORKED

in locations around the world. The campaign employs a range of tactics including street actions, guerrilla theater, culture jamming, social media work, traditional media outreach, and consumer education. The campaign acts as an omnipresent mosquito buzzing around the head of the company, a target chosen because its practices contravene international law. A core group developed the campaign — the web site, the tools and resources — and coalition activists around the world were able to use them in their locales.

- -

KEY TACTICS
used

OTHER TACTICS USED:
Boycott web
Détournement/Culture
jamming p. 28
Media-jacking p. 72
Street theater web
Creative disruption p. 18
Distributed action p. 36

CREATIVE DISRUPTION: Stolen Beauty activists get attention and tell a story with outrageous costumes, direct action and clever yet clear messaging. Stores that sell illegal settlement products come to a standstill when we enter singing in bathrobes, smeared with mud or performing marriage ceremonies pledging ourselves to the pursuit of Palestinian human rights.

DISTRIBUTED ACTION: Stolen Beauty has succeeded in getting a diverse set of tools into the hands of high numbers of activists to wage a multi-pronged, global campaign. The script and song sheets for actions like performing a marriage ceremony pledging to boycott settlement products in front of the Bed, Bath & Beyond Bridal Registry are easily downloadable from the Stolen Beauty website. We provide Twitter suggestions via email for the lone wolf and tips for indoor Valentine's Day parties when the weather is bad to clog the comment threads of beauty sites that sell Ahava.

KEY PRINCIPLES
at work

USE THE LAW, DON'T BE AFRAID OF IT: Occupation is illegal. It directly contravenes international law, the Geneva Conventions and existing United Nations resolutions. Stolen Beauty puts the onus where it belongs: Israeli companies are breaking the law and profiting from the occupation, and should be held to account. While bringing attention to these facts, activists dressed in bathrobes, bikinis or bridal wear risk arrest in order to creatively disrupt business as usual.

MAKE THE INVISIBLE VISIBLE: People shopping for high-end cosmetics, as well as passersby, store clerks and managers, are made aware of the Israeli occupation

CASE STUDY: The Stolen Beauty boycott campaign

when they are exposed to Stolen Beauty's actions. The campaign undermines the legitimacy of the "Made in Israel" stamp, and makes visible illegal profiteering from occupation.

PICK BATTLES BIG ENOUGH TO MATTER, SMALL ENOUGH TO WIN: Will activists stop the Israeli occupation of Palestine by boycotting a cosmetic company? No. But the campaign is affecting Ahava's reputation and bottom line by exposing its ugly secrets, and contributing to the much larger Boycott, Divestment and Sanctions campaign. Activists have convinced many local stores to stop carrying Ahava, and the British Boycott, Divestment and Sanctions campaign was able, after months of continual protest, to get the Ahava flagship store to close its Covent Garden location.

OTHER PRINCIPLES AT WORK:

Reframe p. 168
Create levels of participation web
Lead with sympathetic characters p. 146
Show, don't tell p. 174
Always have an ask or next step web
By any media necessary web

CASE STUDY:
Streets into gardens

WHEN
1999

WHERE
New York City

PRACTITIONERS
Reclaim the Streets NYC
More Gardens! Coalition
Lower East Side Collective

CONTRIBUTED BY
Mark Read

In the spring of 1999, real estate values in New York's East Village and Lower East Side neighborhoods were skyrocketing, in no small part due to the beautiful network of communitygardens in the area. In a massive giveaway to corporate developers, then-Mayor Rudolph Giuliani announced he would auction off 198 community gardens. Gardeners and their supporters began organizing to stop it from happening.

On a gray and quiet Saturday afternoon weeks before the auction, two "tripod teams" were anxiously milling about on Avenue A in the East Village, anticipating the arrival of a boisterous crowd assembling several blocks away. All the constituent parts of the tripod, along with several plant boxes and other sundry items, had been stashed in strategic and discrete locations along the sidewalk.

Meanwhile, the diverse and growing crowd was in the garden finishing its face-painting, elf-costuming and other preparations. Lace-winged children and leaf-adorned stilt-walkers made their way into the street. The brass notes of trombones, tubas and saxophones rang out as the throng of garden protectors proceeded westward along 7th Street and turned the corner onto Avenue A. When the crowd arrived, the teams quickly erected the tripods. The designated"perchers" quickly ascended the rope that hung from the center and installed themselves in the cradle formed at the top. Traffic was thus effectively and immediately shut down. Marchers dragged the plant boxes into the street, gave packages of seeds to the children and began teaching them how to make roses grow. With a bit of rope and some ingenuity, others were able to turn several misplaced police barricades into a seesaw. Beautifully wrapped packages were opened to the delight of all as the crowd, which had been asked to bring gifts to share, bestowed one another with presents. A sound crew wheeled a massive set of speakers into the street and began broadcasting a pirate radio signal that was transmitting from a nearby apartment. Dancing began in earnest, and the crowd soon swelled to 300, then 400, then 500.

For the next several hours, a city block became the sort of public space that Giuliani was planning to eliminate by selling the gardens. One banner above all others summed up the driving logic of the action: "If they're going to pave over the places where we play, then we will play in the places they've paved over." The frame stuck, and was repeated in the mainstream media that night and the next day. By the time the auction was scheduled to take place, public sentiment had shifted strongly against the mayor on this issue. He was ultimately forced to stop the auction and sell the gardens to private land trusts instead of greedy developers, and all of the gardens were preserved in perpetuity.

Related:

THEORIES

Temporary Autonomous Zone p. 270

Action Logic p. 208

Ethical Spectacle p. 230

A Reclaim the Streets' festival of resistance in support of Streets into Gardens action.

The "streets into gardens" action viscerally demonstrated what would be lost were Giuliani to succeed in paving over the community gardens of New York City. By taking the city's position on gardens (pave them over) and inverting that logic in the streets (play on the pavement), organizers were able to reveal the outrageous injustice of the auction itself while simultaneously embodying the world they were fighting to preserve. The action was also, crucially, one part of a much larger, broad-based campaign. It was thus clearly understood within the context of that campaign to save the gardens. Lastly, the action was able to draw in passersby and turn them into participants because it was bold, innovative, daring, and most of all, fun!

CARNIVAL-PROTEST: This action was a "festival of resistance" or a carnival-protest, and it certainly benefited from the use of this tactic in the expected ways: the

WHY IT WORKED

protest didn't feature a long list of speakers, it didn't insist on using angry chants to drive its message, it was participatory and it was fun! People from around the neighborhood actually joined in the action and stayed in the street with the demonstrators. The tactic of carnival protest was especially well-suited to the frame of the action, which was all about maintaining and protecting public spaces that are themselves cites of celebration and community participation.

OTHER TACTICS USED:

Mass street action p. 68
Prefigurative intervention p. 82
Direct action p. 32

KEY PRINCIPLES
at work

OTHER PRINCIPLES AT WORK:

Escalate strategically p. 134
*No one wants to watch a
drum circle* p. 156
Reframe p. 168
Show, don't tell p. 174
*Lead with sympathetic
characters* p. 146
Create levels of participation web

TURN THE TABLES: By arbitrarily repurposing a street and symbolically transforming it into a community garden, neighborhood residents exposed an analogously arbitrary act of repurposing by then-Mayor Rudolph Giuliani. Through that analogy, the action was made coherent, and the action's very audacity, by echoing the audacity of Giuliani's move to sell off so many gardens at once, lent a moral credibility to a stunt that might otherwise have come off as merely uncivil.

MAKE THE INVISIBLE VISIBLE: The mechanisms of power are often obscured behind layers of bureaucracy and unquestioned assumptions. By making visible and tangible the community's need for accessible green space, and clearly identifying the source of the threat to those spaces, the action clarified the terms of the struggle, terms that had previously been murky.

BE AN ETHICAL PRANKSTER: The utopian edge of this action is a world that values — prizes even — human relationships and community life over profits and losses. For an afternoon, participants created that world in the street. People gave gifts instead of exchanging money, sang and laughed and talked instead of passively consuming. It was prefigurative politics at its best.

PICK BATTLES BIG ENOUGH TO MATTER BUT SMALL ENOUGH TO WIN:
Although saving the 198 gardens that were up for auction was an uphill climb, we always felt the fight was winnable. There was wide support for community gardens throughout the city, including allies on the city council and within the mainstream media. Our action was one part of a broad and powerful campaign that was well organized and well connected. We were not shocked that we won, but it was a big enough win to warrant widespread celebration.

A poster for Reclaim the Streets' festival of resistance in support of Streets into Gardens action.

CASE STUDY:
Taco Bell boycott

WHEN

2001–2005

WHERE

Across North America

PRACTITIONERS

Coalition of Immokalee Workers
Student/Farmworker Alliance
Interfaith Action of South-
west Florida
Just Harvest USA

FURTHER INSIGHT

Yutaka Dirks, "From the jaws of
defeat: Four thoughts on social
change strategy," Briarpatch
Magazine (Nov./Dec., 2011)
Coalition of Immokalee Workers
http://www.ciw-online.org/

CONTRIBUTED BY

Yutaka Dirks

For years, workers in Florida's tomato fields have endured poverty wages and terrible working conditions. In 1993, a small, community-based organization called the Coalition of Immokalee Workers (CIW) formed to demand an end to these unfair labor practices. By 2005, they had won a boycott campaign against Taco Bell, one of the largest fast-food corporations in the world, raising wages by almost seventy-five percent and setting an inspiring precedent for farm worker organizing.

"The boycott win was an unqualified victory. All demands were met, including the first-ever ongoing, direct payment to farm workers."

The Coalition of Immokalee Workers began by developing a list of concrete demands that, if met, would realize their vision of social justice in the fields. These were later refined into "fair food principles" which would bring tangible benefits to their base, and were sufficiently clear that the workers could know whether or not they had succeeded in their campaign.

Once they had established their goals, the CIW identified tomato growers as the group that had the power to give them what they wanted. The CIW fought a well-organized campaign targeting the growers, engaging in three community-wide work stoppages and a high-profile hunger strike. The CIW was able to win the first wage increase in twenty years, but wages were still well below the poverty level. They realized that they, the workers alone, did not have the power to force their target to capitulate, so they looked for another target.

The CIW identified the corporations that bought from the growers, including Taco Bell, as a secondary target. Taco Bell's success, unlike that of the growers, depended on its public image. The CIW also identified potential allies that could help them put pressure on their target. They reached out to students, because Taco Bell targeted them as consumers. They also allied themselves with social justice-oriented religious groups.

In 2001, the CIW launched the boycott of Taco Bell, calling on the fast-food giant to take responsibility for human rights violations in their supply chain, to improve wages and working conditions by passing on a penny-per-pound pay increase to the workers, and to buy only from Florida growers who passed this penny per pound payment on to the farm workers.

The CIW-led campaign organized cross-country caravans that held rallies outside Taco Bell restaurants; students organized petitions to "Boot the Bell" from campus food courts; religious, labor and community leaders were approached to publicly endorse the boycott and further isolate Taco Bell from support; and they directly targeted Taco Bell headquarters with public hunger strikes and marches.

After four years of actions by the CIW and their allies, Taco Bell conceded. The boycott win was an unqualified victory. All demands were met, including the first-ever ongoing, direct payment to farm workers, substantially raising their wages, and an enforceable code of conduct. The agreement was a clear victory for the workers who struggled for it against an intransigent target, and helped bring renewed energy to the fair-food movement.

Related:

THEORIES
Points of intervention *p. 250*
Anti-oppression *p. 212*
Narrative power analysis *p. 244*

WHY IT WORKED

The Taco Bell boycott was successful because the Coalition of Immokalee Workers succeeded in identifying who was responsible for their low wages and poor working conditions and then crafted a strategy that targeted the weakest link. The fast-food corporations that bought the Florida tomatoes were vulnerable in a way that growers, the primary targets, were not. Ultimately, by offering leadership and opportunities for active participation to a strong network of allies, the CIW was able to harness enough power to force Taco Bell to concede to its demands.

. . . .

BOYCOTT: While the Taco Bell Boycott went beyond asking people not to purchase Taco Bell products, it was a useful centerpiece for the campaign, tapping into a rich history of boycotts led by exploited and oppressed people, including the Montgomery bus boycott and the California grape boycott. Recalling those powerful examples, the public easily understood the key issues and saw how it could lend its support to the CIW.

KEY TACTIC
used

OTHER TACTICS USED:
Trek *p. 90*
Mass street action *p. 68*

KEY PRINCIPLES
at work

CHOOSE YOUR TARGET WISELY: The CIW's first actions targeted the growers responsible for wages and working conditions, but after winning their first wage increase in 1998, it became apparent that the CIW did not have sufficient power to extract further concessions. Recognizing that the growers could be made vulnerable through pressure from the corporations that bought their tomatoes, the CIW crafted a campaign that played to their strengths.

SHIFT THE SPECTRUM OF ALLIES: The CIW built a broad-based campaign that exposed the consumers of Taco Bell's products to the reality of the working conditions of tomato pickers. The CIW was able to offer leadership to supporters who were not farm workers and encourage them to become active, allowing them space to craft their own actions putting pressure on Taco Bell.

Coalition of Immokalee workers rally for justice on a secondary target's doorstep.

CASE STUDY:
Tar sands action

WHEN

August–November 2011

WHERE

United States and Canada

PRACTITIONERS

The Tar Sands Action
Indigenous Environmental Network
BOLD Nebraska
350.org
Bill McKibben

FURTHER INSIGHT

Tar Sands Action website
http://www.tarsandsaction.org/

CONTRIBUTED BY

Duncan Meisel
Joshua Kahn Russell

Because tar sands oil emits four times the carbon dioxide as standard crude, renowned climate scientist James Hanson has declared that if the Canadian tar sands were fully developed, it would be "essentially game over for the climate." Seeking to draw a line in the (tar) sands, activists successfully organized to delay, and possibly stop, TransCanada's plans to build the Keystone XL pipeline, which would have carried 800,000 barrels a day of tar sands oil to Texas refineries. As of this writing it is unclear if the project will re-emerge in another form, but the movement is girding to defeat any attempted resurrection.

Indigenous communities in northern Alberta, Canada, have been organizing to stop tar sands expansion for decades, and while many U.S. environmental groups began to join the fight around 2007, they had a hard time popularizing the issue in the United States. This changed in June 2011, when a group of prominent authors, scientists, Indigenous leaders, and activists, spearheaded by Bill McKibben, released a joint letter calling on climate activists to participate in two weeks of daily non-violent direct action at the White House in Washington, D.C.

The action quickly became a rallying point for activists working on climate change issues. From August 20 to September 3, 1,253 farmers, teachers, mothers, scientists, celebrities, Indigenous elders, faith leaders and students were arrested outside the White House, garnering international media attention and galvanizing the environmental movement's opposition to the pipeline.

Because building the Keystone XL pipeline required a Presidential Permit to go ahead, organizers chose to target President Obama as the focus of the action *see PRINCIPLES: Choose your target wisely, Points of intervention*. Activists were clear to distinguish between Obama as the *target* and TransCanada as the *enemy*. This distinction yielded a tone that was assertive but friendly. Even as the campaign interrupted his public speeches, flooded campaign offices and staged mass arrests, the emphasis was always on Obama's campaign promises to "end the tyranny of oil" and slow the rise of the oceans. By repeating his own words back to him, activists framed the issue in such a way that Obama had both a serious liability and a huge opportunity on his hands: he could side with the people, or with the polluters.

Of all the tactics employed on the campaign, Obama officials said they were rattled most by "bird-doging" interruptions at high-priced fundraisers because these actions eroded the confidence of Obama's key financial backers. Even in disruptive actions, the message was always inviting, remixing Obama's own messaging: "President Obama, Yes You Can Stop the Keystone XL Pipeline." The goal was to emphasize the political risks of alienating his environmentalist and climate-conscious base. This risk was further amplified by protests around the world, including a mass arrestable sit-in at the Canadian parliament.

Building on this momentum, a second invitation to action was issued, this time for thousands of people to surround the White House on November 6, one year before the next presidential election. This event brought 12,000 people to Obama's front door and showcased a wide segment of the environmental movement, from Indigenous leaders to Nebraska ranchers to college students. Four days later, President Obama sent the pipeline back for a full 18-month re-review. In response, Republicans in Congress legislatively forced an accelerated timeline for approval, which led to the president choosing to *outright deny* the rushed permit. This was a definitive victory against the pipeline, and while TransCanada can still reapply — forcing us to fight the battle again, it reminds us that most environmental victories are temporary on their own, and require continued organizing and pressure (alongside systemic change) to remain durable.

The tar sands action effectively used Obama's own words and supporters against him, framing the issue around the political risk Obama would be taking if he approved the pipeline. Photos from the August action accompanied a huge majority of the stories written or broadcast about the pipeline. The arrests demonstrated the depth of opposition to the pipeline, with dispersed actions across the country showing the breadth of opposition. In addition, some of the actions — at Obama 2012 campaign offices and fundraising events — posed an immediate threat of disrupting Obama's political machinery while continuing to raise the profile of the issue.

Related:

THEORIES
Points of intervention p. 250
Ethical spectacle p. 230
Hashtag politics p. 238

WHY IT WORKED

WHAT DIDN'T WORK

The action was highly successful communicating its message *despite* having no action logic *see PRINCIPLE: Action Logic*. Those sitting-in were violating a random law — it is illegal to stand still in front of the White House because it inhibits tourists from taking clear pictures. It is illogical for scientists to sit in front of the White House and get arrested so tourists can take pictures. But because the action had two weeks to build momentum, had strict image and tone-discipline, ultra-clear messaging on banners and signs, and highly sympathetic spokespeople, the power of this action overcame what it lacked in action logic. It was highly successful in capturing the public imagination, getting a remarkable amount of clear media attention, and it put into motion a campaign that eventually beat back a multi-billion dollar oil pipeline.

. . . .

KEY TACTIC
used

OTHER TACTICS USED:
Direct action p. 32
Creative disruption p. 18
Bird-dogging web
Mass street action p. 68

KEY PRINCIPLES
at work

OTHER PRINCIPLES AT WORK:
Choose your target wisely p. 114
Use the power of ritual p. 198
Make the invisible visible p. 152
Make new folks welcome p. 150
Kill them with kindness p. 140

SIT-IN: One thousand two hundred and fifty three arrests over two weeks generated a drumbeat of news stories, trained and empowered a dedicated core of activists, and provided the visual and narrative campaign hook for the months to come. The sit-ins set a fire underneath the environmental movement.

HOPE IS A MUSCLE: By simply using Barack Obama's own words as organizing slogans, the Tar Sands Action vividly spotlighted his shortcomings on environmental issues, re-activating a core of volunteers and supporters from 2008. The campaign positively affirmed his hopeful statements, holding out the promise of the same support from environmentalists he enjoyed in 2008 if he were able to live up to those words in his response to the pipeline.

SHIFT THE SPECTRUM OF ALLIES: This action would not have worked a year earlier. The tactics and message were suited to their moment and context. Obama's environmentalist base was disillusioned with his failure to live up to his promises, social movements were riding a global wave of revolutions, and Occupy Wall Street was just taking off and giving popular voice to the efficacy of mass protest. The sit-ins were highly choreographed and made as "safe" as possible. While to some they may have appeared insufficiently "hardcore," they effectively gave passive allies an entry point into action, identifying the key social blocs in need of shifting. The vast majority of participants in the tar sands action indicated it was their first protest experience, let alone their first direct action. This was paired with a grassroots-led organizing strategy that emphasized local autonomy within a clear framework. Each stage of the campaign was designed for participants to take themselves to the next level.

The Tar Sands Action, Washingto, DC, September 3rd,2011. Over 1,200 people were arrested during this two-week long action that culminated in President Obama rejecting the permit for the Keystone XL pipeline in January of 2012. Photo by Milan Ilnyckyj of Tar Sands Action.

DO THE MEDIA'S WORK FOR THEM: During the August sit-ins, organizers extensively documented both the actions and participants. Photos from the event were made freely available online and became a key part of news stories about the pipeline for months to come. Also, every participant had a personal photo taken at a photo booth at the action training, giving everyone something to share and remember from the action.

ESCALATE STRATEGICALLY: In a fight over fossil fuel infrastructure, there is a tendency to jump immediately to physical blockade tactics. By proactively setting the tone with disciplined arrestable actions, the campaign successfully focused energy from different segments of the environmental movement. The sit-ins held the promise of escalated actions, but maintained a tone that discouraged runaway escalation.

CASE STUDY:
The teddy bear catapult

WHEN
April 2001

WHERE
Québec City

PRACTITIONERS
The Deconstructionist
Institute for Surreal Topology

FURTHER INSIGHT
The Deconstructionist Institute
for Surreal Topology website
http://trb.la/wHr1wq

Press release: "We made the catapult, Judy Rebick got the $&$"
http://trb.la/zsdG6c

CONTRIBUTED BY
Dave Oswald Mitchell

It was a classic summit protest at the height of the anti-globalization movement. Thirty-four heads of state from across the Americas were gathering in Québec City to negotiate the Free Trade Area of the Americas (FTAA), a sweeping trade deal with deeply anti-democratic provisions. Protests had been called, tens of thousands were expected to fill the streets, and a giant fence defended by thousands of riot police was to be erected around the Old City to keep protesters far from the convention center.

The teddy-bear catapult and ursine comrades in police custody. Photo by Gareth Lind.

As the summit drew closer and heated debates raged in activist circles about how to oppose the FTAA most effectively, a group calling themselves the Deconstructionist Institute for Surreal Topology (DIST) circulated a satirical booklet promoting more creative protest tactics: "For those who yawn every time they see yet another Black Bloc, the Deconstructionist Institute for Surreal Topology presents this brief list of alternatives, to help spark discussion and inject a bit of creativity and derisive laughter into the mix."

Their list of protest ideas included the Gary Coleman Bloc (tactic of choice: continuously walking up to cops and demanding, "Whatchu talkin' bout, Willus?"), the Mascot Bloc, the Bloc Parents and the Fuchsia Bloc ("dressed in tights and pink tutus, the Fuchsia Bloc's role is to follow the Black Bloc and tease them mercilessly"). DIST also jokingly proposed challenging the fence around the conference area with a Monty-Pythonesque

Medieval Bloc: "If the *man* is gonna turn the summit into a fortress, the Medieval Bloc will lay siege with gusto. Beautiful battering rams, ladders, siege towers, Trojan donuts, catapults, and dead cows infected with the plague."

It was a good laugh, but seemingly nothing more — until a public figure sympathetic to the cause contacted the group and said, "if you can find someone to build a catapult, I'll pay for it." A group of catapult enthusiasts in Ottawa agreed to build the prop (rigged to ensure it couldn't launch anything very far on the off-chance it was actually taken for a weapon), and DIST smuggled it into the city. On the day of the march, activists with pots and colanders on their heads pulled the full-size catapult up to the fence and began gently lobbing teddy bears into lines of riot cops. Meanwhile, other activists dismantled the offending fence with bolt-cutters as cameras rolled.

The stunt complete, the activists disabled the prop and abandoned it to the police who were advancing through clouds of tear gas. Everyone thought that would be the end of it, but the police couldn't bear to be outflanked on the absurdist front: they retaliated by sending plainclothes officers to snatch a prominent activist, Jaggi Singh, who had had nothing to do with the catapult, and charge him with possession of a "dangerous weapon": the prop itself. Singh was held for seventeen days before being released.

The spurious weapons charge only added fuel to DIST's fire, setting off a whole new round of press releases and media stunts mocking the security establishment, with activists turning in their "stuffed comrades" (i.e. teddy bears) to local police stations across the country and sending them to the Canadian Prime Minister's office to protest the absurd charge.

The catapult action was not just good theater, but also effective activism. It attacked, both physically and symbolically, the fence that kept civil society away from trade deal negotiations that would impact everyone. In the end, the protests were a success: the Summit was a public relations nightmare for the Canadian government,

> "Activists with pots and colanders on their heads pulled the full-size catapult up to the fence and began gently lobbing teddy bears into lines of riot cops."

Related:

TACTICS
Direct action p. 32
Mass street action p. 68
Media-jacking p. 72
Hoax p. 54
Street theater web

THEORIES
Action logic p. 208
Ethical spectacle p. 230
Hamoq & hamas p. 236
Narrative power analysis p. 244
Temporary Autonomous Zone (TAZ) p. 270

WHY IT WORKED

public sympathy swung toward the protesters and the hemisphere-wide trade deal was never signed.

While the literal target of the airborne teddy bears was the riot police and the politicians behind them, the real target lay outside the fence. Firstly, the action captivated the public imagination with a media spectacle that exposed the absurdity of democratic leaders literally "besieged" by citizens asking reasonable questions. Secondly, the action engaged other activists with two important messages: first, *don't be afraid to confront state power, and second, when you do so, don't lose your sense of humor or lose sight of the broader optics of your actions.*

. . . .

KEY PRINCIPLES
at work

OTHER PRINCIPLES AT WORK:
Lead with sympathetic characters p. 146
The real action is your target's reaction web
Know your cultural terrain p. 142
Use your radical fringe to slide the Overton window p. 200
Reframe p. 168
Play to the audience that isn't there p. 160
Kill them with kindness p. 140
Turn the tables p. 190
Escalate strategically p. 134

SAY IT WITH PROPS: Whether it's a giant Earth Mother puppet, a rented woodchipper redecorated into an outsized Enron stock shredder or a teddy-bear catapult, well-chosen larger-than-life props can help create a media spectacle and tell a story. By choosing an absurdist siege engine, DIST neatly exposed the absurdity of the larger situation: democratic leaders forced to meet "under siege" by their constituents when making hugely unpopular decisions.

USE ABSURDITY TO UNDERMINE THE AURA OF AUTHORITY: To operate, power requires the aura of authority. The man in the uniform or the business suit has everything under control. He's sober, serious, knows best, and maybe above all, is needed (to protect you). Nothing quite undermines this aura (and the rationale for state violence that goes with it) like laughter, especially in the context of an absurd situation they don't know how to handle. If they react to it according to their normal logic, they look ridiculous and/or paranoid—whether it's the Polish police deciding whether to arrest a bunch of dwarves for going to a meeting or Canadian police confiscating a teddy bear as a dangerous weapon.

USE THE MATERIALS AT HAND: As Yogi Berra said, "When you come to a fork in the road, take it!" This action succeeded because those involved responded intelligently and creatively to the unexpected opportunities that presented themselves: first, a serious offer of funding in response to an absurd proposal, and second, a police overreaction that further emphasized the absurdity of the situation.

SHOW, DON'T TELL: The Canadian security establishment justified its unprecedented mobilization by stirring fears of violent protests. But what is more non-violent than a teddy bear? By building an actual engine of war and choosing to gently fling teddy bears off of it, DIST found a playful and unexpected way to demonstrate their commitment to nonviolence and expose the government's trumped-up fears as unwarranted.

CASE STUDY:
Trail of Dreams

WHEN

January 1, 2010—May 1, 2010

WHERE

Miami to Washington D.C.

PRACTITIONERS

Students Working for Equal Rights

FURTHER INSIGHT

Trail of Dreams website
http://trail2010.org/

CONTRIBUTED BY

Gaby Pacheco

On January 1, 2010, four immigrant youth leaders (Carlos Roa, Felipe Matos, Juan Rodriguez and myself) embarked on a 1,500 mile walk from Miami, Florida to Washington, D.C. The long-term goal of this arduous journey was to put a human face on the immigration debate and counteract the effect of anti-immigrant portrayals in the mainstream media. The short-term goal was to put pressure on Washington to fix a failed system that has kept millions of undocumented members of our communities and families in the shadows.

We had four requests. The first was for President Obama, through an executive action, to stop the detentions and deportations of students for two years and halt removal proceedings for people with immediate family members who are U.S. citizens. The second was the passage of the DREAM Act ("Development, Relief and Education for Alien Minors") to allow access to higher education. Third, protection of immigrant workers' rights, and last, the passage of just and humane immigration reform.

At the core of the Trail of Dreams trek was the desire to escalate our activism by publicly sharing stories and struggles, inspiring others to take up similar actions throughout the United States. The goal was to open hearts and change minds in order to create much-needed policy change. Over four months we walked through Florida, Georgia, South Carolina, North Carolina, and Virginia, finally arriving in Washington, D.C., on May 1. Each day we walked sixteen to eighteen miles. Every encounter was an opportunity to share our story, to plant a seed.

With the help of hosting communities, we held events where we broke bread and invited people to share their stories, and to organize and fight for their dreams. We were weclcomed by congregations from various faiths, including the Lutherans, Unitarian Universalists, United Methodists, Christ Churchers, Catholics, Baptists and others. We spoke to crowds of white conservatives, conducted a joint event with African-Americans in Georgia, and of course reached out to the Latino base, immigrants and citizens alike. The trek would have not been possible without the support of a small but dedicated group, including a project manager, a logistics coordinator, a driver and an on-site coordinator. Our organization, Students Working

The Trail of Dreams, 2010.

Related:

THEORIES
Hamoq & hamas p. 236
Action logic p. 208
Points of intervention p. 250

for Equal Rights, set up local teams along the route to ensure our safety and well-being.

We faced many challenges. One was blisters, body aches and walking through one of the coldest winters in recent memory. The other was the backlash from anti-immigrant hate groups, including the Klu Klux Klan, which targeted the Trail with a rally in an unsuccessful attempt to intimidate the walkers. Additionally, three of us faced the constant risk of deportation by coming into direct contact with federal immigration authorities.

WHY IT WORKED

The Trail of Dreams inspired a sleeping giant, immigrant youth, to take their stories to the streets. It inspired young people to share their dreams publicly, including youth in Illinois who organized "coming-out actions" declaring, "we are undocumented and unafraid." In Arizona, five immigrant youths sat-in at Senator John McCain's office, while several solidarity walks took place across the country. The Trail of Dreams caught the eye of both local and national media, with over 300 articles written about the walk and interviews with trekkers on several major networks. The trek inspired a nation of DREAMers and allies to fight for the passage of the DREAM Act, which, while not yet passed into law, remains within reach.

TREK: By creating a national support network and taking our demands on the road, we were able to directly challenge racist and anti-immigrant policies. As openly undocumented youth with the legitimacy of a broad-based movement behind us, we were able to meet with sheriffs, police officers, immigration agents and other officials without being detained or deported. We proved that the power of people is stronger than inhumane laws and a broken immigration system.

EVERYONE HAS BALLS/OVARIES OF STEEL: There is nothing more powerful than letting your heart lead you. If we had listened to all the people who told us this walk was "crazy," "suicidal," "not real organizing" or "impossible," the trek never would have happened. We didn't let fear paralyze us; we knew that if we opened our hearts to the community, people would listen and respond. We followed our hearts and sparked a movement.

SHIFT THE SPECTRUM OF ALLIES: Although one of our goals was to inspire our community, another was to reach out to people who were misguided by the media. We wanted to speak to those who felt that we did not belong. We wanted to share with them our stories and allow them to decide for themselves. After talking with us, many anti-immigrants shifted their position.

KILL THEM WITH KINDNESS: We didn't fight hate with hate but rather with love. When a man told Felipe he was less than human because all he was an "illegal," Felipe responded, "God bless you." When a group of young people came to disrupt our walk with a big Confederate flag, we walked with them and shared our stories until they folded the flag and left. When we went to Arizona and met with Sheriff Joe Arpaio, "America's toughest sheriff" and a tireless crusader against liberal immigration policies, I hugged him. I told him that he was our brother who had gone astray, that he and I were equals, and that our "papers" were in our blood. I touched his heart with my right hand and said that I hoped he would change. He didn't arrest us, and that day we faced each other as equals.

A SOUND BITE

IS MERELY AN EXTRMLY ABBRVIATD FORM OF STRY — TLLING.

—*Charlotte Ryan*

CASE STUDY:
Virtual Streetcorners

WHEN
June 2010

WHERE
Greater Boston

PRACTITIONERS
John Ewing

FURTHER INSIGHT

Virtual Streetcorners website
www.virtualcorners.net

Front page story on Boston Globe
http://tinyurl.com/25zgepk

Blog entry on PBS.org
http://www.pbs.org/
idealab/john_ewing/

Profile piece on WGBH TV
http://bit.ly/v8OtkD

Atlantic Magazine online interview
http://bit.ly/tSD9qO

CONTRIBUTED BY
John Ewing

From "red-lining" in the '50s to busing in the '70s and recent police harassment of Harvard professor Henry Louis Gates, Boston has been a crucible of racial tension in America for decades. Typical of many large cities, segregation along ethnic and class lines still often determines where people live and how they navigate the city. It is common for people living in one neighborhood to know very little about, or to never have traveled to, adjacent areas of the city.

"The concept was simple and easily understood, but at the same time led to profound experiences."

Coolidge Corner in Brookline and Dudley Square in Roxbury are hubs of their respective communities. Brookline has a large Jewish population that migrated in the 1960s from the Dudley area in Roxbury, so there's a historical connection. Roxbury is now a black and Latino neighborhood. Despite being just over two miles apart and connected by a city bus, people living in these neighborhoods rarely visit the other.

Virtual Streetcorners was a public art installation inviting people to close that gap and experience the city in a new way. Using technology developed to bridge much larger geographical distances, the project instead traversed the social boundaries that separate two neighborhoods.

Throughout the month of June 2010, large glass storefronts in both neighborhoods were transformed into giant video screens providing pedestrians at each location a portal into the others' world. Running 24/7, these life-size screen images and AV technology facilitated real-time interaction between residents of the two communities. A passerby could look into the window in one location and see out the window in the other, and be able to converse with whomever might be standing there.

In addition to spontaneous interactions, there were many programmed activities. Local politicians — from city councilors to former presidential nominee Michael Dukakis — joined artists, educators, activists and religious leaders in street corner dialogues on a range of issues. Citizen journalists were hired to come to the screens and deliver daily news reports about what was happening in each neighborhood.

The project generated a great deal of excitement and attracted a wide range of participants. Ironically in this era of technology, people treated it as something magical when it was simply a street corner from across town appearing in the window. Many found it entertaining to connect in this way. Others used the opportunity to tackle more philosophical or socio-political issues. "There was an odd sense of safety in talking with someone I had never met," said one participant. "It's as if the virtuality of the whole thing emboldened us to say things we'd never say if we simply sat next to each other on a bus."

Related:

THEORIES
Anti-oppression p. 212
Environmental justice p. 228
Points of intervention p. 250
Action logic p. 208
The tactics of everyday life p. 268
Story of self web
Social sculpture web
Art as life web

The piece touched a nerve and tackled an issue rarely addressed head-on. The concept was simple and easily understood — "connecting neighborhoods which are next to each other yet 'worlds apart' " — but at the same time led to profound experiences. It invited people to participate in a solution ratherthan attacking them for being racist and classist. We hired community organizers in advance who worked for months laying the groundwork, and had strong coalitions with trusted local organizations bridging class and race lines. It worked on different levels, from simple commentary and observation to involved participation.

WHY IT WORKED

The tech was complex and far from foolproof. If tech is going to be put to use by the public, it needs to be rock-solid, even if it means sacrificing some utility.

WHAT DIDN'T WORK

· ·

ART INTERVENTION: Public art is one of the few ways to have a large art project seen by tens of thousands of people without having to shoehorn your ideas into the art gallery system. One of the advantages of contemporary art is that it can include almost anything, including activism, education, science and community organizing. The project relied on audience participation to create its meaning, and was accessible to audiences that wouldn't necessarily attend galleries.

KEY TACTIC
used

NAME THE ELEPHANT IN THE ROOM: Virtual Streetcorners spotlighted issues that are always in front of us but

KEY PRINCIPLES
at work

OTHER PRINCIPLES AT WORK:

Create levels of participation web
*Take direction from the
most impacted* web
Consider your audience p. 118
Make cross-class alliances web

that we tend to ignore on a day-to-day basis. Passersby were brought face to face with people from a different class and race background, pointing up how lack of diversity, rather than diversity, is in fact the social norm.

SHOW, DON'T TELL: The project concisely visualizes the problem but leaves an opening for people to respond based on their own experience. Statistics could convey a similar message, but the compelling narrative and reliance on community participation made the project more engaging than yet another opinion piece on Boston's racial problems.

SIMPLE RULES CAN HAVE GRAND RESULTS: Virtual Streetcorners provided a medium and an underlying narrative, but then left it up to participants to determine their own experience. It facilitated a discussion rather than voicing an opinion.

LAY THE GROUNDWORK: On the face of things, the project was very simple — set up video conferencing between two street corners so people can talk to each other. In reality, however, it took years of background work: researching history, thinkingthrough the interactive design and building relationships with residents and community organizations in both neighborhoods.

Virtual Streetcorners bus ad.

CASE STUDY:
Whose Tea Party?

WHEN

April 15, 1998 (Tax Day)

WHERE

Boston

PRACTITIONERS

United for a Fair Economy (UFE)
Art for a Fair Economy
Rich People's Liberation Front

CONTRIBUTED BY

Andrew Boyd

Two Republican Congressmen, Dick Armey from Texas and Billy Tauzin of Louisiana, have come to Boston to promote their snake oil proposals for a flat tax and national sales tax, two initiatives that would dramatically shift the tax burden off the wealthy and onto low- and moderate-income working families.

They've set up a classic photo opportunity by inviting national TV and print media to the Boston Harbor Tea Party Ship Museum, where they plan to symbolically throw the entire IRS tax code into Boston Harbor. With the cameras rolling, they step up to the railing of the Tea Party boat, ready to heave forth an enormous trunk containing the tax code.

Suddenly, two protesters from United for a Fair Economy, a Boston-based NGO working for greater economic equality, paddle into sight in a small dinghy. One of them is in a hard hat, the other clutching a plastic baby doll. They paddle the precarious "Working Family Life Raft" into position directly below where Armey and Tauzin are standing and plead, "Your flat tax will sink the working family!" and "You'll drown us with your sales tax!" Other UFE protesters, who have snuck onto the Tea Party ship and are dressed in fancy suits and dresses, start egging on the Congressmen, chanting, "Sink 'em with the sales tax!" and "Drown 'em with the flat tax!"

Armey and Tauzin stand paralyzed on the boat. Their handlers go into a panic as UFE staff approach the media with press releases, explaining the symbolism of the protest and offering evidence of how both the flat tax and the national sales tax will sink working families.

Finally, not knowing what else to do, they throw the tax code trunk into the harbor, swamping the fragile life raft and plunging UFE Education Director Chris Hartman, UFE financial manager Kristin Barralli, and plastic baby doll Veronica into Boston Harbor.

Their media stunt hijacked out from under them, Representatives Tauzin and Armey retreat to their limousine, which is now surrounded by cheering members of the Rich People's Liberation Front, a UFE theater group, holding signs reading, "We love you Armey and Tauzin!" "Tax cuts for us, not our maids," "Free the Forbes 400," and "Rich folks love the flat tax!"

Quickly, images of the upended Working Families Life Raft are broadcast around the planet through hourly runs on CNN and other networks. The Reuters International story is titled, "GOP Tax Photo Op Backfires." The Associated Press reports, "Protesters Use Tax Day For Batting Practice." Rush Limbaugh chortles that he was glad the UFE protesters got wet. UFE staff conduct live TV interviews and radio feeds all afternoon describing the protest and why the flat tax and sales tax will hurt working families. The next day, the *Boston Globe* and dozens of other daily papers run a three-photo sequence of the raft's demise.

"The protesters understood the symbolism of the GOP event, and instead of disrupting or denouncing it, they participated in it, and thus were able to reframe it."

Related:

THEORIES
Action logic p. 208
Ethical spectacle p. 230
Narrative power analysis p. 244
Points of intervention p. 250
Activist realpolitik web

For UFE activists, it's just another day fighting the power by combining education, humor, direct action, research, media savvy, and nautical skills.

WHY IT WORKED

"Pranks are symbolic warfare," Abbie Hoffman once said, and this action is a perfect illustration of that maxim. The protesters understood the symbolism of the GOP event, and instead of disrupting or denouncing it, they participated in it. By accepting the original symbolism at face value, UFE was able to extend and reinterpret it. What was initially posed, however disingenuously, as an act of liberation from a despised tax code, was revealed as a dumping of society's tax burden onto the shoulders of ordinary people.

KEY TACTIC
used

MEDIA-JACKING: The congressmen set up the event and sent out the press releases. It was their name recognition (and PR budget) that drew the media coverage. But the UFE stunt hijacked it out from under them. Two ordinary people (and a doll) getting capsized by a couple of congressmen is far more interesting than the hokey set-piece event the suits had planned. If the intervention hadn't been so ballsy, dramatic, and entertaining, the media wouldn't have followed UFE as they flipped the event away from GOP talking points.

OTHER TACTICS USED:
Direct Action p. 32
Guerrilla Theatre p. 52

Republican lawmakers had their media event hijacked out from under them in this classic example of media-jacking. The "Working Family Life Raft" was capsized seconds later as the lawmakers dropped the tax code into Boston Harbor. (United for a Fair Economy)

KEY PRINCIPLES
at work

OTHER PRINCIPLES AT WORK:

Think narratively p. 186
Deploy sympathetic characters p. 146
Reframe p. 168
Make the invisible visible p. 152
Play to the audience that isn't there p. 160
Show, don't tell p. 174
Make it funny web
Stay on message p. 178
Everyone has balls/ovaries of steel p. 136

PUT YOUR TARGET IN A DECISION DILEMMA: Once the congressmen were caught by surprise, they had two choices: go ahead with their plan and drop the trunk of tea onto the life raft, or back down, sparing the ordinary folks down below the consequences of their selfish actions. Either way, they would lose: either they participated in demonstrating the damage their policies would cause, or they conceded the truth of that damage and were seen as rethinking their controversial stance.

DO YOUR RESEARCH: The UFE activists sleuthed out the crucial details by calling up the congressmen's office and pretending to be supporters planning to show up and cheer them on, and designed their action accordingly. UFE also scoped out the physical site beforehand, identifying a good hiding place for the raft.

CAPTURE THE ELEMENT OF SURPRISE: The congressmen didn't know tht the little raft was coming. They didn't realize that the Rich People's Liberation Front was in their midst until the trap had been sprung. Seizing the

CASE STUDY: Whose Tea Party?

initiative allowed UFE to steal the show. The congressmen being caught by surprise itself became part of the media story.

DO THE MEDIA'S WORK FOR IT: UFE didn't just pull off the prank and hope for the best from the media, they guided the media through every element of the story. The organization's codirector (in a straight, nontheatrical role) worked the media both before and after the stunt. He handed out press releases and gave the cameramen a heads-up, suggesting they set a wide angle to capture the larger scene that was about to unfold. Afterwards, he was available on the spot (and the rest of the day by phone) for expert commentary addressing both the prank and the deeper issues to which it spoke.

CASE STUDY:
Wisconsin Capitol occupation

WHEN
Spring 2011

WHERE
Madison, Wisconsin

CONTRIBUTED BY
Duncan Meisel

From February 14 to early March 2011, opponents of GovernorScott Walker's legislation to strip civic unions of collective bargaining rights filled Wisconsin's state capitol with a non-stop protest that became one of the largest labor mobilizationsin the U.S. in a generation. Though the protests were ultimately unsuccessful, they heralded a major watershed in the labor movement's resistance to austerity cuts.

Protests began shortly after Gov. Walker proposed his legislation. On February 14, a group of unionized teaching assistants from the University of Wisconsin at Madison led a Valentine's Day-themed protest at the capitol, joined by labor and student groups. Labor-student collaboration became a model for the remainder of the organizing, as state employeesused their workplaces and community roles to contact peoplenot immediately affected, widening the struggle and helping provoke a political crisis in the state.

Wisconsin state law allowed for the capitol to remain open as long as public debate continued about a pending bill. The teaching assistants noticed that the senate had failed to set a limit on the number of speakers on a floor debate about Walker's bill, and so signed up thousands of people to offer testimony. This kept debate open indefinitely, as well as the capitol itself, and eventually turned the occupation into a twenty-four-hour speak-out, with a microphone set up in the middle of the rotunda. The microphone served as an invitation to everyone to be heard at the protest, and triggered an important shift in tone and approach. What had begun as a simple defense of workers' rights now shifted to become an inclusive forum for multiple groups hurt by budget cuts. The boldness and persistence of the tactic galvanized thousands of people to join in, and within days 70,000 people were marching to oppose the Governor's budget.

Protests were also well-coordinated with progressive and Democratic legislators. Three days after protests began, fourteen senate Democrats fled the state of Wisconsin to deny the GOP a quorum. This bought political space and time in addition to the literal space and time that had been seized in the capitol building.

Additionally, the occupation focused attention and support by connecting with other movements and national progressive media networks. The Egyptian

Protesters crowd the rotunda of the state Capitol in Madison, Wisconsin in early 2011. The mass outpouring of both labor and students was a key to the power of the occupation. Photo by Emily Mills.

Related:

THEORIES

Pillars of support p. 248
The shock doctrine p. 262
Points of intervention p. 250
Cultural hegemony p. 222

revolution was in full flower at the time and lent energy and inspiration to the Wisconsin encampment. Protesters carried Egyptian flags, and several Egyptian revolutionaries sent support in the form of pizzas ordered from local business to be delivered to the capitol. Solidarity pizzas then rolled in from across the world. The occupation was also one of the first to use continuous livestreaming to document itself.

Eventually, Governor Walker's legislation was passed in a legally suspect parliamentary gambit, and the occupation forces switched to an electoral recall strategy.

WHY IT WORKED

Buoyed by both a proud Wisconsin progressive tradition and a national sense of disenfranchisement, the Wisconsin Capitol Occupation effectively transformed an iconic public space into an accessible forum to voice multiple grievances against budget austerity in America. The protests became a symbol of how and why to fight back against budget cuts, as public employees connected with community members.

WHAT DIDN'T WORK

After the bill was passed, the fourteen senators returned. A debate ensued. Mainstream organized labor encouraged protesters to bring the occupation to a close, in order to focus energy on an electoral strategy to recall Republican state senators and Governor Walker. Other coalition groups and individuals, notably the International Workers of the World (IWW) contingent, argued for expanding the people-powered dimension of the struggle into a statewide general strike. The IWW was outvoted. The senate recall effort fell short, and at the time of this writing, the fate of the gubernatorial recall effort is unknown. The people-power path not pursued…well, we'll never quite know.

. . . .

KEY TACTIC
used

OTHER TACTICS USED:

Mass street action p. 68
Blockade p. 14
Direct action p. 32
Public filibuster p. 86
Creative disruption p. 18

KEY PRINCIPLES
at work

OTHER PRINCIPLES AT WORK:

Shift the spectrum of allies p. 172
Use the law, don't be
afraid of it p. 196
Escalate strategically p. 134
If protest is made illegal, make
daily life a protest p. 138
Be both expressive and
insturmental web
Put your target in a
decision dilemma p. 166
We are all leaders p. 202
Use your radical fringe to slide
the Overton window p. 200
Take leadership from the
most impacted p. 180

OCCUPATION: The occupation of the capitol itself provided a focal point for protesters trying to unite broad communities against the budget cuts and created a space for diverse groups to work together to solve common problems. Holding the space and filling it with sound and people united diverse voices, while also giving them a way to be heard.

NO ONE WANTS TO WATCH A DRUM CIRCLE: Although the occupation did use drums to quite a useful effect, the cliquish "drum circle" was never the model. Instead, everyone was invited to participate. The microphone at the center of the Capitol rotunda was a microcosm of the rest of the protest. Participants spoke through through the mic and could hear their voices amplified by the movement that surrounded them.

LEAD WITH SYMPATHETIC CHARACTERS: The protests gained strength by placing public employees front and center, emphasizing their role in the community. Madison teachers were some of the first to join the initial protests en masse, and their connection to students and parents helped humanize a struggle otherwise trapped in the abstraction of budgetary issues and collective bargaining. The visuals of firemen in full gear on the steps of the capitol gave the protests a heroic and all-American legitimacy.

MAINTAIN NONVIOLENT DISCIPLINE: The dedicated nonviolence of the protests made cooperation with police easier and kept the capitol open longer. Madison and capitol police supported the occupation by refusing to enforce illegal orders to shut down the capitol, and even sent off-duty officers to sleep in the capitol to show support.

Photo by Jena Pope.

CASE STUDY:
Yomango

WHEN
July 2002–present

WHERE
Spain, then global

PRACTITIONERS
Yomango

FURTHER INSIGHT
Yomango
http://yomango.net

Wired, "Shoplifting as Social
Commentary," August 25, 2005
http://trb.la/yqtQFj

CONTRIBUTED BY
Leónidas Martín Saura

On July 5, 2002, a strange new brand began cropping up in the streets of Barcelona. That day, at the height of sales season, more than fifty people rushed through the center of Barcelona to the Bershka clothing store to perform the very first Yomango fashion show.

The show lived up to its "magical" billing: a simple object was turned into a symbol of another way of living. To be more precise, a ten-euro dress was spirited from the store, later to show up as a work of art at one of the most important art museums in the city. All the activities of Yomango were open, public and publicized.

The name "Yomango" and the lifestyle it celebrates refers to *mangar*, a Spanish slang term meaning "to shoplift," particularly from multinational corporations. The concept of *ethical shoplifting* had suddenly acquired public visibility.

The Yomango brand is itself a reappropriation, or *détournement*, of the wildly popular Mango brand *see TACTIC: Détournement/Culture jamming*. By adding a pronominal prefix (*yo*, or "I" in Spanish) to the clothing company's name, the modified brand takes on a different meaning entirely: *I swipe*. Yomango disrupts the primary goal of the original brand, turning it into a new direct-action practice based on the widespread habit of shoplifting.

At first glance, this may seem like a simple surrender to the greedy logic of capitalism, but nothing could be further from the truth. As Yomango states on its website, its only interest in commodities is "to make something new happen in their midst, to push them to the point of turning them into something else, something that has nothing to do with producing a way of life that is dedicated to consumption, but rather moves toward inventing new possible ways of living."

Through its actions and its philosophy, but also through its style and design, Yomango turns the impulse to shoplift into a movement, a method, an art. For instance, Yomango introduced designs that were not only cool, but also served as gear for shoplifting, such as a "jacket of a thousand pockets," in which all the many pockets were interconnected. When an object is surreptitiously placed in the jacket, it simply disappears, only to be discovered again sometime later, perhaps in the safety of your own home.

YOMANGO

Related:

THEORIES

Ethical spectacle p. 230
Action logic p. 20
The tactics of everyday life p. 268
The commons p. 220
Capitalism p. 216

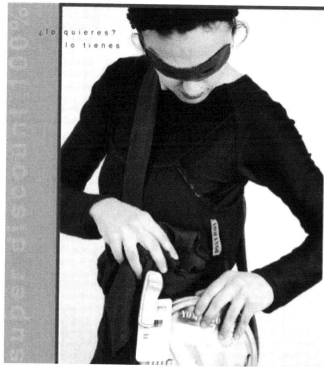

The Cookie Bag (Yomango Fashion)

Thanks to a proliferation of workshops in arts institutions and social organizations in cities around the world, Yomango's actions have expanded since the anti-brand first debuted. The website — built on an open-publishing framework enabling people to exchange information and experiences with anyone else captivated by the Yomango brand — also contributed to its spread. Various Yomango communities began appearing in different parts of the world: Argentina, Chile, Mexico, Germany, Italy, as well as other Spanish cities including Madrid and Bilbao.

Though it celebrates individual acts of self-liberation, the Yomango brand also gestures toward mass political action, with actions targeting various multinational corporations, such as the "Yomango-Tango," in which a crowd of Yomango dancers in Argentina liberated hundreds of bottles of Champagne from a

Carrefour supermarket, and then uncorked and drank them in a branch of Banco Santander — both entities directly implicated in the Argentinian economic crisis.

These actions have served as brand advertisements as enticing as the glittering billboards in the heart of the metropolis. In this way, the Yomango brand spreads through direct-action events and highly diverse avenues of communication: from the alternative media to the official press, from supermarkets to activist meetings, and from art catalogs to the Internet. The anti-brand is designed so that any person or group can reappropriate it in whatever manner he/she/it chooses, transforming it, plagiarizing it, elaborating on it.

Yomango. You want it? You got it!

WHY IT WORKED

Before Yomango, shoplifting was a clandestine practice. Yomango's actions, designs, and advertisements made the action visible, celebrating it as a way of life. Yomango worked both on a personal level by offering practical tools to liberate products from the multinationals, and on a collective level by creating an international community united by collective actions and workshops.

KEY TACTIC
used

OTHER TACTICS USED:
Détournement/Culture jamming p. 28
Distributed action p. 36
Direct action p. 32
Identity correction p. 60
Flash mob p. 46

ETHICAL SHOPLIFTING: Yomango celebrates stealing — not from people, but from large transnational corporations which show no respect for workers' rights, the environment, or anything other than their bottom line. In many cases Yomango's actions have been supported or directly fostered by employees of these large chains, some of whom have become active members of Yomango chapters.

Stealing (labor, time, ideas, lives) is what transnationals do. What Yomango does is *ethical shoplifting*: returning to the people what the transnationals have stolen.

BRAND OR BE BRANDED: Yomango is a brand that appropriates and undermines other brands. Yomango captures the desires these brands harness and liberates them from the power of the market. Like other brands, it promises a lifestyle, except what Yomango is "selling" costs nothing at all. Yomango is a brand that exists outside the market.

CREATE LEVELS OF PARTICIPATION: Yomango opens up a broad and diverse participatory process. All the ideas and

CASE STUDY: Yomango

tools, as well as the Yomango brand itself, were created with the anonymous participation of many people. In this sense, Yomango is what organizers call a "social brand." By making its tools freely available, Yomango offers a kind of participation that may be less visible than your average multinational brand, but much more extensive and integrated into the day-to-day lives of participants.

MAKE THE INVISIBLE VISIBLE: Shoplifting is widespread, but remains largely invisible. Yomango makes shoplifting visible, transforming a clandestine gesture of non-cooperation with consumer culture into a brand, a fashion and a lifestyle that embodies a critique of consumer capitalism.

KEY PRINCIPLES
at work

OTHER PRINCIPLES AT WORK:

CASE STUDY
Write your own CASE STUDY

WHEN *What happened?*

WHERE

EPIGRAPH

PRACTITIONERS

FURTHER INSIGHT

CONTRIBUTED BY

WHY IT WORKED

KEY TACTIC
used

OTHER TACTICS USED:

KEY PRINCIPLES
at work

OTHER PRINCIPLES AT WORK:

Related:

THEORIES

. . . .

The modular format of *Beautiful Trouble* allows the collection to expand endlessly to reflect new tactical breakthroughs, underrepresented areas of struggle and overlooked pearls of wisdom.

Become part of *Beautiful Trouble*. Use this template to write up your own creative-activism insights. Submit your own module for publication on the *Beautiful Trouble* website here: http://beautifultrouble.org.

PRACTITIONERS

SOME OF THE SHOULDERS
WE STAND ON

Brief write-ups of some of the people and groups that inspire us to be better changemakers.

"I'd rather be a lightning bolt than a seismograph."
—Ken Kesey (when asked why he'd rather be a cultural activist than a writer)

Whether it's groups (Greenpeace, The Center for Tactical Magic), lone artists (Banksy), mini-movements (Orange Alternative, The Dutch Provos) or tiny collectives (Gran Fury), a vast tapestry of pranksters and rebel dreamers, both living and dead, have given our movements their singular style and sense. The tour starts now...

ASSEMBLED BY *ZACK MALITZ* / **WRITTEN BY** *ZACK MALITZ, MAXINE SCHOEFER-WULF & JESSE BARRON*

ACT-UP

TACTIC

Direct action *p. 32*
Mass street action *p. 68*

PRINCIPLE

Use your radical fringe
to slide the Overton window *p. 200*

SOURCES

ACT-UP website
http://www.actupny.org
Global Nonviolent Action Database,
"U.S. AIDS Coalition to Unleash
Power (ACT-UP)
demands access to drugs, 1987-89"
http://trb.la/yhXiOu

Detailed scenes from ACT-UP
actions
http://www.actupny.org/
divatv/synopsis75.html

Founded in 1987, AIDS Coalition to Unleash Power (ACT-UP) is an international non-partisan group dedicated to ending the AIDS crisis. ACT-UP utilizes direct action and devotes itself to political agitation around legislation and policy changes that can make a difference in the lives of AIDS-affected individuals. During its peak years, ACT-UP spent much of its time focused on drug availability and pricing, placing significant pressure on the FDA through visible protest and demonstration. These actions gained considerable media attention and contributed to a twenty percent reduction in price of the drug AZT. ACT-UP stunts have included chaining themselves to the VIP balcony of the New York Stock Exchange, shutting down the FDA, and storming of a CBS Evening News broadcast. The organization emphasizes the need for public education as well as policies to prohibit discrimination in areas like housing, insurance, treatment and employment. ACT-UP has seen a recent decline in membership, but chapters continue to meet and its creative protest tactics have had a lasting influence on subsequent protest movements.

Adbusters

TACTIC

Détournement/Culture
jamming *p. 28*

THEORY

Society of the spectacle *p. 266*

CASE

Occupy Wall Street *web*

SOURCES

Adbusters website
http://www.adbusters.org

Activist Cash, "Adbusters"
http://trb.la/yl8Q1S

Kalle Lasn was in a supermarket, about to pay a quarter for use of a shopping cart, when the idea of *Adbusters* came to him. Soon after, in 1989, Adbusters magazine was released in Vancouver as a local quarterly, chock-full of "culture jamming" design: the alteration and parody of advertisements for political effect. Adbusters' editorial line is decidedly anti-consumerist, aiming to promote media literacy and resist corporate power. The magazine is perhaps best known as the source of the call to action that inspired the occupation of Zuccotti Park and the Occupy Wall Street protests in 2011.

April 6 Youth Movement (Egypt)

The April 6 Youth Movement played a key role in ending Hosni Mubarak's twenty-nine-year stint as Egypt's president. It began as a Facebook group expressing solidarity with protesting industrial workers in al-Mahalla al-Kubra. The protests escalated to calls for a national strike, and on April 6, 2008, thousands of Egyptians flooded the streets. They were met with violent repression by police forces, resulting in four deaths and 400 arrests. For the next two years, members studied the nonviolent tactics of Serbian and Ukrainian youth movements as well as methods for evading government surveillance and harassment. In 2009 and 2010 they attempted to replicate the April 6, 2008 strike, but the regime was able to obstruct most of the group's activities. Finally, galvanized by the success of the Tunisian revolution, the April 6 Youth Movement's leaders announced a day of action: January 25, 2011. The subsequent protests, which centered on Cairo's Tahrir Square, ultimately toppled Mubarak's regime and led to a transfer of power to the Egyptian military. According to Mohamad Adel, a founding member of the April 6 Youth Movement, the group is now focused on "the building of the nation and (exerting) pressure on government and society in order to complete the process of democratic reform in Egypt."

TACTIC
Occupation p. 78
Flash mob p. 46

PRINCIPLE
Shift the spectrum of allies p. 172

SOURCES
Carnegie Endowment for International Peace, "Egypt 6 Youth Movement" http://trb.la/zbDHym
April 6 Youth Movement Facebook http://trb.la/xOID3m

Art and Revolution Collective

The Art and Revolution Collective was a San Francisco group that worked in the carnivalesque puppet-and-mask performance style made famous by Bread and Puppet Theater. Their first major action was at the Democratic National Convention in Chicago in 1996 and involved a twenty-foot-tall puppet called the "Corporate Tower of Power." To draw attention to Chevron Texaco, they brought kids to the gates of a California oil refinery to hold up paintings of their visions of the future. They also dressed up like salmon and "swam" in a forest to protest logging. Like Bread and Puppet, Art and Revolution often displayed generalized messages on large banners as part of their performances, tying the action to larger political and philosophical ideas ("restorative justice"). Often these messages snuck into newspapers when photographers, snapping the giant puppets, captured the banners without meaning to.

TACTIC
Carnival protest web

PRINCIPLE
Balance art and message p. 100
Make your actions concrete and communicative p. 154

SOURCES
Sierra Club, "Street Theater, Puppet Politics" http://trb.la/zkosHO

Artist Network of Refuse & Resist!

The Artist Network (AN) of Refuse & Resist! (R&R!) used art to create a colorful culture and community of resistance. R&R! was a non-partisan, national activist organization, founded in New York in 1987 by lawyers, artists, activists, students and other youth who saw a trend in the U.S. toward greater state control. Founded in 1997, AN connected engaged artists to members of the resistance movement and put out calls to artists to use their tools for the cause. Some AN projects include "Inside the Culture of Resistance," an ongoing series of interviews with socially conscious artists, and "Not in Our Name," a statement resisting the political direction the U.S. has taken since 9/11. On September 22, 2001, 100 artists wearing all black stood in silence in Union Square, holding signs reading "OUR GRIEF IS NOT A CRY FOR WAR." Two more such performances took place at Union Square, and a larger number of artists repeated the action in Times Square.

Bread and Puppet Theater

The Bread and Puppet Theater wrote in their 1984 Cheap Art Manifesto: "ART IS FOOD. You can't EAT it BUT it FEEDS you." Their name refers to the practice of giving out free bread after each of their performances. Although their early work focused on issues specific to New York, their huge puppets on stilts were a fixture of anti-Vietnam War and other major protests. In 1970, Bread and Puppet left New York for Vermont, where they set up first at Goddard College and later on farmland in Glover. It was there that their most famous event, "Our Domestic Resurrection Circus," drew tens of thousands of people for one weekend each year until 1998. Since then, the Theater has produced a carnival every weekend from June through September. Bread and Puppet is a nonprofit, sustaining itself largely with revenues from European and American tours of their productions. The group's puppets are displayed at the Bread and Puppet Museum, an old red barn in Glover.

The Center for Tactical Magic

The Center for Tactical Magic (CTM) is a Bay Area collective that creates installations and exhibits that subvert the role of illegitimate power in society. Notable for the historical and technological components of their actions, CTM often re-purposes established symbols of oppressive power in unexpected, anti-oppressive ways. One such action involved a Merry Pranksters-like VW bus filled with waterbeds and suspended from a crane — a participatory experience that was also an allusion to a form of medieval torture called a "witch net." Not all their actions have grim back stories; CTM exhibited "magic wands" of all kinds (including vibrators and airport security metal detectors) at the Los Angeles County Museum of Art, and designed a system that could detect illegal logging by recording the distressed chirps of crickets. Their patron saint would be the early twentieth-century magician and polymath Aleister Crowley, whom the group frequently quotes in their erudite and sometimes arcane literature.

TACTIC
Advanced leafleting p. 8
Détournement/Culture jamming p. 28

PRINCIPLE
Know your cultural terrain p. 142

SOURCES
Center for Tactical Magic website
http://www.tacticalmagic.org

The Coalition of Immokalee Workers

The Coalition of Immokalee Workers (CIW) is a community-based farmworker organization headquartered in Immokalee, Florida, with over 4,000 members. The CIW seeks modern working conditions and fair treatment for farmworkers, and empowers individual members and Florida farmworkers as a whole through continual reflection, analysis and education. In 2001 the CIW launched the Campaign for Fair Food, an innovative worker-led campaign to address human rights abuses in the Florida tomato industry. The campaign identifies the links between brutal farm labor conditions in the fields and the multi-billion-dollar retail food brands that buy the produce grown in those fields. By mobilizing both farmworkers and consumers, the Campaign for Fair Food seeks to pressure retail food giants to improve farmworker wages and to reward growers who respect farmworker rights. This ongoing effort is bringing about considerable industry-wide change and improving conditions at 34,000 harvesting jobs in Florida's tomato fields.

PRINCIPLE
Choose your target wisely p. 114

CASE
Modern-Day Slavery Museum p. 338
Taco Bell boycott p. 372

SOURCES
Coalition of Immokalee Workers website
http://www.ciw-online.org

Left Turn, "Coalition of Immokalee Workers – A Model of Strategic Organizing: An Interview with the Coalition of Immokalee Workers," August 1, 2005
http://trb.la/xIEmSu

SmartMeme, Re:Imagining Change: An Introduction to Story-Based Strategy, by Doyle Canning and Patrick Reinsborough, 2009
http://trb.la/ABaDFt

Robbie Conal

Robbie Conal is an LA-based guerrilla poster artist known for his grotesque portraits of political figures. Conal studied art at Stanford in the '70s, but his politics led him outside the traditional art establishment and toward guerrilla art. The filmmaker Clay Walker made a documentary about him in 1992 ("Post No Bills"), and in 2004 he worked with Mear One and Shepard Fairey on the "Be the Revolution" national postering campaign, protesting Bush and the Bush wars. His latest work focuses on the financial crisis: one poster shows the CEOs of Goldman, JP Morgan, etc., wrapped in the tentacles of a giant pink squid while testifying before Congress, which itself is underwater. The caption reads "Big Fish Eat Little Fish: You Can Bank On It." In his "Guerrilla Etiquette + Postering Techniques" manifesto, Conal lays out three key principles of his work: mass distribution, counter-infotainment and empowerment. He also reminds volunteers not to poster on privately guarded property because the folks in uniform could lose their jobs.

The Deconstructionist Institute for Surreal Topology

The Deconstructionist Institute for Surreal Topology (DIST), a loose-knit group based in Canada and the UK, specializes in "Revolutionary Studies and the advancement of Applied Autonomy." At the Free Trade Area of the Americas protests in Québec City in 2001, their Permanent Revolution pamphlet inspired the formation of a Medieval Bloc of protesters who built a giant teddy-bear-launching catapult. In 2002, when the G8 chose to meet in the mountain resort of Kananaskis in Western Canada to avoid protests, DIST issued a White Paper calling for protesters to adapt "Ewok tactics" à la Return of the Jedi to shut down the summit: "Maximum disruption combined with maximum cuddliness." DIST has shown that research and a sense of humor can be the perfect antidote to both stale tactics and state repression.

Design Studio for Social Intervention

Design Studio for Social Intervention (DS4SI) describes itself as a research-and-development unit of the nonprofit sector. Founded in 2005 by Kenneth Bailey, then a fellow at MIT's Department of Urban Design, DS4SI tries to create methods for changing the way people experience cities and public spaces. Their actions frequently use spectacle to reclaim public space that has become hostile or inaccessible to those who need it: they organized giant tug-of-war games in violent Boston neighborhoods and subway stations, for example. Their "Let's Flip It" campaign turned a well-known symbol of Boston gang violence — baseball hats whose colors indicate allegiance to a particular block or project — into a symbol of nonviolence, by designing an all-white, no-allegiances hat and a youth-to-youth network to distribute it. They also repurpose familiar actions in new theoretical frameworks; their Food Not Bombs-like Public Kitchen was billed as an effort to dissociate the connotations of "cheap" and "run-down" from the word "public."

PRINCIPLE
Reframe p. 168
Take leadership from the
most impacted p. 180

THEORY
Action logic p. 208

SOURCES
Design Studio for Social
Innovation website
http://ds4si.org

The (new) Diggers

Named for a group of seventeenth-century English agrarian communists, the Diggers were a San Francisco-based anarchist guerrilla action group active in the mid to late 1960s. Opposed to private property and market exchanges, the Diggers promoted a Free City through artistic direct actions and street theater, as well as by opening free clinics, providing free housing, distributing free food and opening free stores. Their media-savvy street happenings helped to publicize the hippie counterculture. For instance, a 1967 parade called "The Death of Hippie" involved carrying a coffin with the words "Hippie—Son of Media," thereby forcing the news media to communicate the Diggers' message that "hippie" was a media fabrication.

TACTIC
Prefigurative intervention p. 82

PRINCIPLE
No one wants to watch
a drum circle p.156

THEORY
Temporary Autono-
mous Zone p. 270

SOURCES
The Diggers archives
http://www.diggers.
org/overview.htm

Ricardo Dominguez

Ricardo Dominguez is a theorist and practitioner of electronic civil disobedience, the co-founder of Electronic Disturbance Theater (EDT), and the co-director of thing.net, an ISP for artists and activists. EDT created the FloodNet System, a participatory network for conducting "virtual sit-ins" — denial-of-service attacks in which large numbers of activists slow down or crash a target website by simultaneously and repetitively attempting to access it. Between 1998 and 1999, in over sixteen virtual sit-ins carried out in solidarity with protesting Zapatista communities, Dominguez targeted the official websites of the U.S. Border Patrol, White House, G8, and Mexican Embassy. Dominguez also deployed virtual sit-ins in solidarity with students protesting at UC San Diego, where he teaches visual art. His technology continuously reloaded the UC president's home page as hundreds of protesters typed "transparency" into its search box. The jammed website responded with an error message: "File not found." More recently, EDT 2.0 modified the GPS applet of low-cost mobile phones to become a compass-like "Transborder Immigrant Tool" for undocumented immigrants completing border crossings.

Earth First!

Earth First! is a worldwide movement of small, bioregionally-based groups of radical environmentalists. Formed in 1979, Earth First! claims to have no members, only "believers" — self-proclaimed deep ecologists who equally value and protect all life by acting locally. Their actions range from public education, grassroots organizing and involvement in the legal process, to blockades, tree sits and demonstrations. In alignment with their motto, "No compromise in defense of Mother Earth," some Earth First!ers go a step beyond civil disobedience, sabotaging industrial equipment in ecodefense. Such nonviolent and "productive" forms of property destruction include road reclamation, destruction of genetically modified crops and tree spiking. *Ecodefense: A Field Guide to Monkeywrenching* — a compilation of articles and letters sent to the *Earth First!* Journal by dozens of individuals, edited by Dave Foreman and published by Earth First! Books — outlines methods for decommissioning bulldozers, flattening tires, burning machinery and pulling out survey stakes, and discusses the security, safety, strategy and justification behind such actions.

Eve Ensler

Eve Ensler is a Tony Award-winning author, playwright and anti-violence feminist activist. She wrote *The Vagina Monologues*, a play inspired by conversations with friends and based on interviews with over 200 women about their experiences of sexuality. The play has been translated into over forty-eight languages and performed in 140 countries, and inspired Ensler to create V-Day, a global activist movement to end violence against women. V-Day educates and raises funds and public attention through media campaigns, annual gatherings and benefit productions of Eve's plays. V-Day also built the City of Joy, a community for survivors of gender violence in Bukavo, Democratic Republic of Congo. Eve Ensler has written *The Good Body*, a play about obsession with women's appearance, and *I Am an Emotional Creature: The Secret Life of Girls Around The World*, a collection of original monologues about and for girls. She writes regularly for *Glamour Magazine*, *The Guardian*, *Marie Claire*, *Huffington Post*, *Washington Post*, *Utne Reader* and *O Magazine*.

PRINCIPLE

Think narratively p.186
Challenge the patriarchy
as you organize p.108
Make the invisible visible p.152

SOURCES

V-day website
www.vday.org

Huffington Post, "Eve Ensler"
http://www.huffington-post.com/eve-ensler

Coco Fusco

Coco Fusco is a New York-based, Cuban-American interdisciplinary artist and writer, and the director of Intermedia Initiatives at Parsons The New School for Design. Her videos, multimedia installations and public performances address issues of race and international relations. For example, she issued replicas of passbooks, once required of black South Africans entering white neighborhoods during apartheid, to serve as proof of payment for the 1997 Johannesburg Biennial. Her more recent work deals with the role of female interrogators in the war on terror. In her 2005 public performance "Bare Life Study #1," Fusco dressed as a military police-woman, assumed authoritative positions over fifty shackled young people (played by drama students) in orange inmate uniforms, and commanded them to scrub the floor in front of the U.S. Consulate in São Paulo, Brazil, with their toothbrushes. The performance was based on reports that American soldiers order prisoners to clean their cells with their toothbrushes for hours at a time.

PRINCIPLE

Make the invisible visible p.152
Balance art and message p.100

CASE

The Couple in the Cage p. 312

SOURCES

Coco Fusco website
http://www.thing.net/~cocofusco

MuseumMuseum, "Coco Fusco"
http://trb.la/yNTxoh

Guillermo Gómez-Peña & La Pocha Nostra

Guillermo Gómez-Peña is a Mexico City-born performance artist, activist and writer who came to the United States in 1978. A MacArthur Fellow and American Book Award recipient, his mixed-genre work ranges from short videos and public and interactive performances to newspaper and radio commentaries. He explores cross-cultural issues, including borders, citizenship, immigration and the politics and power of language. For example, in his video "El Leonard Cojen (Cohen) de Tijuana" he mixes Spanish and English with the intention of making a monolingual American feel incompetent. In 1993 Gómez-Peña founded the international collaboration and network of artists "La Pocha Nostra," with over thirty associates worldwide. Their perhaps most significant contributions are interactive "living museums" that parody colonial practices of representation, much like Gómez-Peña's earlier "Couple in the Cage."

Gran Fury

Gran Fury formed after members of ACT-UP came together in 1987 to create the art installation "Let the Record Show...." In the New Museum's window on Broadway they displayed a neon sign reading "SILENCE=DEATH" underneath a pink triangle. This is today perhaps the emblem most associated with ACT-UP and AIDS activism in general. Several ACT-UP members decided to continue creating visuals and worked continuously from 1988 to 1994 as Gran Fury, named after the Plymouth automobile favored by the New York City Police Department. Their posters and printed ads intervened in public spaces widely covered by the media and were soon largely accepted and funded by the institutional art world. Examples are the "Kissing Doesn't Kill" (1989) poster series Gran Fury plastered on NYC buses, depicting kissing couples of mixed race and sex along with the words "Kissing Doesn't Kill: Greed and Indifference Do." For the forty-fourth Venice Biennale they created two controversial pieces: one of the pope, and the adjacent image of a gigantic erect penis titled "Sexism Rears Its Unprotected Head."

Greenpeace

Greenpeace is the largest environmental NGO in the world, and the most publicly visible. Today it's based in Amsterdam and works in forty-five countries, but it started with Vancouver activists sailing to Amchitka Island in 1971 to protest nuclear testing. Greenpeace's hallmark is a combination of disruptive action and "bearing witness," best evidenced by their fleet of three ocean-faring boats used to interrupt and document everything from coal mining to Arctic oil dumping. They're also good in court. One amazing example is the 2008 Kingsnorth Case, in which six Greenpeace activists were arrested for painting "Gordon" — meaning then-Prime Minister Gordon Brown — on the smokestack of a coal power plant before trying to shut the plant down. The defense argued that stopping emissions from Kingsnorth would ultimately protect property elsewhere in the world, and in an unprecedented application of the "lawful excuse" defense, the six were acquitted. Greenpeace's policy of refusing donations from corporations and governments is well publicized, and it supports itself mostly through individual contributions solicited online and by its street teams.

TACTIC
Blockade p. 14

PRINCIPLE
Maintain nonviolent discipline p. 148
Do the media's work for them p. 124

SOURCES
Greenpeace USA website
www.greenpeace.org/usa/en

Guerrilla Girls

The Guerrilla Girls, a group of anonymous women who take the names of deceased female artists as pseudonyms, describe themselves as the "conscience of the art world." Wearing gorilla masks, they use humor, facts and "outrageous visuals" to expose sexism, racism and corruption and "show that feminists can be funny." In time for the 2002 Oscars, they unveiled anti-film industry billboards in Hollywood depicting the "Anatomically Correct Oscar: He's white & male, just like the guys who win!" Their actions were inspired by a 1985 MOMA exhibit titled "An International Survey of Painting and Sculpture" that featured all white artists, of which thirteen out of 169 were women. No one took responsibility for the discrepancy, so the Guerrilla Girls publicly showed these records on posters in the streets of SoHo. Since then, they have created stickers, billboards, and posters, taught workshops internationally and written several books including *The Guerrilla Girls' Bedside Companion to the History of Western Art.*

TACTIC
Détournement/Culture jamming p. 28

PRINCIPLE
Challenge patriarchy as you organize p. 108

THEORY
Cultural hegemony p. 222

SOURCES
Guerrilla Girls website
http://www.guerrillagirls.com

Abbie Hoffman

Abbie Hoffman (1936–1989) was an activist, writer and founder of the Youth International Party (Yippies). Hoffman's creative pranks and protests, which combined civil disobedience with the whimsical spirit of the counter-culture, made him a national symbol of the 1960s rebellions. In 1967 Hoffman and a group of collaborators showered the NYSE trading floor with handfuls of dollar bills thrown from the gallery above, creating chaos among traders and temporarily suspending trading. Later that year, during a massive anti-war demonstration in Washington, D.C., Hoffman led a group of protesters in an attempt to levitate the Pentagon and dispel evil spirits from the building by singing and chanting. In the wake of the 1968 riot in Chicago, Hoffman, along with seven others, was arrested on conspiracy charges. Hoffman's antics during the trial effectively conveyed his political message and turned him into a household name.

I Dream Your Dream

"I Dream Your Dream" is an interactive ritual designed to be performed on the anniversary of Dr. Martin Luther King, Jr.'s "I Have A Dream" speech, each August 28. Participants write down their own dreams for a better world on a colored ribbon, then exchange these dreams with a stranger. The other person's dream is tied around the participant's wrist. By promising to wear it until it falls off, the participant in effect makes a promise to protect the other's dream. In doing so, participants recommit themselves to the cause and to each other; the political is personalized in a very intimate way. "I Dream Your Dream" was inspired by the art installation "I Wish Your Wish" by Rivane Neuenschwander.

Improv Everywhere

Improv Everywhere (IE) is a New York group that stages choreographed but spontaneous-looking performances in public spaces, often with assistance from their huge army of loyal volunteers. IE was founded in 2001 by Charlie Todd, who met many of his "Senior Agents" while performing at the Upright Citizens Brigade. Their performances, which they call "missions," have no particular political goals. Instead, IE tries to turn the boring monotony of urban life on its head and instill a sense of wonder and absurdity in the familiar scenes of city life. Past actions included the famous "Frozen Grand Central," in which hundreds of volunteers simultaneously "paused" for five minutes in the middle of the station; the "MP3 Experiments," where people followed recorded instructions to dance, jump, and sing in sync; site-specific mini-musicals; a fake U2 concert; and a tuxedo-wearing bathroom attendant at the Times Square McDonald's.

TACTIC
Flash mob p. 46
Invisible theater p. 66

PRINCIPLE
Anyone can act p. 98

SOURCES
Improv Everywhere website
http://improveverywhere.com

Improv Everywhere
youtube channel
www.youtube.com/user/
ImprovEverywhere

Iraq Veterans Against the War (IVAW)

Founded in 2004, Iraq Veterans Against the War (IVAW) is an advocacy group comprising around 1,800 active-duty military personnel and veterans from all branches of the military who have served since 9/11, particularly in Iraq and Afghanistan. The group calls for withdrawal of all occupying forces in Iraq and Afghanistan, reparations for the human and structural damage suffered in Iraq and Afghanistan, and full benefits, adequate healthcare (including mental health) and other support for returning servicemen and women. Named for the 1971 Winter Soldier hearings, "Winter Solider: Iraq & Afghanistan — Eyewitness Accounts of the Occupations" was a four-day event organized in 2008 by the IVAW at which more than 200 veterans gave testimony about their experiences as soldiers. "Operation First Casualty" was a series of dramatic IVAW actions, designed to demonstrate the reality of war, in which uniformed veterans conducted mock patrols in major American cities.

PRINCIPLE
Bring the issue home p. 106
Take leadership from those
most impacted p. 180

THEORY
Ethical Spectacle p. 230

SOURCES
Iraq Veterans Against
the War website
http://ivaw.org

Video: "Operation First Casualty"
http://trb.la/yM1SIV

Allan Kaprow

Allan Kaprow (1927–2006) was an American performance artist and teacher whose "Happenings" helped shape the New York performance art scene in the 1950s and '60s, and were hugely influential on later artists. Happenings are characterized by lack of formal structure and defiance of the traditional performer/audience relationship; everyone is an audience member and a performer simultaneously. Here are some typical examples of the more than 200 Happenings: Participants took Polaroids of each other and left them in the performance space; a giant room made of ice gradually melted from visitors' body heat; fife and drum music played in a high school gym while people kicked balls around; visitors rearranged the furniture in a gallery at the New York Museum of Modern Art; participants tied greenhouse-grown leaves to the bare branches of trees. "Objects of every sort are materials for the new art," Kaprow wrote. "Paint, food, chairs, electric and neon lights, smoke, water, old socks, a dog, movies, a thousand other things which will be discovered by the present generation of artists…"

Paul Krassner

Paul Krassner is a satirist and journalist who played a major role in the evolution of late twentieth-century American political humor. He's best known as founder and editor of *The Realist*, the taboo-exploding satirical magazine that ran for forty years. Though he was a stylistically versatile writer, he'd worked at *Mad* magazine in college and retained a sense of the satirical grotesque. One of his articles, "The Parts That Were Left Out of the Kennedy Book," described Lyndon Johnson penetrating the dying JFK's bullet hole wound — and for a while many people thought it was true. As a prankster, he distributed "Fuck Communism" bumper stickers at the height of the Vietnam War. As an editor, he worked with Norman Mailer, Joseph Heller and Ken Kesey (Krassner was a member of Kesey's Merry Pranksters), and as an activist he co-founded the Yippies with Abbie Hoffman.

Suzanne Lacy

A California-based feminist activist, teacher, and leading figure in the public art movement, Suzanne Lacy creates socially oriented artworks that engage with community and audience members on multiple levels. Her projects include and combine exhibits, live performances, narratives, video and audio, workshops, public speak-outs, symposia and demonstrations. Lacy largely creates her work within a specific community and spatial context and collaborates with local politicians, grassroots activists, artists and other people directly affected by the chosen subject. Her work has mainly focused on feminist and urban issues. "3 Weeks in May" (Los Angeles, 1977) addressed rape by combining personal narratives and performative healing rituals with help hotlines, public self-defense classes and the mapped display of locations of rapes reported to the Los Angeles Police Department in a three-week time frame. Since 1991 Lacy has been the executive director of TEAM (Teens + Educators + Artists + Media Makers) in Oakland, California. She served in then-Mayor Jerry Brown's education cabinet and was an arts commissioner for the city. Lacy is the Chair of Fine Arts at Otis College of Art and Design, Los Angeles, and edited the book *Mapping the Terrain: New Genre Public Art* (1995).

TACTIC
Artistic vigl p. 10

PRINCIPLE
Use the power of ritual p. 198

THEORY
Intellectuals and power p. 240

SOURCES
Suzanne Lacy website
http://www.suzannelacy.com

"Nature, Culture, Public Space,"
Artist Statement by Suzanne Lacy
http://trb.la/zp6DOu

Ladies Against Women

Ladies Against Women (LAW) was a street performance group that used satire to ridicule the anti-feminist backlash of 1980s Reagan-era America. In ruffled dresses, white gloves and pillbox hats, the Ladies would hand out consciousness-lowering manifestos that included such action items as "Restore virginity as a high-school graduation requirement" and "Eliminate the gender gap by repealing the Ladies' Vote (Babies, Not Ballots)." LAW welcomed new recruits, but only if they brought pink permission slips signed by their husbands.

PRINCIPLE
Make it funny web
Don't dress like a protestor p. 126

CASE
Billionaires for Bush p. 296

SOURCES
Ladies Against Women website
http://www.ladies-
againstwomen.com

The Lesbian Avengers

TACTIC
Mass street action p. 68

PRINCIPLE
Make the invisible visible p. 152

THEORY
Expressive and
instrumental actions p. 232

SOURCES
Lesbian Avengers website
http://www.lesbianavengers.com

ACT-UP NY, "The Lesbian
Avengers Handbook"
http://trb.la/yejnyC

The direct action group Lesbian Avengers was founded in 1992 by longtime New York lesbian activists Ana Simo, Sarah Schulman, Maxine Wolfe, Anne-christine D'Adesky, Marie Honan and Anne Maguire, who focused on issues of lesbian survival and visibility in public life. Their goal: avoid "stale tactics" and create daring and participatory confrontation that flaunts "lesbionic outrageousness" instead. At its peak mid-decade, the Avengers had more than fifty chapters worldwide. At the NYC memorial of a lesbian and a gay man, both killed by skinheads throwing a Molotov cocktail into their Oregon home, the newly organized Avengers ate fire and chanted, "The fire will not consume us. We take it and make it our own." Fire eating has since become an Avenger trademark. Their most enduring legacy, however, is the Dyke March, still held across the country annually one day before the Pride Parade. The first Dyke March, organized without a permit in Washington, D.C., on April 24, 1993, in collaboration with ACT-UP and other Washington, D.C., area groups, was "the largest lesbian event in the history of the world," according to Sarah Schulman.

The Living Theater

TACTIC
Street theater web

PRINCIPLE
Balance art and message p. 100

THEORY
The tactics of everday life p. 268

SOURCES
Living Theater website
http://www.livingtheater.org

A major player in the establishment of an experimental and politically engaged Off-Broadway culture, the Living Theater was founded in 1947 by Judith Malina and Julian Beck. Their early work was legendary in New York for its willingness to push boundaries: everyone who saw "Paradise Now" in 1968 remembers the piles of naked audience members and actors (some of whom were arrested for indecent exposure). They're also important as early American adopters of playwrights like Brecht, Lorca, Pirandello, William Carlos Williams and Gertrude Stein. After four of their New York theaters were closed by government bureaucracies, the troupe went nomadic, embarking on what became a forty-year tour of Europe and the world. Their sacred text is French playwright Antonin Artaud's manifesto *The Theater and Its Double*, which exalts immediate emotional experience. Although they've frequently performed political theater in unconventional venues like prisons and steel mills, today they have a home again in the Lower East Side.

Los Angeles Poverty Department (LAPD)

The Los Angeles Poverty Department, a community theater company, was founded in 1985 by director/performer John Malpede. The first performance group in the nation made up principally of homeless people, the group is committed to creating high-quality, challenging performances and multi-disciplinary artworks that tell the first-hand narrative of Skid Row's community. Projects include "The Skid Row History Museum" at the Box Gallery in LA's Chinatown, the "Festival for All Skid Row Artists," and large-scale collaborations like "UTOPIA/dystopia — 220 Glimpses" and "Agents and Assets," which integrated panel discussions with the community. The LAPD has created residency projects internationally, working with community drug recovery programs, shelters, policy advocates and arts organizations, and has won awards including the LA Weekly Theater Award, New York's Bessie Creation Award, and the Otto Award for Political Theater.

PRINCIPLE
Think narratively p. 186
Take leadership from the most impacted p. 180

THEORY
Theater of the Oppressed p. 272

SOURCES
Los Angeles Poverty Department website
http://lapovertydept.org

Mothers of the Plaza de Mayo

Mothers of the Plaza de Mayo is a group of Argentine human rights activists formed in response to the campaign of disappearances, torture and murder carried out during the military junta's 1976–1983 "dirty war." The junta "disappeared" over 30,000 people while denying any knowledge of their whereabouts. Day after day, the Mothers assembled in the Plaza de Mayo, facing the presidential palace, to protest the disappearance of their children. They wore headscarves with the names of their children and often carried photographs of the disappeared. Mothers of the Plaza de Mayo played a critical role in organizing resistance to the junta and in its eventual collapse in 1983.

TACTIC
Artistic vigil p. 10

PRINCIPLE
Make the invisible visible p. 152
Use the power of ritual p. 198

SOURCES
University of Texas at Austin, "Madres de Plaza de Mayo"
http://trb.la/wjaP8H

International Center on Nonviolent Conflict, "Madres de Plaza de Mayo"
http://trb.la/ylckaV

Operation SalAMI

TACTIC
Nonviolent search and
seizure p. 76

PRINCIPLE
Make the invisible visible p. 152

THEORY
Points of intervention p. 250

SOURCES
Operation SalAMI, "Resist the AMI!"
http://www.ainfos.ca/98/
apr/ainfos00293.html

Multi-Monde Productions,
"Operation SalAMI"
http://www.pmm.qc.ca/salami/
ENGLISH/opers.html

Global Nonviolent Action Database,
"Canadian Activists Demand
Transparency
in FTAA negotiations, 2000-2001"
http://trb.la/xigN8r

Operation SalAMI was a Montréal-based direct action group conceived as a campaign against the Multilateral Agreement on Investment (MAI). The MAI was a global investment treaty being privately worked out between member countries of the Organization for Economic Co-operation and Development and the International Chamber of Commerce. The name SalAMI includes this agreement's French acronym AMI (or "friend") preceded by "Sal," meaning bad or dirty. In May 1998 SalAMI surrounded and delayed the Conférence de Montréal on Globalized Economies. The ensuing global mobilizations actually led to the shelving of the agreement. Since then, Operation SalAMI has collaborated to organize conferences, teach-ins and two festive May 1 vigils in front of the Montréal Stock Exchange. In 2001, after the government failed to produce secret negotiating texts for the Free Trade Area of the Americas (FTAA) treaty, Operation SalAMI surrounded the Department of International Trade and Foreign Affairs. Climbing barricades, they declared they had a "Citizens' Warrant for Search and Seizure." Five days later, the International Trade Minister released the full FTAA draft. Negotiators missed the 2005 deadline for the implementation of the FTAA.

The Orange Alternative

TACTIC
Happening web

PRINCIPLE
Don't dress like a protestor p. 126
The real action is
your target's reaction web

SOURCES
Swarthmore College Computer
Society, "Orange Alternative"
http://trb.la/wdPc3V

The Orange Alternative was a 1980s-era underground protest movement in Poland. It used street happenings and absurdist provocations to ridicule the Communist regime and promote independent thinking. Their actions, enormously popular with students who often found Solidarity marches stiff and boring, included graffiti, distributing toilet paper (a consumer product in short supply at the time), and singing Stalinist hymns while holding hands around the orangutan cage at the Warsaw Zoo. Most memorably, they organized a march of 10,000 people in orange dwarf hats. "How can you treat a police officer seriously," notes founder Waldemar Fydrych, "when he is asking you the question: 'Why did you participate in an illegal meeting of dwarfs?'"

Otpor

Otpor — "resistance" in Serbian — was a civic youth movement started by a small group of student activists at Belgrade University that was active from 1998 until 2003. Otpor played a key role in overthrowing Slobodan Milošević's government and in Serbia's transition to democracy. In just two years of struggle against Milošević, Otpor's numbers grew from eleven to 60,000. Otpor used street theater, dilemma actions, poster propagation and pranks to satirize, embarrass and undermine the legitimacy of the government. For example, activists in Nis held a "birthday party" for Milošević with prank gifts like a one-way ticket to the Hague, a prison uniform and a cake in the shape of a red star. Even the group's iconic clenched fist logo lampooned the WWII Serb Partisans' symbol. Although the group was provocative, they maintained a staunch and disciplined commitment to non-violence which ultimately dissuaded security forces from attacking them, regardless of orders. Since Milošević's ouster in 2000, the group has disseminated the lessons and tactics of their movement through trainings and consultations. Most recently, Egypt's April 6 Movement received training from Otpor on how to conduct peaceful demonstrations, how to respond to the threat of state violence and how to mobilize people.

PRINCIPLE
Maintain nonviolent discipline p. 148
Take leadership from the most impacted p.180

THEORY
Pillars of support p. 248
The social cure p. 264

SOURCES
Foreign Policy, "Revolution U," February 16, 2011
http://trb.la/yqbSKx

A Force More Powerful (film)
http://www.aforcemore-powerful.org

Preemptive Media

Founded in 2002, Preemptive Media (PM) is a group of artists, activists and technologists that produces projects drawing attention to the ubiquity and invisibility of consumer data. PM's goal is to make their audiences more aware of the information they unknowingly divulge to governments and corporations and the ways in which the collection of that data often occurs without consent. One of PM's most famous projects, the "Swipe Bar," was a mobile installation designed to look like a local watering hole. When customers showed their IDs and swiped their Visas, Preemptive Media served them not only beer but also a report of all the data stored on those cards. PM thinks of its projects as "beta tests," and some of them — like a website to aggregate short news reports sent from hundreds of cell phones — resemble pared-down precursors of more popular technologies (like Twitter). But the "beta" quality of their actions, and the willingness to experiment, is very much the point.

TACTIC
Détournement/Culture jamming p. 28

PRINCIPLE
Make the invisible visible p. 152
By any media necessary web

SOURCES
Preemptive Media website
http://preemptivemedia.net

ArtSlant, "Preemptive Media"
http://trb.la/zhOXnz

The Provos

TACTIC
Prefigurative intervention p. 82
Hoax p. 54

PRINCIPLE
Put your target in a
decision dilemma p. 166

SOURCES
High Times, "Dutch Provos,"
January 1990
http://trb.la/xqYElu

The Provos, active in the mid-1960s, were a Dutch counterculture movement heavily influenced by anarchism. The Provos undermined the legitimacy of the authorities with nonviolent pranks and happenings designed to provoke violent police responses. A royal wedding in 1965 was the occasion for the most audacious prank. Before the wedding, the Provos spread wild rumors about schemes to dump LSD into Amsterdam's water supply, drug the royal horses, and the like. The government responded by mobilizing 25,000 troops to guard the royal parade. On the day of the wedding, it took nothing but a few smoke bombs to provoke a massive riot. The Provos also devised a series of White Plans: utopian, often whimsical schemes and policy proposals that targeted absurd and undesirable aspects of capitalist society. The White Bicycle Plan, for instance, called for Amsterdam to ban cars from the central city and to distribute thousands of free, white bicycles for public use. The Provos began implementing the plan by placing fifty white bicycles on the street, which were promptly confiscated by the police, who asserted that free bicycles were an invitation for thieves.

Reverend Billy and the Church of Earthalujah

TACTIC
Détournement/Culture
jamming p. 28
Street theater web

THEORY
Commodity fetishism p. 218

SOURCES
Reverend Billy and The Church
of Earthalujah website
http://www.revbilly.com

Village Voice, "Rage Against the
Caffeine: Reverend Billy Preaches
the Anticorporate
Gospel to Starbucks," April 18, 2000
http://trb.la/xUEo1K

New York Times Magazine, "Reverend Billy's Unholy War," August
22, 2004
http://www.nytimes.
com/2004/08/22/
magazine/reverend-billy-s-unholy-
war.html

Reverend Billy is part performance art, part guerrilla theater and part political activism. Devised by Billy Talen in 1997 as a one-man performance piece, the Reverend Billy character first appeared in Times Square preaching that "Mickey Mouse is the Antichrist!" Styled after conservative televangelists in his white dinner jacket over a black T-shirt, priest's collar and Elvis-esque hairdo, Reverend Billy and the Church of Earthalujah — a group of green-robed gospel singers formerly known as The Church of Stop Shopping — have performed countless retail interventions in the United States and abroad. Their targets have included Disney Stores, Starbucks, Walmart, Nike, Home Depot, Barnes & Noble, JPMorgan Chase and UBS.

Cindy Sheehan

Cindy Lee Miller Sheehan, or the "Peace Mom," is best known for her peaceful anti-war vigil "Camp Casey." After her 24-year-old son, U.S. Army Specialist Casey Sheehan, was killed in the Iraq war in April 2004, President Bush met in Fort Lewis with Cindy and other grieving parents to pay them his respects. According to Sheehan, Bush behaved disrespectfully at this meeting, forgetting her deceased son's name and leaving her questions unanswered. In response she co-founded Gold Star Families for Peace, and in August 2005 she camped outside then-President Bush's Crawford Texas ranch for twenty-six days demanding answers and another meeting with him (neither of which occurred). With her action, Sheehan attracted national and international support and media attention. She has since participated in anti-war protests across the nation, given speeches, written articles, and run against House Speaker Nancy Pelosi as an independent candidate after Pelosi did not take initiative to impeach Bush.

PRINCIPLE
Put your target in a decision dilemma p. 166
Lead with sympathetic character p. 146
Shift the spectrum of allies p. 172

SOURCES
Gold Star Families For Peace website
http://www.gsfp.org

Situationist International

Situationist International (SI) was either one of the twentieth century's most important and successful cadres of anti-capitalist revolutionaries, or a bunch of petty, self-marginalized megalomaniacs waging an inconsequential decades-long war of words — depending on your perspective. SI began as a group of avant-garde artists but rapidly evolved into a political organization that, at its peak, heavily influenced the May 1968 general strike in France. SI's organizational culture was persistently tumultuous. Recounting its history of backbiting, excommunications, factional splits, personal feuds, esoteric debates and bitter polemics would require a separate book. For instance, Letterist International, one of SI's parent organizations, emerged out of a heated debate over the artistic status of Charlie Chaplin. Having expelled all of SI's founding members, the group's intellectual leader Guy Debord dissolved the group in 1972. SI's chief legacy is its social and political theory, which has influenced a broad range of individuals, organizations and movements, including Reclaim the Streets, the Weathermen and *Adbusters*.

THEORY
Society of the Spectacle p. 266
Political identity paradox p. 254

CASE
Reclaim the Streets p. 350

SOURCES
Situationist International Archives
http://www.nothingness.org/SI

Bureau of Public Secrets,
"May 1968 Graffiti"
http://www.bopsecrets.
org/CF/graffiti.htm

Joey Skaggs

TACTIC

Hoax p. 54

PRINCIPLE

Play to the audience that isn't there p. 160
Make it funny web

SOURCES

*Joey Skaggs website
http://joeyskaggs.com*

Joey Skaggs (born 1945) is an American artist notable for his prolific hoaxes and media pranks. In one (in)famous hoax, Skaggs put an ad in the *Village Voice* advertising a dog brothel. After receiving a blizzard of interested phone calls, he hired actors (dogs and people) and invited reporters to tour the facility. WABC TV even aired a piece on the brothel that was slated to win an Emmy but was disqualified when Skaggs revealed the hoax. Other pranks over the last several decades have included taking hippies on sightseeing tours of suburban Queens after Skaggs became annoyed at suburbanites touring the Lower East Side to gawk at hippies, attempting to burn a "Vietnamese nativity scene" to protest the war in Vietnam, tying a fifty-foot bra to the U.S. Treasury building on Wall Street, and dozens of others.

Mitch Snyder

TACTIC

Direct action p. 32

PRINCIPLE

Take leadership from the most impacted p. 180

THEORY

Action logic p. 208

SOURCES

*The Gelman Library at George Washington University, "Mitch Snyder"
http://trb.la/zsCqYW*

*First Church Shelter, "Mitch Snyder"
http://trb.la/A2M3AD*

*National Coalition for the Homeless, "Remembering Mitch Snyder"
http://trb.la/wvpfOo*

Mitch Snyder (1946–1990) was an American advocate for the rights of homeless folks. His career as an organizer began while he was serving time in prison following a 1970 arrest for auto theft. Snyder, along with Phillip and Daniel Berrigan, participated in hunger strikes to protest the treatment of prisoners in Vietnam. In 1973 Snyder joined the Community for Creative Non-Violence (CCNV) in Washington, D.C., then an anti-war group. After the end of the Vietnam war, CCNV began to administer services to homeless Washingtonians, and Snyder began the work that ultimately made him famous. In addition to participating in hunger strikes, holding public funerals for homeless people, and organizing housing takeovers to protest municipal and federal housing policy, Snyder participated in numerous pranks and artistic hijinks. In one case, he and several of his colleagues dressed in business suits, infiltrated a National Conservative Caucus and dove into the world's largest apple pie — intended by the NCC to symbolize a bigger piece of the pie for everyone — howling "It's all for me!'"

El Teatro Campesino

El Teatro Campesino — "The Peasants' Theater" — is a California-based company whose performances focus on the social and political experience of Latinos in the U.S. They staged their first productions on flatbed trucks as part of César Chávez's Delano Grape Strike in 1965, and collaborated with Peter Brook to stage performances for farm workers in the early 1970s. In the late '70s they shifted into more heavily produced spectacles, the most famous being artistic director Luis Valdez's "Zoot Suit," about the false murder conviction of twenty-one young Chicanos in Los Angeles, which became the first play by a Latino to go to Broadway. Their latest work has expanded to address broader political questions like corporate power and the environment.

TACTIC
Street theater web

PRINCIPLE
Balance art and message p. 100
Know your cultural terrain p. 142

SOURCES
El Teatro Campesino website
http://www.elteatrocampesino.com

Video archive of El

Teatro Campesino
http://cemaweb.library.ucsb.edu/ETCList.html

UK Uncut

UK Uncut is a tax justice movement that emerged in late 2010 in response to proposals by the British government to sharply reduce social spending. UK Uncut highlights the disparity between the government's aggressive austerity measures and the preferential tax treatment enjoyed by big businesses by targeting retail stores and bank branches owned by the worst corporate tax dodgers. Its colorful, creative actions have shut down dozens of banks and stores through banging pots, blowing whistles, chanting and singing. To highlight cuts to specific social services, protesters have held read-ins to protest library closures and sleep-ins to protest cuts to housing subsidies, and they have transformed targeted stores into hospitals, daycares, classrooms and homeless shelters. UK Uncut has also inspired similar actions in the United States, carried out under the name U.S. Uncut, which began with a national day of action on February 26, 2011.

TACTIC
Flash mob p. 46

PRINCIPLE
Choose your target wisely p. 114

THEORY
Hashtag politics p. 238

SOURCES
UK Uncut website
http://www.ukuncut.org.uk

Voina

TACTIC

Guerilla theater web

PRINCIPLE

Reframe p. 168
Use your radical fringe to slide
the Overton window p. 200

SOURCES

Free Voina
http://en.free-voina.org

Don't Panic Online, "Russian Art
Anarchists Explain Themselves"
http://trb.la/zWZr9o

Voina ("war") is a Russian performance art collective that uses guerrilla street theater as a vehicle for political protest. The group has projected a skull and crossbones onto the national government building, painted a 65-meter erect penis on a drawbridge facing the state security agency's headquarters, overturned police cars, and thrown chickens at McDonald's workers to "alleviate their boredom." One performance, staged a few days before Dmitry Medvedev was elected president, consisted of six couples having sex in Moscow's state biological museum under a banner that read "Fuck for the heir, Little Bear," a play on Medvedev's surname, which means "bear" in Russian. In 2010, the group's co-founders, Oleg Vorotnikov and Leonid Nikolayev, were arrested for an anti-corruption performance that involved overturning seven police cars and were held for three months before being charged with a crime. At the time of this writing, they are charged with inciting hatred against a social group — the police — and face up to seven years in prison.

Washington Action Group

TACTIC

Mass street action p. 68
Street theater web

PRINCIPLE

This ain't the Sistine Chapel p. 188

SOURCES

Washington Action Group website
www.wagthis.org

Since 1998, Washington Action Group (WAG) has creatively harnessed the energy of cultural work to nonviolently build people and community power with street theater, stilt walking, graphic visuals, banners, giant props/puppets, pageantry and civil resistance actions and trainings. WAG formed the core of the organizing, training and art teams for the World Bank / IMF actions in 2000 that brought 40,000 protesters along with a fifteen-foot tall Goddess of Liberation and a humongous papier-mâché Structural Adjustment Machine into the DC streets. They have provided guidance to many national and local groups looking to make a splash effectively and safely at the intersection of art and politics. WAG is dedicated to using a diversity of creative resistance and cultural expression to help activists be more effective.

Women in Black

Women in Black (WiB) began in 1988 in Israel as a response to the Israeli occupation of the West Bank and Gaza and to the Palestinian Intifada, but spread rapidly to countries all around the world. WiB's website states: "Women in Black is a world-wide network of women committed to peace with justice and actively opposed to injustice, war, militarism and other forms of violence.... We are not an organization, but a means of communicating and a formula for action." WiB actions often take the form of regularly scheduled silent vigils where participating women wear all black, stand in a public place, carry placards and pass out leaflets. WiB groups have also used many forms of nonviolent direct action, including blocking roads and trespassing on military bases.

TACTIC
Artistic vigil p. 10

PRINCIPLE
Simple rules can have
grand results p. 176

THEORY
Memes p. 242

SOURCES
Women in Black website
http://www.womenin-
black.org/en/vigil

The Ya Basta Association

The Ya Basta Association was an organization of Italian anti-capitalists. The group is famous primarily for originating the *tute bianche* tactic. In 1994, the mayor of Milan ordered the eviction of protesters from the Leoncavallo social center, declaring, "From now on, squatters will be nothing more than ghosts wandering about in the city!" Protesters responded by wearing tutes bianches — white overalls — to reconquer the center. The meme spread rapidly and tute bianche blocs were a visible component of many subsequent anti-globalization protests. Symbolically, the white overalls were meant to challenge the invisibility of people on the margins of social life — the unemployed, the homeless and the illegal immigrants. Practically, the white overalls were often padded or worn along with shields made of plexiglas and helmets to resist the blows of police while the bloc marched through barrier lines and perimeter fences. Tute bianche blocs became a kind of collective protection force, marching in compact formations to prevent dissipation by security forces, creating a sense of security for protesters who feared injury. As a result, protester injuries decreased significantly, and police were forced to shift from a dissipation to a containment tactic.

PRINCIPLE
Don't dress like a
protester p. 126
Maintain nonviolent dis-
cipline p. 148
Take risks, but take care p. 182

SOURCES
The Fifth International, "Tute
Bianche"
http://trb.la/zGYB3b

Dario Azzellini, "Tute Bianche"
http://www.azzellini.net/node/2466

The Zapatista Army of National Liberation

THEORY

Expressive and instrumen-
tal actions p. 232
Floating signifier p. 234
Revolutionary nonviolence p. 260

SOURCES

Ejército Zapatista de
Liberación Nacional
http://ezln.org.mx

Wikipedia, "Zapatista Army
of National Liberation"
http://trb.la/wgAtud

Although the Zapatista Army of National Liberation (EZLN) began as, and in many ways remains, an armed uprising against the Mexican state, the EZLN frames its goals and actions in political, rather than military, terms. The movement's anti-leader Subcomandante Marcos has written: "In a war, the decisive thing is not the military confrontation but the politics at stake in the confrontation. We didn't go to war to kill or be killed. We went to war in order to be heard." Marcos' prolific writing, along with the movement's persistent outreach efforts and savvy media campaigns, have inspired radicals all over the world to demand autonomy and rise up against their governments and corporate overlords.

Write your own practitioner profile

The modular format of *Beautiful Trouble* allows the collection to expand endlessly to reflect new tactical breakthroughs, underrepresented areas of struggle and overlooked pearls of wisdom.

Become part of *Beautiful Trouble*. Use this template to write up your own creative-activism insights. Submit your own module for publication on the *Beautiful Trouble* website here: http://beautifultrouble.org.

RESOURCES
50 MINDBOMBS NO BEAUTIFUL
TROUBLEMAKER SHOULD DO WITHOUT

· ·

10 GOOD BOOKS ABOUT BIG IDEAS

Grace Lee Boggs with Scott Kurashige, *The Next American Revolution: Sustainable Activism for the Twenty-First Century* (Berkeley and Los Angeles: University of California Press, 2011)

Jan Cohen-Cruz, ed., *Radical Street Performance: An International Anthology* (New York: Routledge, 1998)

Stephen Duncombe, ed., *The Cultural Resistance Reader* (London and New York: Verso, 2002)

David Harvey, *The Enigma of Capital and the Crises of Capitalism* (New York: Oxford University Press, 2010)

Paul Hawken, *Blessed Unrest* (New York: Penguin Group, 2007)

bell hooks, *Feminist Theory From Margin to Center* (London: Pluto Press, 2000)

Naomi Klein, *The Shock Doctrine: The Rise of Disaster Capitalism* (New York: Picador, 2007)

Vijay Prashad, *The Darker Nations: A People's History of the Third World* (New York: New Press, 2008)

David Solnit, *Globalize Liberation: How to Uproot the System and Build a Better World* (San Francisco: City Lights Books, 2004)

Clay Shirky, *Here Comes Everybody: The Power of Organizing Without Organizations* (New York: Penguin, 2008)

· ·

10 GOOD BOOKS ABOUT ORGANIZING

Kim Bobo, Jackie Kendall and Steve Max, *Organizing for Social Change* (Santa Ana, CA: Seven Locks Press, 1996)

Doyle Canning and Patrick Reinsborough, *Re:Imagining Change: An Introduction to Story-Based*

Strategy (Oakland, CA: PM Press, 2010)

Robert Bray, *SPIN Works: A Media Guidebook for Communicating Values and Shaping Opinion* (San Francisco: Independent Media Institute, 2000)

Si Kahn, *Organizing: A Guide for Grassroots Leaders* (Silver Spring, MD: National Association of Social Workers, 1991)

Rinku Sen, *Stir It Up: Lessons in Community Organizing and Advocacy* (Hoboken, NJ: Jossey-Bass [Wiley and Sons], 2003)

INCITE! Women of Color Against Violence, *The Revolution Will Not be Funded: Beyond the Non-Profit Industrial Complex* (Brooklyn, NY: South End Press, 2007)

Hillary Moore and Joshua Kahn Russell. *Organizing Cools the Planet: Tools and Reflections to Navigate the Climate Crisis* (Oakland, CA: PM Press, 2011)

Paulo Freire, *Pedagogy of the Oppressed* (New York and London: Continuum, 2006)

Judy Ancel and Jane Slaughter, *A Troublemaker's Handbook 2: How To Fight Back Where You Work — and Win!* (Detroit: Labor Notes, 2005)

CrimethInc, *Recipes for Disaster: An Anarchist Cookbook* (Salem, OR: CrimethInc Far East, 2006)

. . . .

10 GOOD ORGANIZING WEBSITES

Beyond the Choir
http://beyondthechoir.org

Colours of Resistance Archive
http://www.coloursofresistance.org

Midnight Special Law Collective
http://www.midnightspecial.net

New Organizing Institute
http://neworganizing.com

Organizing for Power
http://organizingforpower.wordpress.com

Organizing Upgrade
http://www.organizingupgrade.com

Praxis Makes Perfect
http://joshuakahnrussell.wordpress.com

The Ruckus Society
http://ruckus.org

Training for Change
http://www.trainingforchange.org

Waging Nonviolence
http://wagingnonviolence.org

10 GOOD RESEARCH WEBSITES

Center for Media Justice
http://centerformediajustice.org

CorpWatch
http://www.corpwatch.org

Global Nonviolent Action Database
http://nvdatabase.swarthmore.edu

International Center on Nonviolent Conflict
http://www.nonviolent-conflict.org

Know Your Meme
http://knowyourmeme.com

Little Sis
littlesis.org

The Meta-Activism Project
http://www.meta-activism.org

Multinational Monitor
http://multinationalmonitor.org

Open Secrets
http://www.opensecrets.org

Tactical Media Files
http://www.tacticalmediafiles.net

10 Tactics. Directed by the Tactical Technology Collective. 2009.
http://www.informationactivism.org/en

10 GOOD FILMS

After Stonewall. Directed by John Scagliotti. New York: First Run Features, 1999.
http://firstrunfeatures.com/afterstonewalldvd.html

Bringing Down a Dictator. Directed by Steve York. A Force More Powerful Films, 2002.
http://www.aforcemorepowerful.org/films/bdd

The Corporation. Directed by Mark Achbar and Jennifer Abbott. New York: Zeitgeist Films, 2003.
http://www.zeitgeistfilms.com/film.php?directoryname=corporation

The Fourth World War. Directed by Rick Rowley. New York: Big Noise Films, 2003.
http://www.bignoisefilms.com/films/features/89-fourth-world-war

A Force More Powerful. Directed by Steve York. A Force More Powerful Films, 1999.
http://www.aforcemorepowerful.org/films/afmp

Harlan County U.S.A. Directed by Barbara Kopple. New York: Cabin Creek Films, 1976.
http://www.cabincreekfilms.com/films_harlancounty.html

Manufacturing Consent: Noam Chomsky and the Media. Directed by Mark Achbar and Peter Wintonick. New York: Zeitgeist Films, 1992.
http://www.zeitgeistfilms.com/film.php?directoryname=manufacturingconsent

This is What Democracy Looks Like. Directed by Jill Friedberg and Rick Rowley. New York: Big Noise Films, 2000.
http://www.bignoisefilms.org/films/features/100-whatdemocracylookslike

We: A Documentary Featuring the Words of Arundhati Roy. Created anonymously.
http://www.weroy.org

CONTRIBUTOR BIOS

EDITORS   **ANDREW BOYD** is an author, humorist and veteran of creative campaigns for social change. He led the decade-long satirical media campaign "Billionaires for Bush." He co-founded Agit-Pop Communications, an award-winning "subvertising" agency, and the netroots movement The Other 98%. He's the author of three books: *Daily Afflictions*, *Life's Little Deconstruction Book* and the creative action manual *The Activist Cookbook*. Unable to come up with with his own lifelong ambition, he's been cribbing Milan Kundera's: "to unite the utmost seriousness of question with the utmost lightness of form." You can find him at andrewboyd.com.

DAVE OSWALD MITCHELL is a writer, editor and researcher camped out at the intersection of the economic and ecological crises. He edited the Canadian activist publication *Briarpatch Magazine* from 2005 to 2010, and his writing has been published in *Rabble, Reality Sandwich, Rolling Thunder* and *Upping the Anti*. His interests include brevity, tactical media and going elsewhere.

CONTRIBUTORS   **RAE ABILEAH** is the co-director of CODEPINK Women for Peace, a peace and justice group working to redirect the nation's resources from militarism to healthcare, education, green jobs and other life-affirming activities. Rae lives in San Francisco, and is a contributing author to several books including: *10 Excellent Reasons Not to Join the Military; Sisters Singing; Beyond Tribal Loyalties: Personal Stories of Jewish Peace Activists*; and *Corporate Complicity in Israel's Occupation*. When not raising a ruckus for justice, she enjoys surfing, hiking and cooking quiches. She can be reached at rae@codepink.org

RYAN ACUFF grew up in Chicago, IL but has been in Rochester, NY for the last six years participating in community organizing and pursuing graduate work in psychology (M.A). Currently his organizing is focused on homelessness, foreclosure and affordable housing rights, including work with University of Rochester Students for a Democratic Society (SDS), Genesee Valley Earth First!, Food Not Bombs, Rochester Free School, Healthcare Education Project, 1199 SEIU United Healthcare Workers East, Rochester Police Accountability Coalition, Rochester Copwatch, Occupy Rochester and Take Back the Land Rochester.

CELIA ALARIO is a communications strategist, spokesperson coach and seasoned troublemaker. She enjoys collaborating with grassroots organizations, filmmakers, artists and authors, and scheming about how to engage key audiences and change the world with stories, while tapping both traditional media/marketing and new media/web 2.0

tools. Alario teaches Environmental Communications Strategies and Tactics at UC Santa Barbara, and serves on the board of directors of the Independent Television Service (ITVS) and the smartMeme Training and Strategy Collective, and on the advisory boards of BEN (Business Ethics Network) and IVAW (Iraq Veterans Against the War). Her sock puppet alias tweets at www.twitter.com/celiaalario

PHIL ARONEANU been working on solving the climate crisis since he was sixteen. In 2008, with author/activist Bill McKibben and a small group of fellow students, he helped launch the innovative 350.org campaign. In the lead-up to the 2009 United Nations climate talks in Copenhagen, 350.org pulled off over 5,200 simultaneous public events in 181 countries in what CNN called "the most widespread day of political action in history." Since then, Phil has led national and global campaigns to push back against corporate polluters and build an authentic grassroots climate movement. Phil currently serves as U.S. Campaign Director at 350.org

PETER BARNES is an entrepreneur and writer who has founded and led several successful companies. Barnes began his career as a reporter on *The Lowell* (Mass.) *Sun*, and was subsequently a Washington correspondent for *Newsweek* and West Coast correspondent for *The New Republic*. In 1976 he cofounded a worker-owned solar energy company in San Francisco, and in 1985 he cofounded Working Assets Long Distance (now Credo Mobile). His books include *Capitalism 3.0: A Guide to Reclaiming the Commons* (2006), *Who Owns the Sky?* (2001), and *Pawns: The Plight of the Citizen-Soldier* (1972).

JESSE BARRON is a fiction writer and critic living in Brooklyn. His reviews have appeared in the *New York Observer* and the *Daily*, and he worked with The Faster Times on the media campaign for the One Young World activists' summit in Zurich. Since graduating from Harvard in 2009, he's been at work on a novel about Americans in Dubai.

ANDY BICHLBAUM (AKA Jacques Servin) got his start as an activist when, as a computer programmer, he inserted a swarm of kissing boys in a shoot-'em-up video game just before it shipped to store shelves, and found himself fired, famous, and hugely amused. Now, Andy helps run the Yes Lab for Creative Activism as part of his job as professor of subversion at New York University. Bichlbaum once flew down the Nile in a two-seater airplane, bringing a live goat to a remote Sudanese village as a hostess gift for a homecoming party. (The party was fun and the goat was insanely delicious.)

NADINE BLOCH has walked hundreds of miles, trained volunteers, built giant puppets, climbed skyscrapers, dangled off bridges, wrangled spokecouncils, juggled media, developed curricula, and sailed oceans, all in support of social and economic justice. Her affiliations include work with Bread & Puppet Theater, Greenpeace, Labor Heritage Foundation, Nonviolence International, Ruckus Society, HealthGAP and Housing Works. Nadine's work explores the potent intersection of art and politics; where creative cultural resistance is not only effective political action, but also a powerful way to reclaim agency over our own lives, fight oppressive systems, and invest in our communities — all while having more fun than the other side!

KATHRYN BLUME grew up improvising radio dramas on a tape recorder and pretending the trees were talking back. A little while later, she finagled a self-designed degree from Yale in environmental studies and theater, and it's been pretty much stuff like that ever since. She is co-founder of the radio show *Earth on the Air*, and the Lysistrata Project, the first worldwide theatrical event for peace. She has had essays published in numerous books, blogs, and magazines. Kathryn's also a solo performer, climate activist, yoga teacher, wedding officiant, haphazard gardener, and irresponsible cat owner. Visit her at kathrynblume.com.

L.M. BOGAD is a lifelong creative strategist (guided and goaded by Harpo, Groucho and Zero), co-founder of the Rebel Clown Army, founding director of the Center for Artistic Activism (West Coast), and professor of political performance at the University of California at Davis. He writes, performs, and strategizes with the Yes Men, Agit-Pop, and La Pocha Nostra. Author of *Electoral Guerrilla Theater: Radical Ridicule and Social Movements, Tactical Performance* (forthcoming), the play *COINTELSHOW: A Patriot Act*, and works about the Spanish Civil War, Haymarket Square Riot, Pinochet coup, and the Egyptian revolution, he has led his Tactical Performance workshops in revolutionary Cairo, Reykjavik, Buenos Aires, and across the USA and Europe.

JOSH BOLOTSKY is an online organizer, blogger, comedic performer/ writer and occasional voiceover artist, currently serving as new media director for Agit-Pop Communications and its Other 98% Project. While at Agit-Pop, he has worked on creating and spreading projects that include the RepubliCorp effort for MoveOn, and Target Ain't People, the very first Depeche-Mode-inspired take on the Citizens United decision to break a million views on YouTube. Josh also serves as part of the national volunteer collective that manages Living Liberally, a network of progressive social groups and activist resources in all fifty states. He enjoys vegan chili and writing about himself in the third person. More at JoshBolotsky.com

MIKE BONANNO (né Igor Vamos) is a guy from Troy, New York, who spent his formative post-childhood years making mischief. Mike once purchased hundreds of talking GI Joe and Barbie dolls, switched out their voice boxes, and created a media firestorm that had God-fearing Americans up in arms about the shadowy "Barbie Liberation Front." This escapade caught the attention of lazy queer hackers like Bichlbaum, and together they formed the Yes Men. When not involved in tomfoolery, Bonanno is also a professor of media art at Rensselaer Polytechnic Institute, with a Scottish wife and two babies.

KEVIN BUCKLAND is an artist, artivist organizer and the "Arts Ambassador" for the grassroots global network 350.org. He has worked with the International Youth Climate Network to promote creative communication and beauty in the call for climate justice across the globe. Harkening on the call to "make this movement as beautiful as the planet we are fighting to save," he employs comedy, tragedy, farce, satire and a great deal of cardboard in his attempts to end empire and globalize justice. Videos, writings and participatory projects can be seen at www.ctrlartshift.org

MARGARET CAMPBELL is a freelancer of many trades, but carries with her the spirit of engaged journalism, and a closely-held belief in the capacity of public art to heal and unite. She has had the opportunity to travel toward a deep understanding of her home community of Minneapolis/ St. Paul, and to work extensively on the White Earth Ojibwe Reservation in Northwestern MN on media and environmental justice initiatives. She is a staunch supporter and budding practitioner of the earnestly-funny approach to activism advocated in this book. She is currently stuck somewhere between the Mini Apple and the Big Apple.

DOYLE CANNING was struck by a tear gas canister in the streets of Seattle in 1999, and has never been the same since. She is a creative strategist with a deep commitment to building broad-based movements for social justice and an ecological future. Doyle is co-director of smartMeme.org, a national strategy center. She delivers training, coaching, facilitation and framing to high-impact networks who are taking on greedy corporations, corrupt politicians, racist laws and polluting policies. Doyle is co-author of *Re:Imagining Change* with Patrick Reinsborough. She lives with her husband in Boston, where she enjoys practicing yoga, cooking, and making music.

SAMANTHA CORBIN is actions director for The Other 98% and national coordinator of the U.S. Uncut network, as well as a non-violent direct action trainer with The Ruckus Society and a founding member of the New York Action Network. She has coordinated scores of affinity group actions including banner hangs, blockades, and street theater actions; led several large-scale actions including the 5,000-strong Powershift 2011; and developed and delivered countless trainings in creative non-violent direct action, affinity group organizing, strategic planning, scouting, and high tech action. Throughout the fall of 2011, she has been organizing and training with Occupy Wall Street. Sam is based in New York City.

YUTAKA DIRKS is a tenant and community organizer and writer living in Toronto, Ontario, Canada. He has been active in anti-poverty, workers rights and international solidarity movements, as well as offering legal support to social justice movements through the Movement Defence Committee of the Law Union of Ontario. His writing has appeared in *Upping the Anti* and *Briarpatch Magazine* as well as *Alfred Hitchcock's Mystery Magazine*.

STEPHEN DUNCOMBE teaches the history and politics of media at New York University. He is the author or editor of six books, including Dream: Re-Imagining Progressive Politics in an Age of Fantasy and the Cultural Resistance Reader. Duncombe is a life-long political activist, co-founding a community-based advocacy group in the Lower East Side of Manhattan and working as an organizer for the NYC chapter of the international direct action group, Reclaim the Streets. He co-created the School for Creative Activism in 2011 and is presently co-director of the Center for Artistic Activism www.artisticactivism.org He can be found at www.stephenduncombe.com

MARK ENGLER is a senior analyst with Foreign Policy in Focus and author of *How to Rule the World: The Coming Battle Over the Global Economy* (Nation Books). He can be reached via the website http://www.DemocracyUprising.com.

SIMON ENOCH is director of the Saskatchewan Office of the Canadian Centre for Policy Alternatives. He holds a PhD in Communication and Culture from Ryerson University in Toronto. Simon has previously published in *Foucault Studies, Cultural Logic, Capitalism, Nature, Socialism* and Socialist Studies. He can be reached at simon@policyalternatives.ca More here: http://www.policyalternatives.ca/offices/saskatchewan

JODIE EVANS has been a peace, environmental, women's rights and social justice activist for forty years. She has traveled to war zones, promoting and learning about peaceful resolution to conflict. She served in the administration of California Governor Jerry Brown and ran his presidential campaigns. She published two books, *Stop the Next War Now* and *Twilight of Empire*, and produced several documentary films, including the Oscar and Emmy-nominated *The Most Dangerous Man in America* and *The People Speak*. Jodie co-founded CODEPINK: Women for Peace, is the board chair of Women's Media Center and sits on many other boards, including Rainforest Action Network, Institute for Policy Studies, and Drug Policy Alliance.

JOHN EWING is a new media artist merging public art with activism and education. He worked for two years in El Salvador, using the arts to organize and inspire dialogue about human rights. Recent projects include Virtual Street Corners (www.virtualcorners.net), winner of the Knight News Challenge Award and selected by Americans for the Arts as one of the most significant public art projects of 2010. He was a co-founder of Ghana Thinktank (www.ghanathinktank.org), a collaborative, decade-long project that was a finalist for the Cartier Award. Ewing has a BFA from Cornell and an MFA from Rhode Island School of Design.

BRIAN FAIRBANKS began his professional journalism career at the age of fifteen as a staff writer for *The Hartford Courant*. After serving as an assistant/librarian to Dr. Stephen Ambrose and Douglas Brinkley, and working on the collected letters of Hunter S. Thompson and the journals of Jack Kerouac, he became an activist with Billionaires For Bush and local grassroots campaigns in New York City. After several years in the Nixon-esque political wilderness, he ended up where most of society's outcasts do: in television. You can haunt him on Twitter.

BRYAN FARRELL is an editor for *Waging Nonviolence*, a blog that documents the many ways people affect positive change around the world every day. His work has also appeared in *The Guardian, The Nation, Mother Jones, Slate*, and *Grist*.

JANICE FINE is associate professor of labor studies and employment relations at the School of Management and Labor Relations, Rutgers University where she teaches and writes about low wage immigrant labor in the U.S., historical and contemporary debates regarding federal immigration policy, dilemmas of labor standards enforcement and innovative union and community organizing strategies. She is the author of *Worker Centers: Organizing Communities at the Edge of the Dream* (2006) published by Cornell University Press and the Economic Policy Institute. Before becoming a professor, Fine worked as a community, labor, coalition and electoral organizer for more than twenty-five years.

LISA FITHIAN has organized since 1975, weaving together strategic creative nonviolent actions, anti-oppression work and sustainable practices in student, environmental justice, workers rights and peace and global justice struggles. Whether it was shutting down the CIA, White House, Supreme Court or the WTO or working on Justice of Janitors, Camp Casey, Common Ground Relief or Wall Street banks, Lisa has supported tens of thousands of people in accessing their power and gaining the experience and skills they need to fight for justice, no matter how great or small the cause. Her website organizingforpower.org chronicles much of her work and offers great resources.

CRISTIAN FLEMING is a graphic designer, creative strategist, mischief enthusiast, and founder of The Public Society, an ethically grounded branding and design company based in Brooklyn, NY. He also works often with activist groups like The Yes Men to make stuff happen in the service of making the world a little better.

ELISABETH GINSBERG holds a master's in cultural studies and journalism from NYU. Being an over-educated Dane, she just finished her second Master's degree, this time from the University of Copenhagen. In an attempt not to dry out completely, she wrote her thesis on Jon Stewart and Stephen Colbert. She lives in Copenhagen, always in close proximity to her Mac.

STAN GOFF spent over two decades in the U.S. Army, mostly special operations, from 1970-1996. He has worked as Organizing Director for Democracy South, a 12-state coalition working on money and politics (1996-2001), and as an Organizational Development Consultant with Iraq Veterans Against the War (2004-2006). Married, with four grown children and four grandchildren, he is the author of four books including *Hideous Dream: A Soldier's Memoir of the U.S. Invasion of Haiti* (Soft Skull Press, 2001) and *Sex & War* (Lulu Press, 2006). He blogs at feralscholar.org.

ARUN GUPTA is a founding editor of *The Indypendent.*

SILAS HARREBYE is finishing up a PhD on creative activism and its potential to facilitate new forms of democratic participation. He has a master's degree in political philosophy and international development. Today the consultancy skills that he acquired as a project manager in Africa and Eastern Europe are used to advance social entrepreneurship. Silas writes for international journals and is frequently used by the Danish media to comment on the implications of social movements around the world. He lectures widely on the same topic. He currently lives in Copenhagen with his partner and their two kids. Write him (silas@ruc.dk) or google his name to find his profile.

JUDITH HELFAND, a Peabody Award-winning filmmaker, is best known for her ability to take the dark, cynical worlds of chemical exposure, heedless corporate behavior and environmental injustice and make them personal, resonant, highly charged and entertaining. Her films include *A Healthy Baby Girl*, its sequel *Blue Vinyl* (co-directed with Daniel B. Gold) and *Everything's Cool* (also co-directed with Gold). Educator, "field explorer" and social entrepreneur, Judith co-founded both Working Films and Chicken & Egg Pictures.

DANIEL HUNTER is a trainer and organizer with Training for Change, which practices a direct education style rooted in popular education, helping each person find their own wisdom and strategic brilliance. He has trained thousands of activists including ethnic minorities in Burma/Myanmar, pastors in Sierra Leone, independence activists in northeast India, environmentalists in Australia, and Indonesian religious leaders. As an organizer, he recently pioneered a successful nonviolent direct action campaign to halt a politically-connected $560 million casino development project — and has led direct action campaigns with local community groups, national unions, and broad coalitions. His home is west Philadelphia.

SARAH JAFFE is a journalist, rabblerouser, and Internet junkie. She is currently an associate editor at AlterNet.org, where she writes about economic justice, activism, and more. She lives in Brooklyn with a rescue dog and too many books. You can follow her exploits on Twitter at @seasonothebitch.

JOHN JORDAN was co-founder of Reclaim the Streets (1995–2001) and now works with the Laboratory of Insurrectionary Imagination, a collective that merges art, activism and permaculture. He loves to apply creativity to social movements such as Climate Camps and has invented various new direct action methodologies such as the Rebel Clown Army. Co-author of *We Are Everywhere: The Irresistible Rise of Global Anti-capitalism* (Verso), he has just brought out a new book-film with Isabelle Fremeaux exploring Europe's utopian communities, *Les sentiers de l'utopie* (Editions Zones/La Découverte). Balancing on the tightrope between art and activism, creativity and resistance, is where he's most at home.

DMYTRI KLEINER is the author of *The Telekommunist Manifesto*, and a contributing artist to the "Miscommunication Technologies" continuing series of artworks in collaboration with the Telekommunisten Network. "Miscommunication Technologies" address the social relations embedded in communications technologies by creating platforms that don't quite work as expected, or work in unexpected ways. Most recently, Dmytri has started an initiative to create an International Debtors' Party. He can be followed at http://dmytri.info

SALLY KOHN makes the world safe for radical ideas. As a veteran community organizer turned political commentator, Sally makes complex political issues accessible for everyday audiences. Sally is a grass-roots strategist actively engaged in movement building for equality and justice. She is a regular on Fox News and MSNBC. Her writing has appeared in the *Washington Post, USA Today*, CNN.com, FoxNews.com, *Reuters, The Guardian* and the *American Prospect*, among other outlets. You can find her at sallykohn.com

STEVE LAMBERT's father, a former Franciscan monk, and mother, an ex-Dominican nun, imbued in him the values of dedication, study, poverty, and service to others — qualities which prepared him for life as an artist. He co-founded the Center for Artistic Activism, was a senior fellow at New York's Eyebeam Center for Art and Technology from 2006–2010, developed workshops for Creative Capital Foundation, and is a faculty member at the School of the Museum of Fine Arts, Boston. Steve is a perpetual autodidact with (if it matters) advanced degrees from a reputable art school and well-respected state university. He dropped out of high school in 1993.

ANNA LEE is manager of filmmaker and partner services at Working Films, one of the leading independent media organizations focused on the art of engagement. Co-founded by Judith Helfand and Robert West, Working Films brings persuasive and provocative documentary films to long-term community organizing and activism. Since joining Working Films, Anna has worked on national audience engagement strategies for numerous high profile documentaries. She currently coordinates Reel Engagement (http://workingfilms.org/article.php?id=302), a ground-breaking, thematic residency series for filmmakers and non-profits. Anna is also an organizer for educational, racial and environmental justice in Working Films' hometown of Wilmington, NC where she lives with her husband and son.

STEPHEN LERNER is architect of the Justice for Janitors campaign. He serves on the executive board of the Service Employees International Union. He has been a labor and community organizer for over thirty years and is working with labor and community groups in campaigns that challenge Wall Street's and big corporations' domination of the political and economic life of the U.S. and global economy. His latest thinking here: http://www.alternet.org/story/153541/the_99_versus_wall_street%3A_stephen_lerner_on_how_we_can_mobilize_to_be_the_greedy_1%27s_worst_nightmare/

ZACK MALITZ, a New Yorker, thinks that fossil fuels belong underground.

NANCY L. MANCIAS is a campaign organizer for CODEPINK. An anti-war advocate, Mancias has been actively trying to bring the troops home from their overseas misadventures. She has also been part of the movement against torture and a proponent of closing the prison in Guantánamo. She is a believer in accountability for war crimes. She alerts people around the country when war criminals will be speaking, encouraging them to try to make a citizen's arrest or some ruckus. Like many in the anti-war movement, Mancias views her work against drones as a natural extension of her peace efforts.

DUNCAN MEISEL is a strategic troublemaker who lives in Brooklyn, where he conspires on how to respond to the impending end of the world. He is particularly interested in trying to stop the warming of the earth, ending the impoverishment of America by corporate power, and putting an end to the prison system as we know it. He is honored to have been a part of campaigns such as Tar Sands Action, U.S. Uncut, The Other 98% and several different "Billionaires for X or Y" efforts.

MATT MEYER is a long-time leader of the War Resisters League and a founder of the anti-imperialist collective Resistance in Brooklyn (RnB). His solidarity and writing includes co-authorship with Pan-African pacifist Bill Sutherland of *Guns and Gandhi in Africa*, of which Archbishop Tutu commented: "Sutherland and Meyer have begun to develop a language which looks at the roots of our humanness." Meyer's work in education includes a ten-year stint as Multicultural Coordinator for NYC's Alternative High Schools, and work on the Board of the Peace and Justice Studies Association. He can be reached at mmmsrnb@igc.org.

TRACEY MITCHELL facilitates creative and courageous conversations for community organizations. Based in Saskatoon, Saskatchewan, Canada, Tracey uses engaging techniques to help groups establish and accomplish goals, build teams, develop leadership skills and make decisions together. Tracey is also a forum theater practitioner (aka a "joker") and has developed plays with groups around issues of poverty and social justice. She is also a campaigner, zinester, organizer, reader and board game player. Tracey lives and works from her home in Saskatoon. For more about Tracey's work, see www.facilitrace.com.

GEORGE MONBIOT is an English writer, known for his environmental and political activism. He writes a weekly column for *The Guardian*, and is the author of a number of books, including *Captive State: The Corporate Takeover of Britain* (2000) and *Bring on the Apocalypse: Six Arguments for Global Justice* (2008). He is the founder of The Land is Ours campaign, which campaigns peacefully for the right of access to the UK countryside and its resources. In January 2010, Monbiot founded the Arrest-Blair.org website which offers a reward to people attempting a peaceful citizen's arrest of former British prime minister Tony Blair for crimes against peace. Find him at monbiot.com.

BRAD NEWSHAM is the author of two round-the-world travel memoirs (*All the Right Places* and *Take Me With You*). Since 1985 he has been a San Francisco taxicab driver, and is currently the owner/driver of Green Cab #914. His first human mural (one thousand people spelling out "IMPEACH!" in 100-foot lettering) was created on Ocean Beach in San Francisco, on January 6, 2007 — two days after San Francisco's Nancy Pelosi became Speaker of the U.S. House of Representatives. More info at bradnewsham.com.

GABY PACHECO is an undocumented American and an immigrant rights leader from Miami, Florida. In 2010, she and three friends walked 1,500 miles to bring to light the plight of immigrants in this country, and to urge President Obama to stop the separations of families and deportations of DREAM (Development, Relief and Education for Alien Minors) Act–eligible youth. This walk was dubbed the Trail of DREAMs. She currently leads a national project, Education not Deportation (END), to stop the deportation of DREAMers. Gaby is in the process of publishing two children's books and aspires to be a musical therapist and work with people with mental disabilities.

MARK READ is a filmmaker and professor of Media Studies at NYU, with a focus on video as a tactical tool in community organizing. In other incarnations, he has also been: a community gardens activist; a Union Square Park defender; a Critical Mass rider and organizer; a coordinator of large spectacles in public spaces such as subway train parties; and a core organizer and propagandist for Reclaim the Streets NYC.

PATRICK REINSBOROUGH is a strategist, organizer and creative provocateur with over twenty years of experience campaigning for peace, justice, indigenous rights and ecological sanity. Patrick has helped organize countless creative interventions, including mass direct actions that shut down the Seattle WTO meeting in 1999 and protested the U.S. invasion of Iraq in 2003. He is the author of numerous essays on social change theory and practice, including co-writing *Re:Imagining Change* (PM Press 2010). He is the co-founder of smartMeme, a movement support organization which harnesses the power of narrative for fundamental social change. He lives with his family in the San Francisco Bay area. More at www.smartMeme.org

SIMON ROEL holds a BA in Philosophy from the University of Copenhagen where he did not only studied, but also got to socialize with all sorts of crazies (i.e., philosophers), including the founders of the Nihilist Democratic Party. Determined to become a film director, he did an intense one-year filmmaking program at the New York Film Academy, and has recently completed his short film *Urban Caveman*, dealing with a dangerous mix of pizza, porn, and philosophy. Bon appétit.

JOSHUA KAHN RUSSELL is an organizer and strategist serving movements for social justice and ecological balance. He is an action coordinator, facilitator & trainer with the Ruckus Society, and has trained thousands of activists. Joshua has written numerous movement strategy essays, chapters for several books, and a few organizing manuals, most recently *Organizing Cools the Planet: Tools and Reflections to Navigate the Climate Crisis,* with Hilary Moore (PM Press 2011). He has helped win campaigns against banks, oil companies, logging corporations, and coal barons; worked with a wide variety of groups in a breadth of arenas, from local resiliency projects, to national coalitions, to the United Nations Climate Negotiations.

LEÓNIDAS MARTIN SAURA is a professor at Barcelona University where he teaches New Media and Political Art. For many years, he has been developing collective projects between art and activism, some of them well known internationally (Las Agencias, Yomango, Prêt à Revolter, New Kids on the Black Block...). He writes about art and politics for blogs, journals and newspapers, has created several documentaries and movies for television and internet, and is a member of the cultural collective Enmedio (www.enmedio.info). Last but not least, he is an expert at telling jokes, often using this divine gift to get free beers and avoid police arrest.

LEVANA SAXON is an organizer and educator with Practicing Freedom, using participatory action research, popular education and Theater of the Oppressed to generate collaborative community-led change. Over the last seventeen years she has trained and facilitated thousands of children, youth and adults. Some of the groups she has worked with include the Paulo Freire Institute, Rainforest Action Network, Center for Political Education, Ella Baker Center for Human Rights, Youth In Focus, El Teatro Campesino and multiple Oakland Public Schools. She currently co-coordinates the Ruckus Society's Arts Core and facilitates trainings and dialogues with the White Noise Collective (www.conspireforchange.org), which she co-founded. She can be found at www.practicingfreedom.org

NATHAN SCHNEIDER is an editor of Waging Nonviolence, a blog about nonviolent conflict and militarism, as well as of *Killing the Buddha*, an online literary magazine about religion and culture. He has written for *Harper's, The New York Times, The Nation, The Catholic Worker, the Boston Review, The Guardian, Religion Dispatches,* and elsewhere. Most recently, he covered Occupy Wall Street from the early planning stages, and is finishing a book for University of California Press about the search for proof of the existence of God, past and present. His website is www.therowboat.com.|

MAXINE SCHOEFER-WULF recently moved eastward, from the CA Bay Area to NYC, in search of adventure and a more rugged climate. In her studies, she focused on art, critical pedagogy, and women's studies and worked closely with the UCLA Art|Global Health Center to bring arts-based sexual health education to L.A. high schools. She has taught self-defense to youth in Oakland, literacy to children in L.A., and English to tots in Rodenäs, rural northern Germany. She is a firm believer in art that sparks laughs and conversation and leaves a mark.

KRISTEN ESS SCHURR took her first professional journalism job as a rock critic in Seattle. She moved on to be Palestine Bureau Chief for KPFA's Flashpoints and also corresponded for several Pacifica affiliates while running the English department of the Palestine News Network in the West Bank and Gaza Strip. Her writing has been translated into seven languages and can be found in independent journals and the anthology Live From Palestine. She is now residing in Los Angeles and working on CODEPINK's Stolen Beauty (www.stolenbeauty.org) and Boycott SodaStream campaigns (www.codepink.org/boycottsodastream).

JOHN SELLERS is co-founder of The Other 98%, a founding partner of Agit-Pop Communications, and president of the Ruckus Society. John worked for Greenpeace in the early '90s before leaving to help start Ruckus. He has had the great fortune to be integrally involved in powerful peaceful actions all over the world: from the high seas with the Rainbow Warrior to the streets of Seattle in the uprising against the WTO. He works from home on Vashon island in the Puget Sound where he and wife Genevieve unschool their seven-year-old twins Sam and Hazel. Check him out at Agit-Pop.com.

RAJNI SHAH is an artist working in performance and live art. Whether online, in a public space or in a theater, her work aims to open up new spaces for conversation and the meeting of diverse voices. From 2006–2010, she conducted a three-year inquiry into the relationship between gift and conversation in public spaces called small gifts. From 2005–2012 she produced a trilogy of large-scale performances (Mr. Quiver, Dinner with America and Glorious) addressing the complexities of cultural identity in the twenty-first century. If you'd like to know more, please visit www.rajnishah.com.

BROOKE SINGER creates platforms for local knowledge to connect, inform and conflict with official data descriptions. She works across media and disciplines, engaging technoscience as an artist, educator, nonspecialist and collaborator. Her work lives on- and offline in the form of websites, workshops, photographs, maps, installations and performances that involve public participation in pursuit of social change. She is associate professor of new media at Purchase College, State University of New York, fellow at Eyebeam Art + Technology Center, and co-founder of the art, technology and activist group Preemptive Media. For more visit www.bsing.net.

MATTHEW SKOMAROVSKY is optimistic and googleable.

ANDREW SLACK is a creator, co-founder, and executive director of the Harry Potter Alliance (HPA). Andrew was a founding partner, performer, and writer in a traveling comedy group where he produced three videos that have been seen more than eleven million times. Andrew has presented his theory of social change, cultural acupuncture, at TEDx in Rome, NPR's *Morning Edition*, Australia's *Today Show*, and is being studied at the University of Southern California. He has written for the *LA Times*, CNN.com, Huffington Post, and In These Times. Check out more at http://thehpalliance.org

PHILLIP SMITH is a digital publishing consultant, online advocacy specialist, and strategic convener.

JONATHAN MATTHEW SMUCKER is a long-time participant and organizer in grassroots movements for social justice, economic equality, ecological sanity, and human rights — especially within the global justice movement and the anti-war movement. He has trained thousands of activists in campaign strategy, messaging, direct action, and other people-powered frameworks and skills. He is co-founder and director of Beyond the Choir, a strategy and training organization. On October 12, 2011, Smucker went to Occupy Wall Street, where — as *Beautiful Trouble* goes to print — he remains, working primarily with the press and movement building working groups. For more of his writing: http://beyondthechoir.org

STARHAWK is an author, activist, permaculture designer, and one of the foremost voices in earth-based spirituality. Her twelve books include *The Spiral Dance, The Fifth Sacred Thing*, and *The Earth Path*, and her first picture book for children, *The Last Wild Witch*. She has lived and worked collectively for thirty years, and her book on group dynamics is just out: *The Empowerment Manual: A Guide for Collaborative Groups*. She directs and teaches Earth Activist Trainings, www.earthactivisttraining.org, which combine a permaculture design certificate course with a grounding in spirit and a focus on organizing and activism. Her website is www.starhawk.org.

ERIC STONER is an adjunct professor at St. Peter's College and an editor at *Waging Nonviolence*, a blog that covers nonviolent action around the world. His articles have appeared in *The Guardian, Mother Jones, The Nation, Sojourners, In These Times* and the *Pittsburgh Post-Gazette*, among other publications. He is on the national board of the War Resisters League and can be found at ericstoner.net.

JEREMY VARON is a professor of history at the New School. He is author of *Bringing the War Home: The Weather Underground, the Red Army Faction, and Revolutionary Violence in the Sixties and Seventies* (2004) and teaches classes on social movements and civil disobedience. He is also a longtime activist, having worked with Billionaires for Bush and, most recently, Witness Against Torture. He therefore favors, by turns, comedy and tragedy.

VIRGINIA VITZTHUM has written for the *Village Voice, Ms., the Washington City Paper, Elle, Time Out New York* and was a columnist for salon.com and for washingtonpost.com. She's also written two books, including *I Love You, Let's Meet*, a screenplay, and a play and edited many publications. She was recently dramaturg/actor/songwriter for *Pedagogy of the Oppressed: The Musical!* — an original production by Falconworks theater in Red Hook, Brooklyn: http://www.redhooktheater.org/ . She currently edits *Represent*, a national magazine written by and for youth in foster care: http://www.representmag.org/. Her website is virginiavitzthum.com.

HARSHA WALIA is a South Asian activist, facilitator, writer and legal researcher based in Vancouver, occupied Indigenous Coast Salish territories. She has been active in (unpaid) community-based grassroots migrant justice, feminist, anti-racist, Indigenous solidarity, anti-capitalist, Palestinian liberation, and anti-imperialist movements for over a decade. She works with women in Vancouver's Downtown Eastside, the poorest neighbourhood in Canada. Her writings have appeared in a number of newspapers, anthologies and academic journals, and she recently co-created a short film on poverty and violence against women. Harsha believes in overgrowing the logic of the state. You can find her at https://twitter.com/#!/HarshaWalia

JEFFERY R. WEBBER teaches politics at Queen Mary, University of London. He is the author of *Red October: Left-Indigenous Struggles in Modern Bolivia* (Brill), and *From Rebellion to Reform in Bolivia: Class Struggle, Indigenous Liberation and the Politics of Evo Morales* (Haymarket, 2011). He is a socialist activist in London and sits on the editorial boards of *Historical Materialism, Latin American Perspectives,* and *Capitalism, Nature, Socialism.*

THE COALITION OF IMMOKALEE WORKERS is a community-based farmworker organization headquartered in Immokalee, Florida. The CIW's Campaign for Fair Food identifies the links between the brutal farm labor conditions in the fields and the multi-billion dollar retail food brands that buy the produce grown in those fields. By mobilizing farmworkers and consumers, the campaign seeks to enlist the resources of retail food giants to improve farmworker wages and to harness their demand to reward growers who respect their workers' rights. This ongoing effort is bringing about considerable industry-wide change and improving conditions at tens of thousands of harvesting jobs in Florida's tomato fields.

PARTNER ORGANIZATIONS

CONVENER

AGIT-POP COMMUNICATIONS is a one-stop creative shop for the progressive movement. We produce smart real world actions and cutting edge new media (and now, books, it seems!) for social change campaigns. We use engaging messages with state-of-the-art tools to inspire people to take action. Our work has won a Webby, two Contagious Festivals, YouTube's Best Political Video of the Year, and Zug's (Second) Best Political Prank of the Year. agit-pop.com

THE OTHER 98% was founded on the premise that our economy and democracy should work for everyday Americans, not the elite 2% of bankers, CEOs and lobbyists who've hijacked our democracy and rigged the system to serve themselves. It's the middle class that's too big to fail, and we're using creative tactics — both online and in the streets — to, well, rally ourselves to our own cause. We stand in solidarity with Occupy Wall Street and allied efforts to build a people-powered movement that can break the corporate stranglehold on our democracy and achieve true economic justice. other98.com

Note: Our "98%" framing preceded the OWS "99%" by more than a year, but we are happy to see a slightly tweaked version of this meme taking off worldwide. :-)

ORGANIZATIONAL PARTNERS

THE YES MEN, called "the Jonathan Swift of the Jackass Generation" by author Naomi Klein, are best known for infiltrating the world of big business and doing incredibly stupid things to expose the world's biggest corporate criminals. Although fronted by Andy Bichlbaum and Mike Bonanno, their membership includes hundreds or perhaps thousands of secret agents, all of whom were recently acquired in a hostile takeover by the Yes Lab.

At the moment, the **YES LAB** is mainly a series of brainstorms and trainings to help activist groups carry out media-getting creative actions, focused on their own campaign goals. It's a way for social justice organizations to take advantage of all that we Yes Men have learned — not only about our own ways of doing things, but those we've come in contact with over the decade and a half we've been doing this sort of thing. The Yes Lab has offices and workshopping space at NYU's Hemispheric Institute in New York. yeslab.org

SMARTMEME is a national strategy center that offers social justice networks and organizations the analysis, training and strategic support to win the battle of ideas with narrative strategies. SmartMeme re-imagines methods to achieve fundamental social change with effective story-based approaches to framing that amplify the impact of grassroots organizing and challenge the underlying assumptions that shape the status quo. smartmeme.org

THE CENTER FOR ARTISTIC ACTIVISM is the home for artists, activists and scholars to explore, discuss, reflect upon, and strengthen connections between social activism and artistic practice. We facilitate projects and strengthen networks. Our goal is to make more creative and more effective citizen activists. artisticactivism.org

BEYOND THE CHOIR is an online space for grassroots change agents — folks who are engaged in grassroots organizing, activism, advocacy, etc. — to share practical strategies, tactics and tools. It's also a place to dig into deeper social change theory — and to make it practical. There are lots of great websites that cover and critique the news. BeyondtheChoir.org is more about figuring out how we can organize ourselves and strategically intervene. beyondthechoir.org

THE RUCKUS SOCIETY has trained and assisted thousands of activists in the use of nonviolent direct action. We see ourselves as a toolbox of experience, training and skills. We provide instruction on the application of tactical and strategic tools to a growing number of organizations and individuals from around the world via skill shares and trainings that are designed to move a campaign forward. ruckus.org

CODEPINK is a woman-initiated grassroots peace and social justice movement working to end U.S.-funded wars and occupations, to challenge militarism globally, and to redirect our resources into health care, education, green jobs and other life-affirming activities. http://www.codepink.org

ALLIANCE OF COMMUNITY TRAINERS offers knowledge, tools and skills to individuals, organizations and communities to empower sustainable transformation. Whether it be community or organizational development, problem solving or conflict resolution, consensus decision-making, facilitation, strategic campaigns, media and public speaking, alternative technology, nonviolent action or environmental sustainability, we support people starting where they are and learning their vision of what they want. trainersalliance.org

WAGING NONVIOLENCE is a source for news, analysis and original reporting about nonviolent activism, as well as for discussion of the theory behind it. These stories often go overlooked by the mainstream media, yet people are using nonviolent strategies and tactics all around us in response to the most pressing challenges — and reshaping our world in the process. wagingnonviolence.org

NONVIOLENCE INTERNATIONAL researches and promotes nonviolent action and seeks to reduce the use of violence worldwide. They believe that every cultural and religious tradition can discover and employ culturally appropriate nonviolent methods for positive social change and international peace that can break the cycle of violence in favor of constructive rather than destructive outcomes. nonviolenceinternational.net

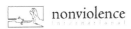

ACKNOWLEDGMENTS

. . . .

This project would never have seen the light of day without the generous contributions of a horde of people, including, but not limited to, the following. Kerrie Maynes, Virginia Vitzthum and Amy X. Neuberg who provided expert copy editing; Joe Keady helped with Spanish-to-English translation; Jason Schultz (UC Berkeley) served as volunteer legal consultant; Andy Menconi lent his graphic design wizardry.

Marisa Jahn deserves thanks for kindly loaning us her digital projector and not getting too pissed-off when Andrew took way too long to get it back to her. Thanks to Andrew's pals at Agit-Pop for letting him take off in the midst of a revolution to work on this book. A tip o' the hat to Crimeth.Inc and their beautifully designed book Recipes for Disaster, which was an inspiration for the design of our own. http://crimethinc.com/books/rfd.html

Thanks to Lauren Kelley for surviving Cristian's hyper-passion, and to Stephanie Lukito for typesetting 'till 3am and then dreaming about the book. Also a big thank you to Bob Meyers of Greenpeace for invaluable assistance sourcing photos of direct actions from around the world, and to the many photographers who put the "beautiful" in Beautiful Trouble by generously making their images available to us, with big unrequited love to those who were unreachable.

Thanks to Avaaz.org for trusting us (four times!) with the keys to their beautiful office space, which served as the perfect base-of-operations for conducting our book sprints (one in the middle of a hurricane!). Thanks to the Millay Artist Colony and the Blue Mountain Center for providing Andrew a place to write and wrangle. And thanks to the whole team at OR Books who not only tolerated but encouraged our very unorthodox approach to collaborative writing and print/digital publishing.

We are extremely grateful for the essential financial support provided by the Lambent Foundation Fund of the Tides Foundation, the Communications, Energy and Paperworks Union of Canada, Jeff Reifman, and our Kickstarter supporters, especially our three Kickstarter co-publishers:

Chris Simpson
Larry Sakin
Yvonne Tasker-Rothenberg

Finally, thanks to the extraordinarily talented and dedicated group of authors who volunteered their time, words and best ideas to sing and sweat this book into existence. Thanks also to Jessica Assaf, Sabrina Banes, Paul Bartlett, Chris Carlsson, Marco Ceglie, Jasmine Chalashtori, Chuck Collins, Melanie Crean, Sidd Joag, Lauren Kelley, Joel Kovel, Lauren Larken, Todd Lester, Margaret Maloney, Lissette Olivares, Michael Pineschi, Gideon Rosenblatt, Lisa Savage, Marina Sitrin and Alison Thomas.

Photo by Fonta Feingold, modifications by Andy Menconi.

INDEX

INDEX

INDEX

INDEX